ALL CREATURES
GREAT AND SMALL

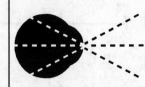

This Large Print Book carries the
Seal of Approval of N.A.V.H.

ALL CREATURES GREAT AND SMALL

JAMES HERRIOT

THORNDIKE PRESS

A part of Gale, Cengage Learning

GALE
CENGAGE Learning®

Detroit • New York • San Francisco • New Haven, Conn • Waterville, Maine • London

GALE
CENGAGE Learning®

LIBRARY OF CONGRESS CATALOGING-IN-PUBLICATION DATA

Herriot, James.
    All creatures great and small / by James Herriot.
        p. cm. — (Thorndike Press large print famous authors)
    ISBN 978-1-4104-4834-7 (hardcover) — ISBN 1-4104-4834-7
(hardcover) 1. Herriot, James. 2. Veterinarians—England—
Yorkshire—Biography. I. Title.
SF613.H44A28 2012
636.089092—dc23
[B]   2012002844

Published in 2012 by arrangement with St. Martin's Press, LLC.

Printed in Mexico
6 7 8 9 10 11 20 19 18 17 16

To
EDDIE STRAITON
with gratitude and affection

and
DONALD AND BRIAN SINCLAIR
still my friends

All things bright and beautiful,
All creatures great and small,
All things wise and wonderful,
The Lord God made them all.

Cecil Frances Alexander
1818–1895

CHAPTER 1

They didn't say anything about this in the books, I thought, as the snow blew in through the gaping doorway and settled on my naked back.

I lay face down on the cobbled floor in a pool of nameless muck, my arm deep inside the straining cow, my feet scrabbling for a toe hold between the stones. I was stripped to the waist and the snow mingled with the dirt and the dried blood on my body. I could see nothing outside the circle of flickering light thrown by the smoky oil lamp which the farmer held over me.

No, there wasn't a word in the books about searching for your ropes and instruments in the shadows; about trying to keep clean in a half bucket of tepid water; about the cobbles digging into your chest. Nor about the slow numbing of the arms, the creeping paralysis of the muscles as the fingers tried to work against the cow's powerful expulsive efforts.

There was no mention anywhere of the

gradual exhaustion, the feeling of futility and the little far-off voice of panic.

My mind went back to that picture in the obstetrics book. A cow standing in the middle of a gleaming floor while a sleek veterinary surgeon in a spotless parturition overall inserted his arm to a polite distance. He was relaxed and smiling, the farmer and his helpers were smiling, even the cow was smiling. There was no dirt or blood or sweat anywhere.

That man in the picture had just finished an excellent lunch and had moved next door to do a bit of calving just for the sheer pleasure of it, as a kind of dessert. He hadn't crawled shivering from his bed at two o'clock in the morning and bumped over twelve miles of frozen snow, staring sleepily ahead till the lonely farm showed in the headlights. He hadn't climbed half a mile of white fell-side to the doorless barn where his patient lay.

I tried to wriggle my way an extra inch inside the cow. The calf's head was back and I was painfully pushing a thin, looped rope towards its lower jaw with my finger tips. All the time my arm was being squeezed between the calf and the bony pelvis. With every straining effort from the cow the pressure became almost unbearable, then she would relax and I would push the rope another inch. I wondered how long I would be able to keep this up. If I didn't snare that jaw soon I would never get the calf away. I groaned, set my teeth and reached forward again.

Another little flurry of snow blew in and I could almost hear the flakes sizzling on my sweating back. There was sweat on my forehead too, and it trickled into my eyes as I pushed.

There is always a time at a bad calving when you begin to wonder if you will ever win the battle. I had reached this stage.

Little speeches began to flit through my brain. 'Perhaps it would be better to slaughter this cow. Her pelvis is so small and narrow that I can't see a calf coming through', or 'She's a good fat animal and really of the beef type, so don't you think it would pay you better to get the butcher?' or perhaps 'This is a very bad presentation. In a roomy cow it would be simple enough to bring the head round but in this case it is just about impossible.'

Of course, I could have delivered the calf by embryotomy — by passing a wire over the neck and sawing off the head. So many of these occasions ended with the floor strewn with heads, legs, heaps of intestines. There were thick textbooks devoted to the countless ways you could cut up a calf.

But none of it was any good here, because this calf was alive. At my furthest stretch I had got my finger as far as the commissure of the mouth and had been startled by a twitch of the little creature's tongue. It was unexpected because calves in this position are usually dead, asphyxiated by the acute flexion of the neck and the pressure of the dam's powerful contractions. But this one had a spark of life in it and if it came out it would have to be in one piece.

I went over to my bucket of water, cold now and bloody, and silently soaped my arms. Then I lay down again, feeling the cobbles harder than ever against my chest. I worked my toes between the stones, shook the sweat from my eyes and for the hundredth time thrust an arm that felt like spaghetti into the cow; alongside the little dry legs of the calf, like sandpaper tearing against my flesh, then to the bend in the neck and so to the ear and then, agonisingly, along the side of the face towards the lower jaw which had become my major goal in life.

It was incredible that I had been doing this for nearly two hours; fighting as my strength ebbed to push a little noose round that jaw. I had tried everything else — repelling a leg, gentle traction with a blunt hook in the eye socket, but I was back to the noose.

It had been a miserable session all through. The farmer, Mr Dinsdale, was a long, sad, silent man of few words who always seemed to be expecting the worst to happen. He had a long, sad, silent son with him and the two of them had watched my efforts with deepening gloom.

But worst of all had been Uncle. When I had first entered the hillside barn I had been surprised to see a little bright-eyed old man in a pork pie hat settling down comfortably on a bale of straw. He was filling his pipe and clearly looking forward to the entertainment.

'Now then, young man,' he cried in the nasal twang of the West Riding. 'I'm Mr Dinsdale's brother. I farm over in Listondale.'

I put down my equipment and nodded. 'How do you do? My name is Herriot.'

The old man looked me over, piercingly. 'My vet is Mr Broomfield. Expect you'll have heard of him — everybody knows him, I reckon. Wonderful man, Mr Broomfield, especially at calving. Do you know, I've never seen 'im beat yet.'

I managed a wan smile. Any other time I would have been delighted to hear how good my colleague was, but somehow not now, not now. In fact, the words set a mournful little bell tolling inside me.

'No, I'm afraid I don't know Mr Broomfield,' I said, taking off my jacket and, more reluctantly, peeling my shirt over my head. 'But I haven't been around these parts very long.'

Uncle was aghast. 'You don't know him! Well you're the only one as doesn't. They think the world of him in Listondale, I can tell you.' He lapsed into a shocked silence

13

and applied a match to his pipe. Then he shot a glance at my goose-pimpled torso. 'Strips like a boxer does Mr Broomfield. Never seen such muscles on a man.'

A wave of weakness coursed sluggishly over me. I felt suddenly leaden-footed and inadequate. As I began to lay out my ropes and instruments on a clean towel the old man spoke again.

'And how long have you been qualified, may I ask?'

'Oh, about seven months.'

'Seven months!' Uncle smiled indulgently, tamped down his tobacco and blew out a cloud of rank, blue smoke. 'Well, there's nowt like a bit of experience, I always says. Mr Broomfield's been doing my work now for over ten years and he really knows what he's about. No, you can 'ave your book learning. Give me experience every time.'

I tipped some antiseptic into the bucket and lathered my arms carefully. I knelt behind the cow.

'Mr Broomfield always puts some special lubricating oils on his arms first,' Uncle said, pulling contentedly on his pipe. 'He says you get infection of the womb if you just use soap and water.'

I made my first exploration. It was the burdened moment all vets go through when they first put their hand into a cow. Within seconds I would know whether I would be

14

putting on my jacket in fifteen minutes or whether I had hours of hard labour ahead of me.

I was going to be unlucky this time; it was a nasty presentation. Head back and no room at all; more like being inside an undeveloped heifer than a second calver. And she was bone dry — the 'waters' must have come away from her hours ago. She had been running out on the high fields and had started to calve a week before her time; that was why they had had to bring her into this half-ruined barn. Anyway, it would be a long time before I saw my bed again.

'Well now, what have you found, young man?' Uncle's penetrating voice cut through the silence. 'Head back, eh? You won't have much trouble, then. I've seen Mr Broomfield do 'em like that — he turns calf right round and brings it out back legs first.'

I had heard this sort of nonsense before. A short time in practice had taught me that all farmers were experts with other farmers' livestock. When their own animals were in trouble they tended to rush to the phone for the vet, but with their neighbours' they were confident, knowledgeable and full of helpful advice. And another phenomenon I had observed was that their advice was usually regarded as more valuable than the vet's. Like now, for instance; Uncle was obviously an accepted sage and the Dinsdales listened with deference to everything he said.

'Another way with a job like this,' continued Uncle, 'is to get a few strong chaps with ropes and pull the thing out, head back and all.'

I gasped as I felt my way around. 'I'm afraid it's impossible to turn a calf completely round in this small space. And to pull it out without bringing the head round would certainly break the mother's pelvis.'

The Dinsdales narrowed their eyes. Clearly they thought I was hedging in the face of Uncle's superior knowledge.

And now, two hours later, defeat was just round the corner. I was just about whacked. I had rolled and grovelled on the filthy cobbles while the Dinsdales watched me in morose silence and Uncle kept up a non-stop stream of comment. Uncle, his ruddy face glowing with delight, his little eyes sparkling, hadn't had such a happy night for years. His long trek up the hillside had been repaid a hundredfold. His vitality was undiminished; he had enjoyed every minute.

As I lay there, eyes closed, face stiff with dirt, mouth hanging open, Uncle took his pipe in his hand and leaned forward on his straw bale. 'You're about beat, young man,' he said with deep satisfaction. 'Well, I've never seen Mr Broomfield beat but he's had a lot of experience. And what's more, he's strong, really strong. That's one man you couldn't tire.'

Rage flooded through me like a draught of strong spirit. The right thing to do, of course, would be to get up, tip the bucket of bloody water over Uncle's head, run down the hill and drive away; away from Yorkshire, from Uncle, from the Dinsdales, from this cow.

Instead, I clenched my teeth, braced my legs and pushed with everything I had; and with a sensation of disbelief I felt my noose slide over the sharp little incisor teeth and into the calf's mouth. Gingerly, muttering a prayer, I pulled on the thin rope with my left hand and felt the slipknot tighten. I had hold of that lower jaw.

At last I could start doing something. 'Now hold this rope, Mr Dinsdale, and just keep a gentle tension on it. I'm going to repel the calf and if you pull steadily at the same time, the head ought to come round.'

'What if the rope comes off?' asked Uncle hopefully.

I didn't answer. I put my hand in against the calf's shoulder and began to push against the cow's contractions. I felt the small body moving away from me. 'Now a steady pull, Mr Dinsdale, without jerking.' And to myself, 'Oh God, don't let it slip off.'

The head was coming round. I could feel the neck straightening against my arm, then the ear touched my elbow. I let go the shoulder and grabbed the little muzzle. Keeping the teeth away from the vaginal wall with my hand, I guided the head till it was resting where it should be, on the fore limbs.

Quickly I extended the noose till it reached behind the ears. 'Now pull on the head as she strains.'

'Nay, you should pull on the legs now,' cried Uncle.

'Pull on the bloody head rope, I tell you!' I bellowed at the top of my voice and felt immediately better as Uncle retired, offended, to his bale.

With traction the head was brought out and the rest of the body followed easily. The little animal lay motionless on the cobbles, eyes glassy and unseeing, tongue blue and grossly swollen.

'It'll be dead. Bound to be,' grunted Uncle, returning to the attack.

I cleared the mucus from the mouth, blew hard down the throat and began artificial respiration. After a few pressures on the ribs, the calf gave a gasp and the eyelids flickered. Then it started to inhale and one leg jerked.

Uncle took off his hat and scratched his head in disbelief. 'By gaw, it's alive. I'd have thowt it'd sure to be dead after you'd messed about all that time.' A lot of the fire had gone out of him and his pipe hung down empty from his lips.

'I know what this little fellow wants,' I said. I grasped the calf by its fore legs and pulled it up to its mother's head. The cow was stretched out on her side, her head extended wearily along the rough floor. Her ribs heaved, her eyes were almost closed; she looked past caring about anything. Then she felt the calf's body against her face and there was a transformation; her eyes opened wide and her muzzle began a snuffling exploration of the new object. Her interest grew with every sniff and she struggled on to her chest, nosing and probing all over the calf, rumbling deep in her chest. Then she began to lick him methodically. Nature provides the perfect stimulant massage for a time like this and the little creature arched his back as the coarse papillae on the tongue dragged along his skin. Within a minute he was shaking his head and trying to sit up.

I grinned. This was the bit I liked. The little miracle. I felt it was something that would never grow stale no matter how often I saw it. I cleaned as much of the dried blood and filth from my body as I could, but most of it had caked on my skin and not even my finger nails would move it. It would have to wait for the hot bath at home. Pulling my shirt over my head, I felt as though I had been beaten for a long time with a thick stick. Every muscle ached. My mouth was dried out, my lips almost sticking together.

A long, sad figure hovered near. 'How about a drink?' asked Mr Dinsdale.

I could feel my grimy face cracking into an

incredulous smile. A vision of hot tea well laced with whisky swam before me. 'That's very kind of you, Mr Dinsdale, I'd love a drink. It's been a hard two hours.'

'Nay,' said Mr Dinsdale looking at me steadily, 'I meant for the cow.'

I began to babble. 'Oh yes, of course, certainly, by all means give her a drink. She must be very thirsty. It'll do her good. Certainly, certainly, give her a drink.'

I gathered up my tackle and stumbled out of the barn. On the moor it was still dark and a bitter wind whipped over the snow, stinging my eyes. As I plodded down the slope, Uncle's voice, strident and undefeated, reached me for the last time.

'Mr Broomfield doesn't believe in giving a drink after calving. Says it chills the stomach.'

CHAPTER 2

It was hot in the rickety little bus and I was on the wrong side where the July sun beat on the windows. I shifted uncomfortably inside my best suit and eased a finger inside the constricting white collar. It was a foolish outfit for this weather but a few miles ahead, my prospective employer was waiting for me and I had to make a good impression.

There was a lot hanging on this interview; being a newly qualified veterinary surgeon in this year of 1937 was like taking out a ticket for the dole queue. Agriculture was depressed by a decade of government neglect, the draught horse which had been the mainstay of the profession was fast disappearing. It was easy to be a prophet of doom when the young men emerging from the colleges after a hard five years' slog were faced by a world indifferent to their enthusiasm and bursting knowledge. There were usually two or three situations vacant in the *Record* each week and an average of eighty applicants for each one.

It hadn't seemed true when the letter came from Darrowby in the Yorkshire Dales. Mr Siegfried Farnon M.R.C.V.S. would like to see me on the Friday afternoon; I was to come to tea and if we were mutually suited I could stay on as assistant. I had grabbed at the lifeline unbelievingly; so many friends who had qualified with me were unemployed or working in shops or as labourers in the shipyards that I had given up hope of any other future for myself.

The driver crashed his gears again as he went into another steep bend. We had been climbing steadily now for the last fifteen miles or so, moving closer to the distant blue swell of the Pennines. I had never been in Yorkshire before but the name had always raised a picture of a county as stodgy and unromantic as its pudding; I was prepared for solid worth, dullness and a total lack of charm. But as the bus groaned its way higher I began to wonder. The formless heights were resolving into high, grassy hills and wide valleys. In the valley bottoms, rivers twisted among the trees and solid greystone farmhouses lay among islands of cultivated land which pushed bright green promontories up the hillsides into the dark tide of heather which lapped from the summits.

I had seen the fences and hedges give way to dry stone walls which bordered the roads, enclosed the fields and climbed endlessly over the surrounding fells. The walls were everywhere, countless miles of them, tracing their patterns high on the green uplands.

But as I neared my destination the horror stories kept forcing their way into my mind; the tales brought back to college by veterans hardened and embittered by a few months of practice. Assistants were just little bits of dirt to be starved and worked into the ground by the principals who were heartless and vicious to a man. Dave Stevens, lighting a cigarette with trembling hand: 'Never a night off or a half day. He made me wash the car, dig the garden, mow the lawn, do the family shopping. But when he told me to sweep the chimney I left.' Or Willie Johnstone: 'First job I had to do was pass the stomach tube on a horse. Got it into the trachea instead of the oesophagus. Couple of quick pumps and down went the horse with a hell of a crash — dead as a hammer. That's when I started these grey hairs.' Or that dreadful one they passed around about Fred Pringle. Fred had trocharised a bloated cow and the farmer had been so impressed by the pent up gas hissing from the abdomen that Fred had got carried away and applied his cigarette lighter to the canula. A roaring sheet of flame had swept on to some straw bales and burned the byre to the ground. Fred had taken up a colonial appointment immediately afterwards — Leeward Islands wasn't it?

Oh hell, that one couldn't be true. I cursed my fevered imagination and tried to shut out the crackling of the inferno, the terrified bellowing of the cattle as they were led to safety. No, it couldn't be as bad as that; I rubbed my sweating palms on my knees and tried to concentrate on the man I was going to meet.

Siegfried Farnon. Strange name for a vet in the Yorkshire Dales. Probably a German who had done his training in this country and decided to set up in practice. And it wouldn't have been Farnon in the beginning; probably Farrenen. Yes, Siegfried Farrenen. He was beginning to take shape; short, fat, roly-poly type with merry eyes and a bubbling laugh. But at the same time I had trouble with the obtruding image of a hulking, cold-eyed, bristle-skulled Teuton more in keeping with the popular idea of the practice boss.

I realised the bus was clattering along a narrow street which opened on to a square where we stopped. Above the window of an unpretentious grocer shop I read 'Darrowby Co-operative Society'. We had arrived.

I got out and stood beside my battered suitcase, looking about me. There was something unusual and I couldn't put my finger on it at first. Then I realised what it was — the silence. The other passengers had dispersed, the driver had switched off his engine and there was not a sound or a movement anywhere. The only visible sign of life was a group of old men sitting round the clock tower in the centre of the square but they might have been carved from stone.

Darrowby didn't get much space in the guide books but when it was mentioned it was described as a grey little town on the river Darrow with a cobbled market place and little of interest except its two ancient bridges. But when you looked at it, its setting was beautiful on the pebbly river where the houses clustered thickly and straggled unevenly along the lower slopes of Herne Fell. Everywhere in Darrowby, in the streets, through the windows of the houses you could see the Fell rearing its calm, green bulk more than two thousand feet above the huddled roofs.

There was a clarity in the air, a sense of space and airiness that made me feel I had shed something on the plain, twenty miles behind. The confinement of the city, the grime, the smoke — already they seemed to be falling away from me.

Trengate was a quiet street leading off the square and I had my first sight of Skeldale House. I knew it was the right place before I was near enough to read 'S. Farnon M.R.C.V.S.' on the old-fashioned brass plate hanging slightly askew on the iron railings. I knew by the ivy which climbed untidily over the mellow brick to the topmost windows. It was what the letter had said — the only house with ivy; and this could be where I would work for the first time as a veterinary surgeon.

Now that I was here, right on the doorstep, I felt breathless, as though I had been running. If I got the job, this was where I would find out about myself. There were many things to prove.

But I liked the look of the old house. It was Georgian with a fine, white-painted doorway. The windows, too, were white — wide and graceful on the ground floor and first storey but small and square where they peeped out from under the overhanging tiles far above. The paint was flaking and the mortar looked crumbly between the bricks, but there was a changeless elegance about the place. There was no front garden and only the railings separated the house from the street a few feet away.

I rang the doorbell and instantly the afternoon peace was shattered by a distant baying like a wolf pack in full cry. The upper half of the door was of glass and, as I peered through, a river of dogs poured round the corner of a long passage and dashed itself with frenzied yells against the door. If I hadn't been used to animals I would have turned and run for my life. As it was I stepped back warily and watched the dogs as they appeared, sometimes two at a time, at the top of their leap, eyes glaring, jaws slavering. After a minute or two of this I was able to sort them out and I realised that my first rough count of about fourteen was exaggerated. There were, in fact, five; a huge fawn greyhound who appeared most often as he hadn't so far to jump as the others, a cocker spaniel, a Scottie, a whippet and a tiny, short-legged hunt terrier. This terrier was seldom seen since the glass was rather high for him, but when he did make it he managed to get an even more frantic note into his bark before he disappeared.

I was thinking of ringing the bell again when I saw a large woman in the passage. She rapped out a single word and the noise stopped as if by magic. When she opened the door the ravening pack was slinking round her feet ingratiatingly, showing the whites of their eyes and wagging their tucked-in tails. I had never seen such a servile crew.

'Good afternoon,' I said with my best smile. 'My name is Herriot.'

The woman looked bigger than ever with the door open. She was about sixty but her hair, tightly pulled back from her forehead, was jet black and hardly streaked with grey. She nodded and looked at me with grim benevolence, but she seemed to be waiting for further information. Evidently, the name struck no answering spark.

'Mr Farnon is expecting me. He wrote asking me to come today.'

'Mr Herriot?' she said thoughtfully. 'Surgery is from six to seven o'clock. If you wanted to bring a dog in, that would be your best time.'

'No, no,' I said, hanging on to my smile. 'I'm applying for the position of assistant. Mr Farnon said to come in time for tea.'

'Assistant? Well, now, that's nice.' The lines in her face softened a little. 'I'm Mrs Hall. I keep house for Mr Farnon. He's a bachelor, you know. He never said anything to me about you, but never mind, come in and have a cup of tea. He shouldn't be long before he's back.'

I followed her between whitewashed walls, my feet clattering on the tiles. We turned right at the end into another passage and I was beginning to wonder just how far back the house extended when I was shown into a sunlit room.

It had been built in the grand manner, high-ceilinged and airy with a massive fireplace flanked by arched alcoves. One end was taken up by a french window which gave on a long, high-walled garden. I could see unkempt lawns, a rockery and many fruit trees. A great bank of peonies blazed in the hot sunshine and at the far end, rooks cawed in the branches of a group of tall elms. Above and beyond were the green hills with their climbing walls.

Ordinary-looking furniture stood around on a very worn carpet. Hunting prints hung on the walls and books were scattered everywhere, some on shelves in the alcoves but others piled on the floor in the corners. A pewter pint pot occupied a prominent place at one end of the mantelpiece. It was an interesting pot. Cheques and bank notes had been stuffed into it till they bulged out of the top and overflowed on to the hearth beneath. I was studying this with astonishment when Mrs Hall came in with a tea tray.

'I suppose Mr Farnon is out on a case,' I said.

'No, he's gone through to Brawton to visit his mother. I can't really say when he'll be back.' She left me with my tea.

The dogs arranged themselves peacefully around the room and, except for a brief dispute between the Scottie and the cocker spaniel about the occupancy of a deep chair, there was no sign of their previous violent behaviour. They lay regarding me with friendly boredom and, at the same time, fighting a losing battle against sleep. Soon the last nodding head had fallen back and a chorus of heavy breathing filled the room.

But I was unable to relax with them. A feeling of let-down gripped me; I had screwed myself up for an interview and I was left dangling. This was all very odd. Why should anyone write for an assistant, arrange a time to meet him and then go to visit his mother? Another thing — if I was engaged, I would be living in this house, yet the housekeeper had no instructions to prepare a room for me. In fact, she had never even heard of me.

My musings were interrupted by the door bell ringing and the dogs, as if touched by a live wire, leaped screaming into the air and launched themselves in a solid mass through the door. I wished they didn't take their duties so seriously. There was no sign of Mrs Hall so I went out to the front door where the dogs were putting everything into their fierce act.

'Shut up!' I shouted and the din switched itself off. The five dogs cringed abjectly round my ankles, almost walking on their knees. The big greyhound got the best effect by drawing his lips back from his teeth in an apologetic grin.

I opened the door and looked into a round, eager face. Its owner, a plump man in Wellington boots, leaned confidently against the railings.

'Hello, 'ello, Mr Farnon in?'

'Not at the moment. Can I help you?'

'Aye, give 'im a message when he comes in. Tell 'im Bert Sharpe of Barrow Hills has a cow wot wants borin' out?'

'Boring out?'

'That's right, she's nobbut going on three cylinders.'

'Three cylinders?'

'Aye and if we don't do summat she'll go

wrang in 'er ewer, won't she?'

'Very probably.'

'Don't want felon, do we?'

'Certainly not.'

'O.K., you'll tell 'im, then. Ta-ta.'

I returned thoughtfully to the sitting-room. It was disconcerting but I had listened to my first case history without understanding a word of it.

I had hardly sat down when the bell rang again. This time I unleashed a frightening yell which froze the dogs when they were still in mid air; they took the point and returned, abashed, to their chairs.

This time it was a solemn gentleman with a straightly adjusted cloth cap resting on his ears, a muffler knotted precisely over his adam's apple and a clay pipe growing from the exact centre of his mouth. He removed the pipe and spoke with a rich, unexpected accent.

'Me name's Mulligan and I want Misther Farnon to make up some midicine for me dog.'

'Oh, what's the trouble with your dog, Mr Mulligan?'

He raised a questioning eyebrow and put a hand to his ear. I tried again with a full blooded shout.

'What's the trouble?'

He looked at me doubtfully for a moment. 'He's womitin', sorr. Womitin' bad.'

I immediately felt on secure ground now and my brain began to seethe with diagnostic procedures. 'How long after eating does he vomit?'

The hand went to the ear again. 'Phwhat's that?'

I leaned close to the side of his head, inflated my lungs and bawled: 'When does he womit — I mean vomit?'

Comprehension spread slowly across Mr Mulligan's face. He gave a gentle smile. 'Oh aye, he's womitin'. Womitin' bad, sorr.'

I didn't feel up to another effort so I told him I would see to it and asked him to call later. He must have been able to lipread me because he seemed satisfied and walked away.

Back in the sitting-room, I sank into a chair and poured a cup of tea. I had taken one sip when the bell rang again. This time, a wild glare from me was enough to make the dogs cower back in their chairs; I was relieved they had caught on so quickly.

Outside the front door a lovely, red-haired girl was standing. She smiled, showing a lot of very white teeth.

'Good afternoon,' she said in a loud, well-bred voice. 'I am Diana Brompton. Mr Farnon is expecting me for tea.'

I gulped and clung to the door handle. 'He's asked YOU to tea?'

The smile became fixed. 'Yes, that is correct,' she said, spelling the words out carefully. 'He asked me to tea.'

'I'm afraid Mr Farnon isn't at home. I can't say when he'll be back.'

The smile was plucked away. 'Oh,' she said, and she got a lot into the word. 'At any rate, perhaps I could come in.'

'Oh, certainly, do come in. I'm sorry,' I babbled, suddenly conscious that I had been staring, open mouthed at her.

I held open the door and she brushed past me without a word. She knew her way about because, when I got to the first corner, she had disappeared into the room. I tiptoed past the door and broke into a gallop which took me along another thirty yards or so of twisting passage to a huge, stone-flagged kitchen. Mrs Hall was pottering about there and I rushed at her.

'There's a young lady here, a Miss Brompton. She's come to tea, too.' I had to fight an impulse to pluck at her sleeve.

Mrs Hall's face was expressionless. I thought she might have started to wave her arms about, but she didn't even seem surprised.

'You go through and talk to her and I'll bring a few more cakes,' she said.

'But what the heck am I going to talk to her about? How long is Mr Farnon going to be?'

'Oh, just chat to her for a bit. I shouldn't think he'll be very long,' she said calmly.

33

Slowly, I made my way back to the sitting-room and when I opened the door the girl turned quickly with the makings of another big smile. She made no attempt to hide her disgust when she saw it was only me.

'Mrs Hall thinks he should be back fairly soon. Perhaps you would join me in a cup of tea while you're waiting.'

She gave me a quick glance which raked me from my rumpled hair to my scuffed old shoes. I realised suddenly how grimy and sweaty I was after the long journey. Then she shrugged her shoulders and turned away. The dogs regarded her apathetically. A heavy silence blanketed the room.

I poured a cup of tea and held it out to her. She ignored me and lit a cigarette. This was going to be tough, but I could only try.

I cleared my throat and spoke lightly. 'I've only just arrived myself. I hope to be the new assistant.'

This time she didn't trouble to look round. She just said 'Oh' and again the monosyllable carried a tremendous punch.

'Lovely part of the world, this,' I said, returning to the attack.

'Yes.'

'I've never been in Yorkshire before, but I like what I've seen.'

'Oh.'

'Have you known Mr Farnon very long?'

'Yes.'

'I believe he's quite young — about thirty?'

'Yes.'

'Wonderful weather.'

'Yes.'

I kept at it with courage and tenacity for about five minutes, hunting for something original or witty, but finally, Miss Brompton, instead of answering, took the cigarette from her mouth, turned towards me and gave me a long, blank stare. I knew that was the end and shrank into silence.

After that, she sat staring out of the french window, pulling deeply at her cigarette, narrowing her eyes as the smoke trickled from her lips. As far as she was concerned, I just wasn't there.

I was able to observe her at will and she was interesting. I had never met a living piece of a society magazine before. Cool, linen dress, expensive-looking cardigan, elegant legs and the glorious red hair falling on her shoulders.

And yet here was a fascinating thought. She was sitting there positively hungering for a little fat German vet. This Farnon must have something.

The tableau was finally broken up when Miss Brompton jumped to her feet. She hurled her cigarette savagely into the fireplace and marched from the room.

Wearily, I got out of my chair. My head began to ache as I shuffled through the french window into the garden. I flopped down among the knee deep grass on the lawn and rested my back against a towering acacia tree. Where the devil was Farnon? Was he really expecting me or had somebody played a horrible practical joke on me? I felt suddenly cold. I had spent my last few pounds getting here and if there was some mistake I was in trouble.

But, looking around me, I began to feel better. The sunshine beat back from the high old walls, bees droned among the bright masses of flowers. A gentle breeze stirred the withered blooms of a magnificent wistaria which almost covered the back of the house. There was peace here.

I leaned my head against the bark and closed my eyes. I could see Herr Farrenen, looking just as I had imagined him, standing over me. He wore a shocked expression.

'Wass is dis you haff done?' he spluttered, his fat jowls quivering with rage. 'You kom to my house under false pretences, you insult Fräulein Brompton, you trink my tea, you eat my food. Vat else you do, hein? Maybe you steal my spoons. You talk about assistant but I vant no assistant. Is best I telephone the police.'

Herr Farrenen seized the phone in a pudgy hand. Even in my dream, I wondered how the man could use such a completely corny

36

accent. I heard the thick voice saying 'Hello, hello.'

And I opened my eyes. Somebody was saying 'Hello', but it wasn't Herr Farrenen. A tall, thin man was leaning against the wall, his hands in his pockets. Something seemed to be amusing him. As I struggled to my feet, he heaved himself away from the wall and held out his hand. 'Sorry you've had to wait. I'm Siegfried Farnon.'

He was just about the most English-looking man I had ever seen. Long, humorous, strong-jawed face. Small, clipped moustache, untidy, sandy hair. He was wearing an old tweed jacket and shapeless flannel trousers. The collar of his check shirt was frayed and the tie carelessly knotted. He looked as though he didn't spend much time in front of a mirror.

Studying him, I began to feel better despite the ache in my neck where it had rested against the tree. I shook my head to get my eyes fully open and tufts of grass fell from my hair. 'There was a Miss Brompton here,' I blurted out. 'She came to tea. I explained you had been called away.'

Farnon looked thoughtful, but not put out. He rubbed his chin slowly. 'Mm, yes — well, never mind. But I do apologise for being out when you arrived. I have a shocking memory and I just forgot.'

It was the most English voice, too.

Farnon gave me a long, searching look, then he grinned. 'Let's go inside. I want to show you round the place.'

CHAPTER 3

The long offshoot behind the house had been
the servants' quarters in grander days. Here,
everything was dark and narrow and poky as
if in deliberate contrast with the front.

Farnon led me to the first of several doors
which opened off a passage where the smell
of ether and carbolic hung on the air. 'This,'
he said, with a secret gleam in his eye as
though he were about to unveil the mysteries
of Aladdin's cave, 'is the dispensary.'

The dispensary was an important place in
the days before penicillin and the sulphon-
amides. Rows of gleaming Winchester bottles
lined the white walls from floor to ceiling. I
savoured the familiar names: Sweet Spirits of
Nitre, Tincture of Camphor, Chlorodyne,
Formalin, Salammoniac, Hexamine, Sugar of
Lead, Linimentum Album, Perchloride of
Mercury, Red Blister. The lines of labels were
comforting.

I was an initiate among old friends. I had
painfully accumulated their lore, ferreting out

their secrets over the years. I knew their origins, actions and uses, and their maddeningly varied dosage. The examiner's voice — 'And what is the dose for the horse? — and the cow? — and the sheep? — and the pig? — and the dog? — and the cat?'

These shelves held the vet's entire armoury against disease and, on a bench under the window, I could see the instruments for compounding them; the graduated vessels and beakers, the mortars and pestles. And underneath, in an open cupboard, the medicine bottles, piles of corks of all sizes, pill boxes, powder papers.

As we moved around, Farnon's manner became more and more animated. His eyes glittered and he talked rapidly. Often, he reached up and caressed a Winchester on its shelf; or he would lift out a horse ball or an electuary from its box, give it a friendly pat and replace it with tenderness.

'Look at this stuff, Herriot,' he shouted without warning. 'Adrevan! This is the remedy, par excellence, for red worms in horses. A bit expensive, mind you — ten bob a packet. And these gentian violet pessaries. If you shove one of these into a cow's uterus after a dirty cleansing, it turns the discharges a very pretty colour. Really looks as though it's doing something. And have you seen this trick?'

He placed a few crystals of resublimated

iodine on a glass dish and added a drop of turpentine. Nothing happened for a second then a dense cloud of purple smoke rolled heavily to the ceiling. He gave a great bellow of laughter at my startled face.

'Like witchcraft, isn't it? I use it for wounds in horses' feet. The chemical reaction drives the iodine deep into the tissues.'

'It does?'

'Well, I don't know, but that's the theory, and anyway, you must admit it looks wonderful. Impresses the toughest client.'

Some of the bottles on the shelves fell short of the ethical standards I had learned in college. Like the one labelled 'Colic Drench' and featuring a floridly drawn picture of a horse rolling in agony. The animal's face was turned outwards and wore an expression of very human anguish. Another bore the legend 'Universal Cattle Medicine' in ornate script — 'A sovereign Remedy for coughs, chills, scours, pneumonia, milk fever, gargett and all forms of indigestion.' At the bottom of the label, in flaring black capitals, was the assurance, 'Never Fails to Give Relief.'

Farnon had something to say about most of the drugs. Each one had its place in his five years' experience of practice; they all had their fascination, their individual mystique. Many of the bottles were beautifully shaped, with heavy glass stoppers and their Latin names cut deeply into their sides; names

41

familiar to physicians for centuries, gathering fables through the years.

The two of us stood gazing at the gleaming rows without any idea that it was nearly all useless and that the days of the old medicines were nearly over. Soon they would be hustled into oblivion by the headlong rush of the new discoveries and they would never return.

'This is where we keep the instruments.' Farnon showed me into another little room. The small animal equipment lay on green baize shelves, very neat and impressively clean. Hypodermic syringes, whelping forceps, tooth scalers, probes, searchers, and, in a place of prominence, an ophthalmoscope.

Farnon lifted it lovingly from its black box. 'My latest purchase,' he murmured, stroking its smooth shaft. 'Wonderful thing. Here, have a peep at my retina.'

I switched on the bulb and gazed with interest at the glistening, coloured tapestry in the depths of his eye. 'Very pretty. I could write you a certificate of soundness.'

He laughed and thumped my shoulder. 'Good, I'm glad to hear it. I always fancied I had a touch of cataract in that one.'

He began to show me the large animal instruments which hung from hooks on the walls. Docking and firing irons, bloodless castrators, emasculators, casting ropes and hobbles, calving ropes and hooks. A new, silvery embryotome hung in the place of honour, but many of the instruments, like the drugs, were museum pieces. Particularly the blood stick and fleam, a relic of medieval times, but still used to bring the rich blood spouting into a bucket.

'You still can't beat it for laminitis,' Farnon declared seriously.

We finished up in the operating room with its bare white walls, high table, oxygen and ether anaesthetic outfit and a small steriliser.

'Not much small animal work in this district.' Farnon smoothed the table with his palm. 'But I'm trying to encourage it. It makes a pleasant change from lying on your belly in a cow house. The thing is, we've got to do the job right. The old castor oil and prussic acid doctrine is no good at all. You probably know that a lot of the old hands won't look at a dog or a cat, but the profession has got to change its ideas.'

He went over to a cupboard in the corner and opened the door. I could see glass shelves with a few scalpels, artery forceps, suture needles and bottles of catgut in spirit. He took out his handkerchief and flicked at an auroscope before closing the doors carefully.

'Well, what do you think of it all?' he asked as he went out into the passage.

'Great,' I replied. 'You've got just about everything you need here. I'm really impressed.'

He seemed to swell visibly. The thin cheeks

43

flushed and he hummed softly to himself. Then he burst loudly into song in a shaky baritone, keeping time with our steps as we marched along.

Back in the sitting-room, I told him about Bert Sharpe. 'Something about boring out a cow which was going on three cylinders. He talked about her ewer and felon — I didn't quite get it.'

Farnon laughed. 'I think I can translate. He wants a Hudson's operation doing on a blocked teat. Ewer is the udder and felon the local term for mastitis.'

'Well, thanks. And there was a deaf Irishman, a Mr Mulligan . . .'

'Wait a minute.' Farnon held up a hand. 'Let me guess — womitin'?'

'Aye, womitin' bad, sorr.'

'Right, I'll put up another pint of bismuth carb for him. I'm in favour of long-range treatment for this dog. He looks like an airedale but he's as big as a donkey and has a moody disposition. He's had Joe Mulligan on the floor a few times — just gets him down and worries him when he's got nothing better to do. But Joe loves him.'

'How about the womitin'?'

'Doesn't mean a thing. Natural reaction from eating every bit of rubbish he finds. Well, we'd better get out to Sharpe's. And there are one or two other visits — how about coming with me and I'll show you a bit of the district.'

Outside the house, Farnon motioned me towards a battered Hillman and, as I moved round to the passenger's side, I shot a startled glance at the treadless tyres, the rusty body-work, the almost opaque windscreen with its network of fine cracks. What I didn't notice was that the passenger seat was not fixed to the floor but stood freely on its sledge-like runners. I dropped into it and went over backwards, finishing with my head on the rear seat and my feet against the roof. Farnon helped me up, apologising with great charm, and we set off.

Once clear of the market place, the road dipped quite suddenly and we could see all of the Dale stretching away from us in the evening sunshine. The outlines of the great hills were softened in the gentle light and a broken streak of silver showed where the Darrow wandered on the valley floor.

Farnon was an unorthodox driver. Apparently captivated by the scene, he drove slowly down the hill, elbows resting on the wheel, his chin cupped in his hands. At the bottom of the hill he came out of his reverie and spurted to seventy miles an hour. The old car rocked crazily along the narrow road and my movable seat slewed from side to side as I jammed my feet against the floorboards.

Then he slammed on the brakes, pointed out some pedigree shorthorns in a field and jolted away again. He never looked at the road in front; all his attention was on the countryside around and behind him. It was that last bit that worried me, because he spent a lot of time driving fast and looking over his shoulder at the same time.

We left the road at last and made our way up a gated lane. My years of seeing practice had taught me to hop in and out very smartly as students were regarded primarily as gate-opening machines. Farnon, however, thanked me gravely every time and once I got over my surprise I found it refreshing.

We drew up in a farmyard. 'Lame horse here,' Farnon said. A strapping Clydesdale gelding was brought out and we watched attentively as the farmer trotted him up and down.

'Which leg do you make it?' my colleague asked. 'Near fore? Yes, I think so, too. Like to examine it?'

I put my hand on the foot, feeling how much hotter it was than the other. I called for a hammer and tapped the wall of the hoof. The horse flinched, raised the foot and held it trembling for a few seconds before replacing it carefully on the ground. 'Looks like pus in the foot to me.'

'I'll bet you're right,' Farnon said. 'They call it gravel around here, by the way. What do you suggest we do about it?'

'Open up the sole and evacuate the pus.'

46

'Right.' He held out a hoof knife. 'I'll watch your technique.'

With the uncomfortable feeling that I was on trial, I took the knife, lifted the foot and tucked it between my knees. I knew what I had to do — find the dark mark on the sole where the infection had entered and follow it down till I reached the pus. I scraped away the caked dirt and found not one, but several marks. After more tapping to find the painful area I selected a likely spot and started to cut.

The horn seemed as hard as marble and only the thinnest little shaving came away with each twist of the knife. The horse, too, appeared to appreciate having his sore foot lifted off the ground and gratefully leaned his full weight on my back. He hadn't been so comfortable all day. I groaned and dug him in the ribs with my elbow and, though it made him change his position for a second, he was soon leaning on again.

The mark was growing fainter and, after a final gouge with the knife, it disappeared altogether. I swore quietly and started on another mark. With my back at breaking point and the sweat trickling into my eyes, I knew that if this one petered out, too, I would have to let the foot go and take a rest. And with Farnon's eye on me I didn't want to do that.

Agonisingly, I hacked away and, as the hole

47

deepened, my knees began an uncontrollable trembling. The horse rested happily, his fifteen hundredweight cradled by this thoughtful human. I was wondering how it would look when I finally fell flat on my face when, under the knife blade, I saw a thin spurt of pus followed by a steady trickle.

'There it goes,' the farmer grunted. 'He'll get relief now.'

I enlarged the drainage hole and dropped the foot. It took me a long time to straighten up and when I stepped back, my shirt clung to my back.

'Well done, Herriot.' Farnon took the knife from me and slipped it into his pocket. 'It just isn't funny when the horn is as hard as that.'

He gave the horse a shot of tetanus anti-toxin then turned to the farmer. 'I wonder if you'd hold up the foot for a second while I disinfect the cavity.' The stocky little man gripped the foot between his knees and looked down with interest as Farnon filled the hole with iodine crystals and added some turpentine. Then he disappeared behind a billowing purple curtain.

I watched, fascinated, as the thick pall mounted and spread. I could locate the little man only by the spluttering noises from somewhere in the middle.

As the smoke began to clear, a pair of round, startled eyes came into view. 'By gaw,

Mr Farnon, I wondered what the 'ell had happened for a minute,' the farmer said between coughs. He looked down again at the blackened hole in the hoof and spoke reverently: 'It's wonderful what science can do nowadays.'

We did two more visits, one to a calf with a cut leg which I stitched, dressed and bandaged, then to the cow with the blocked teat.

Mr Sharpe was waiting, still looking eager. He led us into the byre and Farnon gestured towards the cow. 'See what you can make of it.'

I squatted down and palpated the teat, feeling the mass of thickened tissue half up. It would have to be broken down by a Hudson's instrument and I began to work the thin metal spiral up the teat. One second later, I was sitting gasping in the dung channel with the neat imprint of a cloven hoof on my shirt front, just over the solar plexus.

It was embarrassing, but there was nothing I could do but sit there fighting for breath, my mouth opening and shutting like a stranded fish.

Mr Sharpe held his hand over his mouth, his innate politeness at war with his natural amusement at seeing the vet come to grief. 'I'm sorry, young man, but I owt to 'ave told you that this is a very friendly cow. She allus likes to shake hands.' Then, overcome by his own wit, he rested his forehead on the cow's back and went into a long paroxysm of silent mirth.

I took my time to recover, then rose with dignity from the channel. With Mr Sharpe holding the nose and Farnon lifting up the tail, I managed to get the instrument past the fibrous mass and by a few downward tugs I cleared the obstruction; but, though the precautions cramped the cow's style a little, she still got in several telling blows on my arms and legs.

When it was over, the farmer grasped the teat and sent a long white jet frothing on the floor. 'Capital! She's going on four cylinders now!'

CHAPTER 4

'We'll go home a different way.' Farnon leaned over the driving wheel and wiped the cracked windscreen with his sleeve. 'Over the Brenkstone Pass and down Sildale. It's not much further and I'd like you to see it.'

We took a steep, winding road, climbing higher and still higher with the hillside falling away sheer to a dark ravine where a rocky stream rushed headlong to the gentler country below. On the top, we got out of the car. In the summer dusk, a wild panorama of tumbling fells and peaks rolled away and lost itself in the crimson and gold ribbons of the western sky. To the east, a black mountain overhung us, menacing in its naked bulk. Huge, square-cut boulders littered the lower slopes.

I whistled softly as I looked around. This was different from the friendly hill country I had seen on the approach to Darrowby.

Farnon turned towards me. 'Yes, one of the wildest spots in England. A fearsome place in winter. I've known this pass to be blocked for weeks on end.'

I pulled the clean air deeply into my lungs. Nothing stirred in the vastness, but a curlew cried faintly and I could just hear the distant roar of the torrent a thousand feet below.

It was dark when we got into the car and started the long descent into Sildale. The valley was a shapeless blur but points of light showed where the lonely farms clung to the hillsides.

We came to a silent village and Farnon applied his brakes violently. I tobogganed effortlessly across the floor on my mobile seat and collided with the windscreen. My head made a ringing sound against the glass but Farnon didn't seem to notice. 'There's a grand little pub here. Let's go in and have a beer.'

The pub was something new to me. It was, simply, a large kitchen, square and stone-flagged. An enormous fireplace and an old black cooking range took up one end. A kettle stood on the hearth and a single large log hissed and crackled, filling the room with its resinous scent.

About a dozen men sat on the high-backed settles which lined the walls. In front of them, rows of pint mugs rested on oak tables which were fissured and twisted with age.

There was a silence as we went in. Then somebody said 'Now then, Mr Farnon,' not enthusiastically, but politely, and this brought some friendly grunts and nods from the company. They were mostly farmers or farm workers taking their pleasure without fuss or excitement. Most were burnt red by the sun and some of the younger ones were tieless, muscular necks and chests showing through the open shirt fronts. Soft murmurs and clicks rose from a peaceful domino game in the corner.

Farnon guided me to a seat, ordered two beers and turned to face me. 'Well, you can have this job if you want it. Four quid a week and full board. O.K.?'

The suddenness struck me silent. I was in. And four pounds a week! I remembered the pathetic entries in the *Record.* 'Veterinary surgeon, fully experienced, will work for keep.' The B.V.M.A. had had to put pressure on the editor to stop him printing these cries from the heart. It hadn't looked so good to see members of the profession offering their services free. Four pounds a week was affluence.

'Thank you,' I said, trying hard not to look triumphant. 'I accept.'

'Good.' Farnon took a hasty gulp at his beer. 'Let me tell you about the practice. I bought it a year ago from an old man of eighty. Still practising, mind you, a real tough old character. But he'd got past getting up in the middle of the night, which isn't surprising. And, of course, in lots of other ways he had let things slide — hanging on to all the old ideas. Some of those ancient instruments in the surgery were his. One way and another, there was hardly any practice left and I'm trying to work it up again now. There's very little profit in it so far, but if we stick in for a few years, I'm confident we'll have a good business. The farmers are pleased to see a younger man taking over and they welcome new treatments and operations. But I'm having to educate them out of the three and sixpenny consulting fee the old chap used to charge and it's been a hard slog. These Dalesmen are wonderful people and you'll like them, but they don't like parting with their brass unless you can prove they are getting something in return.'

He talked on enthusiastically of his plans for the future, the drinks kept coming and the atmosphere in the pub thawed steadily. The place filled up as the regulars from the village streamed in, the noise and heat increased and by near closing time I had got separated from my colleague and was in the middle of a laughing group I seemed to have known for years.

But there was one odd character who swam repeatedly into my field of vision. An elderly little man with a soiled white panama perched above a smooth, brown, time-worn face like an old boot. He was dodging round the edge of the group, beckoning and winking.

I could see there was something on his mind, so I broke away and allowed myself to be led to a seat in the corner. The old man sat opposite me, rested his hands and chin on the handle of his walking stick and regarded me from under drooping eyelids.

'Now then, young man, ah've summat to tell thee. Ah've been among beasts all me life and I'm going to tell tha summat.'

My toes began to curl. I had been caught this way before. Early in my college career I had discovered that all the older inhabitants of the agricultural world seemed to have the idea that they had something priceless to impart. And it usually took a long time. I looked around me in alarm but I was trapped. The old man shuffled his chair closer and began to talk in a conspiratorial whisper. Gusts of beery breath hit my face from six inches range.

There was nothing new about the old man's tale — just the usual recital of miraculous cures he had wrought, infallible remedies known only to himself and many little side-tracks about how unscrupulous people had tried in vain to worm his secrets from him. He paused only to take expert pulls at his pint pot; his tiny frame seemed to be able to accommodate a surprising amount of beer.

But he was enjoying himself and I let him ramble on. In fact I encouraged him by expressing amazement and admiration at his feats.

The little man had never had such an audience. He was a retired smallholder and it had been years since anybody had shown him the appreciation he deserved. His face wore a lopsided leer and his swimmy eyes were alight with friendship. But suddenly he became serious and sat up straight.

'Now, afore ye go, young man, I'm going to tell thee summat nobody knows but me. Ah could've made a lot o' money out o' this. Folks 'ave been after me for years to tell 'em but I never 'ave.'

He lowered the level in his glass by several inches then narrowed his eyes to slits. 'It's the cure for mallenders and sallenders in 'osses.'

I started up in my chair as though the roof had begun to fall in. 'You can't mean it,' I gasped. 'Not mallenders and sallenders.'

The old man looked smug. 'Ah, but ah do mean it. All you have to do is rub on this salve of mine and the 'oss walks away sound. He's better by that!' His voice rose to a thin shout and he made a violent gesture with his arm which swept his nearly empty glass to the floor.

I gave a low, incredulous whistle and ordered another pint. 'And you're really going to tell me the name of this salve?' I whispered.

'I am, young man, but only on one condition. Tha must tell no one. Tha must keep it to thaself, then nobody'll know but thee and me.' He effortlessly tipped half of his fresh pint down his throat. 'Just thee and me, lad.'

'All right, I promise you. I'll not tell a soul. Now what is this wonderful stuff?'

The old man looked furtively round the crowded room. Then he took a deep breath, laid his hand on my shoulder and put his lips close to my ear. He hiccuped once, solemnly, and spoke in a hoarse whisper. 'Marshmallow ointment.'

I grasped his hand and wrung it silently. The old man, deeply moved, spilled most of his final half pint down his chin.

But Farnon was making signals from the door. It was time to go. We surged out with our new friends, making a little island of noise and light in the quiet village street. A tow-haired young fellow in shirt sleeves opened the car door with natural courtesy and, waving a final good night, I plunged in. This time, the seat went over quicker than usual and I hurtled backwards, coming to rest with my head among some Wellingtons and my knees tucked underneath my chin.

A row of surprised faces peered in at me through the back window, but soon, willing hands were helping me up and the trick seat was placed upright on its rockers again. I wondered how long it had been like that and if my employer had ever thought of having it fixed.

We roared off into the darkness and I looked back at the waving group. I could see the little man, his panama gleaming like new in the light from the doorway. He was holding his finger to his lips.

CHAPTER 5

The past five years had been leading up to one moment and it hadn't arrived yet. I had been in Darrowby for twenty-four hours now and I still hadn't been to a visit on my own.

Another day had passed in going around with Farnon. It was a funny thing, but, for a man who seemed careless, forgetful and a few other things, Farnon was frustratingly cautious about launching his new assistant.

We had been over into Lidderdale today and I had met more of the clients — friendly, polite farmers who received me pleasantly and wished me success. But working under Farnon's supervision was like being back at college with the professor's eye on me. I felt strongly that my professional career would not start until I, James Herriot, went out and attended a sick animal, unaided and unobserved.

However, the time couldn't be very far away now. Farnon had gone off to Brawton to see his mother again. A devoted son, I thought wonderingly. And he had said he would be back late, so the old lady must keep unusual hours. But never mind about that — what mattered was that I was in charge.

I sat in an armchair with a frayed loose cover and looked out through the french window at the shadows thrown by the evening sun across the shaggy lawn. I had the feeling that I would be doing a lot of this.

I wondered idly what my first call would be. Probably an anticlimax after the years of waiting. Something like a coughing calf or a pig with constipation. And maybe that would be no bad thing — to start with something I could easily put right. I was in the middle of these comfortable musings when the telephone exploded out in the passage. The insistent clamour sounded abnormally loud in the empty house. I lifted the receiver.

'Is that Mr Farnon?' It was a deep voice with a harsh edge to it. Not a local accent; possibly a trace of the South West.

'No, I'm sorry, he's out. This is his assistant.'

'When will he be back?'

'Not till late, I'm afraid. Can I do anything for you?'

'I don't know whether you can do anything for me or not.' The voice took on a hectoring tone. 'I am Mr Soames, Lord Hulton's farm manager. I have a valuable hunting horse with colic. Do you know anything about colic?'

I felt my hackles rising. 'I am a veterinary surgeon, so I think I should know something about it.'

There was a long pause, and the voice barked again. 'Well, I reckon you'll have to do. In any case, I know the injection the horse wants. Bring some arecoline with you. Mr Farnon uses it. And for God's sake, don't be all night getting here. How long will you be?'

'I'm leaving now.'

'Right.'

I heard the receiver bang down on to its rest. My face felt hot as I walked away from the phone. So my first case wasn't going to be a formality. Colics were tricky things and I had an aggressive know-all called Soames thrown in for good measure.

On the eight-mile journey to the case, I reread from memory that great classic, Caulton Reeks' *Common Colics of the Horse*. I had gone through it so often in my final year that I could recite stretches of it like poetry. The well-thumbed pages hovered in front of me, phantom-like, as I drove.

This would probably be a mild impaction or a bit of spasm. Might have had a change of food or too much rich grass. Yes, that would be it; most colics were like that. A quick shot of arecoline and maybe some chlorodyne to relieve the discomfort and all would be well. My mind went back to the cases I had met while seeing practice. The horse standing quietly except that it occasionally eased a hind leg or looked round at its side. There was nothing to it, really.

I was elaborating this happy picture when I arrived. I drove into a spotless, gravelled yard surrounded on three sides by substantial loose boxes. A man was standing there, a broad-shouldered, thick-set figure, very trim in check cap and jacket, well-cut breeches and shiny leggings.

The car drew up about thirty yards away and, as I got out, the man slowly and deliberately turned his back on me. I walked across the yard, taking my time, waiting for the other to turn round, but he stood motionless, hands in pockets, looking in the other direction.

I stopped a few feet away but still the man did not turn. After a long time, and when I had got tired of looking at the back, I spoke.

'Mr Soames?'

At first the man did not move, then he turned very slowly. He had a thick, red neck, a ruddy face and small, fiery eyes. He made no answer but looked me over carefully from head to foot, taking in the worn raincoat, my youth, my air of inexperience. When he had completed his examination he looked away again.

'Yes, I am Mr Soames.' He stressed the 'Mr' as though it meant a lot to him. 'I am a very great friend of Mr Farnon.'

'My name is Herriot.'

Soames didn't appear to have heard. 'Yes, a clever man is Mr Farnon. We are great friends.'

'I understand you have a horse with colic.' I wished my voice didn't sound so high and unsteady.

Soames' gaze was still directed somewhere into the sky. He whistled a little tune softly to himself before replying. 'In there,' he said, jerking his head in the direction of one of the boxes. 'One of his lordship's best hunters. In need of expert assistance, I think.' He put a bit of emphasis on the 'expert'.

I opened the door and went inside. And I stopped as though I had walked into a wall. It was a very large box, deeply bedded with peat moss. A bay horse was staggering round and round the perimeter where he had worn a deep path in the peat. He was lathered in sweat from nose to tail, his nostrils were dilated and his eyes stared blankly in front of him. His head rolled about at every step and, through his clenched teeth, gobbets of foam dripped to the floor. A rank steam rose from his body as though he had been galloping.

My mouth had gone dry. I found it difficult to speak and when I did, it was almost in a whisper. 'How long has he been like this?'

'Oh, he started with a bit of belly ache this morning. I've been giving him black draughts all day, or at least this fellow has. I wouldn't be surprised if he's made a bloody mess of it like he does everything.'

I saw that there was somebody standing in the shadows in the corner; a large, fat man with a head collar in his hand.

'Oh, I got the draughts down him, right enough, Mr Soames, but they haven't done 'im no good.' The big man looked scared.

'You call yourself a horseman,' Soames said, 'but I should have done the damn job myself. I reckon he'd have been better by now.'

'It would take more than a black draught to help him,' I said. 'This is no ordinary colic'

'What the hell is it, then?'

'Well, I can't say till I've examined him, but severe, continuous pain like that could mean a torsion — a twisted bowel.'

'Twisted bowel, my foot! He's got a bit of belly ache, that's all. He hasn't passed anything all day and he wants something to shift him. Have you got the arecoline with you?'

'If this is a torsion, arecoline would be the worst thing you could give him. He's in agony now, but that would drive him mad. It acts by contracting the muscles of the intestines.'

'God dammit,' snarled Soames, 'don't start giving me a bloody lecture. Are you going to start doing something for the horse or aren't you?'

I turned to the big man in the corner. 'Slip on that head collar and I'll examine him.'

With the collar on, the horse was brought

to a halt. He stood there, trembling and groaning as I passed a hand between ribs and elbows, feeling for the pulse. It was as bad as it could be — a racing, thready beat. I everted an eyelid with my fingers; the mucous membrane was a dark, brick red. The thermometer showed a temperature of a hundred and three.

I looked across the box at Soames. 'Could I have a bucket of hot water, soap and a towel, please?'

'What the devil for? You've done nothing yet and you want to have awash?'

'I want to make a rectal examination. Will you please bring me the water?'

'God help us, I've never seen anything like this.' Soames passed a hand wearily over his eyes then swung round on the big man.

'Well, come on, don't stand around there. Get him his water and we'll maybe get something done.'

When the water came, I soaped my arm and gently inserted it into the animal's rectum. I could feel plainly the displacement of the small intestine on the left side and a tense, tympanitic mass which should not have been there. As I touched it, the horse shuddered and groaned again.

As I washed and dried my arms, my heart pounded. What was I to do? What could I say?

Soames was stamping in and out of the box,

muttering to himself as the pain-maddened animal writhed and twisted. 'Hold the bloody thing,' he bellowed at the horseman who was gripping the head collar. 'What the bloody hell are you playing at?'

The big man said nothing. He was in no way to blame but he just stared back stolidly at Soames.

I took a deep breath. 'Everything points to the one thing. I'm convinced this horse has a torsion.'

'All right then, have it your own way. He's got a torsion. Only for God's sake do something, will you? Are we going to stand in here all night?'

'There's nothing anybody can do. There is no cure for this. The important thing is to put him out of his pain as quickly as possible.'

Soames screwed up his face. 'No cure? Put him out of his pain? What rubbish is this you're talking? Just what are you getting at?'

I took a hold on myself. 'I suggest you let me put him down immediately.'

'What do you mean?' Soames' mouth fell open.

'I mean that I should shoot him now, straight away. I have a humane killer in the car.'

Soames looked as if he was going to explode. 'Shoot him! Are you stark raving mad? Do you know how much that horse is worth?'

'It makes no difference what he's worth,

Mr Soames. He has been going through hell all day and he's dying now. You should have called me out long ago. He might live a few hours more but the end would be the same. And he's in dreadful pain, continuous pain.'

Soames sunk his head in his hands. 'Oh God, why did this have to happen to me? His lordship is on holiday or I'd call him out to try to make you see some sense. I tell you, if your boss had been here he'd have given that horse an injection and put him right in half an hour. Look here, can't we wait till Mr Farnon gets back tonight and let him have a look at him?'

Something in me leaped gladly at the idea. Give a shot of morphine and get away out of it. Leave the responsibility to somebody else. It would be easy. I looked again at the horse. He had recommenced his blind circling of the box, stumbling round and round in a despairing attempt to leave his agony behind. As I watched, he raised his lolling head and gave a little whinny. It was a desolate, uncomprehending, frantic sound and it was enough for me.

I strode quickly out and got the killer from the car. 'Steady his head,' I said to the big man and placed the muzzle between the glazing eyes. There was a sharp crack and the horse's legs buckled. He thudded down on the peat and lay still.

I turned to Soames who was staring at the

body in disbelief. 'Mr Farnon will come round in the morning and carry out a post-mortem. I'd like Lord Hulton to have my diagnosis confirmed.'

I put on my jacket and went out to the car. As I started the engine, Soames opened the door and pushed his head in. He spoke quietly but his voice was furious. 'I'm going to inform his lordship about this night's work. And Mr Farnon too. I'll let him know what kind of an assistant he's landed himself with. And let me tell you this. You'll be proved wrong at that post-mortem tomorrow and then I'm going to sue you.' He banged the door shut and walked away.

Back at the surgery, I decided to wait up for my boss and I sat there trying to rid myself of the feeling that I had blasted my career before it had got started. Yet, looking back, I knew I couldn't have done anything else. No matter how many times I went over the ground, the conclusion was always the same.

It was 1 a.m. before Farnon got back. His evening with his mother had stimulated him. His thin cheeks were flushed and he smelt pleasantly of gin. I was surprised to see that he was wearing evening dress and though the dinner jacket was of old-fashioned cut and hung in loose folds on his bony frame, he still managed to look like an ambassador.

He listened in silence as I told him about

the horse. He was about to comment when the phone rang. 'A late one,' he whispered, then 'Oh, it's you, Mr Soames.' He nodded at me and settled down in his chair. He was a long time saying 'Yes' and 'No' and 'I see', then he sat up decisively and began to speak.

'Thank you for ringing, Mr Soames, and it seems as though Mr Herriot did the only possible thing in the circumstances. No, I cannot agree. It would have been cruel to leave him. One of our duties is to prevent suffering. Well, I'm sorry you feel like that, but I consider Mr Herriot to be a highly capable veterinary surgeon. If I had been there I have no doubt I'd have done the same thing. Good night, Mr Soames, I'll see you in the morning.'

I felt so much better that I almost launched into a speech of gratitude, but in the end, all I said was 'Thanks'.

Farnon reached up into the glass-fronted cupboard above the mantelpiece and pulled out a bottle of whisky. He carelessly slopped out half a tumblerful and pushed it at me. He gave himself a similar measure and fell back into the armchair.

He took a deep swallow, stared for a few seconds at the amber fluid in the glass then looked up with a smile. 'Well, you certainly got chucked in at the deep end tonight, my boy. Your first case! And it had to be Soames, too.'

'Do you know him very well?'

'Oh, I know all about him. A nasty piece of work and enough to put anybody off their stroke. Believe me, he's no friend of mine. In fact, rumour has it that he's a bit of a crook. They say he's been feathering his nest for a long time at his lordship's expense. He'll slip up one day, I expect.'

The neat whisky burned a fiery path down to my stomach but I felt I needed it. 'I wouldn't like too many sessions like tonight's, but I don't suppose veterinary practice is like that all the time.'

'Well, not quite,' Farnon replied, 'but you never know what's in store for you. It's a funny profession, ours, you know. It offers unparalleled opportunities for making a chump of yourself.'

'But I expect a lot depends on your ability.'

'To a certain extent. It helps to be good at the job, of course, but even if you're a positive genius humiliation and ridicule are lurking just round the corner. I once got an eminent horse specialist along here to do a rig operation and the horse stopped breathing half way through. The sight of that man dancing frantically on his patient's ribs taught me a great truth — that I was going to look just as big a fool at fairly regular intervals throughout my career.'

I laughed. 'Then I might as well resign myself to it right at the beginning.'

'That's the idea. Animals are unpredictable

things so our whole life is unpredictable. It's a long tale of little triumphs and disasters and you've got to really like it to stick it. Tonight it was Soames, but another night it'll be something else. One thing, you never get bored. Here, have some more whisky.'

I drank the whisky and then some more and we talked. It seemed no time at all before the dark bulk of the acacia tree began to emerge from the grey light beyond the french window, a blackbird tried a few tentative pipes and Farnon was regretfully shaking the last drops from the bottle into his glass.

He yawned, jerked the knot out of his black tie and looked at his watch. 'Well, five o'clock. Who would have thought it? But I'm glad we had a drink together — only right to celebrate your first case. It was a right one, wasn't it?'

CHAPTER 6

Two and a half hours' sleep was a meagre ration but I made a point of being up by seven thirty and downstairs, shaved and scrubbed, by eight.

But I breakfasted alone. Mrs Hall, impassively placing scrambled eggs before me, told me that my employer had left some time ago to do the P.M. on Lord Hulton's horse. I wondered if he had bothered to go to bed at all.

I was busy with the last of the toast when Farnon burst into the room. I was getting used to his entrances and hardly jumped at all as he wrenched at the door handle and almost leaped into the middle of the carpet. He looked rosy and in excellent spirits.

'Anything left in that coffee pot? I'll join you for a cup.' He crashed down on a protesting chair. 'Well, you've nothing to worry about. The P.M. showed a classical torsion. Several loops of bowel involved — black and tympanitic. I'm glad you put the poor beggar down straight away.'

'Did you see my friend Soames?'

'Oh, he was there, of course. He tried to get in a few digs about you but I quietened him. I just pointed out that he had delayed far too long in sending for us and that Lord Hulton wasn't going to be too pleased when he heard how his horse had suffered. I left him chewing over that.'

The news did a lot to lighten my outlook. I went over to the desk and got the day book. 'Here are this morning's calls. What would you like me to do?'

Farnon picked out a round of visits, scribbled the list on a scrap of paper and handed it over. 'Here you are,' he said, 'a few nice, trouble-free cases to get yourself worked in.'

I was turning to leave when he called me back. 'Oh, there's one other thing I'd like you to do. My young brother is hitching from Edinburgh today. He's at the Veterinary College there and the term finished yesterday. When he gets within striking distance he'll probably give us a ring. I wonder if you'd slip out and pick him up?'

'Certainly. Glad to.'

'His name is Tristan, by the way.'

'Tristan?'

'Yes. Oh, I should have told you. You must have wondered about my own queer name. It was my father. Great Wagnerian. It nearly ruled his life. It was music all the time — mainly Wagner.'

'I'm a bit partial myself.'

'Ah well, yes, but you didn't get it morning, noon and night like we did. And then to be stuck with a name like Siegfried. Anyway, it could have been worse — Wotan, for instance.'

'Or Pogner.'

Farnon looked startled. 'By golly, you're right. I'd forgotten about old Pogner. I suppose I've a lot to be thankful for.'

It was late afternoon before the expected call came. The voice at the other end was uncannily familiar.

'This is Tristan Farnon.'

'Gosh, you sound just like your brother.'

A pleasant laugh answered me. 'Everybody says that — oh, that's very good of you. I'd be glad of a lift. I'm at the Holly Tree Café on the Great North Road.'

After the voice I had been expecting to find a younger edition of my employer but the small, boyish-faced figure sitting on a rucksack could hardly have been less like him. He got up, pushed back the dark hair from his forehead and held out his hand. The smile was charming.

'Had much walking to do?' I asked.

'Oh, a fair bit, but I needed the exercise. We had a roughish end of term party last night.' He opened the car door and threw the rucksack into the back. As I started the engine he settled himself in the passenger seat as though it were a luxurious armchair, pulled out a paper packet of Woodbines, lit one with tender concentration and gulped the smoke down blissfully. He produced the *Daily Mirror* from a side pocket and shook it open with a sigh of utter content. The smoke, which had been gone a long time, began to wisp from his nose and mouth.

I turned west off the great highway and the rumble of traffic faded rapidly behind us. I glanced round at Tristan. 'You'll have just finished exams?' I said.

'Yes, pathology and parasitology.'

I almost broke one of my steadfast rules by asking him if he had passed, but stopped myself in time. It is a chancy business. But in any case, there was no shortage of conversation. Tristan had something to say about most of the news items and now and then he read out an extract and discussed it with me. I felt a growing conviction that I was in the presence of a quicker and livelier mind than my own. It seemed no time at all before we pulled up outside Skeldale House.

Siegfried was out when we arrived and it was early evening when he returned. He came in through the french window, gave me a friendly greeting and threw himself into an armchair. He had begun to talk about one of his cases when Tristan walked in.

The atmosphere in the room changed as though somebody had clicked a switch. Siegfried's smile became sardonic and he gave his brother a long, appraising look. He grunted a 'hello', then reached up and began to run his finger along the titles of the books in the alcove. He seemed absorbed in this for a few minutes and I could feel the tension building up. Tristan's expression had changed remarkably; his face had gone completely deadpan but his eyes were wary.

Siegfried finally located the book he was looking for, took it down from the shelf and began to leaf through it unhurriedly. Then, without looking up, he said quietly: 'Well, how did the exams go?'

Tristan swallowed carefully and took a deep breath. 'Did all right in parasitology,' he replied in a flat monotone.

Siegfried didn't appear to have heard. He had found something interesting in his book and settled back to read. He took his time over it, then put the book back on the shelf. He began again the business of going along the titles; still with his back to his brother, he spoke again in the same soft voice.

'How about pathology?'

Tristan was on the edge of his chair now, as if ready to make a run for it. His eyes darted from his brother to the book shelves and back again. 'Didn't get it,' he said tonelessly.

There was no reaction from Siegfried. He

kept up his patient search for his book, occasionally pulling a volume out, glancing at it and replacing it carefully. Then he gave up the hunt, lay back in the chair with his arms dangling almost to the floor and looked at Tristan. 'So you failed pathology,' he said conversationally.

I was surprised to hear myself babbling with an edge of hysteria in my voice. 'Well now that's pretty good you know. It puts him in the final year and he'll be able to sit path, at Christmas. He won't lose any time that way and, after all, it's a tough subject.'

Siegfried turned a cold eye on me. 'So you think it's pretty good, do you?' There was a pause and a long silence which was broken by a totally unexpected bellow as he rounded on his brother. 'Well, I don't! I think it is bloody awful! It's a damned disgrace, that's what it is. What the hell have you been doing all this term, anyway? Boozing, I should think, chasing women, spending my money, anything but working. And now you've got the bloody nerve to walk in here and tell me you've failed pathology. You're lazy, that's your trouble, isn't it? You're bloody bone idle!'

He was almost unrecognisable. His face was darkly flushed and his eyes glared. He yelled wildly again at his brother. 'But I've had enough this time. I'm sick of you. I'm not going to work my fingers to the bloody bone to keep you up there idling your time away.

This is the end. You're sacked, do you hear me? Sacked once and for all. So get out of here — I don't want to see you around any more. Go on, get out!'

Tristan, who had preserved an air of injured dignity throughout, withdrew quietly.

Writhing with embarrassment, I looked at Siegfried. He was showing the strain of the interview. His complexion had gone blotchy; he muttered to himself and drummed his fingers on the arm of the chair.

I was aghast at having to witness this break-up and I was grateful when Siegfried sent me on a call and I was able to get out of the room.

It was nearly dark when I got back and I drove round to the back lane and into the yard at the foot of the garden. The creaking of the garage doors disturbed the rooks in the great elms which overhung the buildings. Far up in the darkness there was a faint fluttering, a muffled cawing then silence. As I stood listening, I became aware of a figure in the gloom, standing by the yard door, looking down the garden. As the face turned towards me I saw it was Tristan.

Again, I felt embarrassed. It was an unfortunate intrusion when the poor fellow had come up here to brood alone. 'Sorry about the way things turned out,' I said awkwardly.

The tip of the cigarette glowed brightly as Tristan took a long pull. 'No, no, that's all right. Could have been a lot worse, you know.'

'Worse? Well, it's bad enough, isn't it? What are you going to do?'

'Do? What do you mean?'

'Well, you've been kicked out, haven't you? Where are you going to sleep tonight?'

'I can see you don't understand,' Tristan said. He took his cigarette from his mouth and I saw the gleam of very white teeth as he smiled. 'You needn't worry, I'm sleeping here and I'll be down to breakfast in the morning.'

'But how about your brother?'

'Siegfried? Oh, he'll have forgotten all about it by then.'

'Are you sure?'

'Dead sure. He's always sacking me and he always forgets. Anyway, things turned out very well. The only tricky bit back there was getting him to swallow that bit about the parasitology.'

I stared at the shadowy form by my side. Again, there was a rustling as the rooks stirred in the tall trees then settled into silence.

'The parasitology?'

'Yes. If you think back, all I said was that I had done all right. I wasn't any more specific than that.'

'Then you mean . . . ?'

Tristan laughed softly and thumped my shoulder.

'That's right, I didn't get parasitology. I

failed in both. But don't worry, I'll pass them at Christmas.'

CHAPTER 7

I huddled deeper in the blankets as the strident brreeng-brreeng, brreeng-brreeng of the telephone echoed through the old house.

It was three weeks since Tristan's arrival and life at Skeldale House had settled into a fairly regular pattern. Every day began much the same with the phone ringing between seven and eight o'clock after the farmers had had the first look at their stock.

There was only one phone in the house. It rested on a ledge in the tiled passage downstairs. Siegfried had impressed on me that I shouldn't get out of bed for these early calls. He had delegated the job to Tristan; the responsibility would be good for him. Siegfried had been emphatic about it.

I listened to the ringing. It went on and on — it seemed to get louder. There was neither sound nor movement from Tristan's room and I waited for the next move in the daily drama. It came, as always, with a door crashing back on its hinges, then Siegfried rushed out on to the landing and bounded down the stairs three at a time.

A long silence followed and I could picture him shivering in the draughty passage, his bare feet freezing on the tiles as he listened to the farmer's leisurely account of the animal's symptoms. Then the ting of the phone in its rest and the mad pounding of feet on the stairs as Siegfried made a dash for his brother's room.

Next a wrenching sound as the door was flung open, then a yell of rage. I detected a note of triumph; it meant Tristan had been caught in bed — a definite victory for Siegfried and he didn't have many victories. Usually, Tristan exploited his quick-dressing technique and confronted his brother fully dressed. It gave him a psychological advantage to be knotting his tie when Siegfried was still in pyjamas.

But this morning Tristan had overplayed his hand; trying to snatch the extra few seconds he was caught between the sheets. I listened to the shouts. 'Why didn't you answer the bloody phone like I told you? Don't tell me you're deaf as well as idle! Come on, out of it, out, out!'

But I knew Tristan would make a quick come-back. When he was caught in bed he usually scored a few points by being half way through his breakfast before his brother came in.

Later, I watched Siegfried's face as he entered the dining-room and saw Tristan munching his toast happily, his *Daily Mirror* balanced against the coffee pot. It was as if he had felt a sudden twinge of toothache.

It all made for a strained atmosphere and I was relieved when I was able to escape to collect my things for the morning round. Down the narrow passage with its familiar, exciting smell of ether and carbolic and out into the high-walled garden which led to the yard where the cars were kept.

It was the same every morning but, to me, there was always the feeling of surprise. When I stepped out into the sunshine and the scent of the flowers it was as though I was doing it for the first time. The clear air held a breath of the nearby moorland; after being buried in a city for five years it was difficult to take it all in.

I never hurried over this part. There could be an urgent case waiting but I still took my time. Along the narrow part between the ivy-covered wall and the long offshoot of the house where the wistaria climbed, pushing its tendrils and its withered blooms into the very rooms. Then past the rockery where the garden widened to the lawn, unkempt and lost-looking but lending coolness and soft-ness to the weathered brick. Around its borders flowers blazed in untidy profusion, battling with a jungle of weeds.

And so to the rose garden, then an asparagus bed whose fleshy fingers had grown into tall fronds. Further on were strawberries and raspberries. Fruit trees were everywhere, their branches dangling low over the path. Peaches, pears, cherries and plums were trained against the south wall where they fought for a place with wild-growing rambler roses.

Bees were at work among the flowers and the song of blackbirds and thrushes competed with the cawing of the rooks high up in the elms.

Life was full for me. There were so many things to find out and a lot I had to prove to myself. The days were quick and challenging and they pressed on me with their very newness. But it all stopped here in the garden. Everything seemed to have stopped here a long time ago. I looked back before going through the door into the yard and it was like suddenly coming across a picture in an old book; the empty, wild garden and the tall, silent house beyond. I could never quite believe it was there and that I was a part of it.

And the feeling was heightened when I went into the yard. It was square and cobbled and the grass grew in thick tufts between the stones. Buildings took up two sides; the two garages, once coach houses, a stable and saddle room, a loose box and a pigsty. Against the free wall a rusty iron pump hung over a stone water trough.

Above the stable was a hay loft and over one of the garages a dovecot. And there was old Boardman. He, too, seemed to have been left behind from grander days, hobbling round on his lame leg, doing nothing in particular.

He grunted good morning from his cubby hole where he kept a few tools and garden implements. Above his head his reminders of the war looked down; a row of coloured prints of Bruce Bairnsfather cartoons. He had stuck them up when he came home in 1918 and there they were still, dusty and curled at the edges but still speaking to him of Kaiser Bill and the shell holes and muddy trenches.

Boardman washed a car sometimes or did a little work in the garden, but he was content to earn a pound or two and get back to his yard. He spent a lot of time in the saddle room, just sitting. Sometimes he looked round the empty hooks where the harness used to hang and then he would make a rubbing movement with his fist against his palm.

He often talked to me of the great days. 'I can see t'owd doctor now, standing on top step waiting for his carriage to come round. Big, smart-looking feller he was. Allus wore a top hat and frock coat, and I can remember him when I was a lad, standing there, pulling on 'is gloves and giving his hat a tilt while he waited.'

Boardman's features seemed to soften and a light came into his eyes as though he were talking more to himself than to me. 'The old house was different then. A housekeeper and six servants there were and everything just so. And a full-time gardener. There weren't a blade of grass out of place in them days and the flowers all in rows and the trees pruned, tidy-like. And this yard — it were t'owd doctor's favourite spot. He'd come and look over t' door at me sitting here polishing the harness and pass time o' day, quiet like. He were a real gentleman but you couldn't cross 'im. A few specks o' dust anywhere down here and he'd go nearly mad.

'But the war finished it all. Everybody's rushing about now. They don't care about them things now. They've no time, no time at all.'

He would look round in disbelief at the overgrown cobbles, the peeling garage doors hanging crazily on their hinges. At the empty stable and the pump from which no water flowed.

He was always friendly with me in an absent way, but with Siegfried he seemed to step back into his former character, holding himself up smartly and saying 'Very good, sir,' and saluting repeatedly with one finger. It was as though he recognised something there — something of the strength and authority of t'owd doctor — and reached out eagerly towards the lost days.

'Morning, Boardman,' I said, as I opened the garage door. 'How are you today?'

'Oh, middlin', lad, just middlin'.' He limped across and watched me get the starting handle and begin the next part of the daily routine. The car allotted to me was a tiny Austin of an almost forgotten vintage and one of Boardman's voluntary duties was towing it off when it wouldn't start. But this morning, surprisingly, the engine coughed into life after six turns.

As I drove round the corner of the back lane, I had the feeling, as I did every morning, that this was where things really got started. The problems and pressures of my job were waiting for me out there and at the moment I seemed to have plenty.

I had arrived in the Dales, I felt, at a bad time. The farmers, after a generation of neglect, had seen the coming of a prophet, the wonderful new vet, Mr Farnon. He appeared like a comet, trailing his new ideas in his wake. He was able, energetic and charming and they received him as a maiden would a lover. And now, at the height of the honeymoon, I had to push my way into the act, and I just wasn't wanted.

I was beginning to get used to the questions: 'Where's Mr Farnon?' — 'Is he ill or something?' — 'I expected Mr Farnon.' It was a bit daunting to watch their faces fall when they saw me walking on to their farms. Usually they looked past me hopefully and some even went and peered into the car to see if the man they really wanted was hiding in there.

And it was uphill work examining an animal when its owner was chafing in the background, wishing with all his heart that I was somebody else.

But I had to admit they were fair. I got no effusive welcomes and when I started to tell them what I thought about the case they listened with open scepticism, but I found that if I got my jacket off and really worked at the job they began to thaw a little. And they were hospitable. Even though they were disappointed at having me they asked me into their homes. 'Come in and have a bit o' dinner,' was a phrase I heard nearly every day. Sometimes I was glad to accept and I ate some memorable meals with them.

Often, too, they would slip half a dozen eggs or a pound of butter into the car as I was leaving. This hospitality was traditional in the Dales and I knew they would probably do the same for any visitor, but it showed the core of friendliness which lay under the often unsmiling surface of these people and it helped.

I was beginning to learn about the farmers

and what I found I liked. They had a tough-
ness and a philosophical attitude which was
new to me. Misfortunes which would make
the city dweller want to bang his head against
a wall were shrugged off with 'Aye, well, these
things happen.'

It looked like being another hot day and I
wound down the car windows as far as they
would go. I was on my way to do a tuberculin
test; the national scheme was beginning to
make its first impact in the Dales and the
more progressive farmers were asking for
survey tests.

And this was no ordinary herd. Mr
Copfield's Galloway cattle were famous in
their way. Siegfried had told me about them.
'The toughest lot in this practice. There's
eighty-five of them and none has ever been
tied up. In fact, they've scarcely been touched
by hand. They live out on the fells, they calve
and rear their calves outside. It isn't often
anybody goes near them so they're practically
wild animals.'

'What do you do when there's anything
wrong with them?' I had asked.

'Well, you have to depend on Frank and
George — they're the two Copfield sons.
They've been reared with those cattle since
they were babies — started tackling the little
calves as soon as they could walk, then
worked up to the big ones. They're about as
tough as the Galloways.'

Copfield's place was one of the bleak ones. Looking across the sparse pastures to the bald heights with their spreading smudges of heather it was easy to see why the farmer had chosen a breed hardier than the local short-horns. But this morning the grim outlines were softened by the sunshine and there was a desert peace in the endless greens and browns.

Frank and George were not as I expected. The durable men who helped me in my daily jobs tended to be dark and lean with stringy muscles but the Copfields were golden haired and smooth skinned. They were good-looking young men about my own age and their mas-sive necks and wide spread of shoulder made their heads look small. Neither of them was tall but they looked formidable with their shirt sleeves rolled high to reveal wrestlers' arms and their thick legs encased in cloth gaiters. Both wore clogs.

The cattle had been herded into the build-ings and they just about filled all the avail-able accommodation. There were about twenty-five in a long passage down the side of the fold yard; I could see the ragged line of heads above the rails, the steam rising from their bodies. Twenty more occupied an old stable and two lots of twenty milled about in large loose boxes.

I looked at the black, untamed animals and they looked back at me, their reddish eyes glinting through the rough fringe of hair which fell over their faces. They kept up a menacing, bad-tempered swishing with their tails.

It wasn't going to be easy to get an intra-dermal injection into every one of them. I turned to Frank.

'Can you catch these beggars?' I asked.

'We'll 'ave a bloody good try,' he replied calmly, throwing a halter over his shoulder. He and his brother lit cigarettes before climbing into the passage where the biggest beasts were packed. I followed them and soon found that the tales I had heard about the Galloways hadn't been exaggerated. If I approached them from the front they came at me with their great hairy heads and if I went behind them they kicked me as a matter of course.

But the brothers amazed me. One of them would drop a halter on a beast, get his fingers into its nose and then be carried away as the animal took off like a rocket. They were thrown about like dolls but they never let go; their fair heads bobbed about incongruously among the black backs; and the thing that fascinated me was that through all the contortions the cigarettes dangled undisturbed.

The heat increased till it was like an oven in the buildings and the animals, their bowels highly fluid with their grass diet, ejected greenish-brown muck like non-stop geysers.

The affair was conducted in the spirit of a

game with encouragement shouted to the man in action: 'Thou 'as 'im, Frank.' 'Sniggle 'im, George.' In moments of stress the brothers cursed softly and without heat: 'Get off ma bloody foot, thou awd bitch.' They both stopped work and laughed with sincere appreciation when a cow slashed me across the face with her sodden tail; and another little turn which was well received was when I was filling my syringe with both arms raised and a bullock, backing in alarm from the halter, crashed its craggy behind into my midriff. The wind shot out of me in a sharp hiccup, then the animal decided to turn round in the narrow passage, squashing me like a fly against the railings. I was pop-eyed as it scrambled round; I wondered whether the creaking was coming from my ribs or the wood behind me.

We finished up with the smallest calves and they were just about the most difficult to handle. The shaggy little creatures kicked, bucked, sprang into the air, ran through our legs and even hurtled straight up the walls. Often the brothers had to throw themselves on top of them and bear them to the ground before I could inject them and when the calves felt the needle they stuck out their tongues and bawled deafeningly; outside, the anxious mothers bellowed back in chorus.

It was midday when I reeled out of the buildings. I seemed to have been a month in there, in the suffocating heat, the continuous din, the fusillade of muck.

Frank and George produced a bucket of water and a scrubbing brush and gave me a rough clean-up before I left. A mile from the farm I drove off the unfenced road, got out of the car and dropped down on the cool fellside. Throwing wide my arms I wriggled my shoulders and my sweat-soaked shirt into the tough grass and let the sweet breeze play over me. With the sun on my face I looked through half closed eyes at the hazy-blue sky.

My ribs ached and I could feel the bruises of a dozen kicks on my legs. I knew I didn't smell so good either. I closed my eyes and grinned at the ridiculous thought that I had been conducting a diagnostic investigation for tuberculosis back there. A strange way to carry out a scientific procedure; a strange way, in fact, to earn a living.

But then I might have been in an office with the windows tight shut against the petrol fumes and the traffic noise, the desk light shining on the columns of figures, my bowler hat hanging on the wall.

Lazily I opened my eyes again and watched a cloud shadow riding over the face of the green hill across the valley. No, no . . . I wasn't complaining.

CHAPTER 8

I hardly noticed the passage of the weeks as I rattled along the moorland roads on my daily rounds; but the district was beginning to take shape, the people to emerge as separate personalities. Most days I had a puncture. The tyres were through to the canvas on all wheels; it surprised me that they took me anywhere at all.

One of the few refinements on the car was a rusty 'sunshine roof'. It grated dismally when I slid it back, but most of the time I kept it open and the windows too, and I drove in my shirt sleeves with the delicious air swirling about me. On wet days it didn't help much to close the roof because the rain dripped through the joints and formed pools on my lap and the passenger seat.

I developed great skill in zig-zagging round puddles. To drive through was a mistake as the muddy water fountained up through the gaps in the floorboards.

But it was a fine summer and long days in

the open gave me a tan which rivalled the farmers'. Even mending a puncture was no penance on the high, unfenced roads with the wheeling curlews for company and the wind bringing the scents of flowers and trees up from the valleys. And I could find other excuses to get out and sit on the crisp grass and look out over the airy roof of Yorkshire. It was like taking time out of life. Time to get things into perspective and assess my progress. Everything was so different that it confused me. This countryside after years of city streets, the sense of release from exams and study, the job with its daily challenge. And then there was my boss.

Siegfried Farnon charged round the practice with fierce energy from dawn till dark and I often wondered what drove him on. It wasn't money because he treated it with scant respect. When the bills were paid, the cash went into the pint pot on the mantelpiece and he grabbed handfuls when he wanted it. I never saw him take out a wallet, but his pockets bulged with loose silver and balled-up notes. When he pulled out a thermometer they flew around him in a cloud.

After a week or two of headlong rush he would disappear; maybe for the evening, maybe overnight and often without saying where he was going. Mrs Hall would serve a meal for two, but when she saw I was eating alone she would remove the food without comment.

He dashed off the list of calls each morning with such speed that I was quite often sent hurrying off to the wrong farm or to do the wrong thing. When I told him later of my embarrassment he would laugh heartily.

There was one time when he got involved himself. I had just taken a call from a Mr Heaton of Bronsett about doing a P.M. on a dead sheep.

'I'd like you to come with me, James,' Siegfried said. 'Things are quiet this morning and I believe they teach you blokes a pretty hot post-mortem procedure. I want to see you in action.'

We drove into the village of Bronsett and Siegfried swung the car left into a gated lane.

'Where are you going?' I said. 'Heaton's is at the other end of the village.'

'But you said Seaton's.'

'No, I assure you . . .'

'Look, James, I was right by you when you were talking to the man. I distinctly heard you say the name.'

I opened my mouth to argue further but the car was hurtling down the lane and Siegfried's jaw was jutting. I decided to let him find out for himself.

We arrived outside the farmhouse with a screaming of brakes. Siegfried had left his seat and was rummaging in the boot before the car had stopped shuddering. 'Hell!' he shouted. 'No post-mortem knife. Never mind, I'll borrow something from the house.' He slammed down the lid and bustled over to the door.

The farmer's wife answered and Siegfried beamed on her. 'Good morning to you, Mrs Seaton, have you a carving knife?'

The good lady raised her eyebrows. 'What was that you said?'

'A carving knife, Mrs Seaton, a carving knife, and a good sharp one, please.'

'You want a carving knife?'

'Yes, that's right, a carving knife!' Siegfried cried, his scanty store of patience beginning to run out. 'And I wonder if you'd mind hurrying. I haven't much time.'

The bewildered woman withdrew to the kitchen and I could hear whispering and muttering. Children's heads peeped out at intervals to get a quick look at Siegfried stamping irritably on the step. After some delay, one of the daughters advanced timidly, holding out a long, dangerous-looking knife.

Siegfried snatched it from her hand and ran his thumb up and down the edge. 'This is no damn good!' he shouted in exasperation. 'Don't you understand I want something really sharp? Fetch me a steel.'

The girl fled back into the kitchen and there was a low rumble of voices. It was some minutes before another young girl was pushed round the door. She inched her way up to

Siegfried, gave him the steel at arm's length and dashed back to safety.

Siegfried prided himself on his skill at sharpening a knife. It was something he enjoyed doing. As he stropped the knife on the steel, he warmed to his work and finally burst into song. There was no sound from the kitchen, only the ring of steel on steel backed by the tuneless singing; there were silent intervals when he carefully tested the edge, then the noise would start again.

When he had completed the job to his satisfaction he peered inside the door. 'Where is your husband?' he called.

There was no reply so he strode into the kitchen, waving the gleaming blade in front of him. I followed him and saw Mrs Seaton and her daughters cowering in the far corner, staring at Siegfried with large, frightened eyes.

He made a sweeping gesture at them with the knife. 'Well, come on, I can get started now!'

'Started what?' the mother whispered, holding her family close to her.

'I want to P.M. this sheep. You have a dead sheep, haven't you?'

Explanations and apologies followed.

Later, Siegfried remonstrated gravely with me for sending him to the wrong farm.

'You'll have to be a bit more careful in future, James,' he said seriously. 'Creates a very bad impression, that sort of thing.'

■ ■ ■ ■

Another thing about my new life which
interested me was the regular traffic of
women through Skeldale House. They were
all upper class, mostly beautiful and they had
one thing in common — eagerness. They
came for drinks, for tea, to dinner, but the
real reason was to gaze at Siegfried like
parched travellers in the desert sighting an
oasis.

I found it damaging to my own ego when
their eyes passed over me without recognition or interest and fastened themselves
hungrily on my colleague. I wasn't envious,
but I was puzzled. I used to study him
furtively, trying to fathom the secret of his
appeal. Looking at the worn jacket hanging
from the thin shoulders, the frayed shirt collar and anonymous tie, I had to conclude that
clothes had nothing to do with it.

There was something attractive in the long,
bony face and humorous blue eyes, but a lot
of the time he was so haggard and sunken-
cheeked that I wondered if he was ill.

I often spotted Diana Brompton in the
queue and at these times I had to fight down
an impulse to dive under the sofa. She was
difficult to recognise as the brassy beauty of
that afternoon as she looked up meltingly at
Siegfried, hanging on his words, giggling like

a schoolgirl.

I used to grow cold at the thought that Siegfried might pick her out of the mob and marry her. It worried me a lot because I knew I would have to leave just when I was beginning to enjoy everything about Darrowby.

But Siegfried showed no sign of marrying any of them and the procession continued hopefully. I finally got used to it and stopped worrying.

I got used, too, to my employer's violent changes of front. There was one morning when Siegfried came down to breakfast, rubbing a hand wearily over red-rimmed eyes.

'Out at 4 a.m.,' he groaned, buttering his toast listlessly. 'And I don't like to have to say this, James, but it's all your fault.'

'My fault?' I said, startled.

'Yes, lad, your fault. This was a cow with a mild impaction of the rumen. The farmer had been mucking about with it himself for days; a pint of linseed oil one day, a bit of bicarb and ginger the next, and at four o'clock in the morning he decides it is time to call the vet. When I pointed out it could have waited a few hours more he said Mr Herriot told him never to hesitate to ring — he'd come out any hour of the day or night.'

He tapped the top of his egg as though the effort was almost too much for him. 'Well, it's all very well being conscientious and all that, but if a thing has waited several days it can wait till morning. You're spoiling these chaps, James, and I'm getting the backwash of it. I'm sick and tired of being dragged out of my bed for trifles.'

'I'm truly sorry, Siegfried. I honestly had no wish to do that to you. Maybe it's just my inexperience. If I didn't go out, I'd be worried the animal might die. If I left it till morning and it died, how would I feel?'

'That's all right,' snapped Siegfried. 'There's nothing like a dead animal to bring them to their senses. They'll call us out a bit earlier next time.'

I absorbed this bit of advice and tried to act on it. A week later, Siegfried said he wanted a word with me.

'James, I know you won't mind my saying this, but old Sumner was complaining to me today. He says he rang you the other night and you refused to come out to his cow. He's a good client, you know, and a very nice fellow, but he was quite shirty about it. We don't want to lose a chap like that.'

'But it was just a chronic mastitis,' I said. 'A bit of thickening in the milk, that's all. He'd been dosing it himself for nearly a week with some quack remedy. The cow was eating all right, so I thought it would be quite safe to leave it till next day.'

Siegfried put a hand on my shoulder and an excessively patient look spread over his face. I steeled myself. I didn't mind his impatience; I was used to it and could stand it. But the patience was hard to take.

'James,' he said in a gentle voice, 'there is one fundamental rule in our job which transcends all others, and I'll tell you what it is. YOU MUST ATTEND. That is it and it ought to be written on your soul in letters of fire.' He raised a portentous forefinger. 'YOU MUST ATTEND. Always remember that, James; it is the basis of everything. No matter what the circumstances, whether it be wet or fine, night or day, if a client calls you out, you must go; and go cheerfully. You say this didn't sound like an urgent case. Well, after all, you have only the owner's description to guide you and he is not equipped with the knowledge to decide whether it is urgent or not. No, lad, you have to go. Even if they have been treating the animal themselves, it may have taken a turn for the worse. And don't forget,' wagging the finger solemnly, 'the animal may die.'

'But I thought you said there was nothing like a dead animal to bring them to their senses,' I said querulously.

'What's that?' barked Siegfried, utterly astonished. 'Never heard such rubbish. Let's have no more of it. Just remember — YOU MUST ATTEND.'

Sometimes he would give me advice on how

to live. As when he found me hunched over the phone which I had just crashed down; I was staring at the wall, swearing softly to myself.

Siegfried smiled whimsically. 'Now what is it, James?'

'I've just had a torrid ten minutes with Rolston. You remember that outbreak of calf pneumonia? Well, I spent hours with those calves, poured expensive drugs into them. There wasn't a single death. And now he's complaining about his bill. Not a word of thanks. Hell, there's no justice.'

Siegfried walked over and put his arm round my shoulders. He was wearing his patient look again. 'My dear chap,' he cooed. 'Just look at you. Red in the face, all tensed up. You mustn't let yourself get upset like this; you must try to relax. Why do you think professional men are cracking up all over the country with coronaries and ulcers? Just because they allow themselves to get all steamed up over piffling little things like you are doing now. Yes, yes, I know these things are annoying, but you've got to take them in your stride. Keep calm, James, calm. It just isn't worth it — I mean, it will all be the same in a hundred years.'

He delivered the sermon with a serene smile, patting my shoulder reassuringly like a psychiatrist soothing a violent patient.

I was writing a label on a jar of red blister a

few days later when Siegfried catapulted into the room. He must have kicked the door open because it flew back viciously against the rubber stop and rebounded almost into his face. He rushed over to the desk where I was sitting and began to pound on it with the flat of his hand. His eyes glared wildly from a flushed face.

'I've just come from that bloody swine Holt!' he shouted.

'Ned Holt, you mean?'

'Yes, that's who I mean, damn him!'

I was surprised. Mr Holt was a little man who worked on the roads for the county council. He kept four cows as a sideline and had never been known to pay a veterinary bill; but he was a cheerful character and Siegfried had rendered his unpaid services over the years without objection.

'One of your favourites, isn't he?' I said.

'Was, by God, was,' Siegfried snarled. 'I've been treating Muriel for him. You know, the big red cow second from the far end of his byre. She's had recurrent tympany — coming in from the field every night badly blown — and I'd tried about everything. Nothing did any good. Then it struck me that it might be actinobacillosis of the reticulum. I shot some sodium iodine into the vein and when I saw her today the difference was incredible — she was standing there, chewing her cud, right as rain. I was just patting myself on the back for a smart piece of diagnosis, and do you know what Holt said? He said he knew she'd be better today because last night he gave her half a pound of epsom salts in a bran mash. That was what had cured her.'

Siegfried took some empty cartons and bottles from his pockets and hurled them savagely into the wastepaper basket. He began to shout again.

'Do you know, for the past fortnight I've puzzled and worried and damn nearly dreamt about that cow. Now I've found the cause of the trouble, applied the most modern treatment and the animal has recovered. And what happens? Does the owner express his grateful thanks for my skill? Does he hell — the entire credit goes to the half pound of epsom salts. What I did was a pure waste of time.'

He dealt the desk another sickening blow.

'But I frightened him, James,' he said, his eyes staring. 'By God, I frightened him. When he made that crack about the salts, I yelled out "You bugger!" and made a grab for him. I think I would have strangled him, but he shot into the house and stayed there. I didn't see him again.'

Siegfried threw himself into a chair and began to churn his hair about. 'Epsom salts!' he groaned. 'Oh God, it makes you despair.'

I thought of telling him to relax and pointing out that it would all be the same in a hundred years, but my employer still had an empty serum bottle dangling from one hand. I discarded the idea.

Then there came the day when Siegfried decided to have my car rebored. It had been using a steady two pints of oil a day and he hadn't thought this excessive, but when it got to half a gallon a day he felt something ought to be done. What probably decided him was a farmer on market day saying he always knew when the young vet was coming because he could see the cloud of blue smoke miles away.

When the tiny Austin came back from the garage, Siegfried fussed round it like an old hen. 'Come over here, James,' he called. 'I want to talk to you.'

I saw he was looking patient again and braced myself.

'James,' he said, pacing round the battered vehicle, whisking specks from the paintwork. 'You see this car?'

I nodded.

'Well, it has been rebored, James, rebored at great expense, and that's what I want to talk to you about. You now have in your possession what amounts to a new car.' With an effort he unfastened the catch and the bonnet creaked open in a shower of rust and dirt. He pointed down at the engine, black and oily, with unrelated pieces of flex and rubber tubing hanging around it like garlands. 'You have a piece of fine mechanism here and I want you to treat it with respect. I've seen you belting along like a maniac and it won't do. You've got to nurse this machine for the next two or three thousand miles; thirty miles an hour is quite fast enough. I think it's a crime the way some people abuse a new engine — they should be locked up — so remember, lad, no flogging or I'll be down on you.'

He closed the bonnet with care, gave the cracked windscreen a polish with the cuff of his coat and left.

These strong words made such an impression on me that I crawled round the visits all day almost at walking pace.

The same night, I was getting ready for bed when Siegfried came in. He had two farm lads with him and they both wore silly grins. A powerful smell of beer filled the room.

Siegfried spoke with dignity, slurring his words only slightly. 'James, I met these gentlemen in the Black Bull this evening. We have had several excellent games of dominoes but unfortunately they have missed the last bus. Will you kindly bring the Austin round and I will run them home.'

I drove the car to the front of the house and the farm lads piled in, one in the front, the other in the back. I looked at Siegfried lowering himself unsteadily into the driving seat and decided to go along. I got into the back.

The two young men lived in a farm far up on the North Moors and, three miles out of the town, we left the main road and our headlights picked out a strip of track twisting along the dark hillside.

Siegfried was in a hurry. He kept his foot on the boards, the note of the engine rose to a tortured scream and the little car hurtled on into the blackness. Hanging on grimly, I leaned forward so that I could shout into my employer's ear. 'Remember this is the car which has just been rebored,' I bellowed above the din.

Siegfried looked round with an indulgent smile. 'Yes, yes, I remember, James. What are you fussing about?' As he spoke, the car shot off the road and bounded over the grass at sixty miles an hour. We all bounced around like corks till he found his way back. Unperturbed, he carried on at the same speed. The silly grins had left the lads' faces and they sat rigid in their seats. Nobody said anything.

The passengers were unloaded at a silent farmhouse and the return journey began. Since it was downhill all the way, Siegfried found he could go even faster. The car leaped and bumped over the uneven surface with its engine whining. We made several brief but tense visits to the surrounding moors, but we got home.

It was a month later that Siegfried had occasion to take his assistant to task once more. 'James, my boy,' he said sorrowfully, 'you are a grand chap, but by God, you're hard on cars. Look at this Austin. Newly rebored a short time ago, in tip-top condition, and look at it now — drinking oil. I don't know how you did it in the time. You're a real terror.'

CHAPTER 9

'First, please,' I called as I looked into the waiting-room. There was an old lady with a cat in a cardboard box, two small boys trying to keep hold of a rabbit, and somebody I didn't recognise at first. Then I remembered — it was Soames.

When it was his turn, he came into the surgery but he was a vastly different character from the one I knew. He wore an ingratiating smile. His head bobbed up and down as he spoke. He radiated anxiety to please. And the most interesting thing was that his right eye was puffed and closed and surrounded by an extensive area of bluish-black flesh.

'I hope you don't mind my coming to see you, Mr Herriot,' he said. 'The fact is I have resigned my position with his lordship and am looking for another post. I was wondering if you and Mr Farnon would put in a word for me if you heard of anything.'

I was too astonished at the transformation to say much. I replied that we would do what we could and Soames thanked me effusively and bowed himself out.

I turned to Siegfried after he had gone. 'Well, what do you make of that?'

'Oh, I know all about it.' Siegfried looked at me with a wry smile. 'Remember I told you he was working one or two shady sidelines up there — selling a few bags of corn or a hundredweight of fertiliser here and there. It all mounted up. But it didn't last; he got a bit careless and he was out on his ear before he knew what had happened.'

'And how about the lovely black eye?'

'Oh, he got that from Tommy. You must have seen Tommy when you were there. He's the horseman.'

My mind went back to that uncomfortable night and to the quiet man holding the horse's head. 'I remember him — big fat chap.'

'Yes, he's a big lad and I'd hate to have him punch me in the eye. Soames gave him a hell of a life and as soon as Tommy heard about the sacking he paid a visit just to settle the score.'

I was now comfortably settled into the way of life in Skeldale House. At first I wondered where Tristan fitted into the set up. Was he supposed to be seeing practice, having a holiday, working or what? But it soon became clear that he was a factotum who dispensed and delivered medicines, washed the cars, answered the phone and even, in an emergency, went to a case.

At least, that was how Siegfried saw him and he had a repertoire of tricks aimed at keeping him on his toes. Like returning unexpectedly or bursting into a room in the hope of catching him doing nothing. He never seemed to notice the obvious fact that the college vacation was over and Tristan should have been back there. I came to the conclusion over the next few months that Tristan must have had some flexible arrangement with the college authorities because, for a student, he seemed to spend a surprising amount of time at home.

He interpreted his role rather differently from his brother and, while resident in Darrowby, he devoted a considerable amount of his acute intelligence to the cause of doing as little as possible. Tristan did, in fact, spend much of his time sleeping in a chair. When he was left behind to dispense when we went out on our rounds he followed an unvarying procedure. He half filled a sixteen-ounce bottle with water, added a few drachms of chlorodyne and a little ipecacuanha, pushed the cork in and took it through to the sitting-room to stand by his favourite chair. It was a wonderful chair for his purpose; old fashioned and high backed with wings to support the head.

He would get out his *Daily Mirror,* light a Woodbine and settle down till sleep overcame him. If Siegfried rushed in on him he grabbed the bottle and started to shake it madly, inspecting the contents at intervals. Then he went through to the dispensary, filled up the bottle and labelled it.

It was a sound, workable system but it had one big snag. He never knew whether it was Siegfried or not when the door opened and often I walked in and found him half lying in his chair, staring up with startled, sleep-blurred eyes while he agitated his bottle.

Most evenings found him sitting on a high stool at the bar counter of the Drovers' Arms, conversing effortlessly with the barmaid. At other times he would be out with one of the young nurses from the local hospital which he seemed to regard as an agency to provide him with female company. All in all, he managed to lead a fairly full life.

Saturday night, 10.30 p.m. and I was writing up my visits when the phone rang. I swore, crossed my fingers and lifted the receiver.

'Hello, Herriot speaking.'

'Oh, it's you, is it?' growled a dour voice in broadest Yorkshire. 'Well, ah want Mr Farnon.'

'I'm sorry, Mr Farnon is out. Can I help you?'

'Well, I 'ope so, but I'd far raither 'ave your

113

boss. This is Sims of Beal Close.'

(Oh no, please no, not Beal Close on a Saturday night. Miles up in the hills at the end of a rough lane with about eight gates.)

'Yes, Mr Sims, and what is the trouble?'

'Ah'll tell you, there is some trouble an' all. I 'ave a grand big show 'oss here. All of seventeen hands. He's cut 'isself badly on the hind leg, just above the hock. I want him stitched immediately.'

(Glory be! Above the hock! What a charming place to have to stitch a horse. Unless he's very quiet, this is going to be a real picnic.)

'How big is the wound, Mr Sims?'

'Big? It's a gurt big thing about a foot long and bleedin' like 'ell. And this 'oss is as wick as an eel. Could kick a fly's eye out. Ah can't get near 'im nohow. Goes straight up wall when he sees anybody. By gaw, I tell you I had 'im to t'blacksmith t'other day and feller was dead scared of 'im. Twiltin' gurt 'oss 'e is.'

(Damn you, Mr Sims, damn Beal Close and damn your twiltin' gurt 'oss.)

'Well, I'll be along straight away. Try to have some men handy just in case we have to throw him.'

'Throw 'im? Throw 'im? You'd never throw this 'oss. He'd kill yer first. Anyways, I 'ave no men here so you'll 'ave to manage on your own. Ah know Mr Farnon wouldn't want a

114

lot of men to help 'im.'

(Oh lovely, lovely. This is going to be one for the diary.)

'Very well, I'm leaving now, Mr Sims.'

'Oh, ah nearly forgot. My road got washed away in the floods yesterday. You'll 'ave to walk the last mile and a half. So get a move on and don't keep me waiting all night.'

(This is just a bit much.)

'Look here, Mr Sims, I don't like your tone. I said I would leave now and I will get there just as soon as I can.'

'You don't like ma tone, eh? Well, ah don't like useless young apprentices practising on my good stock, so ah don't want no cheek from you. You know nowt about t'damn job, any road.'

(That finally does it.)

'Now just listen to me, Sims. If it wasn't for the sake of the horse I'd refuse to come out at all. Who do you think you are, anyway? If you ever try to speak to me like that again . . .'

'Now, now, Jim, get a grip on yourself. Take it easy, old boy. You'll burst a blood vessel if you go on like this.'

'Who the devil . . . ?'

'Ah, ah, Jim, calm yourself now. That temper of yours, you know. You'll really have to watch it.'

'Tristan! Where the hell are you speaking from?'

'The kiosk outside the Drovers. Five pints

inside me and feeling a bit puckish. Thought I'd give you a ring.'

'By God, I'll murder you one of these days if you don't stop this game. It's putting years on me. Now and again isn't so bad, but this is the third time this week.'

'Ah, but this was by far the best, Jim. It was really wonderful. When you started drawing yourself up to your full height — it nearly killed me. Oh God, I wish you could have heard yourself.' He trailed off into helpless laughter.

And then my feeble attempts at retaliation; creeping, trembling, into some lonely phone box.

'Is that young Mr Farnon?' in a guttural croak. 'Well, this is Tilson of High Woods. Ah want you to come out here immediately. I 'ave a terrible case of . . .'

'Excuse me for interrupting, Jim, but is there something the matter with your tonsils? Oh, good. Well, go on with what you were saying, old lad. Sounds very interesting.'

There was only one time when I was not on the receiving end. It was Tuesday — my half day — and at 11:30 a.m. a call came in. An eversion of the uterus in a cow. This is the tough job in country practice and I felt the usual chill.

It happens when the cow, after calving, continues to strain until it pushes the entire uterus out and it hangs down as far as the animal's hocks. It is a vast organ and desperately difficult to replace, mainly because the cow, having once got rid of it, doesn't want it back. And in a straightforward contest between man and beast the odds were very much on the cow.

The old practitioners, in an effort to even things up a bit, used to sling the cow up by its hind limbs and the more inventive among them came up with all sorts of contraptions like the uterine valise which was supposed to squeeze the organ into smaller bulk. But the result was usually the same — hours of backbreaking work.

The introduction of the epidural anaesthetic made everything easier by removing sensation from the uterus and preventing the cow from straining but, for all that, the words 'calf bed out' coming over the line were guaranteed to wipe the smile off any vet's face.

I decided to take Tristan in case I needed a few pounds of extra push. He came along but showed little enthusiasm for the idea. He showed still less when he saw the patient, a very fat shorthorn lying, quite unconcerned, in her stall. Behind her, a bloody mass of uterus, afterbirth, muck and straw spilled over into the channel.

She wasn't at all keen to get up, but after we had done a bit of shouting and pushing at her shoulder she rose to her feet, looking bored.

The epidural space was difficult to find among the rolls of fat and I wasn't sure if I had injected all the anaesthetic into the right place. I removed the afterbirth, cleaned the uterus and placed it on a clean sheet held by the farmer and his brother. They were frail men and it was all they could do to keep the sheet level. I wouldn't be able to count on them to help me much.

I nodded to Tristan; we stripped off our shirts, tied clean sacks round our waists and gathered the uterus in our arms.

It was badly engorged and swollen and it took us just an hour to get it back. There was a long spell at the beginning when we made no progress at all and the whole idea of pushing the enormous organ through a small hole seemed ludicrous, like trying to thread a needle with a sausage. Then there were a few minutes when we thought we were doing famously only to find we were feeding the thing down through a tear in the sheet (Siegfried once told me he had spent half a morning trying to stuff a uterus up a cow's rectum. What really worried him, he said, was that he nearly succeeded) and at the end when hope was fading, there was the blissful moment when the whole thing began to slip inside and incredibly disappeared from sight.

Somewhere half way through we both took

a breather at the same time and stood panting, our faces almost touching. Tristan's cheeks were prettily patterned where a spouting artery had sprayed him; I was able to look deep into his eyes and I read there a deep distaste for the whole business.

Lathering myself in the bucket and feeling the ache in my shoulders and back, I looked over at Tristan. He was pulling his shirt over his head as though it cost him the last of his strength. The cow, chewing contentedly at a mouthful of hay, had come best out of the affair.

Out in the car, Tristan groaned. 'I'm sure that sort of thing isn't good for me. I feel as though I've been run over by a steam roller. Hell, what a life this is at times.'

After lunch I rose from the table. 'I'm off to Brawton now, Triss, and I think I'd better mention that you may not have seen the last of that cow. These bad cases sometimes recur and there's a chance that little lot may come out again. If it does, it's all yours because Siegfried won't be back for hours and nothing is going to stop me having my half day.'

For once Tristan's sense of humour failed him. He became haggard, he seemed to age suddenly. 'Oh God,' he moaned, 'don't even talk about it. I'm all in — another session like that would kill me. And on my own! It would be the end of me, I tell you.'

'Ah well,' I said sadistically, 'try not to

worry. It may never happen.'

It was when I saw the phone box about ten miles along the Brawton road that the thought struck me. I slowed down and got out of the car. 'I wonder,' I muttered, 'I wonder if I could do it just once.'

Inside the box, inspiration was strong in me. I wrapped my handkerchief over the mouthpiece, dialled the practice number and when I heard Tristan on the line I shouted at the top of my voice. 'Are you t'young feller that put our cow's calf bed back this morning?'

'Yes, I'm one of them.' Tension sprang into Tristan's voice. 'Why, is there something wrong?'

'Aye, there is summat wrong,' I bawled. 'She's putten it out again.'

'Out again? Out again? All of it?' He was almost screaming.

'Aye, it's a terrible mess. Pourin' blood and about twice size it was this morning. You'll 'ave some job with 'er.'

There was a long silence and I wondered if he had fainted. Then I heard him again, hoarse but resolute. 'Very well, I'll come straight away.'

There was another pause then he spoke again almost in a whisper. 'Is it out completeiy?'

I broke down then. There was a wistful quality about the words which defeated me; a

120

hint of a wild hope that the farmer may have been exaggerating and that there might be only a tiny piece peeping out. I began to laugh. I would have liked to toy with my victim a little longer but it was impossible. I laughed louder and took my handkerchief from the mouthpiece so that Tristan could hear me.

I listened for a few seconds to the frenzied swearing at the other end then gently replaced the receiver. It would probably never happen again but it was sweet, very sweet.

CHAPTER 10

'You want Mr Herriot? Certainly, I'll get him for you.' Siegfried cupped the phone with his hand. 'Come on, James, here's another one prefers you to me.' I glanced at him quickly, but he was smiling. He was pleased.

I thought, as I took the phone, of the tales I had heard of the other kind of boss; the man who couldn't bear to be knocked off his little pedestal. And I thought, too, of the difference a few weeks had made in the farmers' attitude; they didn't look past me now, hoping that Mr Farnon had come with me. They were beginning to accept me, and I liked to think that it wasn't only their hospitable traditions that made them ask me in for a 'bit o' dinner'.

This really meant something, because, with the passage of time, an appreciation of the Dales people had grown in me; a sense of the value of their carefully given friendship. The higher up the country, the more I liked them. At the bottom of the valley, where it widened into the plain, the farmers were like farmers everywhere, but the people grew more interesting as the land heightened, and in the scattered hamlets and isolated farms near the bleak tops I found their characteristics most marked; their simplicity and dignity, their rugged independence and their hospitality.

This Sunday morning it was the Bellerbys and they lived at the top of Halden, a little valley branching off the main Dale. My car bumped and rattled over the last rough mile of an earth road with the tops of boulders sticking up every few yards.

I got out and from where I stood, high at the head, I could see all of the strangely formed cleft in the hills, its steep sides grooved and furrowed by countless streams feeding the boisterous Halden Beck which tumbled over its rocky bed far below. Down there, were trees and some cultivated fields, but immediately behind me the wild country came crowding in on the bowl where the farmhouse lay. Halsten Pike, Alstang, Birnside — the huge fells with their barbarous names were very near.

Up here, the trappings of civilisation seemed far away. The farm buildings had been built massively of stone hundreds of years ago with the simple object of sheltering the animals. Those ancient masons were untroubled by regulations about the light and ventilation and the cow byre was gloomy, thick walled, almost windowless. The floor was broken and pitted, and rotting wooden partitions separated the cows from each other.

I went in, groping my way until my eyes grew accustomed to the dim light. There was nobody there but a roan cow had a label tied to its tail. Since this was a common way of communicating with the vet I lifted the tail and read 'Felon, back quarters'.

I pushed the cow over and began to examine the back teats. I was drawing out the stringy, discoloured milk when a voice addressed me from the doorway: 'Oh, it's you, Mr Herriot. I'm right glad you've come to see us this morning. You could do us such a great favour if you would.'

I looked up and saw Ruth Bellerby, a fine-looking woman in her late thirties. She was the go-ahead member of the family and had an intelligent, questing mind. She was a great believer in self-improvement for the Dales people.

'I'll be glad to help you if I can, Miss Bellerby. What is it you'd like me to do?'

'Well, Mr Herriot, you know they are putting on the *Messiah* at Darrowby church this afternoon and we did badly want to go, but it's such a job getting the pony and trap ready and it's so slow. If you could give us a lift down in your car, I know we'd be able to get a ride back. It would be such a help.'

'Of course I'll run you down,' I replied. 'I'll be delighted to do it. I'm going myself as a matter of fact. You don't get many chances to hear good music in Darrowby.'

It was good to have a chance to help these kindly people. I had always marvelled at the Bellerbys. They seemed to me to be survivors from another age and their world had a timeless quality. They were never in a hurry; they rose when it was light, went to bed when they were tired, ate when they were hungry and seldom looked at a clock.

Ruth led the way over to the house. 'There's just mother and dad and me going. Bob's not interested, I'm afraid.'

I was slightly taken aback when I entered the house. The family were just sitting down to Sunday dinner and were still in their working clothes. I stole a look at my watch; a quarter to twelve and the performance started at 2 p.m. Oh well, I probably had plenty of time.

'Come on, young man,' said little Mr Bellerby. 'Sit down and have a bit o' dinner.'

It was always a bit tricky refusing these invitations without causing offence, but I pointed out that my own meal would be ready when I got back and it would be hard on Mrs Hall if it were wasted.

They were quick to appreciate this argument and settled down round the scrubbed kitchen table. Mrs Bellerby served a large, round Yorkshire pudding to each of them and poured a pool of gravy into it from a quart-size enamel jug. I had had a hard morning and the delicious scent that rose from the gravy as it ran over the golden slabs was a sweet torture. But I consoled myself with the thought that the fact of my sitting there would make them hurry.

The pudding was consumed in leisurely silence, then Bob, an amiable, thick-set youth in his twenties, pushed out his empty plate. He did not say anything, but his mother planked down another pudding on the plate and plied the gravy jug again. His parents and sister watched him benevolently as he methodically demolished the thick, doughy mass.

Next, a tremendous roast appeared from the oven and Mr Bellerby hacked and sawed at it till they all had a heap of thick slices on their plates. Then mountains of mashed potatoes were served from something that looked like a washing-up bowl. Chopped turnip followed and the family went into action again.

There was no sign of haste. They ate calmly and quietly without any small talk. Bob had an extra helping of mashed potatoes.

The Bellerbys were relaxed and happy, but I couldn't say the same about myself. Hunger was tearing fiercely at me and the minutes on my watch were ticking away relentlessly.

There was a decent interval before Mrs Bellerby went over to the old fire oven in the corner, opened the door and pulled forth a great flat baking tin of steaming apple pie. She then proceeded to carve off about a square foot for each of them and deluged it with something like a pint of custard from another towering enamel jug.

The family set to as though they were just beginning the meal and once more a busy silence fell on the group. Bob cleared his plate in effortless style and pushed it wordlessly into the middle of the table. His mother was ready with another great rectangle of pie and another copious libation of custard.

It was going to be a close thing, I thought, but this surely must be the end. They would realise time was getting short and start to change. But, to my consternation, Mrs Bellerby moved slowly over to the fire and put the kettle on, while her husband and Bob pushed their chairs back and stretched out their legs. They both wore corduroy breeches with the lacing undone and on their feet were enormous hobnailed boots. Bob, after a search through his pockets, brought out a battered packet of cigarettes and lay back in a happy coma as his mother put a cup of tea in front of him. Mr Bellerby produced a clasp knife and began to cut up some plug tobacco for his pipe.

As they rearranged themselves round the

table and began to slowly sip the hot tea, I found I had started to exhibit all the classical symptoms of tension. Pounding pulse, tightly clenched jaws and the beginnings of a headache.

After a second cup of tea, there were signs of activity. Mr Bellerby rose with a groan, scratched his shirt front and stretched luxuriously. 'Well, young man, we'll just have a bit of a wash and get changed. Bob'll stay and talk to you — he's not coming with us.'

There was a lot of splashing and spluttering in the big stone sink at the far end of the kitchen as they made their ablutions, then they disappeared upstairs. I was greatly relieved to find that it didn't take them long to change. Mr Bellerby was down very soon, transformed in appearance by a stiff and shiny suit of navy blue serge with a faint greenish tinge. His wife and daughter followed soon in a blaze of flowered cotton.

'Ah well, now here we are. All ready, eh?' There was a note of hysteria in my heartiness. 'Right, then, off we go. After you, ladies.'

But Ruth did not move. She was pulling on a pair of white gloves and looking at her brother sprawled in his chair. 'You know, Bob, you're nowt but a disgrace!' she burst out. 'Here we are going off to hear this lovely music and you're lying there in your muck, not caring. You've no interest in culture at all. You care no more about bettering yourself than one of them bullocks out there.'

Bob stirred uneasily under this sudden attack, but there was more to come.

Ruth stamped her foot. 'Really, it makes my blood boil to look at you. And I know we won't be right out of t'door before you're asleep. Aye, snoring there all afternoon like a pig.' She swung round to Mrs Bellerby. 'Mother! I've made up my mind. I'm not going to leave him snoring here. He's got to come with us!'

I felt the sweat start out on my brow. I began to babble. 'But don't you think, perhaps . . . might be just a little late . . . starts at two o'clock . . . my lunch . . .'

But my words were utterly lost. Ruth had the bit properly between her teeth. 'Get up out of there, Bob! Get up this minute and get dressed!' She shut her mouth tightly and thrust out her lower jaw.

She was too much for Bob. Although an impressive eater, he didn't seem to have much mind of his own. He mumbled sulkily and shuffled over to the sink. He took off his shirt and they all sat down and watched as he lathered his torso with a large block of White Windsor and sluiced his head and neck by working the pump handle by the side of the sink.

The family regarded him happily, pleased that he was coming with them and content in the knowledge that it would be good for him.

Ruth watched his splashings with the light of love in her eyes. She kept looking over at me as if to say 'Isn't this grand?'

For my part, I was only just stopping myself from tearing out my hair in great handfuls. A compulsion to leap up and pace the floor, to scream at the top of my voice showed that I was nearing the end of my tether. I fought this feeling by closing my eyes and I must have kept them closed for a long time because, when I opened them, Bob was standing by my side in a suit exactly like his father's.

I could never remember much about that ride to Darrowby. I had only a vague recollection of the car hurtling down the stony track at forty miles an hour. Of myself staring straight ahead with protruding eyes and the family, tightly packed but cheerful, thoroughly enjoying the ride.

Even the imperturbable Mrs Hall was a little tight lipped as I shot into the house at ten to two and out again at two after bolting her good food.

I was late for the *Messiah*. The music had started as I crept into the church and I ran a gauntlet of disapproving stares. Out of the corner of my eye I saw the Bellerbys sitting very upright, all in a row. It seemed to me that they looked disapproving, too.

CHAPTER 11

I looked again at the slip of paper where I
had written my visits. 'Dean, 3, Thompson's
Yard. Old dog ill.'

There were a lot of these 'yards' in Darrowby. They were, in fact, tiny streets, like
pictures from a Dickens novel. Some of them
opened off the market place and many more
were scattered behind the main thoroughfares
in the old part of the town. From the outside
you could see only an archway and it was
always a surprise to me to go down a narrow
passage and come suddenly upon the uneven
rows of little houses with no two alike, looking into each other's windows across eight
feet of cobbles.

In front of some of the houses a strip of
garden had been dug out and marigolds and
nasturtiums straggled over the rough stones;
but at the far end the houses were in a
tumbledown condition and some were abandoned with their windows boarded up.

Number three was down at this end and

looked as though it wouldn't be able to hold out much longer.

The flakes of paint quivered on the rotten wood of the door as I knocked; above, the outer wall bulged dangerously on either side of a long crack in the masonry.

A small, white-haired man answered. His face, pinched and lined, was enlivened by a pair of cheerful eyes; he wore a much-darned woollen cardigan, patched trousers and slippers.

'I've come to see your dog,' I said, and the old man smiled.

'Oh, I'm glad you've come, sir,' he said. 'I'm getting a bit worried about the old chap. Come inside, please.'

He led me into the tiny living-room. 'I'm alone now, sir. Lost my missus over a year ago. She used to think the world of the old dog.'

The grim evidence of poverty was everywhere. In the worn out lino, the fireless hearth, the dank, musty smell of the place. The wallpaper hung away from the damp patches and on the table the old man's solitary dinner was laid; a fragment of bacon, a few fried potatoes and a cup of tea. This was life on the old age pension.

In the corner, on a blanket, lay my patient, a cross-bred labrador. He must have been a big, powerful dog in his time, but the signs of age showed in the white hairs round his muzzle and the pale opacity in the depth of his eyes. He lay quietly and looked at me without hostility.

'Getting on a bit, isn't he, Mr Dean?'

'Aye he is that. Nearly fourteen, but he's been like a pup galloping about until these last few weeks. Wonderful dog for his age, is old Bob and he's never offered to bite any-body in his life. Children can do anything with him. He's my only friend now — I hope you'll soon be able to put him right.'

'Is he off his food, Mr Dean?'

'Yes, clean off, and that's a strange thing because, by gum, he could eat. He always sat by me and put his head on my knee at meal times, but he hasn't been doing it lately.'

I looked at the dog with growing uneasi-ness. The abdomen was grossly distended and I could read the tell-tale symptoms of pain; the catch in the respirations, the retracted commissures of the lips, the anxious, pre-occupied expression in the eyes.

When his master spoke, the tail thumped twice on the blankets and a momentary inter-est showed in the white old eyes; but it quickly disappeared and the blank, inward look returned.

I passed my hand carefully over the dog's abdomen. Ascites was pronounced and the dropsical fluid had gathered till the pressure was intense. 'Come on, old chap,' I said, 'let's see if we can roll you over.' The dog made no

133

resistance as I eased him slowly on to his other side, but, just as the movement was completed, he whimpered and looked round. The cause of the trouble was now only too easy to find.

I palpated gently. Through the thin muscle of the flank I could feel a hard, corrugated mass; certainly a splenic or hepatic carcinoma, enormous and completely inoperable. I stroked the old dog's head as I tried to collect my thoughts. This wasn't going to be easy.

'Is he going to be ill for long?' the old man asked, and again came the thump, thump of the tail at the sound of the loved voice. 'It's miserable when Bob isn't following me round the house when I'm doing my little jobs.'

'I'm sorry, Mr Dean, but I'm afraid this is something very serious. You see this large swelling. It is caused by an internal growth.'

'You mean . . . cancer?' the little man said faintly.

'I'm afraid so, and it has progressed too far for anything to be done. I wish there was something I could do to help him, but there isn't.'

The old man looked bewildered and his lips trembled. 'Then he's going to die?'

I swallowed hard. 'We really can't just leave him to die, can we? He's in some distress now, but it will soon be an awful lot worse. Don't you think it would be kindest to put

134

him to sleep? After all, he's had a good, long innings.' I always aimed at a brisk, matter-of-fact approach, but the old clichés had an empty ring.

The old man was silent, then he said, 'Just a minute,' and slowly and painfully knelt down by the side of the dog. He did not speak, but ran his hand again and again over the grey old muzzle and the ears, while the tail thump, thump, thumped on the floor.

He knelt there a long time while I stood in the cheerless room, my eyes taking in the faded pictures on the walls, the frayed, grimy curtains, the broken-springed armchair.

At length the old man struggled to his feet and gulped once or twice. Without looking at me, he said huskily, 'All right, will you do it now?'

I filled the syringe and said the things I always said. 'You needn't worry, this is absolutely painless. Just an overdose of an anaesthetic. It is really an easy way out for the old fellow.'

The dog did not move as the needle was inserted, and, as the barbiturate began to flow into the vein, the anxious expression left his face and the muscles began to relax. By the time the injection was finished, the breathing had stopped.

'Is that it?' the old man whispered.

'Yes, that's it,' I said. 'He is out of his pain now.'

135

The old man stood motionless except for the clasping and unclasping of his hands. When he turned to face me his eyes were bright. 'That's right, we couldn't let him suffer, and I'm grateful for what you've done. And now, what do I owe you for your services, sir?'

'Oh, that's all right, Mr Dean,' I said quickly. 'It's nothing — nothing at all. I was passing right by here — it was no trouble.'

The old man was astonished. 'But you can't do that for nothing.'

'Now please say no more about it, Mr Dean. As I told you, I was passing right by your door.' I said goodbye and went out of the house, through the passage and into the street. In the bustle of people and the bright sunshine, I could still see only the stark, little room, the old man and his dead dog.

As I walked towards my car, I heard a shout behind me. The old man was shuffling excitedly towards me in his slippers. His cheeks were streaked and wet, but he was smiling. In his hand he held a small, brown object.

'You've been very kind, sir. I've got something for you.' He held out the object and I looked at it. It was tattered but just recognisable as a precious relic of a bygone celebration.

'Go on, it's for you,' said the old man. 'Have a cigar.'

CHAPTER 12

It was unfortunate that Siegfried ever had the idea of delegating the book-keeping to his brother, because Skeldale House had been passing through a period of peace and I found it soothing.

For nearly a fortnight there had been hardly a raised voice or an angry word except for one unpleasant interlude when Siegfried had come in and found his brother cycling along the passage. Tristan found all the rage and shouting quite incomprehensible — he had been given the job of setting the table and it was a long way from kitchen to dining-room; it seemed the most natural thing in the world to bring his bike in.

Autumn had come with a sharpness in the air and at nights the log fire burned bright in the big room, sending shadows flickering over the graceful alcoves and up to the high, carved ceiling. It was always a good time when the work of the day was through and the three of us lay back in the shabby armchairs and stretched our feet out to the blaze.

Tristan was occupied with the *Daily Telegraph* crossword which he did every night. Siegfried was reading and I was dosing. It embarrassed me to be drawn into the crossword; Siegfried could usually make a contribution after a minute's thought but Tristan could have the whole thing worked out while I wrestled with the first clue.

The carpet round our feet was hidden by the dogs, all five of them, draped over each other in heavy-breathing layers and adding to the atmosphere of camaraderie and content.

It seemed to me that a chill breath struck through the comfort of the room as Siegfried spoke. 'Market day tomorrow and the bills have just gone out. They'll be queuing up to give us their money so I want you, Tristan, to devote the entire day to taking it from them. James and I are going to be busy, so you'll be in sole charge. All you have to do is take their cheques, give them a receipt and enter their names in the receipt book. Now do you think you can manage that without making a bloody hash of it?'

I winced. It was the first discordant note for a long time and it struck deep.

'I think I might just about cope with that,' Tristan replied haughtily.

'Good. Let's get to bed then.'

But, next day, it was easy to see that the assignment was right up Tristan's street. Stationed behind the desk, he took in the money in handfuls; and all the time he talked. But he did not talk at random; each character got a personal approach.

With the upright methodist, it was the weather, the price of cows and the activities of the village institute. The raffish type with his cap on one side, exhaling fumes of market ale, got the latest stories which Tristan kept on the backs of envelopes. But with the ladies he rose to his greatest heights. They were on his side from the first because of his innocent, boyish face, and when he turned the full blast of his charm on them their surrender was complete.

I was amazed at the giggles which came from behind the door. I was pleased the lad was doing well. Nothing was going wrong this time.

Tristan was smug at lunch time and cock-a-hoop at tea. Siegfried, too, was satisfied with the day's takings which his brother presented in the form of a column of neat figures accurately totalled at the bottom. 'Thank you, Tristan, very efficient.' All was sweetness.

At the end of the day I was in the yard, throwing the used bottles from the boot of my car into a bin. It had been a busy day and I had accumulated a bigger than usual load of empties.

Tristan came panting in from the garden.

'Jim, I've lost the receipt book!'

'Always trying to pull my leg, always joking,' I said. 'Why don't you give your sense of humour a rest some time?' I laughed heartily and sent a liniment bottle crashing among the others.

He plucked at my sleeve. 'I'm not joking, Jim, believe me. I really have lost the bloody thing.' For once, his sang-froid had deserted him. His eyes were wide, his face pale.

'But it can't just have disappeared,' I said. 'It's bound to turn up.'

'It'll never turn up.' Tristan wrung his hands and did a bit of pacing on the cobbles. 'Do you know I've spent about two hours searching for it. I've ransacked the house. It's gone, I tell you.'

'But it doesn't matter, does it? You'll have transferred all the names into the ledger.'

'That's just it. I haven't. I was going to do it tonight.'

'So that means that all the farmers who have been handing you money today are going to get the same bill next month?'

'Looks like it. I can't remember the names of more than two or three of them.'

I sat down heavily on the stone trough. 'Then God help us all, especially you. These Yorkshire lads don't like parting with their brass once, but when you ask them to do it twice — oh, brother!'

Another thought struck me and I said with

140

a touch of cruelty: 'And how about Siegfried. Have you told him yet?'

A spasm crossed Tristan's face. 'No, he's just come in. I'm going to do it now.' He squared his shoulders and strode from the yard.

I decided not to follow him to the house. I didn't feel strong enough for the scene which was bound to follow. Instead, I went out into the back lane and round behind the house to the market place where the lighted entrance of the Drovers' Arms beckoned in the dusk.

I was sitting behind a pint when Tristan came in looking as though somebody had just drained half a gallon of blood from him.

'How did it go?' I asked.

'Oh, the usual, you know. Bit worse this time, maybe. But I can tell you this, Jim. I'm not looking forward to a month from today.'

The receipt book was never found and, a month later, all the bills were sent out again, timed, as usual, to arrive on market day morning.

The practice was quiet that particular day and I had finished my round by mid morning. I didn't go into the house, because through the waiting-room window I could see rows of farmers sitting round the walls; they all wore the same offended, self-righteous expression.

I stole away to the market place. When I

had time, I enjoyed moving among the stalls which crowded the ancient square. You could buy fruit, fish, second-hand books, cheeses, clothes, in fact nearly everything; but the china stall was my favourite.

It was run by a Jewish gentleman from Leeds — fat, confident, sweating, and with a hypnotic selling technique. I never got tired of watching him. He fascinated me. He was in his best form today, standing in a little clearing surrounded on all sides by heaps of crockery, while beyond, the farmers' wives listened open-mouthed to his oratory.

'Ah'm not good-lookin',' he was saying. 'Ah'm not clever, but by God ah can talk. Ah can talk the hind leg off a donkey. Now look 'ere.' He lifted a cheap cup and held it aloft, but tenderly, gripping it between his thick thumb and forefinger, his little finger daintily outspread. 'Beautiful, isn't it? Now isn't that lovely?' Then he placed it reverently on the palm of his hand and displayed it to the audience. 'Now I tell you ladies, you can buy this selfsame tea-set in Conners in Bradford for three pound fifteen. I'm not jokin' nor jestin', it's there and that's the price. But my price, ladies?' and here he fished out an old walking stick with a splintered handle. 'My price for this beautiful tea-set?' He held the stick by its end and brought it crashing down on an empty tea-chest. 'Never mind three pound fifteen.' Crash! 'Never mind three pound.' Crash! 'Never mind two pound.' Crash! 'Never mind thirty bob.' Crash! ' 'ere, 'ere, come on, who'll give me a quid?' Not a soul moved. 'All right, all right, I can see ah've met me match today. Go on, seventeen and a tanner the lot.' A final devastating crash and the ladies began to make signals and fumble in their handbags. A little man emerged from the back of the stall and started to hand out the tea-sets. The ritual had been observed and everybody was happy.

I was waiting, deeply content, for the next item from the virtuoso when I saw a burly figure in a check cap waving wildly at me from the edge of the crowd. He had his hand inside his jacket and I knew what he was feeling for. I didn't hesitate but dodged quickly behind a stall laden with pig troughs and wire netting. I had gone only a few steps before another farmer hailed me purposefully. He was brandishing an envelope.

I felt trapped, then I saw a way of escape. Rapidly skirting a counter displaying cheap jewellery, I plunged into the doorway of the Drovers' Arms and, avoiding the bar which was full of farmers, slipped into the manager's office. I was safe; this was one place where I was always welcome.

The manager looked up from his desk, but he did not smile. 'Look here,' he said sharply, 'I brought my dog in to see you some time ago and in due course I received an account from you.' I cringed inwardly. 'I paid by return and was extremely surprised this morning to find that another account had been rendered. I have here a receipt signed by . . .'

I couldn't stand any more. 'I'm very sorry, Mr Brooke, but there's been a mistake. I'll put it right. Please accept our apologies.'

This became a familiar refrain over the next few days, but it was Siegfried who had the most unfortunate experience. It was in the bar of his favourite pub, the Black Swan. He was approached by Billy Breckenridge, a friendly, jocular little character, one of Darrowby's worthies. 'Hey, remember that three and six I paid at your surgery? I've had another bill for it.'

Siegfried made a polished apology — he'd had a lot of practice — and bought the man a drink. They parted on good terms.

The pity of it was that Siegfried, who seldom remembered anything, didn't remember this. A month later, also in the Swan, he ran into Billy Breckenridge again. This time, Billy wasn't so jocular. 'Hey, remember that bill you sent me twice? Well, I've had it again.'

Siegfried did his best, but his charm bounced off the little man. He was offended. 'Right, I can see you don't believe I paid your bill. I had a receipt from your brother, but I've lost it.' He brushed aside Siegfried's protestations. 'No, no, there's only one way to settle this. I say I've paid the three and six, you say I haven't. All right, I'll toss you for it.'

Miserably, Siegfried demurred, but Billy was adamant. He produced a penny and, with great dignity, balanced it on his thumbnail. 'O.K., you call.'

'Heads,' muttered Siegfried and heads it was. The little man did not change expression. Still dignified, he handed the three and six to Siegfried. 'Perhaps we might be able to consider the matter closed.' He walked out of the bar.

Now there are all kinds of bad memories, but Siegfried's was of the inspired type. He somehow forgot to make a note of this last transaction and, at the end of the month, Billy Breckenridge received a fourth request for the amount which he had already paid twice. It was about then that Siegfried changed his pub and started going to the Cross Keys.

CHAPTER 13

As autumn wore into winter and the high tops were streaked with the first snows, the discomforts of practice in the Dales began to make themselves felt.

Driving for hours with frozen feet, climbing to the high barns in biting winds which seared and flattened the wiry hill grass. The interminable stripping off in draughty buildings and the washing of hands and chest in buckets of cold water, using scrubbing soap and often a piece of sacking for a towel.

I really found out the meaning of chapped hands. When there was a rush of work, my hands were never quite dry and the little red fissures crept up almost to my elbows.

This was when some small animal work came as a blessed relief. To step out of the rough, hard routine for a while; to walk into a warm drawing-room instead of a cow house and tackle something less formidable than a horse or a bull. And among all those comfortable drawing-rooms there was none so beguiling as Mrs Pumphrey's.

Mrs Pumphrey was an elderly widow. Her late husband, a beer baron whose breweries and pubs were scattered widely over the broad bosom of Yorkshire, had left her a vast fortune and a beautiful house on the outskirts of Darrowby. Here she lived with a large staff of servants, a gardener, a chauffeur and Tricki Woo. Tricki Woo was a Pekingese and the apple of his mistress' eye.

Standing now in the magnificent doorway, I furtively rubbed the toes of my shoes on the backs of my trousers and blew on my cold hands. I could almost see the deep armchair drawn close to the leaping flames, the tray of cocktail biscuits, the bottle of excellent sherry. Because of the sherry, I was always careful to time my visits for half an hour before lunch.

A maid answered my ring, beaming on me as an honoured guest and led me to the room, crammed with expensive furniture and littered with glossy magazines and the latest novels. Mrs Pumphrey, in the high-backed chair by the fire, put down her book with a cry of delight. 'Tricki! Tricki! Here is your Uncle Herriot.' I had been made an uncle very early and, sensing the advantages of the relationship, had made no objection.

Tricki, as always, bounded from his cushion, leaped on to the back of a sofa and put his paws on my shoulders. He then licked my face thoroughly before retiring, exhausted. He was soon exhausted because he was given roughly twice the amount of food needed for a dog of his size. And it was the wrong kind of food.

'Oh, Mr Herriot,' Mrs Pumphrey said, looking at her pet anxiously. 'I'm so glad you've come. Tricki has gone flop-bott again.'

This ailment, not to be found in any text-book, was her way of describing the symptoms of Tricki's impacted anal glands. When the glands filled up, he showed discomfort by sitting down suddenly in mid walk and his mistress would rush to the phone in great agitation.

'Mr Herriot! Please come, he's going flop-bott again!'

I hoisted the little dog on to a table and, by pressure on the anus with a pad of cotton wool, I evacuated the glands.

It baffled me that the Peke was always so pleased to see me. Any dog who could still like a man who grabbed him and squeezed his bottom hard every time they met had to have an incredibly forgiving nature. But Tricki never showed any resentment; in fact he was an outstandingly equable little animal, bursting with intelligence, and I was genuinely attached to him. It was a pleasure to be his personal physician.

The squeezing over, I lifted my patient from the table, noticing the increased weight, the padding of extra flesh over the ribs. 'You know, Mrs Pumphrey, you're overfeeding him again. Didn't I tell you to cut out all those pieces of cake and give him more protein?'

'Oh yes, Mr Herriot,' Mrs Pumphrey wailed. 'But what can I do? He's so tired of chicken.'

I shrugged; it was hopeless. I allowed the maid to lead me to the palatial bathroom where I always performed a ritual handwashing after the operation. It was a huge room with a fully stocked dressing-table, massive green ware and rows of glass shelves laden with toilet preparations. My private guest towel was laid out next to the slab of expensive soap.

Then I returned to the drawing-room, my sherry glass was filled and I settled down by the fire to listen to Mrs Pumphrey. It couldn't be called a conversation because she did all the talking, but I always found it rewarding.

Mrs Pumphrey was likeable, gave widely to charities and would help anybody in trouble. She was intelligent and amusing and had a lot of waffling charm; but most people have a blind spot and hers was Tricki Woo. The tales she told about her darling ranged far into the realms of fantasy and I waited eagerly for the next instalment.

'Oh Mr Herriot, I have the most exciting news. Tricki has a pen pal! Yes, he wrote a letter to the editor of *Doggy World* enclosing a donation, and told him that even though he was descended from a long line of Chinese emperors, he had decided to come down and mingle freely with the common dogs. He asked the editor to seek out a pen pal for him among the dogs he knew so that they could correspond to their mutual benefit. And for this purpose, Tricki said he would adopt the name of Mr Utterbunkum. And, do you know, he received the most beautiful letter from the editor' (I could imagine the sensible man leaping upon this potential gold mine) 'who said he would like to introduce Bonzo Fotheringham, a lonely dalmatian who would be delighted to exchange letters with a new friend in Yorkshire.'

I sipped the sherry. Tricki snored on my lap. Mrs Pumphrey went on.

'But I'm so disappointed about the new summerhouse — you know I got it specially for Tricki so we could sit out together on warm afternoons. It's such a nice little rustic shelter, but he's taken a passionate dislike to it. Simply loathes it — absolutely refuses to go inside. You should see the dreadful expression on his face when he looks at it. And do you know what he called it yesterday? Oh, I hardly dare tell you.' She looked around the room before leaning over and whispering: 'He called it "the bloody hut"!'

The maid struck fresh life into the fire and refilled my glass. The wind hurled a handful of sleet against the window. This, I thought, was the life. I listened for more.

'And did I tell you, Mr Herriot, Tricki had another good win yesterday? You know, I'm sure he must study the racing columns, he's such a tremendous judge of form. Well, he told me to back Canny Lad in the three o'clock at Redcar yesterday and, as usual, it won. He put on a shilling each way and got back nine shillings.'

These bets were always placed in the name of Tricki Woo and I thought with compassion of the reactions of the local bookies. The Darrowby turf accountants were a harassed and fugitive body of men. A board would appear at the end of some alley urging the population to invest with Joe Downs and enjoy perfect security. Joe would live for a few months on a knife edge while he pitted his wits against the knowledgeable citizens, but the end was always the same; a few favourites would win in a row and Joe would be gone in the night, taking his board with him. Once I had asked a local inhabitant about the sudden departure of one of these luckless nomads. He replied unemotionally: 'Oh, we broke 'im.'

Losing a regular flow of shillings to a dog must have been a heavy cross for these unfortunate men to bear.

'I had such a frightening experience last week,' Mrs Pumphrey continued. 'I was sure

151

I would have to call you out. Poor little Tricki — he went completely crackerdog!'

I mentally lined this up with flop-bott among the new canine diseases and asked for more information.

'It was awful. I was terrified. The gardener was throwing rings for Tricki — you know he does this for half an hour every day.' I had witnessed this spectacle several times. Hodgkin, a dour, bent old Yorkshireman who looked as though he hated all dogs and Tricki in particular, had to go out on the lawn every day and throw little rubber rings over and over again. Tricki bounded after them and brought them back, barking madly till the process was repeated. The bitter lines on the old man's face deepened as the game progressed. His lips moved continually, but it was impossible to hear what he was saying.

Mrs Pumphrey went on: 'Well, he was playing his game, and he does adore it so, when suddenly, without warning, he went crackerdog. He forgot all about his rings and began to run around in circles, barking and yelping in such a strange way. Then he fell over on his side and lay like a little dead thing. Do you know, Mr Herriot, I really thought he was dead, he lay so perfectly still. And what hurt me most was that Hodgkin began to laugh. He has been with me for twenty-four years and I have never even seen him smile, and yet, when he looked down at that still form, he broke into a queer, high-pitched cackle. It was horrid. I was just going to rush to the telephone when Tricki got up and walked away — he seemed perfectly normal.'

Hysteria, I thought, brought on by wrong feeding and overexcitement. I put down my glass and fixed Mrs Pumphrey with a severe glare. 'Now look, this is just what I was talking about. If you persist in feeding all that fancy rubbish to Tricki you are going to ruin his health. You really must get him on to a sensible dog diet of one or, at the most, two small meals a day of meat and brown bread or a little biscuit. And nothing in between.'

Mrs Pumphrey shrank into her chair, a picture of abject guilt. 'Oh, please don't speak to me like that. I do try to give him the right things, but it is so difficult. When he begs for his little titbits, I can't refuse him.' She dabbed her eyes with a handkerchief.

But I was unrelenting. 'All right, Mrs Pumphrey, it's up to you, but I warn you that if you go on as you are doing, Tricki will go crackerdog more and more often.'

I left the cosy haven with reluctance, pausing on the gravelled drive to look back at Mrs Pumphrey waving and Tricki, as always, standing against the window, his wide-mouthed face apparently in the middle of a hearty laugh.

Driving home, I mused on the many advantages of being Tricki's uncle. When he went to the seaside he sent me boxes of oak-smoked kippers; and when the tomatoes ripened in his greenhouse, he sent a pound or two every week. Tins of tobacco arrived regularly, sometimes with a photograph carrying a loving inscription.

But it was when the Christmas hamper arrived from Fortnum and Mason's that I decided that I was on a really good thing which should be helped along a bit. Hitherto, I had merely rung up and thanked Mrs Pumphrey for the gifts, and she had been rather cool, pointing out that it was Tricki who had sent the things and he was the one who should be thanked.

With the arrival of the hamper it came to me, blindingly, that I had been guilty of a grave error of tactics. I set myself to compose a letter to Tricki. Avoiding Siegfried's sardonic eye, I thanked my doggy nephew for his Christmas gifts and for all his generosity in the past. I expressed my sincere hopes that the festive fare had not upset his delicate digestion and suggested that if he did experience any discomfort he should have recourse to the black powder his uncle always prescribed. A vague feeling of professional shame was easily swamped by floating visions of kippers, tomatoes and hampers. I addressed the envelope to Master Tricki Pumphrey, Barlby Grange and slipped it into the post box with only a slight feeling of guilt.

On my next visit, Mrs Pumphrey drew me to one side. 'Mr Herriot,' she whispered, 'Tricki adored your charming letter and he will keep it always, but he was very put out about one thing — you addressed it to Master Tricki and he does insist upon Mister. He was dreadfully affronted at first, quite beside himself, but when he saw it was from you he soon recovered his good temper. I can't think why he should have these little prejudices. Perhaps it is because he is an only dog — I do think an only dog develops more prejudices than one from a large family.'

Entering Skeldale House was like returning to a colder world. Siegfried bumped into me in the passage. 'Ah, who have we here? Why I do believe it's dear Uncle Herriot. And what have you been doing, Uncle? Slaving away at Barlby Grange, I expect. Poor fellow, you must be tired out. Do you really think it's worth it, working your fingers to the bone for another hamper?'

CHAPTER 14

Looking back, I can scarcely believe we used to spend all those hours in making up medicines. But our drugs didn't come to us in proprietary packages and before we could get out on the road we had to fill our cars with a wide variety of carefully compounded and largely useless remedies.

When Siegfried came upon me that morning I was holding a twelve-ounce bottle at eye level while I poured syrup of coccilana into it. Tristan was moodily mixing stomach powders with a mortar and pestle and he stepped up his speed of stroke when he saw his brother's eye on him. He was surrounded by packets of the powder and, further along the bench, were orderly piles of pessaries which he had made by filling cellophane cylinders with boric acid.

Tristan looked industrious; his elbow jogged furiously as he ground away at the ammon carb and nux vomica. Siegfried smiled benevolently.

I smiled too. I felt the strain badly when the brothers were at variance, but I could see that this was going to be one of the happy mornings. There had been a distinct improvement in the atmosphere since Christmas when Tristan had slipped casually back to college and, apparently without having done any work, had re-sat and passed his exams. And there was something else about my boss today; he seemed to glow with inner satisfaction as though he knew for certain that something good was on the way. He came in and closed the door.

'I've got a bit of good news.'

I screwed the cork into the bottle. 'Well, don't keep us in suspense. Let's have it.'

Siegfried looked from one of us to the other. He was almost smirking. 'You remember that bloody awful shambles when Tristan took charge of the bills?'

His brother looked away and began to grind still faster, but Siegfried laid a friendly hand on his shoulder. 'No, don't worry, I'm not going to ask you to do it again. In fact, you'll never have to do it again because, from now on, the job will be done by an expert.' He paused and cleared his throat. 'We're going to have a secretary.'

As we stared blankly at him he went on. 'Yes, I picked her myself and I consider she's perfect.'

'Well, what's she like?' I asked.

Siegfried pursed his lips. 'It's difficult to describe her. But just think — what do we want here? We don't want some flighty young thing hanging about the place. We don't want a pretty little blonde sitting behind that desk powdering her nose and making eyes at everybody.'

'We don't?' Tristan interrupted, plainly puzzled.

'No, we don't!' Siegfried rounded on him. 'She'd be daydreaming about her boy friends half the time and just when we'd got her trained to our ways she'd be running off to get married.'

Tristan still looked unconvinced and it seemed to exasperate his brother. Siegfried's face reddened. 'And there's another thing. How could we have an attractive young girl in here with somebody like you in the house? You'd never leave her alone.'

Tristan was nettled. 'How about you?'

'I'm talking about you, not me!' Siegfried roared. I closed my eyes. The peace hadn't lasted long. I decided to cut in. 'All right, tell us about the new secretary.'

With an effort, he mastered his emotion. 'Well, she's in her fifties and she has retired after thirty years with Green and Moulton in Bradford. She was company secretary there and I've had the most wonderful reference from the firm. They say she is a model of efficiency and that's what we want in this practice — efficiency. We're far too slack. It's just a stroke of luck for us that she decided to come and live in Darrowby. Anyway, you'll be able to meet her in a few minutes — she's coming at ten o'clock this morning.'

The church clock was chiming when the door bell rang. Siegfried hastened out to answer it and led his great discovery into the room in triumph. 'Gentlemen, I want you to meet Miss Harbottle.'

She was a big, high-bosomed woman with a round healthy face and gold-rimmed spectacles. A mass of curls, incongruous and very dark, peeped from under her hat; they looked as if they might be dyed and they didn't go with her severe clothes and brogue shoes.

It occurred to me that we wouldn't have to worry about her rushing off to get married. It wasn't that she was ugly, but she had a jutting chin and an air of effortless command that would send any man running for his life.

I shook hands and was astonished at the power of Miss Harbottle's grip. We looked into each other's eyes and had a friendly trial of strength for a few seconds, then she seemed happy to call it a draw and turned away. Tristan was entirely unprepared and a look of alarm spread over his face as his hand was engulfed; he was released only when his knees started to buckle.

She began a tour of the office while Siegfried hovered behind her, rubbing his hands and looking like a shopwalker with his favourite customer. She paused at the desk, heaped high with incoming and outgoing bills, Ministry of Agriculture forms, circulars from drug firms with here and there stray boxes of pills and tubes of udder ointment.

Stirring distastefully among the mess, she extracted the dog-eared old ledger and held it up between finger and thumb. 'What's this?'

Siegfried trotted forward. 'Oh, that's our ledger. We enter the visits into it from our day book which is here somewhere.' He scrabbled about on the desk. 'Ah, here it is. This is where we write the calls as they come in.'

She studied the two books for a few minutes with an expression of amazement which gave way to a grim humour. 'You gentlemen will have to learn to write if I am going to look after your books. There are three different hands here, but this one is by far the worst. Quite dreadful. Whose is it?'

She pointed to an entry which consisted of a long, broken line with an occasional undulation.

'That's mine, actually,' said Siegfried, shuffling his feet. 'Must have been in a hurry that day.'

'But it's all like that, Mr Farnon. Look here and here and here. It won't do, you know.'

Siegfried put his hands behind his back and hung his head.

'I expect you keep your stationery and envelopes in here.' She pulled open a drawer in the desk. It appeared to be filled entirely with old seed packets, many of which had burst open. A few peas and french beans rolled gently from the top of the heap. The next drawer was crammed tightly with soiled calving ropes which somebody had forgotten to wash. They didn't smell so good and Miss Harbottle drew back hurriedly; but she was not easily deterred and tugged hopefully at the third drawer. It came open with a musical clinking and she looked down on a dusty row of empty pale ale bottles.

She straightened up slowly and spoke patiently. 'And where, may I ask, is your cash box?'

'Well, we just stuff it in there, you know.' Siegfried pointed to the pint pot on the corner of the mantelpiece. 'Haven't got what you'd call a proper cash box, but this does the job all right.'

Miss Harbottle looked at the pot with horror. 'You just stuff . . .' Crumpled cheques and notes peeped over the brim at her; many of their companions had burst out on to the hearth below. 'And you mean to say that you go out and leave that money there day after day?'

'Never seems to come to any harm,' Siegfried replied.

'And how about your petty cash?'

Siegfried gave an uneasy giggle. 'All in there, you know. All cash — petty and otherwise.'

Miss Harbottle's ruddy face had lost some of its colour. 'Really, Mr Farnon, this is too bad. I don't know how you have gone on so long like this. I simply do not know. However, I'm confident I will be able to straighten things out very soon. There is obviously nothing complicated about your business — a simple card index system would be the thing for your accounts. The other little things' — she glanced back unbelievingly at the pot — 'I will put right very quickly.'

'Fine, Miss Harbottle, fine.' Siegfried was rubbing his hands harder than ever. 'We'll expect you on Monday morning.'

'Nine o'clock sharp, Mr Farnon.'

After she had gone there was a silence. Tristan had enjoyed her visit and was smiling thoughtfully, but I felt uncertain.

'You know, Siegfried,' I said, 'maybe she is a demon of efficiency but isn't she just a bit tough?'

'Tough?' Siegfried gave a loud, rather cracked laugh. 'Not a bit of it. You leave her to me. I can handle her.'

CHAPTER 15

There was little furniture in the dining-room but the noble lines and the very size of the place lent grace to the long sideboard and the modest mahogany table where Tristan and I sat at breakfast.

The single large window was patterned with frost and in the street outside, the footsteps of the passers-by crunched in the crisp snow. I looked up from my boiled egg as a car drew up. There was a stamping in the porch, the outer door banged shut and Siegfried burst into the room. Without a word he made for the fire and hung over it, leaning his elbows on the grey marble mantelpiece. He was muffled almost to the eyes in greatcoat and scarf but what you could see of his face was purplish blue.

He turned a pair of streaming eyes to the table. 'A milk fever up at old Heseltine's. One of the high buildings. God, it was cold up there. I could hardly breathe.'

As he pulled off his gloves and shook his

numbed fingers in front of the flames, he darted sidelong glances at his brother. Tristan's chair was nearest the fire and he was enjoying his breakfast as he enjoyed everything, slapping the butter happily on to his toast and whistling as he applied the marmalade. His *Daily Mirror* was balanced against the coffee pot. You could almost see the waves of comfort and contentment coming from him.

Siegfried dragged himself unwillingly from the fire and dropped into a chair. 'I'll just have a cup of coffee, James. Heseltine was very kind — asked me to sit down and have breakfast with him. He gave me a lovely slice of home fed bacon — a bit fat, maybe, but what a flavour! I can taste it now.'

He put down his cup with a clatter. 'You know, there's no reason why we should have to go to the grocer for our bacon and eggs. There's a perfectly good hen house at the bottom of the garden and a pigsty in the yard with a boiler for the swill. All our household waste could go towards feeding a pig. We'd probably do it quite cheaply.'

He rounded on Tristan who had just lit a Woodbine and was shaking out his *Mirror* with the air of ineffable pleasure which was peculiar to him. 'And it would be a useful job for you. You're not producing much sitting around here on your arse all day. A bit of stock keeping would do you good.'

Tristan put down his paper as though the charm had gone out of it. 'Stock keeping? Well, I feed your mare as it is.' He didn't enjoy looking after Siegfried's new hunter because every time he turned her out to water in the yard she would take a playful kick at him in passing.

Siegfried jumped up. 'I know you do, and it doesn't take all day, does it? It won't kill you to take on the hens and pigs.'

'Pigs?' Tristan looked startled. 'I thought you said pig.'

'Yes, pigs. I've just been thinking. If I buy a litter of weaners we can sell the others and keep one for ourselves. Won't cost a thing that way.'

'Not with free labour, certainly.'

'Labour? Labour? You don't know what it means! Look at you lying back there puffing your head off. You smoke too many of those bloody cigarettes!'

'So do you.'

'Never mind me, I'm talking about you!' Siegfried shouted.

I got up from the table with a sigh. Another day had begun.

When Siegfried got an idea he didn't muck about. Immediate action was his watchword. Within forty-eight hours a litter of ten little pigs had taken up residence in the sty and twelve Light Sussex pullets were pecking about behind the wire of the hen house. He was particularly pleased with the pullets. 'Look at them, James; just on point of lay and a very good strain, too. There'll be just a trickle of eggs at first, but once they get cracking we'll be snowed under. Nothing like a nice fresh egg warm from the nest.'

It was plain from the first that Tristan didn't share his brother's enthusiasm for the hens. I often found him hanging about outside the hen house, looking bored and occasionally throwing bread crusts over the wire. There was no evidence of the regular feeding, the balanced diet recommended by the experts. As egg producers, the hens held no appeal for him, but he did become mildly interested in them as personalities. An odd way of clucking, a peculiarity in gait — these things amused him.

But there were no eggs and as the weeks passed, Siegfried became increasingly irritable. 'Wait till I see the chap that sold me those hens. Damned scoundrel. Good laying strain my foot!' It was pathetic to see him anxiously exploring the empty nesting boxes every morning.

One afternoon, I was going down the garden when Tristan called to me. 'Come over here, Jim. This is something new. I bet you've never seen anything like it before.' He pointed upwards and I saw a group of unusually coloured large birds perched in the branches of the elms. There were more of them in the neighbour's apple trees.

I stared in astonishment. 'You're right, I've never seen anything like them. What are they?'

'Oh, come on,' said Tristan, grinning in delight. 'Surely there's something familiar about them. Take another look.'

I peered upwards again. 'No, I've never seen birds as big as that and with such exotic plumage. What is it — a freak migration?'

Tristan gave a shout of laughter. 'They're our hens!'

'How the devil did they get up there?'

'They've left home. Hopped it.'

'But I can only see seven. Where are the rest of them?'

'God knows. Let's have a look over the wall.'

The crumbling mortar gave plenty of toe holds between the bricks and we looked down into the next garden. The other five hens were there, pecking contentedly among some cabbages.

It took a long time to get them all back into the hen house and the tedious business had to be repeated several times a day thereafter. For the hens had clearly grown tired of life under Tristan and decided that they would do better living off the country. They became nomads, ranging ever further afield in their search for sustenance.

At first the neighbours chuckled. They

phoned to say their children were rounding up the hens and would we come and get them; but with the passage of time their jocularity wore thin. Finally Siegfried was involved in some painful interviews. His hens, he was told, were an unmitigated nuisance.

It was after one particularly unpleasant session that Siegfried decided that the hens must go. It was a bitter blow and as usual he vented his fury on Tristan. 'I must have been mad to think that any hens under your care would ever lay eggs. But really, isn't it just a bit hard? I give you this simple little job and one would have thought that even you would be hard put to it to make a mess of it. But look at the situation after only three weeks. Not one solitary egg have we seen. The bloody hens are flying about the countryside like pigeons. We are permanently estranged from our neighbours. You've done a thorough job, haven't you?' All the frustrated egg producer in Siegfried welled out in his shrill tones.

Tristan's expression registered only wounded virtue, but he was rash enough to try to defend himself. 'You know, I thought there was something queer about those hens from the start,' he muttered.

Siegfried shed the last vestiges of his self-control. 'Queer!' he yelled wildly. 'You're the one that's queer, not the poor bloody hens. You're the queerest bugger there is. For God's sake get out — get out of my sight!'

Tristan withdrew with quiet dignity.

It took some time for the last echoes of the poultry venture to die away but after a fortnight, sitting again at the dining-table with Tristan, I felt sure that all was forgotten. So that it was with a strange sense of the workings of fate that I saw Siegfried stride into the room and lean menacingly over his brother. 'You remember those hens, I suppose,' he said almost in a whisper. 'You'll recall that I gave them away to Mrs Dale, that old age pensioner down Brown's Yard. Well, I've just been speaking to her. She's delighted with them. Gives them a hot mash night and morning and she's collecting ten eggs a day.' His voice rose almost to a scream. 'Ten eggs, do you hear, ten eggs!'

I hurriedly swallowed the last of my tea and excused myself. I trotted along the passage, out the back door and up the garden to my car. On the way I passed the empty hen house. It had a forlorn look. It was a long way to the dining-room but I could still hear Siegfried.

CHAPTER 16

'Jim! Come over here and look at these little beggars.' Tristan laughed excitedly as he leaned over the door of the pigsty.

I walked across the yard. 'What is it?'

'I've just given them their swill and it's a bit hot. Just look at them!'

The little pigs were seizing the food, dropping it and walking suspiciously round it. Then they would creep up, touch the hot potatoes with their muzzles and leap back in alarm. There was none of the usual meal time slobbering; just a puzzled grunting.

Right from the start Tristan had found the pigs more interesting than the hens which was a good thing because he had to retrieve himself after the poultry disaster. He spent a lot of time in the yard, sometimes feeding or mucking out but more often resting his elbows on the door watching his charges.

As with the hens, he was more interested in their characters than their ability to produce pork or bacon. After he poured the swill into the long trough he always watched, entranced, while the pigs made their first rush. Soon, in the desperate gobbling there would be signs of uneasiness. The tiny animals would begin to glance sideways till their urge to find out what their mates were enjoying so much became unbearable; they would start to change position frantically, climbing over each other's backs and falling into the swill.

Old Boardman was a willing collaborator, but mainly in an advisory capacity. Like all countrymen he considered he knew all about the husbandry and diseases of animals and, it turned out, pigs were his speciality. There were long conferences in the dark room under the Bairnsfather cartoons and the old man grew animated over his descriptions of the vast, beautiful animals he had reared in that very sty.

Tristan listened with respect because he had solid proof of Boardman's expertise in the way he handled the old brick boiler. Tristan could light the thing but it went out if he turned his back on it; but it was docile in Boardman's hands. I often saw Tristan listening wonderingly to the steady blub-blub while the old man rambled on and the delicious scent of cooking pig potatoes drifted over them both.

But no animal converts food more quickly into flesh than a pig and as the weeks passed the little pink creatures changed with alarming speed into ten solid, no-nonsense porkers. Their characters deteriorated, too. They lost all their charm. Meal times stopped being fun and became a battle with the odds growing heavier against Tristan all the time.

I could see that it brought a lot of colour into old Boardman's life and he always dropped whatever he was doing when he saw Tristan scooping the swill from the boiler.

He obviously enjoyed watching the daily contest from his seat on the stone trough. Tristan bracing himself, listening to the pigs squealing at the rattle of the bucket; giving a few fearsome shouts to encourage himself then shooting the bolt and plunging among the grunting, jostling animals; broad, greedy snouts forcing into the bucket, sharp feet grinding his toes, heavy bodies thrusting against his legs.

I couldn't help smiling when I remembered the light-hearted game it used to be. There was no laughter now. Tristan finally took to brandishing a heavy stick at the pigs before he dared to go in. Once inside his only hope of staying on his feet was to clear a little space by beating on the backs.

It was on a market day when the pigs had almost reached bacon weight that I came upon Tristan sprawled in his favourite chair. But there was something unusual about him; he wasn't asleep, no medicine bottle, no

Woodbines, no *Daily Mirror.* His arms hung limply over the sides of the chair, his eyes were half closed and sweat glistened on his forehead.

'Jim,' he whispered. 'I've had the most hellish afternoon I've ever had in my life.'

I was alarmed at his appearance. 'What's happened?'

'The pigs,' he croaked. 'They escaped today.'

'Escaped! How the devil could they do that?'

Tristan tugged at his hair. 'It was when I was feeding the mare. I gave her her hay and thought I might as well feed the pigs at the same time. You know what they've been like lately — well, today they went berserk. Soon as I opened the door they charged out in a solid block. Sent me up in the air, bucket and all, then ran over the top of me.' He shuddered and looked up at me wide-eyed. 'I'll tell you this, Jim, when I was lying there on the cobbles, covered with swill and that lot trampling on me, I thought it was all over. But they didn't savage me. They belted out through the yard door at full gallop.'

'The yard door was open then?'

'Too true it was. I would just choose this one day to leave it open.'

Tristan sat up and wrung his hands. 'Well, you know, I thought it was all right at first. You see, they slowed down when they got into the lane and trotted quietly round into the front street with Boardman and I hard on their heels. They formed a group there. Didn't seem to know where to go next. I was sure we were going to be able to head them off, but just then one of them caught sight of itself in Robson's shop window.'

He gave a remarkable impression of a pig staring at its reflection for a few moments then leaping back with a startled grunt.

'Well, that did it, Jim. The bloody animal panicked and shot off into the market place at about fifty miles an hour with the rest after it.'

I gasped. Ten large pigs loose among the packed stalls and market day crowds was difficult even to imagine.

'Oh God, you should have seen it.' Tristan fell back wearily into his chair. 'Women and kids screaming. The stallholders, police and everybody else cursing me. There was a terrific traffic jam too — miles of cars tooting like hell while the policeman on point duty concentrated on browbeating me.' He wiped his brow. 'You know that fast-talking merchant on the china stall — well, today I saw him at a loss for words. He was balancing a cup on his palm and in full cry when one of the pigs got its forefeet on his stall and stared him straight in the face. He stopped as if he'd been shot. Any other time it would have been funny but I thought the perishing animal was going to wreck the stall. The counter was beginning to rock when the pig changed its mind and made off.'

'What's the position now?' I asked. 'Have you got them back?'

'I've got nine of them back,' Tristan replied, leaning back and closing his eyes. 'With the help of almost the entire male population of the district I've got nine of them back. The tenth was last seen heading north at a good pace. God knows where it is now. Oh, I didn't tell you — one of them got into the post office. Spent quite some time in there.' He put his hands over his face. 'I'm for it this time, Jim. I'll be in the hands of the law after this lot. There's no doubt about it.'

I leaned over and slapped his leg. 'Oh, I shouldn't worry. I don't suppose there's been any serious damage done.'

Tristan replied with a groan. 'But there's something else. When I finally closed the door after getting the pigs back in their sty I was on the verge of collapse. I was leaning against the wall gasping for breath when I saw the mare had gone. Yes, gone. I'd gone straight out after the pigs and forgot to close her box. I don't know where she is. Boardman said he'd look around — I haven't the strength.'

Tristan lit a trembling Woodbine. 'This is the end, Jim. Siegfried will have no mercy this time.'

As he spoke, the door flew open and his

brother rushed in. 'What the hell is going on?' he roared. 'I've just been speaking to the vicar and he says my mare is in his garden eating his wallflowers. He's hopping mad and I don't blame him. Go on, you lazy young scoundrel. Don't lie there, get over to the vicarage this instant and bring her back!'

Tristan did not stir. He lay inert, looking up at his brother. His lips moved feebly.

'No,' he said.

'What's that?' Siegfried shouted incredulously. 'Get out of that chair immediately. Go and get that mare!'

'No,' replied Tristan.

I felt a chill of horror. This sort of mutiny was unprecedented. Siegfried had gone very red in the face and I steeled myself for an eruption; but it was Tristan who spoke.

'If you want your mare you can get her yourself.' His voice was quiet with no note of defiance. He had the air of a man to whom the future is of no account.

Even Siegfried could see that this was one time when Tristan had had enough. After glaring down at his brother for a few seconds he turned and walked. He got the mare himself.

Nothing more was said about the incident but the pigs were moved hurriedly to the bacon factory and were never replaced. The stock-keeping project was at an end.

CHAPTER 17

When I came in, Miss Harbottle was sitting, head bowed, over the empty cash box; she looked bereaved. It was a new, shiny, black box with the words 'Petty Cash' printed on top in white letters. Inside was a red book with the incomings and outgoings recorded in neat columns. But there was no money.

Miss Harbottle's sturdy shoulders sagged. She listlessly took up the red book between finger and thumb and a lonely sixpence rolled from between its pages and tinkled into the box. 'He's been at it again,' she whispered.

A stealthy footstep sounded in the passage. 'Mr Farnon!' she called out. And to me: 'It's really absurd the way the man always tries to slink past the door.'

Siegfried shuffled in. He was carrying a stomach tube and pump, calcium bottles bulged from his jacket pockets and a bloodless castrator dangled from the other hand.

He smiled cheerfully but I could see he was uncomfortable, not only because of the load he carried, but because of his poor tactical position. Miss Harbottle had arranged her desk across the corner diagonally opposite the door and he had to walk across a long stretch of carpet to reach her. From her point of view it was strategically perfect. From her corner she could see every inch of the big room, into the passage when the door was open and out on to the front street from the window on her left. Nothing escaped her — it was a position of power.

Siegfried looked down at the square figure behind the desk. 'Good morning, Miss Harbottle, can I do anything for you?'

The grey eyes glinted behind the gold-rimmed spectacles. 'You can, indeed, Mr Farnon. You can explain why you have once more emptied my petty cash box.'

'Oh, I'm so sorry. I had to rush through to Brawton last night and I found myself a bit short. There was really nowhere else to turn to.'

'But Mr Farnon, in the two months I have been here, we must have been over this a dozen times. What is the good of my trying to keep an accurate record of the money in the practice if you keep stealing it and spending it?'

'Well, I suppose I got into the habit in the old pint pot days. It wasn't a bad system, really.'

'It wasn't a system at all. It was anarchy.

You cannot run a business that way. But I've told you this so many times and each time you have promised to alter your ways. I feel almost at my wits' end.'

'Oh, never mind, Miss Harbottle. Get some more out of the bank and put it in your box. That'll put it right.' Siegfried gathered up the loose coils of the stomach tube from the floor and turned to go, but Miss Harbottle cleared her throat warningly.

'There are one or two other matters. Will you please try to keep your other promise to enter your visits in the book every day and to price them as you do so? Nearly a week has gone by since you wrote anything in. How can I possibly get the bills out on the first of the month? This is most important, but how do you expect me to do it when you impede me like this?'

'Yes, yes, I'm sorry, but I have a string of calls waiting. I really must go.' He was half way across the floor and the tube was uncoiling itself again when he heard the ominous throat clearing behind him.

'And one more thing, Mr Farnon. I still can't decipher your writing. These medical terms are difficult enough, so please take a little care and don't scribble.'

'Very well, Miss Harbottle.' He quickened his pace through the door and into the passage where, it seemed, was safety and peace. He was clattering thankfully over the tiles

179

when the familiar rumbling reached him. She could project that sound a surprising distance by giving it a bit of extra pressure, and it was a summons which had to be obeyed. I could hear him wearily putting the tube and pump on the floor; the calcium bottles must have been digging into his ribs because I heard them go down too.

He presented himself again before the desk. Miss Harbottle wagged a finger at him. 'While I have you here I'd like to mention another point which troubles me. Look at this day book. You see all these slips sticking out of the pages? They are all queries — there must be scores of them — and I am at a standstill until you clear them for me. When I ask you you never have the time. Can you go over them with me now?'

Siegfried backed away hurriedly. 'No, no, not just now. As I said, I have some urgent calls waiting. I'm very sorry but it will have to be some other time. First chance I get I'll come in and see you.' He felt the door behind him and with a last glance at the massive, disapproving figure behind the desk, he turned and fled.

CHAPTER 18

I could look back now on six months of hard practical experience. I had treated cows, horses, pigs, dogs and cats seven days a week; in the morning, afternoon, evening and through the hours when the world was asleep. I had calved cows and farrowed sows till my arms ached and the skin peeled off. I had been knocked down, trampled on and sprayed liberally with every kind of muck. I had seen a fair cross-section of the diseases of animals. And yet a little voice had begun to niggle at the back of my mind; it said I knew nothing, nothing at all.

This was strange, because those six months had been built upon five years of theory; a slow, painful assimilation of thousands of facts and a careful storage of fragments of knowledge like a squirrel with its nuts. Beginning with the study of plants and the lowest forms of life, working up to dissection in the anatomy lab and physiology and the vast, soulless territory of materia medica. Then pathology which tore down the curtain of ignorance and let me look for the first time into the deep secrets. And parasitology, the teeming other world of the worms and fleas and mange mites. Finally, medicine and surgery, the crystallisation of my learning and its application to the everyday troubles of animals.

And there were many others, like physics, chemistry, hygiene; they didn't seem to have missed a thing. Why then should I feel I knew nothing? Why had I begun to feel like an astronomer looking through a telescope at an unknown galaxy? This sensation that I was only groping about on the fringes of limitless space was depressing. It was a funny thing, because everybody else seemed to know all about sick animals. The chap who held the cow's tail, the neighbour from the next farm, men in pubs, jobbing gardeners; they all knew and were free and confident with their advice.

I tried to think back over my life. Was there any time when I had felt this supreme faith in my own knowledge? And then I remembered.

I was back in Scotland, I was seventeen and I was walking under the arch of the Veterinary College into Montrose Street. I had been a student for three days but not until this afternoon had I felt the thrill of fulfilment. Messing about with botany and zoology was all right but this afternoon had been the real thing; I had had my first lecture in animal husbandry.

The subject had been the points of the horse. Professor Grant had hung up a life size picture of a horse and gone over it from nose to tail, indicating the withers, the stifle, the hock, the poll and all the other rich, equine terms. And the professor had been wise; to make his lecture more interesting he kept throwing in little practical points like 'This is where we find curb', or 'Here is the site for windgalls'. He talked of thoroughpins and sidebones, splints and quittor; things the students wouldn't learn about for another four years, but it brought it all to life.

The words were still spinning in my head as I walked slowly down the sloping street. This was what I had come for. I felt as though I had undergone an initiation and become a member of an exclusive club. I really knew about horses. And I was wearing a brand new riding mac with all sorts of extra straps and buckles which slapped against my legs as I turned the corner of the hill into busy Newton Road.

I could hardly believe my luck when I saw the horse. It was standing outside the library below Queen's Cross like something left over from another age. It drooped dispiritedly between the shafts of a coal cart which stood like an island in an eddying stream of cars and buses. Pedestrians hurried by, uncaring,

183

but I had the feeling that fortune was smiling on me.

A horse. Not just a picture but a real, genuine horse. Stray words from the lecture floated up into my mind; the pastern, cannon bone, coronet and all those markings — snip, blaze, white sock near hind. I stood on the pavement and examined the animal critically.

I thought it must be obvious to every passer-by that here was a true expert. Not just an inquisitive onlooker but a man who knew and understood all. I felt clothed in a visible aura of horsiness.

I took a few steps up and down, hands deep in the pockets of the new riding mac, eyes probing for possible shoeing faults or curbs or bog spavins. So thorough was my inspection that I worked round to the off side of the horse and stood perilously among the racing traffic.

I glanced around at the people hurrying past. Nobody seemed to care, not even the horse. He was a large one, at least seventeen hands, and he gazed apathetically down the street, easing his hind legs alternately in a bored manner. I hated to leave him but I had completed my examination and it was time I was on my way. But I felt that I ought to make a gesture before I left; something to communicate to the horse that I understood his problems and that we belonged to the same brotherhood. I stepped briskly forward and patted him on the neck.

Quick as a striking snake, the horse whipped downwards and seized my shoulder in his great strong teeth. He laid back his ears, rolled his eyes wickedly and hoisted me up, almost off my feet. I hung there helplessly, suspended like a lopsided puppet. I wriggled and kicked but the teeth were clamped immovably in the material of my coat.

There was no doubt about the interest of the passers-by now. The grotesque sight of a man hanging from a horse's mouth brought them to a sudden halt and a crowd formed with people looking over each other's shoulders and others fighting at the back to see what was going on.

A horrified old lady was crying: 'Oh, poor boy! Help him, somebody!' Some of the braver characters tried pulling at me but the horse whickered ominously and hung on tighter. Conflicting advice was shouted from all sides. With deep shame I saw two attractive girls in the front row giggling helplessly.

Appalled at the absurdity of my position, I began to thrash about wildly; my shirt collar tightened round my throat; a stream of the horse's saliva trickled down the front of my mac. I could feel myself choking and was giving up hope when a man pushed his way through the crowd.

He was very small. Angry eyes glared from

a face blackened by coal dust. Two empty sacks were draped over an arm.

'Whit the hell's this?' he shouted. A dozen replies babbled in the air.

'Can ye no leave the bloody hoarse alone?' he yelled into my face. I made no reply, being pop-eyed, half throttled and in no mood for conversation.

The coalman turned his fury on the horse. 'Drop him, ya big bastard! Go on, let go, drop him!'

Getting no response he dug the animal viciously in the belly with his thumb. The horse took the point at once and released me like an obedient dog dropping a bone. I fell on my knees and ruminated in the gutter for a while till I could breathe more easily. As from a great distance I could still hear the little man shouting at me.

After some time I stood up. The coalman was still shouting and the crowd was listening appreciatively. 'Whit d'ye think you're playing at — keep yer hands off ma bloody hoarse — get the poliss tae ye.'

I looked down at my new mac. The shoulder was chewed to a sodden mass. I felt I must escape and began to edge my way through the crowd. Some of the faces were concerned but most were grinning. Once clear I started to walk away rapidly and as I turned the corner the last faint cry from the coalman reached me.

'Dinna meddle wi' things ye ken nuthin' aboot!'

CHAPTER 19

I flipped idly through the morning mail. The usual stack of bills, circulars, brightly coloured advertisements for new drugs; after a few months the novelty had worn off and I hardly bothered to read them. I had almost reached the bottom of the pile when I came on something different; an expensive-looking envelope in heavy, deckle-edged paper addressed to me personally. I ripped it open and pulled out a gilt-bordered card which I scanned quickly. I felt my face redden as I slipped the card into an inside pocket.

Siegfried finished ticking off the visits and looked up. 'What are you looking so guilty about, James? Your past catching up with you? What is it, anyway — a letter from an outraged mother?'

'Go on then,' I said sheepishly, pulling out the card and handing it to him, 'have a good laugh. I suppose you'd find out, anyway.'

Siegfried's face was expressionless as he read the card aloud. 'Tricki requests the pleasure of Uncle Herriot's company on Friday February 5th. Drinks and dancing.' He looked up and spoke seriously. 'Now isn't that nice? You know, that must be one of the most generous Pekingeses in England. Sending you kippers and tomatoes and hampers isn't enough — he has to ask you to his home for a party.'

I grabbed the card and slipped it out of sight. 'All right, all right, I know. But what am I supposed to do?'

'Do? What you do is to sit down right away and get a letter off saying thank you very much, you'll be there on February the fifth. Mrs Pumphrey's parties are famous. Mountains of exotic food, rivers of champagne. Don't miss it whatever you do.'

'Will there be a lot of people there?' I asked, shuffling my feet.

Siegfried struck himself on the forehead with his open hand. 'Of course there'll be a lot of people. What d'you think? Did you expect it would be just you and Tricki? You'd have a few beers together and then you'd dance a slow foxtrot with him? The cream of the county will be there in full regalia but my guess is that there will be no more honoured guest than Uncle Herriot. Why? Because Mrs Pumphrey invited the others but Tricki invited you.'

'O.K., O.K.,' I groaned. 'I'll be on my own and I haven't got a proper evening suit. I don't fancy it.'

Siegfried rose and put a hand on my shoulder. 'My dear chap, don't mess about. Sit down and accept the invitation and then go into Brawton and hire a suit for the night. You won't be on your own for long — the debs will be tramping over each other for a dance with you.' He gave the shoulder a final pat before walking to the door. Before leaving he turned round and his expression was grave. 'And remember for Pete's sake don't write to Mrs Pumphrey. Address your letter to Tricki himself or you're sunk.'

I had a lot of mixed feelings churning around in me when I presented myself at the Pumphrey home on the night of February 5th. A maid led me into the hall and I could see Mrs Pumphrey at the entrance to the ballroom receiving her guests and beyond, an elegant throng standing around with drinks. There was a well-bred clamour, a general atmosphere of wealth. I straightened the tie on my hired outfit, took a deep breath and waited.

Mrs Pumphrey was smiling sweetly as she shook hands with the couple in front of me but when she saw me her face became radiant. 'Oh Mr Herriot, how nice of you to come. Tricki was so delighted to have your letter — in fact we really must go in and see him now.' She led me across the hall.

'He's in the morning-room,' she whispered. 'Between ourselves he finds these affairs rather a bore, but he'll be simply furious if I don't take you in for a moment.'

Tricki was curled up in an armchair by the side of a bright fire. When he saw me he jumped on the back of the chair barking in delight, his huge, laughing mouth bisecting his face. I was trying to fend off his attempts to lick my face when I caught sight of two large food bowls on the carpet. One contained about a pound of chopped chicken, the other a mass of crumbled cake.

'Mrs Pumphrey!' I thundered, pointing at the bowls. The poor woman put her hand to her mouth and shrank away from me.

'Oh do forgive me,' she wailed, her face a picture of guilt. 'It's just a special treat because he's alone tonight. And the weather is so cold, too.' She clasped her hands and looked at me abjectly.

'I'll forgive you,' I said sternly, 'if you will remove half the chicken and all the cake.'

Fluttering, like a little girl caught in naughtiness, she did as I said.

I parted regretfully from the little peke. It had been a busy day and I was sleepy from the hours in the biting cold. This room with its fire and soft lighting looked more inviting than the noisy glitter of the ballroom and I would have preferred to curl up here with Tricki on my knee for an hour or two.

191

Mrs Pumphrey became brisk. 'Now you must come and meet some of my friends.' We went into the ballroom where light blazed down from three cut glass chandeliers and was reflected dazzlingly from the cream and gold, many-mirrored walls. We moved from group to group as Mrs Pumphrey introduced me and I squirmed in embarrassment as I heard myself described as 'Tricki's dear kind uncle'. But either they were people of superb self-control or they were familiar with their hostess's blind spot because the information was received with complete gravity.

Along one wall a five-piece orchestra was tuning up; white-jacketed waiters hurried among the guests with trays of food and drinks. Mrs Pumphrey stopped one of the waiters. 'François, some champagne for this gentleman.'

'Yes, Madame.' The waiter proffered his tray.

'No, no, no, not those. One of the big glasses.'

François hurried away and returned with something like a soup plate with a stem. It was brimming with champagne.

'François.'

'Yes, Madame?'

'This is Mr Herriot. I want you to take a good look at him.'

The waiter turned a pair of sad, spaniel eyes on me and drank me in for a few moments.

'I want you to look after him. See that his glass is full and that he has plenty to eat.'

'Certainly, Madame.' He bowed and moved away.

I buried my face in the ice cold champagne and when I looked up, there was François holding out a tray of smoked salmon sandwiches.

It was like that all the evening. François seemed always to be at my elbow, filling up the enormous glass or pushing dainties at me. I found it delightful; the salty snacks brought on a thirst which I quenched with deep draughts of champagne, then I had more snacks which made me thirsty again and François would unfailingly pop up with the magnum.

It was the first time I had had the opportunity of drinking champagne by the pint and it was a rewarding experience. I was quickly aware of a glorious lightness, a heightening of the perceptions. I stopped being overawed by this new world and began to enjoy it. I danced with everybody in sight — sleek young beauties, elderly dowagers and twice with a giggling Mrs Pumphrey.

Or I just talked. And it was witty talk; I repeatedly amazed myself by my lightning shafts. Once I caught sight of myself in a mirror — a distinguished figure, glass in hand, the hired suit hanging on me with quiet grace. It took my breath away.

Eating, drinking, talking, dancing, the evening winged past. When it was time to go and I had my coat on and was shaking hands with Mrs Pumphrey in the hall, Francois appeared again with a bowl of hot soup. He seemed to be worried lest I grow faint on the journey home.

After the soup, Mrs Pumphrey said: 'And now you must come and say good night to Tricki. He'll never forgive you if you don't.' We went into his room and the little dog yawned from the depths of the chair and wagged his tail. Mrs Pumphrey put her hand on my sleeve. 'While you're here, I wonder if you would be so kind as to examine his claws. I've been so worried in case they might be growing too long.'

I lifted up the paws one by one and scrutinised the claws while Tricki lazily licked my hands. 'No, you needn't worry, they're perfectly all right.'

'Thank you so much, I'm so grateful to you. Now you must wash your hands.'

In the familiar bathroom with the sea green basins and the enamelled fishes on the walls and the dressing-table and the bottles on the glass shelves, I looked around as the steaming water ran from the tap. There was my own towel by the basin and the usual new slab of soap — soap that lathered in an instant and gave off an expensive scent. It was the final touch of balm on a gracious evening. It had been a few hours of luxury and light and I carried the memory back with me to Skeldale House.

I got into bed, switched off the light and lay on my back looking up into the darkness. Snatches of music still tinkled about in my head and I was beginning to swim back to the ballroom when the phone rang.

'This is Atkinson of Beck Cottage,' a far away voice said. 'I 'ave a sow 'ere what can't get pigged. She's been on all night. Will you come?'

I looked at the clock as I put down the receiver. It was 2 a.m. I felt numbed. A farrowing right on top of the champagne and the smoked salmon and those little biscuits with the black heaps of caviare. And at Beck Cottage, one of the most primitive smallholdings in the district. It wasn't fair.

Sleepily, I took off my pyjamas and pulled on my shirt. As I reached for the stiff, worn corduroys I used for work, I tried not to look at the hired suit hanging on a corner of the wardrobe.

I groped my way down the long garden to the garage. In the darkness of the yard I closed my eyes and the great chandeliers blazed again, the mirrors flashed and the music played.

It was only two miles out to Beck Cottage. It lay in a hollow and in the winter the place was a sea of mud. I left my car and squelched through the blackness to the door of the house. My knock was unanswered and I moved across to the cluster of buildings opposite and opened the half door into the byre. The warm, sweet bovine smell met me as I peered towards a light showing dimly at the far end where a figure was standing.

I went inside past the shadowy row of cows standing side by side with broken wooden partitions between them and past the mounds of manure piled behind them. Mr Atkinson didn't believe in mucking out too often.

Stumbling over the broken floor, splashing through pools of urine, I arrived at the end where a pen had been made by closing off a corner with a gate. I could just make out the form of a pig, pale in the gloom, lying on her side. There was a scanty bed of straw under her and she lay very still except for the trembling of her flanks. As I watched, she caught her breath and strained for a few seconds then the straining began again.

Mr Atkinson received me without enthusiasm. He was middle-aged, sported a week's growth of beard and wore an ancient hat with a brim which flopped round his ears. He stood hunched against a wall, one hand deep in a ragged pocket, the other holding a bicycle lamp with a fast-failing battery.

'Is this all the light we've got?' I asked.

'Aye, it is,' Mr Atkinson replied, obviously surprised. He looked from the lamp to me with a 'what more does he want?' expression.

'Let's have it, then.' I trained the feeble beam on my patient. 'Just a young pig, isn't she?'

'Aye, nobbut a gilt. Fust litter.'

The pig strained again, shuddered and lay still.

'Something stuck there, I reckon,' I said. 'Will you bring me a bucket of hot water, some soap and a towel, please?'

'Haven't got no 'ot water. Fire's out.'

'O.K., bring me whatever you've got.'

The farmer clattered away down the byre taking the light with him and, with the darkness, the music came back again. It was a Strauss waltz and I was dancing with Lady Frenswick; she was young and very fair and she laughed as I swung her round. I could see her white shoulders and the diamonds winking at her throat and the wheeling mirrors.

Mr Atkinson came shuffling back and dumped a bucket of water on the floor. I dipped a finger in the water; it was ice cold. And the bucket had seen many hard years — I would have to watch my arms on that jagged rim.

Quickly stripping off jacket and shirt, I sucked in my breath as a villainous draught blew through a crack on to my back.

'Soap, please,' I said through clenched teeth.

'In t'bucket.'

I plunged an arm into the water, shivered, and felt my way round till I found a roundish object about the size of a golf ball. I pulled it out and examined it; it was hard and smooth and speckled like a pebble from the sea shore and, optimistically, I began to rub it between my hands and up my arms, waiting for the lather to form. But the soap was impervious; it yielded nothing.

I discarded the idea of asking for another piece in case this would be construed as another complaint. Instead, I borrowed the light and tracked down the byre into the yard, the mud sucking at my Wellingtons, goose pimples rearing on my chest. I searched around in the car boot, listening to my teeth chattering, till I came on a jar of antiseptic lubricating cream.

Back in the pen, I smeared the cream on my arm, knelt behind the pig and gently inserted my hand into the vagina. I moved my hand forward and as wrist and elbow disappeared inside the pig I was forced to roll over on my side. The stones were cold and wet but I forgot my discomfort when my fingers touched something; it was a tiny tail. Almost a transverse presentation, biggish piglet stuck like a cork in a bottle.

Using one finger, I worked the hind legs back until I was able to grasp them and draw the piglet out. 'This is the one that's been causing the trouble. He's dead, I'm afraid — been squashed in there too long. But there could be some live ones still inside. I'll have another feel.'

I greased my arm and got down again. Just inside the os uteri, almost at arm's length, I found another piglet and I was feeling at the face when a set of minute but very sharp teeth sank into my finger.

I yelped and looked up at the farmer from my stony bed. 'This one's alive, anyway. I'll soon have him out.'

But the piglet had other ideas. He showed no desire to leave his warm haven and every time I got hold of his slippery little foot between my fingers he jerked it away. After a minute or two of this game I felt a cramping in my arm. I relaxed and lay back, my head resting on the cobbles, my arm still inside the pig. I closed my eyes and immediately I was back in the ballroom, in the warmth and the brilliant light. I was holding out my immense glass while Francois poured from the magnum; then I was dancing, close to the orchestra this time and the leader, beating time with one hand, turned round and smiled into my face; smiled and bowed as though he had been looking for me all his life.

I smiled back but the bandleader's face dissolved and there was only Mr Atkinson looking down at me expressionlessly, his unshaven jaw and shaggy eyebrows thrown into sinister relief by the light striking up from the bicycle lamp.

I shook myself and raised my cheek from the floor. This wouldn't do. Falling asleep on the job; either I was very tired or there was still some champagne in me. I reached again and grasped the foot firmly between two fingers and this time, despite his struggles, the piglet was hauled out into the world. Once arrived, he seemed to accept the situation and tottered round philosophically to his mother's udder.

'She's not helping at all,' I said. 'Been on so long that she's exhausted. I'm going to give her an injection.'

Another numbing expedition through the mud to the car, a shot of pituitrin into the gilt's thigh and within minutes the action began with powerful contractions of the uterus. There was no obstruction now and soon a wriggling pink piglet was deposited in the straw; then quite quickly another and another.

'Coming off the assembly line now, all right,' I said. Mr Atkinson grunted.

Eight piglets had been born and the light from the lamp had almost given out when a dark mass of afterbirth welled from the gilt's vulva.

I rubbed my cold arms. 'Well, I should say that's the lot now.' I felt suddenly chilled; I couldn't say how long I had been standing there looking at the wonder that never grew stale; the little pigs struggling on to their legs and making their way unguided to the long double row of teats; the mother with her first family easing herself over to expose as much as possible of her udder to the hungry mouths.

Better get dressed quickly. I had another try at the marble-like soap but it defeated me as easily as the first time. I wondered how long it had been in the family. Down my right side my cheek and ribs were caked with dirt and mucus. I did my best to scrape some off with my finger nails then I swilled myself down with the cold water from the bucket.

'Have you a towel there?' I gasped.

Mr Atkinson wordlessly handed me a sack. Its edges were stiff with old manure and it smelled musty from the meal it had long since contained. I took it and began to rub my chest and as the sour grains of the meal powdered my skin, the last bubbles of champagne left me, drifted up through the gaps in the tiles and burst sadly in the darkness beyond.

I dragged my shirt over my gritty back, feeling a sense of coming back to my own world. I buttoned my coat, picked up the syringe and the bottle of pituitrin and climbed out of the pen. I had a last look before I left. The bicycle lamp was shedding its final faint glow and I had to lean over the gate to see the row of little pigs sucking busily, utterly absorbed. The gilt carefully shifted her position and grunted. It was a grunt of deep content.

Yes, I was back and it was all right. I drove through the mud and up the hill where I had to get out to open a gate and the wind, with the cold, clean smell of the frosty grass in it, caught at my face. I stood for a while looking across the dark fields, thinking of the night which was ending now. My mind went back to my school-days and an old gentleman talking to the class about careers. He had said: 'If you decide to become a veterinary surgeon you will never grow rich but you will have a life of endless interest and variety.'

I laughed aloud in the darkness and as I got into the car I was still chuckling. That old chap certainly wasn't kidding. Variety. That was it — variety.

CHAPTER 20

As I checked my list of calls it occurred to me that, this time, Siegfried didn't look so much like a schoolboy as he faced Miss Harbottle. For one thing, he hadn't marched straight in and stood in front of the desk; that was disastrous and he always looked beaten before he started. Instead, he had veered off over the last few yards till he stood with his back to the window. This way she had to turn her head slightly to face him and besides, he had the light at his back.

He thrust his hands into his pockets and leaned back against the window frame. He was wearing his patient look, his eyes were kind and his face was illumined by an almost saintly smile. Miss Harbottle's eyes narrowed.

'I just wanted a word with you, Miss Harbottle. One or two little points I'd like to discuss. First, about your petty cash box. It's a nice box and I think you were quite right to institute it, but I think you would be the first to agree that the main function of a cash box

203

is to have cash in it.' He gave a light laugh. 'Now last night I had a few dogs in the surgery and the owners wanted to pay on the spot. I had no change and went for some to your box — it was quite empty. I had to say I would send them a bill, and that isn't good business, is it, Miss Harbottle? It didn't look good, so I really must ask you to keep some cash in your cash box.'

Miss Harbottle's eyes widened incredulously. 'But Mr Farnon, you removed the entire contents to go to the hunt ball at . . .'

Siegfried held up a hand and his smile took on an unearthly quality. 'Please hear me out. There is another very small thing I want to bring to your attention. It is now the tenth day of the month and the accounts have not gone out. Now this is a very undesirable state of affairs and there are several points to consider here.'

'But Mr Farnon . . . !'

'Just one moment, Miss Harbottle, till I explain this to you. It is a known fact that farmers pay their bills more readily if they receive them on the first of the month. And there is another, even more important factor.' The beautiful smile left his face and was replaced by an expression of sorrowing gravity. 'Have you ever stopped to work out just how much interest the practice is losing on all the money lying out there because you are late in sending out the accounts?'

'Mr Farnon . . . !'

'I am almost finished, Miss Harbottle, and, believe me, it grieves me to have to speak like this. But the fact is, I can't afford to lose money in this way.' He spread out his hands in a gesture of charming frankness. 'So if you will just apply yourself to this little matter I'm sure all will be well.'

'But will you tell me how I can possibly send the accounts when you refuse to write up the . . .'

'In conclusion, Miss Harbottle, let me say this. I have been very satisfied with your progress since you joined us, and I am sure that with time you will tighten up on those little points I have just mentioned.' A certain roguishness crept into his smile and he put his head on one side. Miss Harbottle's strong fingers closed tightly round a heavy ebony ruler.

'Efficiency,' he said, crinkling his eyes. 'That's what we must have — efficiency.'

CHAPTER 21

I dropped the suture needle into the tray and stepped back to survey the finished job. 'Well though I say it myself, that looks rather nice.'

Tristan leaned over the unconscious dog and examined the neat incision with its row of regular stitches. 'Very pretty indeed, my boy. Couldn't have done better myself.'

The big black labrador lay peacefully on the table, his tongue lolling, his eyes glazed and unseeing. He had been brought in with an ugly growth over his ribs and I had decided that it was a simple lipoma, quite benign and very suitable for surgery. And so it had turned out. The tumour had come away with almost ridiculous ease, round, intact and shining, like a hard-boiled egg from its shell. No haemorrhage, no fear of recurrence.

The unsightly swelling had been replaced by this tidy scar which would be invisible in a few weeks. I was pleased.

'We'd better keep him here till he comes

round,' I said. 'Give me a hand to get him on to these blankets.' We made the dog comfortable in front of an electric stove and I left to start my morning round.

It was during lunch that we first heard the strange sound. It was something between a moan and a howl, starting quite softly but rising to a piercing pitch before shuddering back down the scale to silence.

Siegfried looked up, startled, from his soup. 'What in God's name is that?'

'Must be that dog I operated on this morning,' I replied. 'The odd one does that coming out of barbiturates. I expect he'll stop soon.'

Siegfried looked at me doubtfully. 'Well, I hope so — I could soon get tired of that. Gives me the creeps.'

We went through and looked at the dog. Pulse strong, respirations deep and regular, mucous membranes a good colour. He was still stretched out, immobile, and the only sign of returning consciousness was the howl which seemed to have settled down into a groove of one every ten seconds.

'Yes, he's perfectly all right,' Siegfried said. 'But what a bloody noise! Let's get out of here.'

Lunch was finished hastily and in silence except for the ceaseless background wailing. Siegfried had scarcely swallowed his last mouthful before he was on his feet. 'Well, I must fly. Got a lot on this afternoon. Tristan, I think it would be a good idea to bring that dog through to the sitting-room and put him by the fire. Then you could stay by him and keep an eye on him.'

Tristan was stunned. 'You mean I have to stay in the same room as that noise all afternoon?'

'Yes, I mean just that. We can't send him home as he is and I don't want anything to happen to him. He needs care and attention.'

'Maybe you'd like me to hold his paw or perhaps wheel him round the market place?'

'Don't give me any of your bloody cheek. You stay with the dog and that's an order!'

Tristan and I stretchered the heavy animal along the passage on the blankets, then I had to leave for the afternoon round. I paused and looked back at the big black form by the fire and Tristan crouched miserably in his chair. The noise was overpowering. I closed the door hurriedly.

It was dark when I got back and the old house hung over me, black and silent against the frosty sky. Silent, that is, except for the howling which still echoed along the passage and filtered eerily into the deserted street.

I glanced at my watch as I slammed the car door. It was six o'clock, so Tristan had had four hours of it. I ran up the steps and along the passage and when I opened the sitting-room door the noise jarred in my head.

Tristan was standing with his back to me, looking through the french window into the darkness of the garden. His hands were deep in his pockets; tufts of cotton wool drooped from his ears.

'Well, how is it going?' I asked.

There was no reply so I walked over and tapped him on the shoulder. The effect was spectacular. Tristan leaped into the air and corkscrewed round. His face was ashen and he was trembling violently.

'God help us, Jim, you nearly killed me there. I can't hear a damn thing through these ear plugs — except the dog, of course. Nothing keeps that out.'

I knelt by the labrador and examined him. The dog's condition was excellent but, except for a faint eye reflex, there was no sign that he was regaining consciousness. And all the time there were the piercing, evenly spaced howls.

'He's taking a hell of a time to come out of it,' I said. 'Has he been like this all afternoon?'

'Yes, just like that. Not one bit different. And don't waste any sympathy on him, the yowling devil. He's as happy as a sandboy down by the fire — doesn't know a thing about it. But how about me? My nerves are about shot to bits listening to him hour after hour. Much more of it and you'll have to give me a shot too.' He ran a shaking hand through his hair and a twitching started in his cheek.

I took his arm. 'Well, come through and eat. You'll feel better after some food.' I led him unresisting into the dining-room.

Siegfried was in excellent form over the meal. He seemed to be in a mood of exhilaration and monopolised the conversation but he did not once refer to the shrill obbligato from the other room. There was no doubt, however, that it was still getting through to Tristan.

As they were leaving the room, Siegfried put his hand on my shoulder. 'Remember we've got that meeting in Brawton tonight, James. Old Reeves on diseases of sheep — he's usually very good. Pity you can't come too, Tristan, but I'm afraid you'll have to stay with the dog till he comes round.'

Tristan flinched as if he had been struck. 'Oh not another session with that bloody animal! He's driving me mad!'

'I'm afraid there's nothing else for it. James or I could have taken over tonight but we have to show up at this meeting. It would look bad if we missed it.'

Tristan stumbled back into the room and I put on my coat. As I went out into the street I paused for a moment and listened. The dog was still howling.

The meeting was a success. It was held in one of Brawton's lush hotels and, as usual, the best part was the get together of the vets in the bar afterwards. It was infinitely soothing to hear the other man's problems and mistakes — especially the mistakes.

It amused me to look round the crowded room and try to guess what the little knots of men were talking about. That man over there, bent double and slashing away at the air with one hand — he was castrating a colt in the standing position. And the one with his arm out at full stretch, his fingers working busily at nothing — almost certainly foaling a mare; probably correcting a carpal flexion. And doing it effortlessly too. Veterinary surgery was a childishly simple matter in a warm bar with a few drinks inside you.

It was eleven o'clock before we all got into our cars and headed for our own particular niche in Yorkshire — some to the big industrial towns of the West Riding, others to the seaside places of the east coast and Siegfried and I hurrying thankfully back on the narrow road which twisted between its stone walls into the Northern Pennines.

I thought guiltily that for the last few hours I had completely forgotten about Tristan and his vigil. Still, it must have been better tonight. The dog would surely have quietened down by now. But, jumping from the car in Darrowby, I froze in mid stride as a thin wail came out faintly from Skeldale House. This was incredible; it was after midnight and the dog was still at it. And what of Tristan? I hated to think what kind of shape he'd be in.

Almost fearfully I turned the knob on the sitting-room door.

Tristan's chair made a little island in a sea of empty beer bottles. An upturned crate lay against the wall and Tristan was sitting very upright and looking solemn. I picked my way over the debris.

'Well, has it been rough, Triss? How do you feel now?'

'Could be worse, old lad, could be worse. Soon as you'd gone I slipped over to the Drovers for a crate of pint Magnets. Made all the difference. After three or four the dog stopped worrying me — matter of fact, I've been yowling back at him for hours now. We've had quite an interesting evening. Anyway, he's coming out now. Look at him.'

The big dog had his head up and there was recognition in his eyes. The howling had stopped. I went over and patted him and the long black tail jerked in a fair attempt at a wag.

'That's better, old boy,' I said. 'But you'd better behave yourself now. You've given your Uncle Tristan one hell of a day.'

The labrador responded immediately by struggling to his feet. He took a few swaying steps and collapsed among the bottles.

Siegfried appeared in the doorway and looked distastefully at Tristan, still very upright and wearing a judicial expression, and at the dog scrabbling among the bottles.

'What an infernal mess! Surely you can do a little job without making an orgy out of it.'

At the sound of his voice the labrador staggered up and, in a flush of over-confidence, tried to run towards him, wagging his tail unsteadily. He didn't get very far and went down in a heap, sending a Magnet empty rolling gently up to Siegfried's feet.

Siegfried bent over and stroked the shining black head. 'Nice friendly animal that. I should think he's a grand dog when he's got his senses about him. He'll be normal in the morning, but the problem is what to do with him now. We can't leave him staggering about down here — he could break a leg.' He glanced at Tristan who had not moved a muscle. He was sitting up straighter than ever; stiff and motionless like a Prussian general. 'You know, I think the best thing would be for you to take him up to your room tonight. Now we've got him so far, we don't want him to hurt himself. Yes, that's it, he can spend the night with you.'

'Thank you, thank you very much indeed,' Tristan said in a flat voice, still looking straight to his front.

Siegfried looked at him narrowly for a moment, then turned away. 'Right then, clear away this rubbish and let's get to bed.'

My bedroom and Tristan's were connected by a door. Mine was the main room, huge, square, with a high ceiling, pillared fireplace and graceful alcoves like the ones downstairs. I always felt a little like a duke lying there.

Tristan's had been the old dressing-room and was long and narrow with his small bed crouching at one end as if trying to hide. There were no carpets on the smooth, varnished boards so I laid the dog on a heap of blankets and talked down soothingly at Tristan's wan face on the pillow.

'He's quiet now — sleeping like a baby and looks as though he's going to stay that way. You'll be able to have a well-earned rest now.'

I went back to my own room, undressed quickly and got into bed. I went to sleep immediately and I couldn't tell just when the noises started next door, but I came suddenly wide awake with an angry yell ringing in my ears. Then there was a slithering and a bump followed by another distracted cry from Tristan.

I quailed at the idea of going into the dressing-room — there was nothing I could do, anyway — so I huddled closer into the sheets and listened. I kept sliding into a half sleep then starting into wakefulness as more bumping and shouting came through the wall.

After about two hours the noises began to change. The labrador seemed to have gained mastery over his legs and was marching up and down the room, his claws making a regular tck-a-tck, tck-a-tck, tck-a-tck on the wooden floor. It went on and on, interminably. At intervals, Tristan's voice, hoarse now, burst out. 'Stop it, for Christ's sake! Sit down, you bloody dog!'

I must have fallen into a deeper sleep because when I awoke the room was grey with the cold light of morning. I rolled on to my back and listened. I could still hear the tck-a-tck of the claws but it had become irregular as though the labrador was strolling about instead of blundering blindly from one end of the room to the other. There was no sound from Tristan.

I got out of bed, shivering as the icy air of the room gripped me, and pulled on my shirt and trousers. Tiptoeing across the floor, I opened the connecting door and was almost floored as two large feet were planted on my chest. The labrador was delighted to see me and appeared to be thoroughly at home. His fine brown eyes shone with intelligence and well-being and he showed rows of glittering teeth and a flawlessly pink tongue in a wide, panting grin. Far below, the tail lashed ecstatically.

'Well, you're all right, chum,' I said. 'Let's have a look at that wound.' I removed the horny paws from my chest and explored the line of stitches over the ribs. No swelling, no pain, no reaction at all.

'Lovely!' I cried. 'Beautiful. You're as good as new again.' I gave the dog a playful slap on the rump which sent him into a transport of joy. He leaped all over me, clawing and licking.

I was fighting him off when I heard a dismal groan from the bed. In the dim light Tristan looked ghastly. He was lying on his back, both hands clutching the quilt and there was a wild look in his eyes. 'Not a wink of sleep, Jim,' he whispered. 'Not a bloody wink. He's got a wonderful sense of humour, my brother, making me spend the night with this animal. It'll really make his day when he hears what I've been through. Just watch him — I'll bet you anything you like he'll look pleased.'

Later, over breakfast, Siegfried heard the details of his brother's harrowing night and was very sympathetic. He condoled with him at length and apologised for all the trouble the dog had given him. But Tristan was right. He did look pleased.

CHAPTER 22

As I came into the operating room I saw that Siegfried had a patient on the table. He was thoughtfully stroking the head of an elderly and rather woebegone border terrier.

'James,' he said, 'I want you to take this little dog through to Grier.'

'Grier?'

'Vet at Brawton. He was treating the case before the owner moved into our district. I've seen it a couple of times — stones in the bladder. It needs an immediate operation and I think I'd better let Grier do it. He's a touchy devil and I don't want to stand on his toes.'

'Oh, I think I've heard of him,' I said.

'Probably you have. A cantankerous Aberdonian. Since he practises in a fashionable town he gets quite a few students and he gives them hell. That sort of thing gets around.' He lifted the terrier from the table and handed him to me. 'The sooner you get through there the better. You can see the op and bring the dog back here afterwards. But watch yourself — don't rub Grier the wrong way or he'll take it out of you somehow.'

At my first sight of Angus Grier I thought immediately of whisky. He was about fifty and something had to be responsible for the fleshy, mottled cheeks, the swimmy eyes and the pattern of purple veins which chased each other over his prominent nose. He wore a permanently insulted expression.

He didn't waste any charm on me; a nod and a grunt and he grabbed the dog from my arms. Then he stabbed a finger at a slight, fairish youth in a white coat. 'That's Clinton — final-year student. Do ye no' think there's some pansy-lookin' buggers coming in to this profession?'

During the operation he niggled constantly at the young man and, in an attempt to create a diversion, I asked when he was going back to college.

'Beginning of next week,' he replied.

'Aye, but he's awa hame tomorrow,' Grier rasped. 'Wasting his time when he could be gettin' good experience here.'

The student blushed. 'Well, I've been seeing practice for over a month and I felt I ought to spend a couple of days with my mother before the term starts.'

'Oh, I ken, I ken. You're all the same — canna stay away from the titty.'

The operation was uneventful and as Grier inserted the last stitch he looked up at me. 'You'll no' want to take the dog back till he's out of the anaesthetic. I've got a case to visit — you can come with me to pass the time.'

We didn't have what you could call a conversation in the car. It was a monologue; a long recital of wrongs suffered at the hands of wicked clients and predatory colleagues. The story I liked best was about a retired admiral who had asked Grier to examine his horse for soundness. Grier said the animal had a bad heart and was not fit to ride, whereupon the admiral flew into a fury and got another vet to examine the horse. The second vet said there was nothing the matter with the heart and passed the animal sound.

The admiral wrote Grier a letter and told him what he thought of him in fairly ripe quarter-deck language. Having got this out of his system he felt refreshed and went out for a ride during which, in the middle of a full gallop, the horse fell down dead and rolled on the admiral who sustained a compound fracture of the leg and a crushed pelvis.

'Man,' said Grier with deep sincerity, 'man, I was awfu' glad.'

We drew up in a particularly dirty farmyard and Grier turned to me. 'I've got a cow tae cleanse here.'

'Right,' I said, 'fine.' I settled down in my seat and took out my pipe. Grier paused, half way out of the car. 'Are you no' coming to give me a hand?'

I couldn't understand him. 'Cleansing' of cows is simply the removal of retained afterbirth and is a one-man job.

'Well, there isn't much I can do, is there?' I said. 'And my Wellingtons and coat are back in my car. I didn't realise it was a farm visit — I'd probably get messed up for nothing.'

I knew immediately that I'd said the wrong thing. The toad-skin jowls flushed darker and he gave me a malevolent glance before turning away; but half way across the yard he stopped and stood for a few moments in thought before coming back to the car. 'I've just remembered. I've got something here you can put on. You might as well come in with me — you'll be able to pass me a pessary when I want one.'

It sounded nutty to me, but I got out of the car and went round to the back. Grier was fishing out a large wooden box from his boot.

'Here, ye can put this on. It's a calving outfit I got a bit ago. I haven't used it much because I found it a mite heavy, but it'll keep ye grand and clean.'

I looked in the box and saw a suit of thick, black, shining rubber. I lifted out the jacket; it bristled with zip fasteners and press studs and felt as heavy as lead. The trousers were even more weighty, with many clips and fasteners. The whole thing was a most imposing creation, obviously designed by somebody who had never seen a cow calved and having the disadvantage that anybody wearing it would be pretty well immobilised.

I studied Grier's face for a moment but the watery eyes told me nothing. I began to take off my jacket — it was crazy but I didn't want to offend the man.

And, in truth, Grier seemed anxious to get me into the suit because he was holding it up in a helpful manner. It was a two-man operation. First the gleaming trousers were pulled on and zipped up fore and aft, then it was the turn of the jacket, a wonderful piece of work, fitting tightly round the waist and possessing short sleeves about six inches long with powerful elastic gripping my biceps.

Before I could get it on I had to roll my shirt sleeves to the shoulder, then Grier, heaving and straining, worked me into it. I could hear the zips squeaking into place, the final one being at the back of my neck to close a high, stiff collar which held my head in an attitude of supplication, my chin pointing at the sky.

Grier's heart really seemed to be in his work and, for the final touch, he produced a black rubber skull cap. I shrank away from the thing and began to mouth such objections as the collar would allow, but Grier insisted. 'Stand still a wee minute longer. We might as well do the job right.'

221

When he had finished he stood back admiringly. I must have been a grotesque sight, sheathed from head to foot in gleaming black, my arms, bare to the shoulders, sticking out almost at right angles. Grier appeared well satisfied. 'Well, come on, it's time we got on wi' the job.' He turned and hurried towards the byre; I plodded ponderously after him like an automaton.

Our arrival in the byre caused a sensation. There were present the farmer, two cowmen and a little girl. The men's cheerful greeting froze on their lips as the menacing figure paced slowly, deliberately in. The little girl burst into tears and ran outside.

'Cleansing' is a dirty, smelly job for the operator and a bore for the onlooker who may have to stand around for twenty minutes without being able to see anything. But this was one time the spectators were not bored. Grier was working away inside the cow and mumbling about the weather, but the men weren't listening; they never took their eyes away from me as I stood rigid, like a suit of armour against the wall. They studied each part of the outfit in turn, wonderingly. I knew what they were thinking. Just what was going to happen when this formidable unknown finally went into action? Anybody dressed like that must have some tremendous task ahead of him.

The intense pressure of the collar against

my larynx kept me entirely out of any conversation and this must have added to my air of mystery. I began to sweat inside the suit.

The little girl had plucked up courage and brought her brothers and sisters to look at me. I could see the row of little heads peeping round the door and, screwing my head round painfully, I tried to give them a reassuring smile; but the heads disappeared and I heard their feet clattering across the yard.

I couldn't say how long I stood there, but Grier at last finished his job and called out, 'All right, I'm ready for you now.' The atmosphere became suddenly electric. The men straightened up and stared at me with slightly open mouths. This was the moment they had been waiting for.

I pushed myself away from the wall and did a right turn with some difficulty before heading for the tin of pessaries. It was only a few yards away but it seemed a long way as I approached it like a robot, head in the air, arms extended stiffly on either side. When I arrived at the tin I met a fresh difficulty; I could not bend. After a few contortions I got my hand into the tin, then had to take the paper off the pessary with one hand; a new purgatory. The men watched in fascinated silence.

Having removed the paper, I did a careful about turn and paced back along the byre with measured tread. When I came level with the cow I extended my arm stiffly to Grier who took the pessary and inserted it in the uterus.

I then took up my old position against the wall while my colleague cleaned himself down. I glanced down my nose at the men; their expressions had changed to open disbelief. Surely the mystery man's assignment was tougher than that — he couldn't be wearing that outfit just to hand over a pessary. But when Grier started the complicated business of snapping open the studs and sliding the zips they realised the show was over; and fast on the feeling of let-down came amusement.

As I tried to rub some life back into my swollen arms which had been strangulated by the elastic sleeves, I was surrounded by grinning faces. They could hardly wait, I imagined, to get round to the local that night to tell the tale. Pulling together the shreds of my dignity, I put on my jacket and got into the car. Grier stayed to say a few words to the men, but he wasn't holding their attention; it was all on me, huddling in the seat. They couldn't believe I was true.

Back at the surgery the border terrier was coming out of the anaesthetic. He raised his head and tried bravely to wag his tail when he saw me. I wrapped him in a blanket, gathered him up and was preparing to leave when I saw Grier through the partly open door of a small store room. He had the wooden box on a table and he was lifting out the rubber suit, but there was something peculiar about the way he was doing it; the man seemed to be afflicted by a kind of rigor — his body shook and jerked, the mottled face was strangely contorted and a half stifled wailing issued from his lips.

I stared in amazement. I would have said it was impossible, yet it was happening right in front of me. There was not a shadow of a doubt about it — Angus Grier was laughing.

CHAPTER 23

Milk fever is one of the straightforward conditions, but, looking down into the beck in the dreary dawn light, I realised that this was one of its more bizarre manifestations. The illness had struck immediately after calving and the cow had slithered down the muddy bank into the water. She was unconscious when I arrived, her hindquarters completely submerged, the head resting on a shelf of rock. Her calf, sodden and pathetic in the driving rain, trembled by her side.

Dan Cooper's eyes were anxious as we made our way down. 'I doubt we're too late. She's dead, isn't she? I can't see her breathing.'

'Pretty far gone, I'm afraid,' I replied, 'but I think there's still life there. If I can get some calcium into her vein she might still come round.'

'Damn, I 'ope so,' Dan grunted. 'She's one of my best milkers. It allus happens to the good 'uns.'

'It does with milk fever, anyway. Here, hold these bottles for me.' I pulled out the syringe box and selected a wide-bored needle. My fingers, numb with the special kind of cold you felt in the early morning with your circulation sluggish and your stomach empty, could hardly hold it. The water was deeper than I thought and it was over my Wellington tops at the first stride. Gasping, I bent down and dug my thumb into the jugular furrow at the base of the neck. The vein came up and as I pushed the needle in, the blood ran warm and dark over my hand. I fumbled the flutter valve from my pocket, pushed a bottle into the cup end and inserted the other end into the needle. The calcium began to flow into the vein.

Standing there in the icy beck, holding the bottle aloft with bloody fingers and feeling the rain working its way inside my collar, I tried to keep out the black thoughts; about all those people I knew who were still in bed and would only leave it when their alarm clocks rang; and they would read their papers over breakfast and drive out to their cosy banks or insurance offices. Maybe I should have been a doctor — they treated their patients in nice, warm bedrooms.

I pulled the needle from the vein and threw the empty bottle on to the bank. There was no response to the injection. I took the other bottle and began to run more calcium under

227

the skin. Might as well go through the motions, futile though it seemed now. It was when I was rubbing away the subcutaneous injection that I noticed the eyelids quiver.

A quick ripple of relief and excitement went through me. I looked up at the farmer and laughed. 'She's still with us, Dan.' I flicked her ear and her eyes opened wide. 'We'll wait a few minutes and then try to roll her on to her chest.'

Within a quarter of an hour she was beginning to toss her head about and I knew it was time. I caught hold of her horns and pulled while Dan and his tall son pushed at her shoulder. We made slow progress but after several concerted heaves the cow took over herself and settled on her chest. Immediately everything looked rosier; when a cow is lying on her side she always has the look of death on her.

I was pretty sure then that she would recover, but I couldn't go away and leave her lying in the beck. Milk fever cows can stay down for days on end but I had the feeling this one would be up soon. I decided to stick it out a bit longer.

She didn't seem to relish her situation in the peaty water and began to make determined efforts to rise, but it was another half hour and my teeth were chattering uncontrollably before she finally staggered to her feet.

'Well, that's a licker!' Dan said. 'Ah never

thought she'd stand again. Must be good stuff you gave her.'

'It's a bit quicker than the old bicycle pump,' I laughed. The spectacular effects of intravenous calcium were still enough of a novelty to intrigue me. For generations, cows with milk fever had just died. Then inflation of the udder had saved many; but the calcium was the thing — when they got up within an hour like this one, I always felt like a successful conjurer.

We guided the cow up the bank and at the top, the full force of the wind and rain struck us. The house was only a hundred yards away and we battled towards it, Dan and his son leading, holding the calf in a sack slung between them. The tiny animal swung to and fro, screwing up its eyes against the hard world it had entered. Close behind followed the anxious mother, still rocky on her legs but doing her best to poke her muzzle into the sack. I squelched along in the rear.

We left the cow knee deep in straw in a warm shed, licking her calf vigorously. In the porch of the house, the others dutifully pulled off their Wellingtons; I did the same, pouring about a pint of beck water from each boot. Mrs Cooper had the reputation of being a firebrand who exercised an iron rule over Dan and her family, but from my previous contacts with her I had the feeling that Dan didn't do so badly.

I thought so again as I saw her, square built but comely, plaiting a little girl's pigtails in readiness for school. A crackling fire was mirrored in the gleaming brass of the hearth and above the clean farmhouse smell there was a hint of home-cured bacon just beginning to fry.

Mrs Cooper sent Dan and the boy scurrying upstairs to change their socks then she turned a calm gaze on me as I dripped on her linoleum. She shook her head as though I were a naughty child.

'All right, off with the socks,' she rapped out. 'And your coat, and roll up your trousers, and sit down here, and dry your hair with this.' A clean towel landed on my lap and Mrs Cooper bent over me. 'Don't you ever think of wearing a hat?'

'Not keen on them, I'm afraid,' I mumbled, and she shook her head again.

She poured hot water from a kettle into a large bowl and added mustard from a pound tin. 'Here, stick your feet in this.'

I had obeyed all her commands with alacrity and I gave an involuntary yelp as I made contact with the bubbling mixture. At this, she shot a fierce glance at me and I took care to keep my feet in the bowl. I was sitting, teeth clenched, enveloped in steam, when she pushed a pint pot of tea into my hand.

It was old-fashioned treatment but effective. By the time I was half way down the pint pot I felt as though I were being consumed by fire. The river bed chill was a dream which vanished completely as Mrs Cooper topped up my bowl with another scalding quart from the kettle.

Next, she grabbed chair and bowl and swivelled me round till I was sitting at the table, still with my feet in the water. Dan and the children were already at their breakfast and in front of me was a plate with two eggs, a rough-cut piece of bacon and several sausages. I had learned enough of Dales ways to keep quiet at meals; when I first came to the district I had thought it incumbent on me to provide light conversation in return for their hospitality but the questioning glances they exchanged with each other silenced me effectively.

So this morning, I attacked the food without preamble, but the first mouthful almost made me break my new-found rule. It was the first time I had tasted a home-made Yorkshire sausage and it was an effort to restrain the cries of congratulation which would have been natural in other circles. But Mrs Cooper had been watching me out of the corner of her eye and she must have noticed my rapt expression. Casually, she rose, brought over the frying pan and rolled a few more links on to my plate.

'Killed a pig last week,' she said, pulling open the pantry door. I could see the dishes heaped with chopped meat, spare rib, liver, the rows of pies with the jelly gleaming on their pale gold crusts.

I finished my meal, pulled on a thick pair of socks borrowed from Dan and my dry shoes. I was about to leave when Mrs Cooper tucked a parcel under my arm. I knew it contained further samples from the pantry but her eyes dared me to say much about it. I muttered a few words of thanks and went out to the car.

The church clock was chiming a quarter past nine when I pulled up outside Skeldale House. I felt good — warm, full of superb food and with the satisfying memory of the cow's quick recovery. And there was my parcel on the back seat; it was always a stroke of luck to land on a farm after a pig killing and there was usually a gift from the hospitable farmers, but these sausages were something I would never forget.

I took the surgery steps at a jump and trotted along the passage, but as I rounded the corner my progress was halted. Siegfried was standing there, rigid, his back pressed against the wall. Over his shoulder dangled a long, flexible, leather probang. Between us was the half open door of the office with Miss Harbottle clearly visible at her desk.

I waved cheerfully. 'Hello, hello, off to a choke?'

Siegfried's face twisted in anguish and he

held up a warning hand. Then he began to creep past the door, balancing on the balls of his feet like a tightrope walker. He was beyond the door and the tense lines of his body had begun to relax when the brass end of the swinging probang clattered against the wall and, as if in reply, came the familiar rumble from Miss Harbottle's corner. Siegfried gave me a single despairing glance then, shoulders drooping, he went slowly into the room.

Watching him go, I thought wonderingly of how things had built up since the secretary's arrival. It was naked war now and it gave life an added interest to observe the tactics of the two sides.

At the beginning it seemed that Siegfried must run out an easy winner. He was the employer; he held the reins and it appeared that Miss Harbottle would be helpless in the face of his obstructive strategy. But Miss Harbottle was a fighter and a resourceful one and it was impossible not to admire the way she made use of the weapons at her command.

In fact, over the past week the tide had been running in her favour. She had been playing Siegfried like an expert fisherman with a salmon; bringing him repeatedly back to her desk to answer footling questions. Her throat clearing had developed into an angry bark which could penetrate the full extent of the house. And she had a new weapon; she had taken to writing Siegfried's clerical idiocies on slips of paper; misspellings, errors in addition, wrong entries — they were all faithfully copied down.

Miss Harbottle used these slips as ammunition. She never brought one out when things were slack and her employer was hanging about the surgery. She saved them until he was under pressure, then she would push a slip under his nose and say 'How about this?'

She always kept an expressionless face at these times and it was impossible to say how much pleasure it gave her to see him cower back like a whipped animal. But the end was unvarying — mumbled explanations and apologies from Siegfried and Miss Harbottle, radiating self-righteousness, correcting the entry.

As Siegfried went into the room I watched through the partly open door. I knew my morning round was waiting but I was impelled by morbid curiosity. Miss Harbottle, looking brisk and businesslike, was tapping an entry in the book with her pen while Siegfried shuffled his feet and muttered replies. He made several vain attempts to escape and, as the time passed, I could see he was nearing breaking point. His teeth were clenched and his eyes had started to bulge.

The phone rang and the secretary answered it. Her employer was making again for the door when she called happily, 'Colonel Brent for you.' Like a man in a dream he turned back. The Colonel, a racehorse owner, had been a thorn in our flesh for a long time with his complaints and his continual questioning and probing; a call from him was always liable to send up the blood pressure.

I could see it was that way this morning. The minutes ticked away and Siegfried's face got redder. He made his replies in a choked voice which finally rose almost to a shout. At the end he crashed the receiver down and leaned on the desk, breathing heavily.

Then, as I watched, unbelieving, Miss Harbottle began to open the drawer where she kept her slips. She fished one out, coughed and held it in Siegfried's face.

'How about this?' she asked.

I resisted the impulse to close my eyes and stared in horror. For a few seconds nothing happened and there was a tense interval while Siegfried stood quite motionless. Then his face seemed to break up and with a scything sweep of his arm he snatched the slip from the secretary's hand and began to tear at it with fierce intensity. He didn't say a word but as he tore, he leaned forward over the desk and his glaring eyes approached ever nearer to Miss Harbottle who slowly edged her chair back till it was jammed against the wall.

It was a weird picture. Miss Harbottle straining back, her mouth slightly open, her tinted curls bobbing in alarm, and Siegfried, his ravaged features close to hers, still tearing with insane vigour at the piece of paper. The scene ended when Siegfried, putting every ounce of his strength into an action like a javelin thrower, hurled the torn-up slip at the wastepaper basket. It fell in a gentle shower, like confetti, in and around the basket and Siegfried, still without speaking, wrapped his probang around him and strode from the room.

In the kitchen, Mrs Hall opened the parcel and extracted a pie, a chunk of liver and a cluster of the exquisite sausages. She turned a quizzical eye on me. 'You look kind of pleased with yourself this morning, Mr Herriot.'

I leaned back against the oak dresser. 'Yes, Mrs Hall, I've just been thinking. It must be very nice to be the principal of a practice but, you know, it's not such a bad life being an assistant.'

CHAPTER 24

The day had started badly. Tristan had been trapped by his brother at 4 a.m. returning from the Bellringers' Outing.

This function took place annually when a bus load of the bellringers of all the local churches made a trip to Morecambe. They spent very little time on the beach, however, and when they weren't working their way from one pub to another, they were attacking the crates of beer they had brought with them.

When they rolled into Darrowby in the small hours most of the occupants of the bus were unconscious. Tristan, an honoured guest of the party, had been tipped out in the back lane behind Skeldale House. He waved weakly as the bus moved away, but drew no response from the unseeing faces at the windows. Lurching down the garden path, he was horrified to see a light in Siegfried's room. Escape was impossible and, when asked to explain where he had been, he made a series of attempts to articulate 'Bellringers' Outing' without success.

Siegfried, seeing he was wasting his time, had saved his wrath till breakfast time. That was when Tristan told me the story — just before his brother came into the dining-room and started on him.

But, as usual, it seemed to take more out of Siegfried who went off on his rounds glowering and hoarse from shouting. Ten minutes after he had gone I found Tristan closeted cheerfully in Boardman's cubby hole, Boardman listening to some fresh material from the backs of the envelopes and sniggering appreciatively.

The old man had cheered up greatly since Tristan came home and the two of them spent a lot of time in the gloom where the light from the tiny window picked out the rows of rusting tools, the Bairnsfather cartoons looking down from the wall. The place was usually kept locked and visitors were not encouraged; but Tristan was always welcome.

Often, when I was passing by, I would peep in and see Tristan patiently pulling at a Woodbine while Boardman rambled on. 'We was six weeks up the line. The French was on our right and the Jocks on our left . . .' or 'Poor old Fred — one minute 'e was standing by me and next 'e was gone. Never found as much as a trouser button . . .'

This morning, Tristan hailed me boisterously and I marvelled again at his resilience and his power to bend like a willow before the winds of misfortune and spring back unscathed. He held up two tickets.

'Village dance tonight, Jim, and I can guarantee it. Some of my harem from the hospital are going, so I'll see you're all right. And that's not all — look here.' He went into the saddle room, lifted out a loose board and produced a bottle of sherry. 'We'll be able to have a toothful between dances.'

I didn't ask where the tickets or the sherry had come from. I liked the village dances. The packed hall with the three-piece band at one end — piano, scraping fiddle and drums — and at the other end, the older ladies looking after the refreshments. Glasses of milk, mounds of sandwiches, ham, home-made brawn, trifles heaped high with cream.

That evening, Tristan came out with me on my last visit and, in the car, the talk was all about the dance. The case was simple enough — a cow with an infected eye — but the farm was in a village high up the Dale, and when we finished, it was dusk. I felt good, and everything seemed to stand out, clear and meaningful. The single, empty, grey stone street, the last red streaks in the sky, the dark purple of the enclosing fells. There was no wind, but a soft breath came from the quiet moors, sweet and fresh and full of promise. Among the houses, the thrilling smell of

239

wood smoke was everywhere.

When we got back to the surgery, Siegfried was out but there was a note for Tristan propped up on the mantelpiece. It said simply: 'Tristan. Go home. Siegfried.'

This had happened before, everything in Skeldale House being in short supply, especially beds and blankets. When unexpected visitors arrived, Tristan was packed off to stay with his mother in Brawton. Normally he would board a train without comment, but tonight was different.

'Good God,' he said. 'Somebody must be coming for the night and, of course, I'm the one who's just expected to disappear. It's a nice bloody carry on, I must say! And isn't that a charming letter! It doesn't matter if I've made any private arrangements. Oh no! There's no question of asking me if it's convenient to leave. It's just "Tristan, go home." Polite and thoughtful, isn't it?'

It was unusual for him to get worked up like this. I spoke soothingly. 'Look, Triss. Maybe we'd better just skip this dance. There'll be others.'

Tristan clenched his fists. 'Why should I let him push me around like this?' he fumed. 'I'm a person, am I not? I have my own life to lead and I tell you I am not going to Brawton tonight. I've arranged to go to a dance and I am damn well going to a dance.'

This was fighting talk but I felt a twinge of

240

alarm. 'Wait a minute. What about Siegfried? What's he going to say when he comes in and finds you still here?'

'To hell with Siegfried!' said Tristan. So I left it at that.

Siegfried came home when we were upstairs, changing. I was first down and found him sitting by the fire, reading. I said nothing but sat down and waited for the explosion.

After a few minutes, Tristan came in. He had chosen with care among his limited wardrobe and was resplendent in a dark grey suit; a scrubbed face shone under carefully combed hair; he was wearing a clean collar.

Siegfried flushed as he looked up from his book. 'What the bloody hell are you doing here? I told you to go to Brawton. Joe Ramage is coming tonight.'

'Couldn't go.'

'Why not?'

'No trains.'

'What the hell do you mean, no trains?'

'Just that — no trains.'

The cross-talk was bringing on the usual sense of strain in me. The interview exasperated, his brother expressionless, answering in a flat monotone, was falling into the habitual pattern; Siegfried red faced, fighting a defensive battle with the skill of long practice.

Siegfried sank back in his chair, baffled for the moment, but he kept a slit-eyed gaze on his brother. The smart suit, the slicked hair and polished shoes all seemed to irritate him further.

'All right,' he said suddenly. 'It's maybe just as well you are staying. I want you to do a job for me. You can open that haematoma on Charlie Dent's pig's ear.'

This was a bombshell. Charlie Dent's pig's ear was something we didn't talk about.

A few weeks earlier, Siegfried himself had gone to the smallholding half way along a street on the outskirts of the town to see a pig with a swollen ear. It was an aural haematoma and the only treatment was to lance it, but, for some reason, Siegfried had not done the job but had sent me the following day.

I had wondered about it, but not for long. When I climbed into the sty, the biggest sow I had ever seen rose from the straw, gave an explosive bark and rushed at me with its huge mouth gaping. I didn't stop to argue. I made the wall about six inches ahead of the pig and vaulted over into the passage. I stood there, considering the position, looking thoughtfully at the mean little red eyes, the slavering mouth with its long, yellow teeth.

Usually, I paid no attention when pigs barked and grumbled at me but this one really seemed to mean it. As I wondered what the next step would be, the pig gave an angry roar, reared up on its hind legs and tried to get over the wall at me. I made up my mind quickly.

'I'm afraid I haven't got the right instrument with me, Mr Dent. I'll pop back another day and open the ear for you. It's nothing serious — only a small job. Goodbye.'

There the matter had rested, with nobody caring to mention it till now.

Tristan was aghast. 'You mean you want me to go along there tonight? Saturday night? Surely some other time would do? I'm going to a dance.'

Siegfried smiled bitterly from the depths of his chair. 'It has to be done now. That's an order. You can go to your dance afterwards.'

Tristan started to say something, but he knew he had pushed his luck far enough. 'Right,' he said, 'I'll go and do it.'

He left the room with dignity, Siegfried resumed his book, and I stared into the fire, wondering how Tristan was going to handle this one. He was a lad of infinite resource, but he was going to be tested this time.

Within ten minutes he was back. Siegfried looked at him suspiciously, 'Have you opened that ear?'

'No.'

'Why not?'

'Couldn't find the place. You must have given me the wrong address. Number 98, you said.'

'It's number 89 and you know damn well it

243

is. Now get back there and do your job.'

The door closed behind Tristan and again, I waited. Fifteen minutes later it opened again and Tristan reappeared looking faintly triumphant. His brother looked up from his book.

'Done it?'

'No.'

'Why not?'

'The family are all out at the pictures. Saturday night, you know.'

'I don't care a damn where the family are. Just get into that sty and lance that ear. Now get out, and this time I want the job done.'

Again Tristan retreated and a new vigil began. Siegfried did not say a word, but I could feel the tension building up. Twenty minutes passed and Tristan was with us again.

'Have you opened that ear?'

'No.'

'Why not?'

'It's pitch dark in there. How do you expect me to work? I've only got two hands — one for the knife and one for the torch. How can I hold the ear?'

Siegfried had been keeping a tight hold on himself, but now his control snapped. 'Don't give me any more of your bloody excuses,' he shouted, leaping from his chair. 'I don't care how you do it, but, by God, you are going to open that pig's ear tonight or I've finished with you. Now get to hell out of here and don't come back till it's done!'

My heart bled for Tristan. He had been dealt a poor hand and had played his cards with rare skill, but he had nothing left now. He stood silent in the doorway for a few moments, then he turned and walked out.

The next hour was a long one. Siegfried seemed to be enjoying his book and I even tried to read myself; but I got no meaning out of the words and it made my head ache to sit staring at them. It would have helped if I could have paced up and down the carpet but that was pretty well impossible in Siegfried's presence. I had just decided to excuse myself and go out for a walk when I heard the outer door open, then Tristan's footsteps in the passage.

A moment later, the man of destiny entered but the penetrating smell of pig got into the room just ahead of him, and as he walked over to the fire, pungent waves seemed to billow round him. Pig muck was spattered freely over his nice suit, and on his clean collar, his face and hair. There was a great smear of the stuff on the seat of his trousers but despite his ravaged appearance he still maintained his poise.

Siegfried pushed his chair back hurriedly but did not change expression.

'Have you got that ear opened?' he asked quietly.

'Yes.'

Siegfried returned to his book without comment. It seemed that the matter was closed and Tristan, after staring briefly at his brother's bent head, turned and marched from the room. But even after he had gone, the odour of the pigsty hung in the room like a cloud.

Later, in the Drovers, I watched Tristan draining his third pint. He had changed, and if he didn't look as impressive as when he started the evening, at least he was clean and hardly smelt at all. I had said nothing yet, but the old light was returning to his eye. I went over to the bar and ordered my second half and Tristan's fourth pint and, as I set the glasses on the table, I thought that perhaps it was time.

'Well, what happened?'

Tristan took a long, contented pull at his glass and lit a Woodbine. 'Well now, all in all, Jim, it was rather a smooth operation, but I'll start at the beginning. You can imagine me standing all alone outside the sty in the pitch darkness with that bloody great pig grunting and growling on the other side of the wall. I didn't feel so good, I can tell you.

'I shone my torch on the thing's face and it jumped up and ran at me, making a noise like a lion and showing all those dirty yellow teeth. I nearly wrapped it up and came home there and then, but I got to thinking about the dance and all and, on the spur of the moment, I hopped over the wall.

'Two seconds later, I was on my back. It must have charged me but couldn't see enough to get a bite in. I just heard a bark, then a terrific weight against my legs and I was down.

'Well, it's a funny thing, Jim. You know I'm not a violent chap, but as I lay there, all my fears vanished and all I felt was a cold hatred of that bloody animal. I saw it as the cause of all my troubles and before I knew what I was doing I was up on my feet and booting its arse round and round the sty. And, do you know, it showed no fight at all. That pig was a coward at heart.'

I was still puzzled. 'But the ear — how did you manage to open the haematoma?'

'No problem, Jim. That was done for me.'

'You don't mean to say . . .'

'Yes,' Tristan said, holding his pint up to the light and studying a small foreign body floating in the depths. 'Yes, it was really very fortunate. In the scuffle in the dark, the pig ran up against the wall and burst the thing itself. Made a beautiful job.'

CHAPTER 25

I realised, quite suddenly, that spring had come. It was late March and I had been examining some sheep in a hillside fold. On my way down, in the lee of a small pine wood I leaned my back against a tree and was aware, all at once, of the sunshine, warm on my closed eyelids, the clamour of the larks, the muted sea-sound of the wind in the high branches. And though the snow still lay in long runnels behind the walls and the grass was lifeless and winter-yellowed, there was the feeling of change; almost of liberation, because, unknowing, I had surrounded myself with a carapace against the iron months, the relentless cold.

It wasn't a warm spring but it was dry with sharp winds which fluttered the white heads of the snowdrops and bent the clumps of daffodils on the village greens. In April the roadside banks were bright with the fresh yellow of the primroses.

And in April, too, came the lambing. It

came in a great tidal wave, the most vivid and interesting part of the veterinary surgeon's year, the zenith of the annual cycle, and it came as it always does when we were busiest with our other work.

In the spring the livestock were feeling the effects of the long winter. Cows had stood for months in the same few feet of byre and were in dire need of the green grass and the sun on their backs, while their calves had very little resistance to disease. And just when we were wondering how we could cope with the coughs and colds and pneumonias and acetonaemias the wave struck us.

The odd thing is that for about ten months of the year, sheep hardly entered into the scheme of our lives. They were just woolly things on the hills. But for the other two months they almost blotted out everything else.

First came the early troubles, the pregnancy toxaemias, the prolapses. Then the lambings in a concentrated rush followed by the calcium deficiencies, the horrible gangrenous mastitis when the udder turns black and sloughs away; and the diseases which beset the lambs themselves — swayback, pulpy kidney, dysentery. Then the flood slackened, became a trickle and by the end of May had almost dried up. Sheep became woolly things on the hills again.

But in this first year I found a fascination

in the work which has remained with me. Lambing, it seemed to me, had all the thrill and interest of calving without the hard labour. It was usually uncomfortable in that it was performed in the open; either in draughty pens improvised from straw bales and gates or more often out in the fields. It didn't seem to occur to the farmers that the ewe might prefer to produce her family in a warm place or that the vet may not enjoy kneeling for an hour in his shirt sleeves in the rain.

But the actual job was as easy as a song. After my experiences in correcting the malpresentations of calves it was delightful to manipulate these tiny creatures. Lambs are usually born in twos or threes and some wonderful mix-ups occur; tangles of heads and legs all trying to be first out and it is the vet's job to sort them around and decide which leg belonged to which head. I revelled in this. It was a pleasant change to be for once stronger and bigger than my patient, but I didn't over-stress this advantage; I have not changed the opinion I formed then that there are just two things to remember in lambing — cleanliness and gentleness.

And the lambs. All young animals are appealing but the lamb has been given an unfair share of charm. The moments come back; of a bitterly cold evening when I had delivered twins on a wind-scoured hillside; the lambs shaking their heads convulsively and within minutes one of them struggling upright and making its way, unsteady, knock-kneed, towards the udder while the other followed resolutely on its knees.

The shepherd, his purpled, weather-roughened face almost hidden by the heavy coat which muffled him to his ears, gave a slow chuckle. 'How the 'ell do they know?'

He had seen it happen thousands of times and he still wondered. So do I.

And another memory of two hundred lambs in a barn on a warm afternoon. We were inoculating them against pulpy kidney and there was no conversation because of the high-pitched protests of the lambs and the unremitting deep baa-ing from nearly a hundred ewes milling anxiously around outside. I couldn't conceive how these ewes could ever get their own families sorted out from that mass of almost identical little creatures. It would take hours.

It took about twenty-five seconds. When we had finished injecting we opened the barn doors and the outpouring lambs were met by a concerted rush of distraught mothers. At first the noise was deafening but it died away rapidly to an occasional bleat as the last stray was rounded up. Then, neatly paired off, the flock headed calmly for the field.

Through May and early June my world became softer and warmer. The cold wind dropped and the air, fresh as the sea, carried a faint breath of the thousands of wild flowers which speckled the pastures. At times it seemed unfair that I should be paid for my work; for driving out in the early morning with the fields glittering under the first pale sunshine and the wisps of mist still hanging on the high tops.

At Skeldale House the wistaria exploded into a riot of mauve blooms which thrust themselves through the open windows and each morning as I shaved I breathed in the heady fragrance from the long clusters drooping by the side of the mirror. Life was idyllic.

There was only one jarring note; it was the time of the horse. In the thirties there were still quite a lot of horses on the farms though the tractors had already sounded their warning knell. In the farms near the foot of the Dale where there was a fair amount of arable land the rows of stables were half empty but there were still enough horses to make May and June uncomfortable. This was when the castrations were done.

Before that came the foaling and it was a common enough thing to see a mare with her foal either trotting beside her or stretched flat on the ground as its mother nibbled at the grass. Nowadays the sight of a cart mare and foal in a field would make me pull up my car to have another look.

There was all the work connected with the foalings; cleansing the mares, docking the foals' tails, treating the illnesses of the new born — joint ill, retained meconium. It was hard and interesting but as the weather grew warmer the farmers began to think of having the year-old colts castrated.

I didn't like the job and since there might be up to a hundred to be done, it cast a shadow over this and many subsequent springs. For generations the operation had been done by casting the colt and tying him up very like a trussed chicken. It was a bit laborious but the animal was under complete restraint and it was possible to concentrate entirely on the job; but about the time I qualified, standing castration was coming very much to the fore. It consisted simply of applying a twitch to the colt's upper lip, injecting a shot of local anaesthetic into each testicle and going straight ahead. There was no doubt it was a lot quicker.

The obvious disadvantage was that the danger of injury to the operator and his helpers was increased tenfold, but for all that the method rapidly became more popular. A local farmer called Kenny Bright who considered himself an advanced thinker took the step of introducing it to the district. He engaged Major Farley, the horse specialist, to give a demonstration on one of his colts, and a large gathering of farmers came to spectate. Kenny, smug and full of self-importance, was holding the twitch and beaming round the company as his protégé prepared to disinfect the operation site, but as soon as the major touched the scrotum with his antiseptic the colt reared and brought a forefoot crashing down on Kenny's head. He was carried away on a gate with his skull fractured and spent a long time in hospital. The other farmers didn't stop laughing for weeks but the example failed to deter them. Standing castration was in.

I said it was quicker. It was when everything went smoothly, but there were other times when the colt kicked or threw himself on top of us or just went generally mad. Out of ten jobs nine would be easy and the tenth would be a rodeo. I don't know how much apprehension this state of affairs built up in other vets but I was undeniably tense on castration mornings.

Of course, one of the reasons was that I was not, am not and never will be a horseman. It is difficult to define the term but I am convinced that horsemen are either born or acquire the talent in early childhood. I knew it was no good my trying to start in my mid twenties. I had the knowledge of equine diseases, I believed I had the ability to treat sick horses efficiently but that power the real horseman had to soothe and quieten and mentally dominate an animal was beyond my reach. I didn't even try to kid myself.

It was unfortunate because there is no

doubt horses know. It is quite different with cows; they don't care either way; if a cow feels like kicking you she will kick you; she doesn't give a damn whether you are an expert or not. But horses know.

So on those mornings my morale was never very high as I drove out with my instruments rattling and rolling about on an enamel tray on the back seat. Would he be wild or quiet? How big would he be? I had heard my colleagues airily stating their preference for big horses — the two-year-olds were far easier, they said, you could get a better grip on the testicles. But there was never any doubt in my own mind. I liked them small; the smaller the better.

One morning when the season was at its height and I had had about enough of the equine race, Siegfried called to me as he was going out. 'James, there's a horse with a tumour on its belly at Wilkinson's of White Cross. Get along and take it off — today if possible but otherwise fix your own time; I'll leave it with you.'

Feeling a little disgruntled at fate having handed me something on top of the seasonal tasks, I boiled up a scalpel, tumour spoons and syringe and put them on my tray with local anaesthetic, iodine and tetanus antitoxin.

I drove to the farm with the tray rattling ominously behind me. That sound always had a connotation of doom for me. I wondered about the horse — maybe it was just a yearling; they did get those little dangling growths sometimes — nanberries, the farmers called them. Over the six miles I managed to build up a comfortable picture of a soft-eyed little colt with pendulous abdomen and overlong hair; it hadn't done well over the winter and was probably full of worms — shaky on its legs with weakness, in fact.

At Wilkinson's all was quiet. The yard was empty except for a lad of about ten who didn't know where the boss was.

'Well, where is the horse?' I asked.

The lad pointed to the stable. 'He's in there.'

I went inside. At one end stood a high, open-topped loose box with a metal grill topping the wooden walls and from within I heard a deep-throated whinnying and snorting followed by a series of tremendous thuds against the sides of the box. A chill crept through me. That was no little colt in there.

I opened the top half door and there, looking down at me, was an enormous animal; I hadn't realised horses ever came quite as big as this; a chestnut stallion with a proud arch to his neck and feet like manhole covers. Surging swathes of muscle shone on his shoulders and quarters and when he saw me he laid back his ears, showed the whites of his eyes and lashed out viciously against the wall. A foot-long splinter flew high in the air as the great hoof crashed against the boards.

'God almighty,' I breathed and closed the half door hurriedly. I leaned my back against the door and listened to my heart thumping.

I turned to the lad. 'How old is that horse?'

'Over six years, sir.'

I tried a little calm thinking. How did you go about tackling a man-eater like this? I had never seen such a horse — he must weigh over a ton. I shook myself; I hadn't even had a look at the tumour I was supposed to remove. I lifted the latch, opened the door about two inches and peeped inside. I could see it plainly dangling from the belly; probably a papilloma, about the size of a cricket ball, with a lobulated surface which made it look like a little cauliflower. It swung gently from side to side as the horse moved about.

No trouble to take it off. Nice narrow neck to it; a few c.c.'s of local in there and I could twist it off easily with the spoons.

But the snag was obvious. I would have to go under that shining barrel of an abdomen within easy reach of the great feet and stick a needle into those few inches of skin. Not a happy thought.

But I pulled my mind back to practical things; like a bucket of hot water, soap and a towel. And I'd need a good man on the twitch. I began to walk towards the house.

There was no answer to my knock. I tried

again; still nothing — there was nobody at home. It seemed the most natural thing in the world to leave everything till another day; the idea of going round the buildings and fields till I found somebody never entered my head.

I almost broke into a gallop on my way to the car, backed it round with the tyres squealing and roared out of the yard.

Siegfried was surprised. 'Nobody there? Well that's a damn funny thing. I'm nearly sure they were expecting you today. But never mind, it's in your hands, James. Give them a ring and fix it up again as soon as possible.'

I found it wonderfully easy to forget about the stallion over the days and weeks that followed; except when my defences were down. At least once a night it thundered through my dreams with gaping nostrils and flying mane and I developed an uncomfortable habit of coming bolt awake at five o'clock in the morning and starting immediately to operate on the horse. On an average, I took that tumour off twenty times before breakfast each morning.

I told myself it would be a lot easier to fix the job up and get it over. What was I waiting for, anyway? Was there a subconscious hope that if I put it off long enough something would happen to get me off the hook? The tumour might fall off or shrink away and disappear, or the horse might drop down dead.

I could have passed the whole thing on to Siegfried — he was good with horses — but my confidence was low enough without that.

All my doubts were resolved one morning when Mr Wilkinson came on the phone. He wasn't in the least upset at the long delay but he made it quite clear that he could wait no longer. 'You see, I want to sell this 'oss, young man, but I can't let him go with that thing on him, can I?'

My journey to Wilkinson's wasn't enlivened by the familiar clatter of the tray on the back seat; it reminded me of the last time when I was wondering what was ahead of me. This time I knew.

Stepping out of the car, I felt almost disembodied. It was like walking a few inches above the ground. I was greeted by a reverberating din from the loose box; the same angry whinnies and splintering crashes I had heard before. I tried to twist my stiff face into a smile as the farmer came over.

'My chaps are getting a halter on him,' he said, but his words were cut short by an enraged squealing from the box and two tremendous blows against the wooden sides. I felt my mouth going dry.

The noise was coming nearer; then the stable doors flew open and the great horse catapulted out into the yard, dragging two big fellows along on the end of the halter shank. The cobbles struck sparks from the men's boots as they slithered about but they were unable to stop the stallion backing and plunging. I imagined I could feel the ground shudder under my feet as the hooves crashed down.

At length, after much manoeuvring, the men got the horse standing with his off side against the wall of the barn. One of them looped the twitch on to the upper lip and tightened it expertly, the other took a firm grip on the halter and turned towards me. 'Ready for you now, sir.'

I pierced the rubber cap on the bottle of cocaine, withdrew the plunger of the syringe and watched the clear fluid flow into the glass barrel. Seven, eight, ten c.c.'s. If I could get that in, the rest would be easy; but my hands were trembling.

Walking up to the horse was like watching an action from a film. It wasn't really me doing this — the whole thing was unreal. The near-side eye flickered dangerously at me as I raised my left hand and passed it over the muscles of the neck, down the smooth, quivering flank and along the abdomen till I was able to grasp the tumour. I had the thing in my hand now, the lobulations firm and lumpy under my fingers. I pulled gently downwards, stretching the brown skin joining the growth to the body. I would put the local in there — a few good weals. It wasn't going to be so bad. The stallion laid back his ears and gave a warning whicker.

I took a long, careful breath, brought up the syringe with my right hand, placed the needle against the skin then thrust it in.

The kick was so explosively quick that at first I felt only surprise that such a huge animal could move so swiftly. It was a lightning outward slash that I never even saw and the hoof struck the inside of my right thigh, spinning me round helplessly. When I hit the ground I lay still, feeling only a curious numbness. Then I tried to move and a stab of pain went through my leg.

When I opened my eyes Mr Wilkinson was bending over me. 'Are you all right, Mr Herriot?' The voice was anxious.

'I don't think so.' I was astonished at the matter-of-fact sound of my own words; but stranger still was the feeling of being at peace with myself for the first time for weeks. I was calm and completely in charge of the situation.

'I'm afraid not, Mr Wilkinson. You'd better put the horse back in his box for now — we'll have a go at him another day — and I wonder if you'd ring Mr Farnon to come and pick me up. I don't think I'll be able to drive.'

My leg wasn't broken but it developed a massive haematoma at the point of impact and then the whole limb blossomed into an unbelievable range of colours from delicate orange to deepest black. I was still hobbling like a Crimean veteran when, a fortnight later, Siegfried and I with a small army of helpers went back and roped the stallion, chloroformed him and removed that little growth.

I have a cavity in the muscle of my thigh to remind me of that day, but some good came out of the incident. I found that the fear is worse than the reality and horse work has never worried me as much since then.

CHAPTER 26

The first time I saw Phin Calvert was in the street outside the surgery when I was talking to Brigadier Julian Coutts-Browne about his shooting dogs. The brigadier was almost a stage version of an English aristocrat; immensely tall with a pronounced stoop, hawk features and a high drawling voice. As he spoke, smoke from a narrow cigar trickled from his lips.

I turned my head at the clatter of heavy boots on the pavement. A thick set figure was stumping rapidly towards us, hands tucked behind his braces, ragged jacket pulled wide to display a curving expanse of collarless shirt, wisps of grizzled hair hanging in a fringe beneath a greasy cap. He was smiling widely at nobody in particular and he hummed busily to himself.

The brigadier glanced at him. 'Morning, Calvert,' he grunted coldly.

Phineas threw up his head in pleased recognition. 'Now then, Charlie, 'ow is ta?'

he shouted.

The brigadier looked as though he had swallowed a swift pint of vinegar. He removed his cigar with a shaking hand and stared after the retreating back. 'Impudent devil,' he muttered.

Looking at Phin, you would never have thought he was a prosperous farmer. I was called to his place a week later and was surprised to find a substantial house and buildings and a fine dairy herd grazing in the fields.

I could hear him even before I got out of the car.

'Hello, 'ello, 'ello! Who's this we've got then? New chap eh? Now we're going to learn summat!' He still had his hands inside his braces and was grinning wider than ever.

'My name is Herriot,' I said.

'Is it now?' Phin cocked his head and surveyed me, then he turned to three young men standing by. 'Hasn't he a nice smile, lads? He's a real Happy Harry!'

He turned and began to lead the way across the yard. 'Come on, then, and we'll see what you're made of. I 'ope you know a bit about calves because I've got some here that are right dowly.'

As he went into the calf house I was hoping I would be able to do something impressive — perhaps use some of the new drugs and sera I had in my car; it was going to take something special to make an impact here.

There were six well-grown young animals, almost stirk size, and three of them were behaving very strangely; grinding their teeth, frothing at the mouth and blundering about the pen as though they couldn't see. As I watched, one of them walked straight into the wall and stood with its nose pressed against the stone.

Phin, apparently unconcerned, was humming to himself in a corner. When I started to take my thermometer from its case he burst into a noisy commentary. 'Now what's he doing? Ah, we're off now, get up there!'

The half minute which my thermometer spends in an animal's rectum is usually devoted to hectic thought. But this time I didn't need the time to work out my diagnosis; the blindness made it easy. I began to look round the walls of the calf house; it was dark and I had to get my face close to the stone.

Phin gave tongue again. 'Hey, what's going on? You're as bad as t' calves, nosing about there, dozy like. What d'you think you're lookin' for?'

'Paint, Mr Calvert. I'm nearly sure your calves have got lead poisoning.'

Phin said what all farmers say at this juncture. 'They can't have. I've had calves in here for thirty years and they've never taken any harm before. There's no paint in here, anyway.'

'How about this, then?' I peered into the darkest corner and pulled at a piece of loose board.

'Oh, that's nobbut a bit of wood I nailed down there last week to block up a hole. Came off an old hen house.'

I looked at the twenty-year-old paint hanging off in the loose flakes which calves find so irresistible. 'This is what's done the damage,' I said. 'Look, you can see the tooth marks where they've been at it.'

Phin studied the board at close quarters and grunted doubtfully. 'All right, what do we do now?'

'First thing is to get this painted board out of here and then give all the calves epsom salts. Have you got any?'

Phin gave a bark of laughter. 'Aye, I've got a bloody great sack full, but can't you do owt better than that? Aren't you going to inject them?'

It was a little embarrassing. The specific antidotes to metal poisoning had not been discovered and the only thing which sometimes did a bit of good was magnesium sulphate which caused the precipitation of insoluble lead sulphate. The homely term for magnesium sulphate is, of course, epsom salts.

'No,' I said. 'There's nothing I can inject that will help at all and I can't even guarantee

266

the salts will. But I'd like you to give the calves two heaped tablespoonfuls three times a day.'

'Oh 'ell, you'll skitter the poor buggers to death!'

'Maybe so, but there's nothing else for it,' I said.

Phin took a step towards me so that his face, dark-skinned and deeply wrinkled, was close to mine. The suddenly shrewd, mottled brown eyes regarded me steadily for a few seconds then he turned away quickly. 'Right,' he said. 'Come in and have a drink.'

Phin stumped into the farm kitchen ahead of me, threw back his head and let loose a bellow that shook the windows. 'Mother! Feller 'ere wants a glass o' beer. Come and meet Happy Harry!'

Mrs Calvert appeared with magical speed and put down glasses and bottles. I glanced at the labels — 'Smith's Nutty Brown Ale', and filled my glass. It was a historic moment though I didn't know it then; it was the first of an incredible series of Nutty Browns I was to drink at that table.

Mrs Calvert sat down for a moment, crossed her hands on her lap and smiled encouragingly. 'Can you do anything for the calves, then?' she asked.

Phin butted in before I could reply. 'Oh aye, he can an' all. He's put them on to epsom salts.'

'Epsom salts?'

'That's it, Missis. I said when he came that we'd get summat real smart and scientific like. You can't beat new blood and modern ideas.' Phin sipped his beer gravely.

Over the following days the calves gradually improved and at the end of a fortnight they were all eating normally. The worst one still showed a trace of blindness, but I was confident this too would clear up.

It wasn't long before I saw Phin again. It was early afternoon and I was in the office with Siegfried when the outer door banged and the passage echoed to the clumping of hobnails. I heard a voice raised in song — hi-ti-tiddly-rum-te-tum. Phineas was in our midst once more.

'Well, well, well!' he bawled heartily at Miss Harbottle. 'It's Flossie! And what's my little darlin' doing this fine day?'

There was not a flicker from Miss Harbottle's granite features. She directed an icy stare at the intruder but Phin swung round on Siegfried with a yellow-toothed grin. 'Now, gaffer, 'ow's tricks?'

'Everything's fine, Mr Calvert,' Siegfried replied. 'What can we do for you?'

Phin stabbed a finger at me. 'There's my man. I want him out to my place right sharpish.'

'What's the trouble?' I asked. 'Is it the calves again?'

'Damn, no! Wish it was. It's me good bull. He's puffin' like a bellows — bit like pneumonia but worse than I've known. He's in a 'ell of a state. Looks like he's peggin' out.' For an instant Phin lost his jocularity.

I had heard of this bull; pedigree shorthorn, show winner, the foundation of his herd. 'I'll be right after you, Mr Calvert. I'll follow you along.'

'Good lad. I'm off, then.' Phin paused at the door, a wild figure, tieless, tattered; baggy trousers ballooning from his ample middle. He turned again to Miss Harbottle and contorted his leathery features into a preposterous leer. 'Ta-ra, Floss!' he cried and was gone.

For a moment the room seemed very empty and quiet except for Miss Harbottle's acid 'Oh, that man! Dreadful! Dreadful!'

I made good time to the farm and found Phin waiting with his three sons. The young men looked gloomy but Phin was still indomitable. 'Here 'e is!' he shouted. 'Happy Harry again. Now we'll be all right.' He even managed a little tune as we crossed to the bull pen but when he looked over the door his head sank on his chest and his hands worked deeper behind his braces.

The bull was standing as though rooted to the middle of the pen. His great rib cage rose and fell with the most laboured respirations I had ever seen. His mouth gaped wide, a bubbling foam hung round his lips and his flaring nostrils; his eyes, almost starting from his head in terror, stared at the wall in front of him. This wasn't pneumonia, it was a frantic battle for breath; and it looked like a losing one.

He didn't move when I inserted my thermometer and though my mind was racing I suspected the half minute wasn't going to be long enough this time. I had expected accelerated breathing, but nothing like this.

'Poor aud beggar,' Phin muttered. 'He's bred me the finest calves I've ever had and he's as quiet as a sheep, too. I've seen me little grandchildren walk under 'is belly and he's took no notice. I hate to see him sufferin' like this. If you can't do no good, just tell me and I'll get the gun out.'

I took the thermometer out and read it. One hundred and ten degrees Fahrenheit. This was ridiculous; I shook it vigorously and pushed it back into the rectum.

I gave it nearly a minute this time so that I could get in some extra thinking. The second reading said a hundred and ten again and I had an unpleasant conviction that if the thermometer had been a foot long the mercury would still have been jammed against the top.

What in the name of God was this? Could be Anthrax . . . must be . . . and yet . . . I looked over at the row of heads above the half door; they were waiting for me to say something and their silence accentuated the agonised groaning and panting. I looked above the heads to the square of deep blue and a tufted cloud moving across the sun. As it passed, a single dazzling ray made me close my eyes and a faint bell rang in my mind.

'Has he been out today?' I asked.

'Aye, he's been out on the grass on his tether all morning. It was that grand and warm.'

The bell became a triumphant gong. 'Get a hosepipe in here quick. You can rig it to that tap in the yard.'

'A hosepipe? What the 'ell . . . ?'

'Yes, quick as you can — he's got sunstroke.'

They had the hose fixed in less than a minute. I turned it full on and began to play the jet of cold water all over the huge form — his face and neck, along the ribs, up and down the legs. I kept this up for about five minutes but it seemed a lot longer as I waited for some sign of improvement. I was beginning to think I was on the wrong track when the bull gulped just once.

It was something — he had been unable to swallow his saliva before in his desperate efforts to get the air into his lungs; and I really began to notice a change in the big animal. Surely he was looking just a little less distressed and wasn't the breathing slowing

271

down a bit?

Then the bull shook himself, turned his head and looked at us. There was an awed whisper from one of the young men: 'By gaw, it's working!'

I enjoyed myself after that. I can't think of anything in my working life that has given me more pleasure than standing in that pen directing the life-saving jet and watching the bull savouring it. He liked it on his face best and as I worked my way up from the tail and along the steaming back he would turn his nose full into the water, rocking his head from side to side and blinking blissfully.

Within half an hour he looked almost normal. His chest was still heaving a little but he was in no discomfort. I tried the temperature again. Down to a hundred and five.

'He'll be all right now,' I said. 'But I think one of the lads should keep the water on him for another twenty minutes or so. I'll have to go now.'

'You've time for a drink,' Phin grunted.

In the farm kitchen his bellow of 'Mother' lacked some of its usual timbre. He dropped into a chair and stared into his glass of Nutty Brown. 'Harry,' he said, 'I'll tell you, you've flummoxed me this time.' He sighed and rubbed his chin in apparent disbelief. 'I don't know what the 'ell to say to you.'

It wasn't often that Phin lost his voice, but

he found it again very soon at the next meeting of the farmers' discussion group.

A learned and earnest gentleman had been expounding on the advances in veterinary medicine and how the farmers could now expect their stock to be treated as the doctors treated their human patients, with the newest drugs and procedures.

It was too much for Phin. He jumped to his feet and cried: 'Ah think you're talking a lot of rubbish. There's a young feller in Darrowby not long out of college and it doesn't matter what you call 'im out for he uses nowt but epsom salts and cold water.'

CHAPTER 27

It was during one of Siegfried's efficiency drives that Colonel Merrick's cow picked up a wire. The colonel was a personal friend, which made things even more uncomfortable.

Everybody suffered when Siegfried had these spells. They usually came on after he had been reading a technical work or when he had seen a film of some new technical procedure. He would rampage around, calling on the cowering household to stir themselves and be better men. He would be obsessed, for a time, with a craving for perfection.

'We must put on a better show at these operations on the farms. It just isn't good enough to fish out a few old instruments from a bag and start hacking at the animal. We must have cleanliness, asepsis if possible, and an orderly technique.'

So he was jubilant when he diagnosed traumatic reticulitis (foreign body in the second stomach) in the colonel's cow. 'We'll really show old Hubert something. We'll give him a picture of veterinary surgery he'll never forget.'

Tristan and I were pressed into service as assistants, and our arrival at the farm was really impressive. Siegfried led the procession, looking unusually smart in a brand new tweed jacket of which he was very proud. He was a debonair figure as he shook hands with his friend.

The colonel was jovial. 'Hear you're going to operate on my cow. Take out a wire, eh? Like to watch you do it, if it's all right with you.'

'By all means, Hubert, please do. You'll find it very interesting.'

In the byre, Tristan and I had to bustle about. We arranged tables alongside the cow and on these we placed new metal trays with rows of shining, sterilised instruments. Scalpels, directors, probes, artery forceps, hypodermic syringes, suture needles, gut and silk in glass phials, rolls of cotton wool and various bottles of spirit and other antiseptics.

Siegfried fussed around, happy as a schoolboy. He had clever hands and, as a surgeon, he was worth watching. I could read his mind without much trouble. This, he was thinking, was going to be good.

When all was to his liking, he took off his jacket and donned a brilliantly white smock.

275

He handed the jacket to Tristan and almost instantly gave a roar of anger. 'Hey, don't just throw it down on that meal bin! Here, give it to me. I'll find a safe place for it.' He dusted the new garment down tenderly and hung it on a nail on the wall.

Meanwhile, I had shaved and disinfected the operation site on the flank and everything was ready for the local anaesthetic. Siegfried took the syringe and quickly infiltrated the area. 'This is where we go inside, Hubert. I hope you aren't squeamish.'

The colonel beamed. 'Oh, I've seen blood before. You needn't worry, I shan't faint.'

With a bold sweep of the scalpel, Siegfried incised the skin, then the muscles and finally, with delicate care, the glistening peritoneum. The smooth wall of the rumen (the large first stomach) lay exposed.

Siegfried reached for a fresh scalpel and looked for the best place to cut in. But as he poised his knife, the wall of the rumen suddenly bulged out through the skin incision. 'Unusual,' he muttered. 'Probably a bit of rumenal gas.' Unflurried, he gently thrust back the protrusion and prepared again to make his cut; but as he withdrew his hand, the rumen welled out after it, a pinkish mass bigger than a football. Siegfried pushed it back and it shot out again immediately, ballooning to a startling size. This time, he took two hands to the job, pushing and pressing till he forced the thing once more out of sight. He stood for a moment with his hands inside the cow, breathing heavily. Two beads of sweat trickled down his forehead.

Carefully, he withdrew his hands. Nothing happened. It must have settled down. He was reaching back for his knife when, like a live thing, the rumen again came leaping and surging out. It seemed almost as though the entire organ had escaped through the incision — a slippery, gleaming mass rising and swelling till it was level with his eyes.

Siegfried had dropped all pretence of calm and was fighting desperately, both arms round the thing, pressing downwards with all his strength. I hastened forward to help and, as I drew near, he whispered hoarsely: 'What the hell is it?' Clearly, he was wondering if this pulsating heap of tissue was some part of the bovine anatomy he had never even heard of.

Silently, we fought the mass down till it was level with the skin. The colonel was watching intently. He hadn't expected the operation to be so interesting. His eyebrows were slightly raised.

'It must be gas that's doing this,' panted Siegfried. 'Pass me the knife and stand back.'

He inserted the knife into the rumen and cut sharply downwards. I was glad I had moved away because through the incision shot a high-pressure jet of semi-liquid stomach contents — a greenish-brown, foul-smelling cascade which erupted from the depths of the cow as from an invisible pump.

The first direct hit was on Siegfried's face. He couldn't release his hold of the rumen or it would have slipped back into the abdomen and contaminated the peritoneum. So he hung on to each side of the opening while the evil torrent poured on to his hair, down his neck and all over his lovely white smock.

Now and then, the steady stream would be varied by a sudden explosion which sent the fermenting broth spouting viciously over everything in the immediate vicinity. Within a minute, the trays with their gleaming instruments were thoroughly covered. The tidy rows of swabs, the snowy tufts of cotton wool disappeared without trace, but it was the unkindest cut of all when a particularly powerful jet sent a liberal spray over the new jacket hanging on the wall. Siegfried's face was too obscured for me to detect any change of expression but at this disaster, I saw real anguish in his eyes.

The colonel's eyebrows were now raised to the maximum and his mouth hung open as he gazed in disbelief at the chaotic scene. Siegfried, still hanging grimly on, was the centre of it all, paddling about in a reeking swamp which came half way up his Wellington boots. He looked very like a Fiji Islander with his hair stiffened and frizzled and his eyes rolling whitely in the brown face.

Eventually, the flood slowed to a trickle and stopped. I was able to hold the lips of the wound while Siegfried inserted his arm and felt his way to the reticulum. I watched him as he groped inside the honeycombed organ far out of sight against the diaphragm. A satisfied grunt told me he had located the piercing wire and within seconds he had removed it.

Tristan had been frantically salvaging and washing suture materials and soon the incision in the rumen was stitched. Siegfried's heroic stand had not been in vain; there was no contamination of the peritoneum.

Silently and neatly, he secured the skin and muscles with retention sutures and swabbed round the wound. Everything looked fine. The cow seemed unperturbed; under the anaesthetic she had known nothing of the titanic struggle with her insides. In fact, freed from the discomfort of the transfixing wire, she appeared already to be feeling better.

It took quite a time to tidy up the mess and the most difficult job was to make Siegfried presentable. We did our best by swilling him down with buckets of water while, all the time, he scraped sadly at his new jacket with a flat stick. It didn't make much difference.

The colonel was hearty and full of congratulations. 'Come in, my dear chap. Come in and have a drink.' But the invitation had a hollow ring and he took care to stand at least ten feet away from his friend.

Siegfried threw his bedraggled jacket over his shoulder. 'No thank you, Hubert. It's most kind of you, but we must be off.' He went out of the byre. 'I think you'll find the cow will be eating in a day or two. I'll be back in a fortnight to take out the stitches.'

In the confined space of the car, Tristan and I were unable to get as far away from him as we would have liked. Even with our heads stuck out of the windows it was still pretty bad.

Siegfried drove for a mile or two in silence, then he turned to me and his streaked features broke into a grin. There was something indomitable about him. 'You never know what's round the corner in this game, my boys, but just think of this — that operation was a success.'

CHAPTER 28

There were three of us in the cheerless yard, Isaac Cranford, Jeff Mallock and myself. The only one who looked at ease was Mallock and it was fitting that it should be so, since he was, in a manner of speaking, the host. He owned the knacker yard and he looked on benignly as we peered into the carcass of the cow he had just opened.

In Darrowby the name Mallock had a ring of doom. It was the graveyard of livestock, of farmers' ambitions, of veterinary surgeons' hopes. If ever an animal was very ill somebody was bound to say: 'I reckon she'll be off to Mallock's afore long,' or 'Jeff Mallock'll have 'er in t' finish.' And the premises fitted perfectly into the picture; a group of drab, red-brick buildings standing a few fields back from the road with a stumpy chimney from which rolled endlessly a dolorous black smoke.

It didn't pay to approach Mallock's too closely unless you had a strong stomach, so the place was avoided by the townspeople, but if you ventured up the lane and peeped through the sliding metal doors you could look in on a nightmare world. Dead animals lay everywhere. Most of them were dismembered and great chunks of meat hung on hooks, but here and there you could see a bloated sheep or a greenish, swollen pig which not even Jeff could bring himself to open.

Skulls and dry bones were piled to the roof in places and brown mounds of meat meal stood in the corners. The smell was bad at any time but when Jeff was boiling up the carcasses it was indescribable. The Mallock family bungalow stood in the middle of the buildings and strangers could be pardoned if they expected a collection of wizened gnomes to dwell there. But Jeff was a pink-faced, cherubic man in his forties, his wife plump, smiling and comely. Their family ranged from a positively beautiful girl of nineteen down to a robust five-year-old boy. There were eight young Mallocks and they had spent their lifetimes playing among tuberculous lungs and a vast spectrum of bacteria from Salmonella to Anthrax. They were the healthiest children in the district.

It was said in the pubs that Jeff was one of the richest men in the town but the locals, as they supped their beer, had to admit that he earned his money. At any hour of the day or night he would rattle out into the country in his ramshackle lorry, winch on a carcass, bring it back to the yard and cut it up. A dog food dealer came twice a week from Brawton with a van and bought the fresh meat. The rest of the stuff Jeff shovelled into his boiler to make the meat meal which was in great demand for mixing in pig and poultry rations. The bones went for making fertiliser, the hides to the tanner and the nameless odds and ends were collected by a wild-eyed individual known only as the 'ket feller'. Sometimes, for a bit of variety, Jeff would make long slabs of strange-smelling soap which found a brisk sale for scrubbing shop floors. Yes, people said, there was no doubt Jeff did all right. But, by gaw, he earned it.

My contacts with Mallock were fairly frequent. A knacker's yard had a useful function for a vet. It served as a crude post-mortem room, a place where he could check on his diagnosis in fatal cases; and on the occasions where he had been completely baffled, the mysteries would be revealed under Jeff's knife.

Often, of course, farmers would send in an animal which I had been treating and ask Jeff to tell them 'what had been wrong wi't' and this was where a certain amount of friction arose. Because Jeff was placed in a position of power and seldom resisted the temptation to wield it. Although he could neither read nor write, he was a man of great professional pride; he didn't like to be called a knacker man but preferred 'fellmonger'. He considered in his heart that, after twenty-odd years of cutting up diseased animals, he knew more than any vet alive, and it made things rather awkward that the farming community unhesitatingly agreed with him.

It never failed to spoil my day if a farmer called in at the surgery and told me that, once more, Jeff Mallock had confounded my diagnosis. 'Hey, remember that cow you were treating for magnesium deficiency? She never did no good and ah sent 'er into Mallock's. Well, you know what was really the matter wi' 'er? Worm i' the tail. Jeff said if you'd nobbut cut tail off, that cow would have gotten up and walked away.' It was no good arguing or saying there was no such thing as worm in the tail. Jeff knew — that was all about it.

If only Jeff had taken his priceless opportunities to acquire a commonsense knowledge it wouldn't have been so bad. But instead, he had built up a weird pathology of his own and backed it up by black magic remedies gleaned from his contacts with the more primitive members of the farming community. His four stock diseases were Stagnation of t'lungs, Black Rot, Gastric Ulsters and Golf Stones. It was a quartet which made the vets tremble for miles around.

Another cross which the vets had to bear was his unique gift of being able to take one look at a dead animal on a farm and pronounce immediately on the cause of death. The farmers, awestruck by his powers, were always asking me why I couldn't do it. But I was unable to dislike the man. He would have had to be more than human to resist the chance to be important and there was no malice in his actions. Still, it made things uncomfortable at times and I liked to be on the spot myself whenever possible. Especially when Isaac Cranford was involved.

Cranford was a hard man, a man who had cast his life in a mould of iron austerity. A sharp bargainer, a win-at-all-cost character and, in a region where thrift was general, he was noted for meanness. He farmed some of the best land in the lower Dale, his shorthorns won prizes regularly at the shows but he was nobody's friend. Mr Bateson, his neighbour to the north, summed it up: 'That feller 'ud skin a flea for its hide.' Mr Dickon, his neighbour to the south, put it differently: 'If he gets haud on a pound note, by gaw it's a prisoner.'

This morning's meeting had had its origin the previous day. A phone call mid afternoon from Mr Cranford. 'I've had a cow struck by lightning. She's laid dead in the field.'

I was surprised. 'Lightning? Are you sure? We haven't had a storm today.'

'Maybe you haven't, but we have 'ere.'

'Mmm, all right, I'll come and have a look at her.'

Driving to the farm, I couldn't work up much enthusiasm for the impending interview. This lightning business could be a bit of a headache. All farmers were insured against lightning stroke — it was usually part of their fire policy — and after a severe thunderstorm it was common enough for the vets' phones to start ringing with requests to examine dead beasts.

The insurance companies were reasonable about it. If they received a certificate from the vet that he believed lightning to be the cause of death they would usually pay up without fuss. In cases of doubt they would ask for a post-mortem or a second opinion from another practitioner. The difficulty was that there are no diagnostic post-mortem features to go on; occasionally a bruising of the tissues under the skin, but very little else. The happiest situation was when the beast was found with the tell-tale scorch marks running from an ear down the leg to earth into the ground. Often the animal would be found under a tree which itself had obviously been blasted and torn by lightning. Diagnosis was easy then.

Ninety-nine per cent of the farmers were looking only for a square deal and if their vet found some other clear cause of death they would accept his verdict philosophically. But the odd one could be very difficult.

I had heard Siegfried tell of one old chap who had called him out to verify a lightning death. The long scorch marks on the carcass were absolutely classical and Siegfried, viewing them, had been almost lyrical. 'Beautiful, Charlie, beautiful, I've never seen more typical marks. But there's just one thing.' He put an arm round the old man's shoulder. 'What a great pity you let the candle grease fall on the skin.'

The old man looked closer and thumped a fist into his palm. 'Dang it, you're right, maister! Ah've mucked t'job up. And ah took pains ower it an' all — been on for dang near an hour.' He walked away muttering. He showed no embarrassment, only disgust at his own technological shortcomings.

But this, I thought, as the stone walls flipped past the car windows, would be very different. Cranford was in the habit of getting his own way, right or wrong, and if he didn't get it today there would be trouble.

I drove through the farm gate and along a neat tarmac road across the single field. Mr Cranford was standing motionless in the middle of the yard and I was struck, not for the first time, by the man's resemblance to a big, hungry bird. The hunched, narrow shoulders, the forward-thrust, sharp-beaked face, the dark overcoat hanging loosely on the bony frame. I wouldn't have been surprised if he had spread his wings and flapped his way on to the byre roof. Instead, he nodded impatiently at me and began to hasten with short, tripping steps to a field at the back of the house.

It was a large field and the dead cow lay almost in the centre. There were no trees, no hedges, not even a small bush. My hopeful picture of the body under a stricken tree melted immediately, leaving an anxious void.

We stopped beside the cow and Mr Cranford was the first to speak. 'Bound to be lightning. Can't be owt else. Nasty storm, then this good beast dropping down dead.'

I looked at the grass around the big shorthorn. It had been churned and torn out, leaving patches of bare earth. 'But it hasn't exactly dropped down, has it? It died in convulsions — you can see where its feet have kicked out the grass.'

'All right then, it 'ad a convulsion, but it was lightning that caused it.' Mr Cranford had fierce little eyes and they darted flitting glances at my shirt collar, macintosh belt, Wellingtons. He never could quite bring himself to look anybody in the eye.

'I doubt it, Mr Cranford. One of the signs of lightning stroke is that the beast has fallen without a struggle. Some of them even have grass in their mouths.'

'Oh, I know all about that,' Cranford

snapped, his thin face flushing. 'I've been among livestock for half a century and this isn't the first beast I've seen that's been struck. They're not all t'same, you know.'

'Oh, I realise that, but, you see, this death could have been caused by so many things.'

'What sort o'things?'

'Well, Anthrax for a start, magnesium deficiency, heart trouble — there's quite a list. I really think we ought to do a post-mortem to make sure.'

'Now see here, are you saying I'm trying to do summat I shouldn't?'

'Not at all. I'm only saying we should make sure before I write a certificate. We can go and see her opened at Mallock's and, believe me, if there's no other obvious cause of death you'll get the benefit of the doubt. The insurance people are pretty good about it.'

Mr Cranford's predatory features sank lower into his coat collar. He dug his hands viciously into his pockets. 'I've had vitneries at these jobs afore. Proper, experienced vitneries, too.' The little eyes flashed in the direction of my left ear. 'They've never messed about like this. What's the use of going to all that trouble? Why do you have to be so damn particular?'

Why indeed, I thought. Why make an enemy of this man? He wielded a lot of power in the district. Prominent in the local Farmers' Union, a member of every agricultural

289

committee for miles around. He was a wealthy, successful man and, if people didn't like him, they respected his knowledge and listened to him. He could do a young vet a lot of harm. Why not write the certificate and go home? This is to certify that I have examined the above-mentioned animal and, in my opinion, lightning stroke was the cause of death. It would be easy and Cranford would be mollified. It would be the end of the whole thing. Why antagonise this dangerous character for nothing? Maybe it really was lightning, anyway.

I turned to face Mr Cranford, trying in vain to look into the eyes that always veered away at the last moment. 'I'm sorry, but I feel we ought to have a look inside this cow. I'll ring Mallock and ask him to pick her up and we can see her in the morning. I'll meet you there at ten o'clock. Will that be all right?'

'Reckon it'll have to be,' Cranford spat out. 'It's a piece o' nonsense, but I suppose I've got to humour you. But just let me remind you — this was a good cow, worth all of eighty pounds. I can't afford to lose that amount of money. I want my rights.'

'I'm sure you'll get them, Mr Cranford. And before I have her moved I'd better take a blood film to eliminate Anthrax.'

The farmer had been under a mounting load of pressure. As a pillar of the methodist chapel his range of language was restricted, so he vented his pent-up feelings by kicking out savagely at the carcass. His toe made contact with the unyielding backbone and he hopped around on one leg for a few seconds. Then he limped off towards the house.

I was alone as I nicked the dead ear with my knife and drew a film of blood across a couple of glass slides. It hadn't been a happy session and the one tomorrow didn't hold out much more promise. I enclosed the blood films carefully in a cardboard box and set off for Skeldale House to examine them under the microscope.

So it wasn't a particularly cheerful group which assembled at the knacker yard the following morning. Even Jeff, though he preserved his usual Buddha-like expression, was, in fact, deeply offended. The account he had given me when I first arrived at the yard was fragmentary, but I could piece the scene together. Jeff, leaping from his lorry at Cranford's, sweeping the carcass with a piercing glance and making his brilliant spot diagnosis. 'Stagnation o' t'lungs. I can allus tell by the look in their eyes and the way their hair lies along t'back.' Waiting confidently for the wondering gasps, the congratulatory speeches which always followed his *tour de force*.

Then Mr Cranford, almost dancing with rage. 'Shut your big, stupid mouth, Mallock, tha knows nowt about it. This cow was struck by lightning and you'd better remember that.'

And now, bending my head over the carcass, I couldn't find a clue anyway. No sign of bruising when the skin was removed. The internal organs clean and normal.

I straightened up and pushed my fingers through my hair. The boiler bubbled softly, puffing out odoriferous wisps into the already highly-charged atmosphere. Two dogs licked busily at a pile of meat meal.

Then a chill of horror struck through me. The dogs had competition. A little boy with golden curls was pushing a forefinger into the heap, inserting it in his mouth and sucking with rapt enjoyment.

'Look at that!' I quavered.

The knacker man's face lit up with paternal pride. 'Aye,' he said happily. 'It isn't only the four-legged 'uns wot likes my meal. Wonderful stuff — full of nourishment!'

His good humour completely restored, he struck a match and began to puff appreciatively at a short pipe which was thickly encrusted with evidence of his grisly trade.

I dragged my attention back to the job in hand. 'Cut into the heart, will you, Jeff,' I said.

Jeff deftly sliced the big organ from top to bottom and I knew immediately that my search was over. The auricles and ventricles were almost completely occluded by a cauliflower-like mass growing from the valves.

Verrucose endocarditis, common in pigs but seldom seen in cattle.

'There's what killed your cow, Mr Cranford,' I said.

Cranford aimed his nose at the heart. 'Fiddlesticks! You're not telling me them little things could kill a great beast like that.'

'They're not so little. Big enough to stop the flow of blood. I'm sorry, but there's no doubt about it — your cow died of heart failure.'

'And how about lightning?'

'No sign of it, I'm afraid. You can see for yourself.'

'And what about my eighty pounds?'

'I'm truly sorry about that, but it doesn't alter the facts.'

'Facts! What facts? I've come along this morning and you've shown me nowt to make me change my opinion.'

'Well, there's nothing more I can say. It's a clear-cut case.'

Mr Cranford stiffened in his perching stance. He held his hands against the front of his coat and the fingers and thumbs rubbed together unceasingly as though fondling the beloved bank notes which were slipping away from him. His face, sunk deeper in his collar, appeared still sharper in outline.

Then he turned to me and made a ghastly attempt to smile. And his eyes, trained on my lapels, tried valiantly to inch their way upwards. There was a fleeting instance when they met my gaze before flickering away in alarm.

He drew me to one side and addressed himself to my larynx. There was a wheedling note in the hoarse whisper.

'Now look here, Mr Herriot, we're both men of the world. You know as well as I do that the insurance company can afford this loss a lot better nor me. So why can't you just say it is lightning?'

'Even though I think it isn't?'

'Well, what the hangment does it matter? You can say it is, can't you? Nobody's going to know.'

I scratched my head. 'But what would bother me, Mr Cranford, is that I would know.'

'You would know?' The farmer was mystified.

'That's right. And it's no good — I can't give you a certificate for this cow and that's the end of it.'

Dismay, disbelief, frustration chased across Mr Cranford's features. 'Well, I'll tell you this. I'm not leaving the matter here. I'm going to see your boss about you.' He swung round and pointed at the cow. 'There's no sign of disease there. Trying to tell me it's all due to little things in the heart. You don't know your job — you don't even know what them things are!'

Jeff Mallock removed his unspeakable pipe from his mouth. 'But ah know. It's what ah said. Stagnation o' t'lungs is caused by milk from milk vein getting back into the body. Finally it gets to t'heart and then it's over wi't. Them's milk clots you're looking at.'

Cranford rounded on him. 'Shut up, you great gumph! You're as bad as this feller here. It was lightning killed my good cow. Lightning!' He was almost screaming. Then he controlled himself and spoke quietly to me. 'You'll hear more of this, Mr Knowledge, and I'll just tell you one thing. You'll never walk on to my farm again.' He turned and hurried away with his quick-stepping gait.

I said good morning to Jeff and climbed wearily into my car. Well, everything had worked out just great. If only vetting just consisted of treating sick animals. But it didn't. There were so many other things. I started the engine and drove away.

CHAPTER 29

It didn't take Mr Cranford long to make good his threat. He called at the surgery shortly after lunch the following day and Siegfried and I, enjoying a post-prandial cigarette in the sitting-room, heard the jangle of the door bell. We didn't get up, because most of the farmers walked in after ringing.

The dogs, however, went into their usual routine. They had had a long run on the high moor that morning and had just finished licking out their dinner bowls. Tired and distended, they had collapsed in a snoring heap around Siegfried's feet. There was nothing they wanted more than ten minutes' peace but, dedicated as they were to their self-appointed role of fierce guardians of the house, they did not hesitate. They leaped, baying, from the rug and hurled themselves into the passage.

People often wondered why Siegfried kept five dogs. Not only kept them but took them everywhere with him. Driving on his rounds it was difficult to see him at all among the shaggy heads and waving tails; and anybody approaching the car would recoil in terror from the savage barking and the bared fangs and glaring eyes framed in the windows.

'I cannot for the life of me understand,' Siegfried would declare, thumping his fist on his knee, 'why people keep dogs as pets. A dog should have a useful function. Let it be used for farm work, for shooting, for guiding; but why anybody should keep the things just hanging around the place beats me.'

It was a pronouncement he was continually making, often through a screen of flapping ears and lolling tongues as he sat in his car. His listener would look wonderingly from the huge greyhound to the tiny terrier, from the spaniel to the whippet to the Scottie; but nobody ever asked Siegfried why he kept his own dogs.

I judged that the pack fell upon Mr Cranford about the bend of the passage and many a lesser man would have fled; but I could hear him fighting his way doggedly forward. When he came through the sitting-room door he had removed his hat and was beating the dogs off with it. It wasn't a wise move and the barking rose to a higher pitch. The man's eyes stared and his lips moved continuously, but nothing came through.

Siegfried, courteous as ever, rose and

indicated a chair. His lips, too, were moving, no doubt in a few gracious words of welcome. Mr Cranford flapped his black coat, swooped across the carpet and perched. The dogs sat in a ring round him and yelled up into his face. Usually they collapsed after their exhausting performance but there was something in the look or smell of Mr Cranford that they didn't like.

Siegfried leaned back in his armchair, put his fingers together and assumed a judicial expression. Now and again he nodded understandingly or narrowed his eyes as if taking an interesting point. Practically nothing could be heard from Mr Cranford but occasionally a word or phrase penetrated.

'. . . have a serious complaint to make . . .'
'. . . doesn't know his job . . .'
'. . . can't afford . . . not a rich man . . .'
'. . . these danged dogs . . .'
'. . . won't have 'im again . . .'
'. . . down dog, get bye . . .'
'. . . nowt but robbery . . .'

Siegfried, completely relaxed and apparently oblivious of the din, listened attentively but as the minutes passed I could see the strain beginning to tell on Mr Cranford. His eyes began to start from their sockets and the veins corded on his scrawny neck as he tried to get his message across. Finally it was too much for him; he jumped up and a leaping brown tide bore him to the door. He gave a last defiant cry, lashed out again with his hat and was gone.

Pushing open the dispensary door a few weeks later, I found my boss mixing an ointment. He was working with great care, turning and re-turning the glutinous mass on a marble slab.

'What's this you're doing?' I asked.

Siegfried threw down his spatula and straightened his back. 'Ointment for a boar.' He looked past me at Tristan who had just come in. 'And I don't know why the hell I'm doing it when some people are sitting around on their backsides.' He indicated the spatula. 'Right, Tristan, you can have a go. When you've finished your cigarette, that is.'

His expression softened as Tristan hastily nipped out his Woodbine and began to work away on the slab. 'Pretty stiff concoction, that. Takes a bit of mixing,' Siegfried said with satisfaction, looking at his brother's bent head. 'The back of my neck was beginning to ache with it.'

He turned to me. 'By the way, you'll be interested to hear it's for your old friend Cranford. For that prize boar of his. It's got a nasty sore across its back and he's worried to death about it. Wins him a lot of money at the shows and a blemish there would be disastrous.'

'Cranford's still with us, then.'

'Yes, it's a funny thing, but we can't get rid of him. I don't like losing clients but I'd gladly make an exception of this chap. He won't have you near the place after that lightning job and he makes it very clear he doesn't think much of me either. Tells me I never do his beasts any good — says it would have been a lot better if he'd never called me. And moans like hell when he gets his bill. He's more bother than he's worth and on top of everything he gives me the creeps. But he won't leave — he damn well won't leave.'

'He knows which side his bread's buttered,' I said. 'He gets first-rate service and the moaning is part of the system to keep the bills down.'

'Maybe you're right, but I wish there was a simple way to get rid of him.' He tapped Tristan on the shoulder. 'All right, don't strain yourself. That'll do. Put it into this ointment box and label it: "Apply liberally to the boar's back three times daily, working it well in with the fingers." And post it to Mr Cranford. And while you're on, will you post this faeces sample to the laboratory at Leeds to test for Johne's disease?' He held out a treacle tin brimming with foul-smelling liquid diarrhoea.

It was a common thing to collect such samples and send them away for Johne's tests, worm counts, etc., and there was always one thing all the samples had in common —

they were very large. All that was needed for the tests was a couple of teaspoonfuls but the farmers were lavish in their quantities. They seemed pleasantly surprised that all the vet wanted was a bit of muck from the dung channel; they threw aside their natural caution and shovelled the stuff up cheerfully into the biggest container they could find. They brushed aside all protests; 'take plenty, we've lots of it' was their attitude.

Tristan took hold of the tin gingerly and began to look along the shelves. 'We don't seem to have any of those little glass sample jars.'

'That's right, we're out of them,' said Siegfried. 'I meant to order some more. But never mind — shove the lid on that tin and press it down tight, then parcel it up well in brown paper. It'll travel to the lab all right.'

It took only three days for Mr Cranford's name to come up again. Siegfried was opening the morning mail, throwing the circulars to one side and making a pile of the bills and receipts when he became suddenly very still. He had frozen over a letter on blue notepaper and he sat like a statue till he read it through. At length he raised his head; his face was expressionless. 'James, this is just about the most vitriolic letter I have ever read. It's from Cranford. He's finished with us for good and all and is considering taking legal action against us.'

'What have we done this time?' I asked.

'He accuses us of grossly insulting him and endangering the health of his boar. He says we sent him a treacle tin full of cow shit with instructions to rub it on the boar's back three times daily.'

Tristan, who had been sitting with his eyes half closed, became fully awake. He rose unhurriedly and began to make his way towards the door. His hand was on the knob when his brother's voice thundered out.

'Tristan! Come back here! Sit down — I think we have something to talk about.'

Tristan looked up resolutely, waiting for the storm to break, but Siegfried was unexpectedly calm. His voice was gentle.

'So you've done it again. When will I ever learn that I can't trust you to carry out the simplest task? It wasn't much to ask, was it? Two little parcels to post — hardly a tough assignment. But you managed to botch it. You got the labels wrong, didn't you?'

Tristan wriggled in his chair. 'I'm sorry, I can't think how . . .'

Siegfried held up his hand. 'Oh, don't worry. Your usual luck has come to your aid. With anybody else this bloomer would be catastrophic but with Cranford — it's like divine providence.' He paused for a moment and a dreamy expression crept into his eyes. 'The label said to work it well in with the fingers, I seem to recall. And Mr Cranford says he opened the package at the breakfast table . . . Yes, Tristan, I think you have found the way. This, I do believe, has done it.'

I said, 'But how about the legal action?'

'Oh, I think we can forget about that. Mr Cranford has a great sense of his own dignity. Just think how it would sound in court.' He crumpled the letter and dropped it into the wastepaper basket. 'Well, let's get on with some work.'

He led the way out and stopped abruptly in the passage. He turned to face us. 'There's another thing, of course. I wonder how the lab is making out, testing that ointment for Johne's disease?'

CHAPTER 30

I was really worried about Tricki this time. I had pulled up my car when I saw him in the street with his mistress and I was shocked at his appearance. He had become hugely fat, like a bloated sausage with a leg at each corner. His eyes, bloodshot and rheumy, stared straight ahead and his tongue lolled from his jaws.

Mrs Pumphrey hastened to explain. 'He was so listless, Mr Herriot. He seemed to have no energy. I thought he must be suffering from malnutrition, so I have been giving him some little extras between meals to build him up. Some calf's foot jelly and malt and cod liver oil and a bowl of Horlick's at night to make him sleep — nothing much really.'

'And did you cut down on the sweet things as I told you?'

'Oh, I did for a bit, but he seemed to be so weak. I had to relent. He does love cream cakes and chocolates so. I can't bear to refuse him.'

I looked down again at the little dog. That was the trouble. Tricki's only fault was greed. He had never been known to refuse food; he would tackle a meal at any hour of the day or night. And I wondered about all the things Mrs Pumphrey hadn't mentioned; the pâte on thin biscuits, the fudge, the rich trifles — Tricki loved them all.

'Are you giving him plenty of exercise?'

'Well, he has his little walks with me as you can see, but Hodgkin has been down with lumbago, so there has been no ring-throwing lately.'

I tried to sound severe. 'Now I really mean this. If you don't cut his food right down and give him more exercise he is going to be really ill. You must harden your heart and keep him on a very strict diet.'

Mrs Pumphrey wrung her hands. 'Oh I will, Mr Herriot. I'm sure you are right, but it is so difficult, so very difficult.' She set off, head down, along the road, as if determined to put the new régime into practice immediately.

I watched their progress with growing concern. Tricki was tottering along in his little tweed coat; he had a whole wardrobe of these coats — warm tweed or tartan ones for the cold weather and macintoshes for the wet days. He struggled on, drooping in his harness. I thought it wouldn't be long before I heard from Mrs Pumphrey.

The expected call came within a few days.

Mrs Pumphrey was distraught. Tricki would eat nothing. Refused even his favourite dishes; and besides, he had bouts of vomiting. He spent all his time lying on a rug, panting. Didn't want to go walks, didn't want to do anything.

I had made my plans in advance. The only way was to get Tricki out of the house for a period. I suggested that he be hospitalised for about a fortnight to be kept under observation.

The poor lady almost swooned. She had never been separated from her darling before; she was sure he would pine and die if he did not see her every day.

But I took a firm line. Tricki was very ill and this was the only way to save him; in fact, I thought it best to take him without delay and, followed by Mrs Pumphrey's wailings, I marched out to the car carrying the little dog wrapped in a blanket.

The entire staff was roused and maids rushed in and out bringing his day bed, his night bed, favourite cushions, toys and rubber rings, breakfast bowl, lunch bowl, supper bowl. Realising that my car would never hold all the stuff, I started to drive away. As I moved off, Mrs Pumphrey, with a despairing cry, threw an armful of the little coats through the window. I looked in the mirror before I turned the corner of the drive; everybody was in tears.

Out on the road, I glanced down at the pathetic little animal gasping on the seat by my side. I patted the head and Tricki made a brave effort to wag his tail. 'Poor old lad,' I said, 'you haven't a kick in you but I think I know a cure for you.'

At the surgery, the household dogs surged round me. Tricki looked down at the noisy pack with dull eyes and, when put down, lay motionless on the carpet. The other dogs, after sniffing round him for a few seconds, decided he was an uninteresting object and ignored him.

I made up a bed for him in a warm loose box next to the one where the other dogs slept. For two days I kept an eye on him, giving him no food but plenty of water. At the end of the second day he started to show some interest in his surroundings and on the third he began to whimper when he heard the dogs in the yard.

When I opened the door, Tricki trotted out and was immediately engulfed by Joe the greyhound and his friends. After rolling him over and thoroughly inspecting him, the dogs moved off down the garden. Tricki followed them, rolling slightly with his surplus fat but obviously intrigued.

Later that day, I was present at feeding time. I watched while Tristan slopped the food into the bowls. There was the usual headlong rush followed by the sounds of high-speed eating; every dog knew that if he fell behind the others he was liable to have some competition for the last part of his meal.

When they had finished, Tricki took a walk round the shining bowls, licking casually inside one or two of them. Next day, an extra bowl was put out for him and I was pleased to see him jostling his way towards it.

From then on, his progress was rapid. He had no medicinal treatment of any kind but all day he ran about with the dogs, joining in their friendly scrimmages. He discovered the joys of being bowled over, trampled on and squashed every few minutes. He became an accepted member of the gang, an unlikely, silky little object among the shaggy crew, fighting like a tiger for his share at meal times and hunting rats in the old hen house at night. He had never had such a time in his life.

All the while, Mrs Pumphrey hovered anxiously in the background, ringing a dozen times a day for the latest bulletins. I dodged the questions about whether his cushions were being turned regularly or his correct coat worn according to the weather; but I was able to tell her that the little fellow was out of danger and convalescing rapidly.

The word 'convalescing' seemed to do something to Mrs Pumphrey. She started to bring round fresh eggs, two dozen at a time, to build up Tricki's strength. For a happy period there were two eggs each for breakfast, but when the bottles of sherry began to arrive, the real possibilities of the situation began to dawn on the household.

It was the same delicious vintage that I knew so well and it was to enrich Tricki's blood. Lunch became a ceremonial occasion with two glasses before and several during the meal. Siegfried and Tristan took turns at proposing Tricki's health and the standard of speech-making improved daily. As the sponsor, I was always called upon to reply.

We could hardly believe it when the brandy came. Two bottles of Cordon Bleu, intended to put a final edge on Tricki's constitution. Siegfried dug out some balloon glasses belonging to his mother. I had never seen them before, but for a few nights they saw constant service as the fine spirit was rolled around, inhaled and reverently drunk.

They were days of deep content, starting well with the extra egg in the morning, bolstered up and sustained by the midday sherry and finishing luxuriously round the fire with the brandy.

It was a temptation to keep Tricki on as a permanent guest, but I knew Mrs Pumphrey was suffering and after a fortnight, felt compelled to phone and tell her that the little dog had recovered and was awaiting collection.

Within minutes, about thirty feet of gleaming black metal drew up outside the surgery. The chauffeur opened the door and I could just make out the figure of Mrs Pumphrey almost lost in the interior. Her hands were tightly clasped in front of her; her lips trembled. 'Oh, Mr Herriot, do tell me the truth. Is he really better?'

'Yes, he's fine. There's no need for you to get out of the car — I'll go and fetch him.'

I walked through the house into the garden. A mass of dogs was hurtling round and round the lawn and in their midst, ears flapping, tail waving, was the little golden figure of Tricki. In two weeks he had been transformed into a lithe, hard-muscled animal; he was keeping up well with the pack, stretching out in great bounds, his chest almost brushing the ground.

I carried him back along the passage to the front of the house. The chauffeur was still holding the car door open and when Tricki saw his mistress he took off from my arms in a tremendous leap and sailed into Mrs Pumphrey's lap. She gave a startled 'Ooh!' and then had to defend herself as he swarmed over her, licking her face and barking.

During the excitement, I helped the chauffeur to bring out the beds, toys, cushions, coats and bowls, none of which had been used. As the car moved away, Mrs Pumphrey leaned out of the window. Tears shone in her eyes. Her lips trembled.

'Oh, Mr Herriot,' she cried, 'how can I ever thank you? This is a triumph of surgery!'

CHAPTER 31

I came suddenly and violently awake, my heart thudding and pounding in time with the insistent summons of the telephone. These bedside phones were undoubtedly an improvement on the old system when you had to gallop downstairs and stand shivering with your bare feet on the tiles of the passage; but this explosion a few inches from your ear in the small hours when the body was weak and the resistance low was shattering. I felt sure it couldn't be good for me.

The voice at the other end was offensively cheerful. 'I have a mare on foaling. She doesn't seem to be getting on wi' t'job. Reckon foal must be laid wrong — can you come and give me a hand?'

My stomach contracted to a tight ball. This was just a little bit too much; once out of bed in the middle of the night was bad enough, but twice was unfair, in fact it was sheer cruelty. I had had a hard day and had been glad to crawl between the sheets at midnight.

I had been hauled out at one o'clock to a damned awkward calving and hadn't got back till nearly three. What was the time now? Three fifteen. Good God, I had only had a few minutes' sleep. And a foaling! Twice as difficult as a calving as a rule. What a life! What a bloody awful life!

I muttered into the receiver, 'Right, Mr Dixon, I'll come straight away' and shuffled across the room, yawning and stretching, feeling the ache in my shoulders and arms. I looked down at the pile of clothing in the chair; I had taken them off, put them on again, taken them off already tonight and something in me rebelled at the thought of putting them on yet again. With a weary grunt I took my macintosh from the back of the door and donned it over my pyjamas, went downstairs to where my Wellingtons stood outside the dispensary door and stuck my feet into them. It was a warm night, what was the point of getting dressed up; I'd only have to strip off again at the farm.

I opened the back door and trailed slowly down the long garden, my tired mind only faintly aware of the fragrance that came from the darkness. I reached the yard at the bottom, opened the double doors into the lane and got the car out of the garage. In the silent town the buildings glowed whitely as the headlights swept across the shuttered shop fronts, the tight-drawn curtains. Everybody was asleep. Everybody except me, James Herriot, creeping sore and exhausted towards another spell of hard labour. Why the hell had I ever decided to become a country vet? I must have been crazy to pick a job where you worked seven days a week and through the night as well. Sometimes I felt as though the practice was a malignant, living entity; testing me, trying me out; putting the pressure on more and more to see just when at what point I would drop down dead.

It was a completely unconscious reaction which hoisted me from my bath of self-pity and left me dripping on the brink, regarding the immediate future with a return of some of my natural optimism. For one thing, Dixon's place was down at the foot of the Dale just off the main road and they had that unusual luxury, electric light in the buildings. And I couldn't be all that tired; not at the age of twenty-four with all my faculties unimpaired. I'd take a bit of killing yet.

I smiled to myself and relapsed into the state of half suspended animation which was normal to me at these times; a sleepy blanketing of all the senses except those required for the job in hand. Many times over the past months I had got out of bed, driven far into the country, done my job efficiently and returned to bed without ever having been fully awake.

I was right about Dixon's. The graceful

Clydesdale mare was in a well-lit loose box and I laid out my ropes and instruments with a feeling of deep thankfulness. As I tipped antiseptic into the steaming bucket I watched the mare straining and paddling her limbs. The effort produced nothing; there were no feet protruding from the vulva. There was almost certainly a malpresentation.

Still thinking hard, I removed my macintosh and was jerked out of my reverie by a shout of laughter from the farmer. 'God 'elp us, what's this, the Fol-de-rols?'

I looked down at my pyjamas which were pale blue with an arresting broad red stripe. 'This, Mr Dixon,' I replied with dignity, 'is my night attire. I didn't bother to dress.'

'Oh, I see now.' The farmer's eyes glinted impishly. 'I'm sorry, but I thought I'd got the wrong chap for a second. I saw a feller just like you at Blackpool last year — same suit exactly, but he 'ad a stripy top hat too and a stick. Did a champion little dance.'

'Can't oblige you, I'm afraid,' I said with a wan smile. 'I'm just not in the mood right now.'

I stripped off, noting with interest the deep red grooves caused by the calf's teeth a couple of hours ago. Those teeth had been like razors, peeling off neat little rolls of skin every time I pushed my arm past them.

The mare trembled as I felt my way inside her. Nothing, nothing, then just a tail and the pelvic bones and the body and hind legs disappearing away beyond my reach. Breech presentation; easy in the cow for a man who knew his job but tricky in the mare because of the tremendous length of the foal's legs.

It took me a sweating, panting half hour with ropes and a blunt hook on the end of a flexible cane to bring the first leg round. The second leg came more easily and the mare seemed to know there was no obstruction now. She gave a great heave and the foal shot out on to the straw with myself, arms around its body, sprawling on top of it. To my delight I felt the small form jerking convulsively; I had felt no movement while I was working and had decided that it was dead, but the foal was very much alive, shaking its head and snorting out the placental fluid it had inhaled during its delayed entry.

When I had finished towelling myself I turned to see the farmer, with an abnormally straight face, holding out my colourful jacket like a valet. 'Allow me, sir,' he said gravely.

'O.K., O.K.,' I laughed, 'I'll get properly dressed next time.' As I was putting my things in the car boot the farmer carelessly threw a parcel on to the back seat.

'Bit o' butter for you,' he muttered. When I started the engine he bent level with the window. 'I think a bit about that mare and I've been badly wanting a foal out of her. Thank ye, lad, thank ye very much.'

He waved as I moved away and I heard his parting cry. 'You did all right for a Kentucky Minstrel!'

I leaned back in my seat and peered through heavy lids at the empty road unwinding in the pale morning light. The sun had come up — a dark crimson ball hanging low over the misted fields. I felt utterly content, warm with the memory of the foal trying to struggle on to its knees, its absurdly long legs still out of control. Grand that the little beggar had been alive after all — there was something desolate about delivering a lifeless creature.

The Dixon farm was in the low country where the Dale widened out and gave on to the great plain of York. I had to cross a loop of the busy road which connected the West Riding with the industrial North East. A thin tendril of smoke rose from the chimney of the all night transport café which stood there and as I slowed down to take the corner a faint but piercing smell of cooking found its way into the car; the merest breath but rich in the imagery of fried sausages and beans and tomatoes and chips.

God, I was starving. I looked at my watch; five fifteen, I wouldn't be eating for a long time yet. I turned in among the lorries on the broad strip of tarmac.

Hastening towards the still lighted building I decided that I wouldn't be greedy. Nothing spectacular, just a nice sandwich. I had been

317

here a few times before and the sandwiches were very good; and I deserved some nourishment after my hard night.

I stepped into the warm interior where groups of lorry drivers sat behind mounded plates, but as I crossed the floor the busy clatter died and was replaced by a tense silence. A fat man in a leather jacket sat transfixed, a loaded fork half way to his mouth, while his neighbour, gripping a huge mug of tea in an oily hand, stared with bulging eyes at my ensemble.

It occurred to me then that bright red striped pyjamas and Wellingtons might seem a little unusual in those surroundings and I hastily buttoned my macintosh which had been billowing behind me. Even closed, it was on the short side and at least a foot of pyjama leg showed above my boots.

Resolutely I strode over to the counter. An expressionless blonde bulging out of a dirty white overall on the breast pocket of which was inscribed 'Dora' regarded me blankly.

'A ham sandwich and a cup of Bovril, please,' I said huskily. As the blonde put a teaspoonful of Bovril into a cup and filled it with a hissing jet of hot water I was uncomfortably aware of the silence behind me and of the battery of eyes focused on my legs. On my right I could just see the leather-jacketed man. He filled his mouth and chewed reflectively for a few moments.

'Takes all kinds, don't it, Ernest?' he said in a judicial tone.

'Does indeed, Kenneth, does indeed,' replied his companion.

'Would you say, Ernest, that this is what the Yorkshire country gentleman is wearing this spring?'

'Could be, Kenneth, could be.'

Listening to the titters from the rear, I concluded that these two were the accepted café wags. Best to eat up quickly and get out. Dora pushed the thickly meated sandwich across the counter and spoke with all the animation of a sleep walker. 'That'll be a shillin'.'

I slipped my hand inside my coat and encountered the pocketless flannelette beneath. God almighty, my money was in my trousers back in Darrowby! A wave of sickly horror flooded me as I began a frantic, meaningless search through my macintosh.

I looked wildly at the blonde and saw her slip the sandwich under the counter. 'Look, I've come out without any money. I've been in here before — do you know who I am?'

Dora gave a single bored shake of her head.

'Well, never mind,' I babbled, 'I'll pop in with the money next time I'm passing.'

Dora's expression did not alter but she raised one eyebrow fractionally; she made no effort to retrieve the sandwich from its hiding place.

Escape was the only thing in my mind now. Desperately I sipped at the scalding fluid.

Kenneth pushed back his plate and began to pick his teeth with a match. 'Ernest,' he said as though coming to a weighty conclusion, 'it's my opinion that this 'ere gentleman is eccentric.'

'Eccentric?' Ernest sniggered into his tea. 'Bloody daft, more like.'

'Ah, but not so daft, Ernest. Not daft enough to pay for 'is grub.'

'You 'ave a point there, Kenneth, a definite point.'

'You bet I have. He's enjoying a nice cup of Bovril on the house and if 'e hadn't mistimed his fumble he'd be at the sandwich too.

'Dora moved a bit sharpish for 'im there — another five seconds and he'd have had 'is choppers in the ham.'

'True, true,' muttered Ernest, seemingly content with his role of straight man.

Kenneth put away his match, sucked his teeth noisily and leaned back. 'There's another possibility we 'aven't considered. He could be on the run.'

'Escaped convict, you mean, Kenneth?'

'I do, Ernest, I do indeed.'

'But them fellers allus have arrows on their uniforms.'

'Ah, some of 'em do. But I 'eard somewhere that some of the prisons is going in for stripes now.'

I had had enough. Tipping the last searing drops of Bovril down my throat I made headlong for the door. As I stepped out into the early sunshine Kenneth's final pronouncement reached me.

'Prob'ly got away from a working party. Look at them Wellingtons . . .'

CHAPTER 32

I could see that Mr Handshaw didn't believe a word I was saying. He looked down at his cow and his mouth tightened into a stubborn line.

'Broken pelvis? You're trying to tell me she'll never get up n'more? Why, look at her chewing her cud! I'll tell you this, young man — me dad would've soon got her up if he'd been alive today.'

I had been a veterinary surgeon for a year now and I had learned a few things. One of them was that farmers weren't easy men to convince — especially Yorkshire Dalesmen.

And that bit about his dad. Mr Handshaw was in his fifties and I suppose there was something touching about his faith in his late father's skill and judgement. But I could have done very nicely without it.

It had acted as an additional irritant in a case in which I felt I had troubles enough. Because there are few things which get more deeply under a vet's skin than a cow which won't get up. To the layman it may seem strange that an animal can be apparently cured of its original ailment and yet be unable to rise from the floor, but it happens. And it can be appreciated that a completely recumbent milk cow has no future.

The case had started when my boss, Siegfried Farnon, who owned the practice in the little Dales market town of Darrowby, sent me to a milk fever. This suddenly occurring calcium deficiency attacks high yielding animals just after calving and causes collapse and progressive coma. When I first saw Mr Handshaw's cow she was stretched out motionless on her side, and I had to look carefully to make sure she wasn't dead.

But I got out my bottles of calcium with an airy confidence because I had been lucky enough to qualify just about the time when the profession had finally got on top of this hitherto fatal condition. The breakthrough had come many years earlier with inflation of the udder and I still carried a little blowing-up outfit around with me (the farmers used bicycle pumps), but with the advent of calcium therapy one could bask in a cheap glory by jerking an animal back from imminent death within minutes. The skill required was minimal but it looked very very good.

By the time I had injected the two bottles — one into the vein, the other under the skin

— and Mr Handshaw had helped me roll the cow on to her chest the improvement was already obvious; she was looking about her and shaking her head as if wondering where she had been for the last few hours. I felt sure that if I had had the time to hang about for a bit I could see her on her feet. But other jobs were waiting.

'Give me a ring if she isn't up by dinner time,' I said, but it was a formality. I was pretty sure I wouldn't be seeing her again.

When the farmer rang at midday to say she was still down it was just a pinprick. Some cases needed an extra bottle — it would be all right. I went out and injected her again.

I wasn't really worried when I learned she hadn't got up the following day, but Mr Handshaw, hands deep in pockets, shoulders hunched as he stood over his cow, was grievously disappointed at my lack of success.

'It's time t'awd bitch was up. She's doin' no good laid there. Surely there's summat you can do. I poured a bottle of water into her lug this morning but even that hasn't shifted her.'

'You what?'

'Poured some cold water down her lug 'ole. Me dad used to get 'em up that way and he was a very clever man with stock was me dad.'

'I've no doubt he was,' I said primly. 'But I really think another injection is more likely to help her.'

The farmer watched glumly as I ran yet another bottle of calcium under the skin. The procedure had lost its magic for him.

As I put the apparatus away I did my best to be hearty. 'I shouldn't worry. A lot of them stay down for a day or two — you'll probably find her walking about in the morning.'

The phone rang just before breakfast and my stomach contracted sharply as I heard Mr Handshaw's voice. It was heavy with gloom. 'Well, she's no different. Lyin' there eating her 'ead off, but never offers to rise. What are you going to do now?'

What indeed, I thought as I drove out to the farm. The cow had been down for forty-eight hours now — I didn't like it a bit.

The farmer went into the attack immediately. 'Me dad allus used to say they had a worm in the tail when they stayed down like this. He said if you cut tail end off it did the trick.'

My spirits sagged lower. I had had trouble with this myth before. The insidious thing was that the people who still practised this relic of barbarism could often claim that it worked because, after the end of the tail had been chopped off, the pain of the stump touching the ground forced many a sulky cow to scramble to her feet.

'There's no such thing as worm in the tail, Mr Handshaw,' I said. 'And don't you think it's a cruel business, cutting off a cow's tail? I hear the R.S.P.C.A. had a man in court last week over a job like that.'

The farmer narrowed his eyes. Clearly he thought I was hedging. 'Well, if you won't do that, what the hangment are you going to do? We've got to get this cow up somehow.'

I took a deep breath. 'Well, I'm sure she's got over the milk fever because she's eating well and looks quite happy. It must be a touch of posterior paralysis that's keeping her down. There's no point in giving her any more calcium so I'm going to try this stimulant injection.' I filled the syringe with a feeling of doom. I hadn't a scrap of faith in the stimulant injection but I just couldn't do nothing. I was scraping the barrel out now.

I was turning to go when Mr Handshaw called after me. 'Hey, Mister, I remember summat else me dad used to do. Shout in their lugs. He got many a cow up that way. I'm not very strong in the voice — how about you having a go?'

It was a bit late to stand on my dignity. I went over to the animal and seized her by the ear. Inflating my lungs to the utmost I bent down and bawled wildly into the hairy depths. The cow stopped chewing for a moment and looked at me enquiringly, then her eyes drooped and she returned contentedly to her cudding. 'We'll give her another day,' I said wearily. 'And if she's still down tomorrow we'll have a go at lifting her. Could you get a few of your neighbours to give us a hand?'

Driving round my other cases that day I felt tied up inside with sheer frustration. Damn and blast the thing! What the hell was keeping her down? And what else could I do? This was 1938 and my resources were limited. Thirty years later there are still milk fever cows which won't get up but the vet has a much wider armoury if the calcium has failed to do the job. The excellent Bagshaw hoist which clamps on to the pelvis and raises the animal in a natural manner, the phosphorus injections, even the electric goad which administers a swift shock when applied to the rump and sends many a comfortably ensconced cow leaping to her feet with an offended bellow.

As I expected, the following day brought no change and as I got out of the car in Mr Handshaw's yard I was surrounded by a group of his neighbours. They were in festive mood, grinning, confident, full of helpful advice as farmers always are with somebody else's animals.

There was much laughter and legpulling as we drew sacks under the cow's body and a flood of weird suggestions to which I tried to close my ears. When we all finally gave a concerted heave and lifted her up, the result was predictable; she just hung there placidly with her legs dangling whilst her owner leaned against the wall watching us with deepening gloom.

After a lot of puffing and grunting we lowered the inert body and everybody looked at me for the next move. I was hunting round desperately in my mind when Mr Handshaw piped up again.

'Me dad used to say a strange dog would allus get a cow up.'

There were murmurs of assent from the assembled farmers and immediate offers of dogs. I tried to point out that one would be enough but my authority had dwindled and anyway everybody seemed anxious to demonstrate their dogs' cow-raising potential. There was a sudden excited exodus and even Mr Smedley the village shopkeeper pedalled off at frantic speed for his border terrier. It seemed only minutes before the byre was alive with snapping, snarling curs but the cow ignored them all except to wave her horns warningly at the ones which came too close.

The flash-point came when Mr Handshaw's own dog came in from the fields where he had been helping to round up the sheep. He was a skinny, hard-bitten little creature with lightning reflexes and a short temper. He stalked, stiff-legged and bristling, into the byre, took a single astounded look at the pack of foreigners on his territory and flew into action with silent venom.

Within seconds the finest dog fight I had

ever seen was in full swing and I stood back and surveyed the scene with a feeling of being completely superfluous. The yells of the farmers rose above the enraged yapping and growling. One intrepid man leaped into the mêlée and reappeared with a tiny Jack Russell hanging on determinedly to the heel of his Wellington boot. Mr Reynolds of Clover Hill was rubbing the cow's tail between two short sticks and shouting 'Cush! Cush!' and as I watched helplessly a total stranger tugged at my sleeve and whispered: 'Hasta tried a teaspoonful of Jeyes' Fluid in a pint of old beer every two hours?'

It seemed to me that all the forces of black magic had broken through and were engulfing me and that my slender resources of science had no chance of shoring up the dyke. I don't know how I heard the creaking sound above the din — probably because I was bending low over Mr Reynolds in an attempt to persuade him to desist from his tail rubbing. But at that moment the cow shifted her position slightly and I distinctly heard it. It came from the pelvis.

It took me some time to attract attention — I think everybody had forgotten I was there — but finally the dogs were separated and secured with innumerable lengths of binder twine, everybody stopped shouting, Mr Reynolds was pulled away from the tail and I had the stage.

I addressed myself to Mr Handshaw. 'Would you get me a bucket of hot water, some soap and a towel, please.'

He trailed off, grumbling, as though he didn't expect much from the new gambit. My stock was definitely low.

I stripped off my jacket, soaped my arms and pushed a hand into the cow's rectum until I felt the hard bone of the pubis. Gripping it through the wall of the rectum I looked up at my audience. 'Will two of you get hold of the hook bones and rock the cow gently from side to side.'

Yes, there it was again, no mistake about it. I could both hear and feel it — a looseness, a faint creaking, almost a grating.

I got up and washed my arm. 'Well, I know why your cow won't get up — she has a broken pelvis. Probably did it during the first night when she was staggering about with the milk fever. I should think the nerves are damaged, too. It's hopeless, I'm afraid.' Even though I was dispensing bad news it was a relief to come up with something rational.

Mr Handshaw stared at me. 'Hopeless? How's that?'

'I'm sorry,' I said, 'but that's how it is. The only thing you can do is get her off to the butcher. She has no power in her hind legs. She'll never get up again.'

That was when Mr Handshaw really blew his top and started a lengthy speech. He wasn't really unpleasant or abusive but firmly pointed out my shortcomings and bemoaned again the tragic fact that his dad was not there to put everything right. The other farmers stood in a wide-eyed ring, enjoying every word.

At the end of it I took myself off. There was nothing more I could do and anyway Mr Handshaw would have to come round to my way of thinking. Time would prove me right.

I thought of that cow as soon as I awoke next morning. It hadn't been a happy episode but at least I did feel a certain peace in the knowledge that there were no more doubts. I knew what was wrong, I knew that there was no hope. There was nothing more to worry about.

I was surprised when I heard Mr Handshaw's voice on the phone so soon. I had thought it would take him two or three days to realise he was wrong.

'Is that Mr Herriot? Aye, well, good mornin' to you. I'm just ringing to tell you that me cow's up on her legs and doing fine.'

I gripped the receiver tightly with both hands.

'What? What's that you say?'

'I said me cow's up. Found her walking about byre this morning, fit as a fiddle. You'd think there'd never been owt the matter with her.' He paused for a few moments then spoke with grave deliberation like a disapproving schoolmaster. 'And you stood there and looked at me and said she'd never get up n'more.'

'But . . . but . . .'

'Ah, you're wondering how I did it? Well, I just happened to remember another old trick of me dad's. I went round to t'butcher and got a fresh-killed sheep skin and put it on her back. Had her up in no time — you'll 'ave to come round and see her. Wonderful man was me dad.'

Blindly I made my way into the dining-room. I had to consult my boss about this. Siegfried's sleep had been broken by a 3 a.m. calving and he looked a lot older than his thirty-odd years. He listened in silence as he finished his breakfast then pushed away his plate and poured a last cup of coffee. 'Hard luck, James. The old sheep skin, eh? Funny thing — you've been in the Dales over a year now and never come across that one. Suppose it must be going out of fashion a bit now but you know it has a grain of sense behind it like a lot of these old remedies. You can imagine there's a lot of heat generated under a fresh sheep skin and it acts like a great hot poultice on the back — really tickles them up after a while, and if a cow is lying there out of sheer cussedness she'll often get up just to get rid of it.'

'But damn it, how about the broken pelvis? I tell you it was creaking and wobbling all over the place!'

'Well, James, you're not the first to have been caught that way. Sometimes the pelvic ligaments don't tighten up for a few days after calving and you get this effect.'

'Oh God,' I moaned, staring down at the table cloth. 'What a bloody mess I've made of the whole thing.'

'Oh, you haven't really.' Siegfried lit a cigarette and leaned back in his chair. 'That old cow was probably toying with the idea of getting up for a walk just when old Handshaw dumped the skin on her back. She could just as easily have done it after one of your injections and then you'd have got the credit. Don't you remember what I told you when you first came here? There's a very fine dividing line between looking a real smart vet on the one hand and an immortal fool on the other. This sort of thing happens to us all, so forget it, James.'

But forgetting wasn't so easy. That cow became a celebrity in the district. Mr Handshaw showed her with pride to the postman, the policeman, corn merchants, lorry drivers, fertiliser salesmen, Ministry of Agriculture officials and they all told me about it frequently with pleased smiles. Mr Handshaw's speech was always the same, delivered, they said, in ringing, triumphant tones:

'There's the cow that Mr Herriot said would never get up n'more!'

I'm sure there was no malice behind the farmer's actions. He had put one over on the young clever-pants vet and nobody could blame him for preening himself a little. And in a way I did that cow a good turn; I considerably extended her life span, because Mr Handshaw kept her long beyond her normal working period just as an exhibit. Years after she had stopped giving more than a couple of gallons of milk a day she was still grazing happily in the field by the roadside.

She had one curiously upturned horn and was easy to recognise. I often pulled up my car and looked wistfully over the wall at the cow that would never get up n'more.

CHAPTER 33

Siegfried came away from the telephone; his face was expressionless. 'That was Mrs Pumphrey. She wants you to see her pig.'

'Peke, you mean,' I said.

'No, pig. She has a six-week-old pig she wants you to examine for soundness.'

I laughed sheepishly. My relations with the elderly widow's Peke was a touchy subject. 'All right, all right, don't start again. What did she really want? Is Tricki Woo's bottom playing him up again?'

'James,' said Siegfried gravely. 'It is unlike you to doubt my word in this way. I will repeat the message from Mrs Pumphrey and then I shall expect you to act upon it immediately and without further question. The lady informed me that she has become the owner of a six-week-old piglet and she wants the animal thoroughly vetted. You know how I feel about these examinations and I don't want the job scamped in any way. I should pay particular attention to its wind — have it well galloped round a paddock before you get your stethoscope on it and for heaven's sake don't miss anything obvious like curbs or ringbones. I think I'd take its height while you're about it; you'll find the measuring stick in . . .'

His words trailed on as I hurried down the passage. This was a bit baffling; I usually had a bit of leg-pulling to stand ever since I became Tricki the Peke's adopted uncle and received regular presents and letters and signed photographs from him, but Siegfried wasn't in the habit of flogging the joke to this extent. The idea of Mrs Pumphrey with a pig was unthinkable; there was no room in her elegant establishment for livestock. Oh, he must have got it wrong somehow.

But he hadn't. Mrs Pumphrey received me with a joyful cry. 'Oh, Mr Herriot, isn't it wonderful! I have the most darling little pig. I was visiting some cousins who are farmers and I picked him out. He will be such company for Tricki — you know how I worry about his being an only dog.'

I shook my head vigorously in bewilderment as I crossed the oak-panelled hall. My visits here were usually associated with a degree of fantasy but I was beginning to feel out of my depth.

'You mean you actually have this pig in the house?'

'But of course.' Mrs Pumphrey looked

surprised. 'He's in the kitchen. Come and see him.'

I had been in this kitchen a few times and had been almost awestruck by its shining spotlessness; the laboratory look of the tiled walls and floors, the gleaming surfaces of sink unit, cooker, refrigerator. Today, a cardboard box occupied one corner and inside I could see a tiny pig; standing on his hind legs, his forefeet resting on the rim, he was looking round him appreciatively at his new surroundings.

The elderly cook had her back to us and did not look round when we entered; she was chopping carrots and hurling them into a saucepan with, I thought, unnecessary vigour.

'Isn't he adorable!' Mrs Pumphrey bent over and tickled the little head. 'It's so exciting having a pig of my very own! Mr Herriot, I have decided to call him Nugent.'

I swallowed. 'Nugent?' The cook's broad back froze into immobility.

'Yes, after my great uncle Nugent. He was a little pink man with tiny eyes and a snub nose. The resemblance is striking.'

'I see,' I said, and the cook started her splashing again.

For a few moments I was at a loss; the ethical professional man in me rebelled at the absurdity of examining this obviously healthy little creature. In fact I was on the point of saying that he looked perfectly all right to me when Mrs Pumphrey spoke.

'Come now, Nugent,' she said, 'You must be a good boy and let your Uncle Herriot look at you.'

That did it. Stifling my finer feelings I seized the string-like tail and held Nugent almost upside down as I took his temperature. I then solemnly auscultated his heart and lungs, peered into his eyes, ran my fingers over his limbs and flexed his joints.

The cook's back radiated stiff disapproval but I carried on doggedly. Having a canine nephew, I had found, carried incalculable advantages; it wasn't only the frequent gifts — and I could still taste the glorious kippers Tricki had posted to me from Whitby — it was the vein of softness in my rough life, the sherry before lunch, the warmth and luxury of Mrs Pumphrey's fireside. The way I saw it, if a piggy nephew of the same type had been thrown in my path then Uncle Herriot was going to be the last man to interfere with the inscrutable workings of fate.

The examination over, I turned to Mrs Pumphrey who was anxiously awaiting the verdict. 'Sound in all respects,' I said briskly. 'In fact you've got a very fine pig there. But there's just one thing — he can't live in the house.'

For the first time the cook turned towards me and I read a mute appeal in her face. I could sympathise with her because the excretions of the pig are peculiarly volatile and even such a minute specimen as Nugent had already added his own faint pungency to the atmosphere in the kitchen.

Mrs Pumphrey was appalled at the idea at first but when I assured her that he wouldn't catch pneumonia and in fact would be happier and healthier outside, she gave way.

An agricultural joiner was employed to build a palatial sty in a corner of the garden; it had a warm sleeping apartment on raised boards and an outside run. I saw Nugent installed in it, curled up blissfully in a bed of clean straw. His trough was filled twice daily with the best meal and he was never short of an extra titbit such as a juicy carrot or some cabbage leaves. Every day he was allowed out to play and spent a boisterous hour frisking round the garden with Tricki.

In short, Nugent had it made, but it couldn't have happened to a nicer pig; because, though most of his species have an unsuspected strain of friendliness, this was developed in Nugent to an extraordinary degree. He just liked people and over the next few months his character flowered under the constant personal contact with humans.

I often saw him strolling companionably in the garden with Mrs Pumphrey and in his pen he spent much of the time standing upright with his cloven feet against the wire netting, waiting eagerly for his next visitor.

Pigs grow quickly and he soon left the pink baby stage behind, but his charm was undiminished. His chief delight was to have his back scratched; he would grunt deeply, screwing up his eyes in ecstasy, then gradually his legs would start to buckle until finally he toppled over on his side.

Nugent's existence was sunny and there was only one cloud in the sky; old Hodgkin, the gardener, whose attitude to domestic pets had been permanently soured by having to throw rubber rings for Tricki every day, now found himself appointed personal valet to a pig. It was his duty to feed and bed down Nugent and to supervise his play periods. The idea of doing all this for a pig who was never ever going to be converted into pork pies must have been nearly insupportable for the old countryman; the harsh lines on his face deepened whenever he took hold of the meal bucket.

On the first of my professional visits to his charge he greeted me gloomily with 'Hasta come to see Nudist?' I knew Hodgkin well enough to realise the impossibility of any whimsical wordplay; it was a genuine attempt to grasp the name and throughout my nephew's long career he remained 'Nudist' to the old man.

There is one memory of Nugent which I treasure. The telephone rang one day just after lunch; it was Mrs Pumphrey and I knew by the stricken voice that something momentous had happened; it was the same voice which had described Tricki Woo's unique symptoms of flop-bott and crackerdog.

'Oh, Mr Herriot, thank heavens you are in. It's Nugent! I'm afraid he's terribly ill.'

'Really? I'm sorry to hear that. What's he doing?'

There was a silence at the other end except for gasping breathing then Mrs Pumphrey spoke again. 'Well, he can't manage . . . he can't do . . . do his little jobs.'

I was familiar with her vocabulary of big jobs and little jobs. 'You mean he can't pass his urine?'

'Well . . . well . . .' she was obviously confused. 'Not properly.'

'That's strange,' I said. 'Is he eating all right?'

'I think so, but . . .' then she suddenly blurted out: 'Oh, Mr Herriot, I'm so terribly worried! I've heard of men being dreadfully ill . . . just like this. It's a gland, isn't it?'

'Oh, you needn't worry about that. Pigs don't have that trouble and anyway, I think four months is a bit young for hypertrophy of the prostate.'

'Oh, I'm so glad, but something is . . . stopping it. You will come, won't you!'

'I'm leaving now.'

I had quite a long wait outside Nugent's pen. He had grown into a chunky little porker

341

and grunted amiably as he surveyed me through the netting. Clearly he expected some sort of game and, growing impatient, he performed a few stiff-legged little gallops up and down the run.

I had almost decided that my visit was fruitless when Mrs Pumphrey, who had been pacing up and down, wringing her hands, stopped dead and pointed a shaking finger at the pig.

'Oh God,' she breathed. 'There! There! There it is now!' All the colour had drained from her face leaving her deathly pale. 'Oh, it's awful! I can't look any longer.' With a moan she turned away and buried her face in her hands.

I scrutinised Nugent closely. He had halted in mid gallop and was contentedly relieving himself by means of the intermittent spurting jets of the normal male pig.

I turned to Mrs Pumphrey. 'I really can't see anything wrong there.'

'But he's . . . he's . . .' she still didn't dare to look. 'He's doing it in . . . in fits and starts!'

I had had considerable practice at keeping a straight face in Mrs Pumphrey's presence and it stood me in good stead now.

'But they all do it that way, Mrs Pumphrey.'

She half turned and looked tremblingly out of the corner of her eye at Nugent. 'You mean . . . all boy pigs . . . ?'

'Every single boy pig I have ever known has

done it like that.'

'Oh . . . Oh . . . how odd, how very odd.' The poor lady fanned herself with her handkerchief. Her colour had come back in a positive flood.

To cover her confusion I became very business-like. 'Yes, yes indeed. Lots of people make the same mistake, I assure you. Ah well, I suppose I'd better be on my way now — it's been nice to see the little fellow looking so well and happy.'

Nugent enjoyed a long and happy life and more than fulfilled my expectations of him; he was every bit as generous as Tricki with his presents and, as with the little Peke, I was able to salve my conscience with the knowledge that I was really fond of him. As always, Siegfried's sardonic attitude made things a little uncomfortable; I had suffered in the past when I got the signed photographs from the little dog — but I never dared let him see the one from the pig.

CHAPTER 34

Angus Grier M.R.C.V.S. was never pretty to look at, but the sight of him propped up in bed, his mottled, pop-eyed face scowling above a pink quilted bed jacket was enough to daunt the bravest. Especially at eight in the morning when I usually had the first of my daily audiences with him.

'You're late again,' he said, his voice grating. 'Can ye no' get out of your bed in the morning? I've told you till I'm tired that I want ye out on the road by eight o'clock.'

As I mumbled apologies he tugged fretfully at the counterpane and looked me up and down with deepening distaste. 'And another thing, that's a terrible pair o' breeches you're wearing. If you must wear breeches to your work, for heaven's sake go and get a pair made at a proper tailor. There's nae cut about those things at all — they're not fit to be worn by a veterinary surgeon.'

The knife really went in then. I was attached to those breeches. I had paid thirty shillings for them at the Army and Navy Stores and cherished a private conviction that they gave me a certain air. And Grier's attack on them was all the more wounding when I considered that the man was almost certainly getting my services free; Siegfried, I felt sure, would wave aside any offers of payment.

I had been here a week and it seemed like a lifetime. Somewhere, far back, I knew, there had been a brighter, happier existence but the memory was growing dim. Siegfried had been sincerely apologetic that morning back in Darrowby.

'James, I have a letter here from Grier of Brawton. It seems he was castrating a colt and the thing threw itself on top of him; he has a couple of cracked ribs. Apparently his assistant walked out on him recently, so there's nobody to run his practice. He wants me to send you along there for a week or two.'

'Oh no! There's a mistake somewhere. He doesn't like me.'

'He doesn't like anybody. But there's no mistake, it's down here — and honestly, what can I do?'

'But the only time I met him he worked me into a horrible rubber suit and made me look a right chump.'

Siegfried smiled sadly. 'I remember, James, I remember. He's a mean old devil and I hate to do this to you, but I can't turn him down, can I?'

At the time I couldn't believe it. The whole idea was unreal. But it was real enough now as I stood at the foot of Grier's bed listening to him ranting away. He was at me again.

'Another thing — my wife tells me you didna eat your porridge. Did you not like it?'

I shuffled my feet. 'Oh yes, it was very nice. I just didn't feel hungry this morning.' I had pushed the tasteless mass about with my spoon and done my best with it but it had defeated me in the end.

'There's something wrong with a man that canna eat his good food.' Grier peered at me suspiciously then held out a slip of paper. 'Here's a list of your visits for this morning. There's a good few so you'll no' have to waste your time getting round. This one here of Adamson's of Grenton — a prolapse of the cervix in a cow. What would you do about that, think ye?'

I put my hand in my pocket, got hold of my pipe then dropped it back again. Grier didn't like smoking.

'Well, I'd give her an epidural anaesthetic, replace the prolapse and fasten it in with retention sutures through the vulva.'

'Havers, man, havers!' snorted Grier. 'What a lot of twaddle. There's no need for a' that. It'll just be constipation that's doing it. Push the thing back, build the cow up with some boards under her hind feet and put her on to linseed oil for a few days.'

'Surely it'll come out again if I don't stitch it in?' I said.

'Na, na, na, not at all,' Grier cried angrily. 'Just you do as I tell you now. I ken more about this than you.'

He probably did. He should, anyway — he had been qualified for thirty years and I was starting my second. I looked at him glowering from his pillow and pondered for a moment on the strange fact of our uncomfortable relationship. A Yorkshireman listening to the two outlandish accents — Grier's rasping Aberdeen, my glottal Clydeside — might have expected that some sort of rapport would exist between us, if only on national grounds. But there was none.

'Right, just as you say.' I left the room and went downstairs to gather up my equipment.

As I set off on the round I had the same feeling as every morning — relief at getting out of the house. I had had to go flat out all week to get through the work but I had enjoyed it. Farmers are nearly always prepared to make allowances for a young man's inexperience and Grier's clients had treated me kindly, but I still had to come back to that joyless establishment for meals and it was becoming more and more wearing.

Mrs Grier bothered me just as much as her husband. She was a tight-lipped woman of amazing thinness and she kept a spartan board in which soggy porridge figured prominently. It was porridge for breakfast, porridge for supper and, in between, a miserable procession of watery stews, anaemic mince and nameless soups. Nothing she cooked ever tasted of anything. Angus Grier had come to Yorkshire thirty years ago, a penniless Scot just like myself, and acquired a lucrative practice by the classical expedient of marrying the boss's daughter; so he got a good living handed to him on a plate, but he also got Mrs Grier.

It seemed to me that she felt she was still in charge — probably because she had always lived in this house with its memories of her father who had built up the practice. Other people would seem like interlopers and I could understand how she felt; after all, she was childless, she didn't have much of a life and she had Angus Grier for a husband. I could feel sorry for her.

But that didn't help because I just couldn't get her out of my hair; she hung over my every move like a disapproving spectre. When I came back from a round she was always there with a barrage of questions. 'Where have you been all this time?' or 'I wondered wherever you'd got to, were you lost?' or 'There's an urgent case waiting. Why are you always so slow?' Maybe she thought I'd nipped into a cinema for an hour or two.

There was a pretty full small animal surgery every night and she had a nasty habit of lurking just outside the door so that she could listen to what I was saying to the clients. She really came into her own in the dispensary where she watched me narrowly, criticising my prescriptions and constantly pulling me up for being extravagant with the drugs. 'You're putting in far too much chlorodyne — don't you know it's very expensive?'

I developed a deep sympathy for the assistant who had fled without warning; jobs were hard to come by and young graduates would stand nearly anything just to be at work, but I realised that there had been no other choice for that shadowy figure.

Adamson's place was a smallholding on the edge of the town and maybe it was because I had just been looking at Grier but by contrast the farmer's lined, patient face and friendly eyes seemed extraordinarily warming and attractive. A ragged khaki smock hung loosely on his gaunt frame as he shook hands with me.

'Now then, we've got a new man today, have we?' He looked me over for a second or two. 'And by the look of you you're pretty fresh to t'job.'

'That's right,' I replied. 'But I'm learning fast.'

Mr Adamson smiled. 'Don't worry about that, lad. I believe in new blood and new ideas — it's what we want in farming. We've stood still too long at this game. Come into t'byre and I'll show you the cow.'

There were about a dozen cows, not the usual shorthorns but Ayrshires, and they were obviously well kept and healthy. My patient was easy to pick out by the football-sized rose-pink protrusion of the vaginal wall and the corrugated uterine cervix. But the farmer had wasted no time in calling for assistance; the mass was clean and undamaged.

He watched me attentively as I swabbed the prolapse with antiseptic and pushed it back out of sight, then he helped me build a platform with soil and planks for the cow's hind feet. When we had finished she was standing on a slope with her tail higher than her head.

'And you say that if I give her linseed oil for a few days that thing won't come out again?'

'That's the idea,' I said. 'Be sure to keep her built up like this.'

'I will, young man, and thank you very much. I'm sure you've done a good job for me and I'll look forward to seeing you again.'

Back in the car, I groaned to myself. Good job! How the hell could that thing stay in without stitches? But I had to do as I was told and Grier, even if he was unpleasant, wasn't a complete fool. Maybe he was right. I put it out of my mind and got on with the other visits.

It was less than a week later at the breakfast

table and I was prodding at the inevitable porridge when Grier, who had ventured downstairs, barked suddenly at me.

'I've got a card here frae Adamson. He says he's not satisfied with your work. We'd better get out there this morning and see what's wrong. I dinna like these complaints.' His normal expression of being perpetually offended deepened and the big pale eyes swam and brimmed till I was sure he was going to weep into his porridge.

At the farm, Mr Adamson led us into the byre. 'Well, what do you think of that, young man?'

I looked at the prolapse and my stomach lurched. The innocuous-looking pink projection had been transformed into a great bloated purple mass. It was caked with filth and an ugly wound ran down one side of it.

'It didn't stay in very long, did it?' the farmer said quietly.

I was too ashamed to speak. This was a dreadful thing to do to a good cow. I felt my face reddening, but luckily I had my employer with me; he would be able to explain everything. I turned towards Grier who snuffled, mumbled, blinked his eyes rapidly but didn't say anything.

The farmer went on. 'And you see she's damaged it. Must have caught it on something. I'll tell you I don't like the look of it.'

It was against this decent man's nature to

be unpleasant, but he was upset all right. 'Maybe it would be better if you would take the job on this time, Mr Grier,' he said.

Grier, who still had not uttered an intelligible word, now sprang into action. He clipped the hair over the base of the spine, inserted an epidural anaesthetic, washed and disinfected the mass and, with an effort, pushed it back to its place. Then he fastened it in with several strong retention sutures with little one-inch lengths of rubber tubing to stop them cutting into the flesh. The finished job looked neat and workmanlike.

The farmer took me gently by the shoulder. 'Now that's something like. You can see it's not going to come out again now, can't you? Why didn't you do something like that when you came before?'

I turned again to Grier, but this time he was seized by a violent fit of coughing. I continued to stare at him but when he still said nothing I turned and walked out of the byre.

'No hard feelings, though, young man,' Mr Adamson called after me. 'I reckon we've all got to learn and there's no substitute for experience. That's so, Mr Grier, isn't it?'

'Aye, och aye, that's right enough. Aye, aye, rightly so, rightly so, there's no doubt aboot that,' Grier mumbled. We got into the car.

I settled down and waited for some explanation from him. I was interested to know just what he would say. But the blue-veined nose pointed straight ahead and the bulging eyes fixed themselves blankly on the road ahead of us.

We drove back to the surgery in silence.

CHAPTER 35

It wasn't long before Grier had to return to bed; he began to groan a lot and hold his injured ribs and soon he was reinstalled upstairs with the pillows at his back and the little pink jacket buttoned to the neck. Whisky was the only thing that gave him relief from his pain and the level of his bedside bottle went down with remarkable speed.

Life resumed its dreary pattern. Mrs Grier was usually around when I had to report to her husband; beyond the bedroom door there would be a lot of whispering which stopped as soon as I entered. I would receive my instructions while Mrs Grier fussed round the bed tucking things in, patting her husband's brow with a folded handkerchief and all the time darting little glances of dislike at me. Immediately I got outside the door the whispering started again.

It was quite late one evening — about ten o'clock — when the call from Mrs Mallard came in. Her dog had a bone in its throat and would Mr Grier come at once. I was starting to say that he was ill and I was doing his work but it was too late; there was a click as the receiver went down at the other end.

Grier reacted to the news by going into a sort of trance; his chin sank on his chest and he sat immobile for nearly a minute while he gave the matter careful thought. Then he straightened up suddenly and stabbed a finger at me.

'It'll not be a bone in its throat. It'll only be a touch of pharyngitis making it cough.'

I was surprised at his confidence. 'Don't you think I'd better take some long forceps just in case?'

'Na, na, I've told ye now. There'll be no bone, so go down and put up some of the syrup of squills and ipecacuanha mixture. That's all it'll want. And another thing — if ye can't find anything wrong don't say so. Tell the lady it's pharyngitis and how to treat it — you have to justify your visit, ye ken.'

I felt a little bewildered as I filled a four ounce bottle in the dispensary, but I took a few pairs of forceps with me too; I had lost a bit of faith in Grier's long-range diagnosis.

I was surprised when Mrs Mallard opened the door of the smart semi-detached house. For some reason I had been expecting an old lady, and here was a striking-looking blonde woman of about forty with her hair piled high in glamorous layers as was the fashion at that time. And I hadn't expected the long ball-room dress in shimmering green, the enormous swaying earrings, the heavily made up face.

Mrs Mallard seemed surprised too. She stared blankly at me till I explained the position. 'I've come to see your dog — I'm Mr Grier's locum. He's ill at the moment, I'm afraid.'

It took a fair time for the information to get through because she still stood on the doorstep as if she didn't know what I was talking about; then she came to life and opened the door wide. 'Oh yes, of course, I'm sorry, do come in.' I walked past her through an almost palpable wall of perfume and into a room on the left of the hall. The perfume was even stronger in here but it was in keeping with the single, pink-tinted lamp which shed a dim but rosy light on the wide divan drawn close to the flickering fire. Somewhere in the shadows a radiogram was softly pouring out 'Body and Soul'.

There was no sign of my patient and Mrs Mallard looked at me irresolutely, fingering one of her earrings.

'Do you want me to see him in here?' I asked.

'Oh yes, certainly.' She became brisk and opened a door at the end of the room. Immediately a little West Highland Terrier bounded across the carpet and hurled himself at me with a woof of delight. He tried his best to lick my face by a series of mighty springs and this might have gone on for quite a long time had I not caught him in mid air.

Mrs Mallard smiled nervously. 'He seems a lot better now,' she said.

I flopped down on the divan still with the little dog in my arms and prised open his jaws. Even in that dim light it was obvious that there was nothing in his throat. I gently slid my forefinger over the back of his tongue and the terrier made no protest as I explored his gullet. Then I dropped him down on the carpet and took his temperature — normal.

'Well, Mrs Mallard,' I said, 'there is certainly no bone in his throat and he has no fever.' I was about to add that the dog seemed perfectly fit to me when I remembered Grier's parting admonition — I had to justify my visit.

I cleared my throat. 'It's just possible, though, that he has a little pharyngitis which has been making him cough or retch.' I opened the terrier's mouth again. 'As you see, the back of his throat is rather inflamed. He may have got a mild infection in there or perhaps swallowed some irritant. I have some medicine in the car which will soon put him right.' Realising I was beginning to gabble, I brought my speech to a close.

Mrs Mallard hung on every word, peering anxiously into the little dog's mouth and nodding her head rapidly. 'Oh yes, I do see,' she said. 'Thank you so much. What a good thing I sent for you!'

On the following evening I was half way through a busy surgery when a fat man in a particularly vivid tweed jacket bustled in and deposited a sad-eyed Basset Hound on the table.

'Shaking his head about a bit,' he boomed. 'Think he must have a touch of canker.'

I got an auroscope from the instrument cupboard and had begun to examine the ear when the fat man started again.

'I see you were out our way last night. I live next door to Mrs Mallard.'

'Oh yes,' I said peering down the lighted metal tube. 'That's right, I was.'

The man drummed his fingers on the table for a moment. 'Aye, that dog must have a lot of ailments. The vet's car seems always to be outside the house.'

'Really, I shouldn't have thought so. Seemed a healthy little thing to me.' I finished examining one ear and started on the other.

'Well, it's just as I say,' said the man. 'The poor creature's always in trouble, and it's funny how often it happens at night.'

I looked up quickly. There was something odd in the way he said that. He looked at me for a moment with a kind of wide-eyed in-nocence, then his whole face creased into a knowing leer.

I stared at him 'You can't mean . . .'

'Not with that ugly old devil, you mean, eh? Takes a bit of reckoning up, doesn't it?' The eyes in the big red face twinkled with amusement.

I dropped the auroscope on the table with a clatter and my arms fell by my sides.

'Don't look like that, lad!' shouted the fat man, giving me a playful punch in the chest. 'It's a rum old world, you know!'

But it wasn't just the thought of Grier that was filling me with horror; it was the picture of myself in that harem atmosphere pontificating about pharyngitis against a background of 'Body and Soul' to a woman who knew I was talking rubbish.

In another two days Angus Grier was out of bed and apparently recovered; also, a replacement assistant had been engaged and was due to take up his post immediately. I was free to go.

Having said I would leave first thing in the morning I was out of the house by 6.30 a.m. in order to make Darrowby by breakfast. I wasn't going to face any more of that porridge.

As I drove west across the Plain of York I began to catch glimpses over the hedge tops and between the trees of the long spine of the Pennines lifting into the morning sky; they were pale violet at this distance and still hazy in the early sunshine but they beckoned to me. And later, when the little car pulled harder against the rising ground and the trees became fewer and the hedges gave way to the clean limestone walls I had the feeling I always had of the world opening out, of shackles falling away. And there, at last, was Darrowby sleeping under the familiar bulk of Herne Fell and beyond, the great green folds of the Dales.

Nothing stirred as I rattled across the cobbled market place then down the quiet street to Skeldale House with the ivy hanging in untidy profusion from its old bricks and 'Siegfried Farnon M.R.C.V.S.' on the lopsided brass plate.

I think I would have galloped along the passage beyond the glass door but I had to fight my way through the family dogs, all five of them, who surged around me, leaping and barking in delight.

I almost collided with the formidable bulk of Mrs Hall who was carrying the coffee-pot out of the dining-room. 'You're back then,' she said and I could see she was really pleased because she almost smiled. 'Well, go in and get sat down. I've got a bit of home-cured in the pan for you.'

My hand was on the door when I heard the brothers' voices inside. Tristan was mumbling something and Siegfried was in full cry. 'Where the hell were you last night, anyway?

I heard you banging about at three o'clock in the morning and your room stinks like a brewery. God, I wish you could see yourself — eyes like piss-holes in the snow!'

Smiling to myself, I pushed open the door, I went over to Tristan who stared up in surprise as I seized his hand and began to pump it; he looked as boyishly innocent as ever except for the eyes which, though a little sunken, still held their old gleam. Then I approached Siegfried at the head of the table. Obviously startled at my formal entry, he had choked in mid-chew; he reddened, tears coursed down his thin cheeks and the small sandy moustache quivered. Nevertheless, he rose from his chair, inclined his head and extended his hand with the grace of a marquis.

'Welcome, James,' he spluttered, spraying me lightly with toast crumbs. 'Welcome home.'

CHAPTER 36

I had been away for only two weeks but it was enough to bring it home to me afresh that working in the high country had something for me that was missing elsewhere. My first visit took me up on one of the narrow, unfenced roads which join Sildale and Cosdale and when I had ground my way to the top in bottom gear I did what I so often did — pulled the car on to the roadside turf and got out.

That quotation about not having time to stand and stare has never applied to me. I seem to have spent a good part of my life — probably too much — in just standing and staring and I was at it again this morning. From up here you could see away over the Plain of York to the sprawl of the Hambleton Hills forty miles to the east, while behind me, the ragged miles of moorland rolled away, dipping and rising over the flat fell-top. In my year at Darrowby I must have stood here scores of times and the view across the plain always looked different; sometimes in the winter the low country was a dark trough between the snow-covered Pennines and the distant white gleam of the Hambletons, and in April the rain squalls drifted in slow, heavy veils across the great green and brown dappled expanse. There was a day, too, when I stood in brilliant sunshine looking down over miles of thick fog like a rippling layer of cotton wool with dark tufts of trees and hilltops pushing through here and there.

But today the endless patchwork of fields slumbered in the sun, and the air, even on the hill, was heavy with the scents of summer. There must be people working among the farms down there, I knew, but I couldn't see a living soul; and the peace which I always found in the silence and the emptiness of the moors filled me utterly.

At these times I often seemed to stand outside myself, calmly assessing my progress. It was easy to flick back over the years — right back to the time I had decided to become a veterinary surgeon. I could remember the very moment. I was thirteen and I was reading an article about careers for boys in the Meccano Magazine and as I read, I felt a surging conviction that this was for me. And yet what was it based upon? Only that I liked dogs and cats and didn't care much for the idea of an office life; it seemed a frail basis on which to build a career. I knew nothing about agriculture or about farm animals and though, during the years in college, I learned about these things I could see only one future for myself; I was going to be a small animal surgeon. This lasted right up to the time I qualified — a kind of vision of treating people's pets in my own animal hospital where everything would be not just modern but revolutionary. The fully equipped operating theatre, laboratory and X-ray room; they had all stayed crystal clear in my mind until I had graduated M.R.C.V.S.

How on earth, then, did I come to be sitting on a high Yorkshire moor in shirt sleeves and Wellingtons, smelling vaguely of cows?

The change in my outlook had come quite quickly — in fact almost immediately after my arrival in Darrowby. The job had been a godsend in those days of high unemployment, but only, I had thought, a stepping-stone to my real ambition. But everything had switched round, almost in a flash.

Maybe it was something to do with the incredible sweetness of the air which still took me by surprise when I stepped out into the old wild garden at Skeldale House every morning. Or perhaps the daily piquancy of life in the graceful old house with my gifted but mercurial boss, Siegfried, and his reluctant student brother, Tristan. Or it could be that it was just the realisation that treating cows and pigs and sheep and horses had a fascination I had never even suspected; and this brought with it a new concept of myself as a tiny wheel in the great machine of British agriculture. There was a kind of solid satisfaction in that.

Probably it was because I hadn't dreamed there was a place like the Dales. I hadn't thought it possible that I could spend all my days in a high, clean-blown land where the scent of grass or trees was never far away; and where even in the driving rain of winter I could snuff the air and find the freshness of growing things hidden somewhere in the cold clasp of the wind.

Anyway, it had all changed for me and my work consisted now of driving from farm to farm across the roof of England with a growing conviction that I was a privileged person.

I got back into the car and looked at my list of visits; it was good to be back and the day passed quickly. It was about seven o'clock in the evening, when I thought I had finished, that I had a call from Terry Watson, a young farm worker who kept two cows of his own. One of them, he said, had summer mastitis. Mid-July was a bit early for this but in the later summer months we saw literally hundreds of these cases; in fact a lot of the farmers called it 'August Bag'. It was an unpleasant condition because it was just about incurable and usually resulted in the cow losing a quarter (the area of the udder which supplies each teat with milk) and sometimes even her life.

Terry Watson's cow looked very sick. She had limped in from the field at milking time, swinging her right hind leg wide to keep it away from the painful udder, and now she stood trembling in her stall, her eyes staring anxiously in front of her. I drew gently at the affected teat and, instead of milk, a stream of dark, foul-smelling serum spurted into the tin can I was holding.

'No mistaking that stink, Terry,' I said. 'It's the real summer type all right.' I felt my way over the hot, swollen quarter and the cow lifted her leg quickly as I touched the tender tissue. 'Pretty hard, too. It looks bad, I'm afraid.'

Terry's face was grim as he ran his hand along the cow's back. He was in his early twenties, had a wife and a small baby and was one of the breed who was prepared to labour all day for somebody else and then come home and start work on his own few stock. His two cows, his few pigs and hens made a big difference to somebody who had to live on thirty shillings a week.

'Ah can't understand it,' he muttered. 'It's usually dry cows that get it and this 'uns still giving two gallons a day. I'd have been on with tar if only she'd been dry.' (The farmers used to dab the teats of the dry cows with Stockholm tar to keep off the flies which were blamed for carrying the infection.)

'No, I'm afraid all cows can get it, especially the ones that are beginning to dry off.' I pulled the thermometer from the rectum — it said a hundred and six.

'What's going to happen, then? Can you do owt for her?'

'I'll do what I can, Terry. I'll give her an injection and you must strip the teat out as often as you can, but you know as well as I do that it's a poor outlook with these jobs.'

'Aye, ah know all about it.' He watched me gloomily as I injected the Coryne pyogenes toxoid into the cow's neck. (Even now we are still doing this for summer mastitis because it is a sad fact none of the modern range of antibiotics has much effect on it.) 'She'll lose her quarter, won't she, and maybe she'll even peg out?'

I tried to be cheerful. 'Well, I don't think she'll die, and even if the quarter goes she'll make it up on the other three.' But there was the feeling of helplessness I always had when I could do little about something which mattered a great deal. Because I knew what a blow this was to the young man; a three-teated cow has lost a lot of her market value and this was about the best outcome I could see. I didn't like to think about the possibility of the animal dying.

'Look, is there nowt at all I can do myself? Is the job a bad 'un do you think?' Terry

Watson's thin cheeks were pale and as I looked at the slender figure with the slightly stooping shoulders I thought, not for the first time, that he didn't look robust enough for his hard trade.

'I can't guarantee anything,' I said. 'But the cases that do best are the ones that get the most stripping. So work away at it this evening — every half hour if you can manage it. That rubbish in her quarter can't do any harm if you draw it out as soon as it is formed. And I think you ought to bathe the udder with warm water and massage it well.'

'What'll I rub it with?'

'Oh, it doesn't matter what you use. The main thing is to move the tissue about so that you can get more of that stinking stuff out. Vaseline would do nicely.'

'Ah've got a bowl of goose grease.'

'O.K. use that.' I reflected that there must be a bowl of goose grease on most farms; it was the all-purpose lubricant and liniment for man and beast.

Terry seemed relieved at the opportunity to do something. He fished out an old bucket, tucked the milking stool between his legs and crouched down against the cow. He looked up at me with a strangely defiant expression. 'Right,' he said. 'I'm startin' now.'

As it happened, I was called out early the next morning to a milk fever and on the way home I decided to look in at the Watsons' cottage. It was about eight o'clock and when I entered the little two-stall shed, Terry was in the same position as I had left him on the previous night. He was pulling at the infected teat, eyes closed, cheek resting against the cow's flank. He started as though roused from sleep when I spoke.

'Hello, you're having another go, I see.'

The cow looked round, too, at my words and I saw immediately, with a thrill of pleasure that she was immeasurably improved. She had lost her blank stare and was looking at me with the casual interest of the healthy bovine and best of all, her jaws were moving with that slow, regular, lateral grind that every vet loves to see.

'My God, Terry, she looks a lot better. She isn't like the same cow!'

The young man seemed to have difficulty in keeping his eyes open but he smiled. 'Aye, and come and have a look at this end.' He rose slowly from the stool, straightened his back a little bit at a time and leaned his elbow on the cow's rump.

I bent down by the udder, feeling carefully for the painful swelling of last night, but my hand came up against a smooth, yielding surface and, in disbelief, I kneaded the tissue between my fingers. The animal showed no sign of discomfort. With a feeling of bewilderment I drew on the teat with thumb and forefinger; the quarter was nearly empty but

I did manage to squeeze a single jet of pure white milk on to my palm.

'What's going on here, Terry? You must have switched cows on me. You're having me on, aren't you?'

'Nay, guvnor,' the young man said with his slow smile. 'It's same cow all right — she's better, that's all.'

'But it's impossible! What the devil have you done to her?'

'Just what you told me to do. Rub and strip.'

I scratched my head. 'But she's back to normal. I've never seen anything like it.'

'Aye, I know you haven't.' It was a woman's voice and I turned and saw young Mrs Watson standing at the door holding her baby. 'You've never seen a man that would rub and strip a cow right round the clock, have you?'

'Round the clock?' I said.

She looked at her husband with a mixture of concern and exasperation. 'Yes, he's been there on that stool since you left last night. Never been to bed, never been in for a meal. I've been bringing him bits and pieces and cups of tea. Great fool — it's enough to kill anybody.'

I looked at Terry and my eyes moved from the pallid face over the thin, slightly swaying body to the nearly empty bowl of goose grease at his feet. 'Good Lord, man,' I said. 'You've done the impossible but you must be about all in. Anyway, your cow is as good as new — you don't need to do another thing to her, so you can go in and have a bit of rest.'

'Nay, I can't do that.' He shook his head and straightened his shoulders. 'I've got me work to go to and I'm late as it is.'

CHAPTER 37

I couldn't help feeling just a little bit smug as I squeezed the bright red rubber ball out through the incision in the dog's stomach. We got enough small animal work in Darrowby to make a pleasant break from our normal life around the farms but not enough to make us blasé. No doubt the man with an intensive town practice looks on a gastrotomy as a fairly routine and unexciting event but as I watched the little red ball roll along the table and bounce on the surgery floor a glow of achievement filled me.

The big, lolloping Red Setter pup had been brought in that morning; his mistress said that he had been trembling, miserable and occasionally vomiting for two days — ever since their little girl's ball had mysteriously disappeared. Diagnosis had not been difficult.

I inverted the lips of the stomach wound and began to close it with a continuous suture. I was feeling pleasantly relaxed unlike Tristan who had been unable to light a Woodbine because of the ether which bubbled in the glass bottle behind him and out through the anaesthetic mask which he held over the dog's face; he stared moodily down at the patient and the fingers of his free hand drummed on the table.

But it was soon my turn to be tense because the door of the operating room burst open and Siegfried strode in. I don't know why it was but whenever Siegfried watched me do anything I started to go to pieces; great waves seemed to billow from him — impatience, frustration, criticism, irritation. I could feel the waves buffeting me now although my employer's face was expressionless; he was standing quietly at the end of the table but as the minutes passed I had the growing impression of a volcano on the bubble. The eruption came when I began to stitch the deep layer of the abdominal muscle. I was pulling a length of catgut from a glass jar when I heard a sharp intake of breath.

'God help us, James!' cried Siegfried. 'Stop pulling at that bloody gut! Do you know how much that stuff costs per foot? Well it's a good job you don't or you'd faint dead away. And that expensive dusting powder you've been chucking about — there must be about half a pound of it inside that dog right now.' He paused and breathed heavily for a few moments. 'Another thing, if you want to swab, a little bit of cotton wool is enough — you don't need a square foot at a time like you've been using. Here, give me that needle. Let me show you.'

He hastily scrubbed his hands and took over. First he took a minute pinch of the iodoform powder and sprinkled it daintily into the wound rather like an old lady feeding her goldfish, then he cut off a tiny piece of gut and inserted a continuous suture in the muscle; he had hardly left himself enough to tie the knot at the end and it was touch and go, but he just made it after a few moments of intense concentration.

This process was repeated about ten times as he closed the skin wound with interrupted silk sutures, his nose almost touching the patient as he laboriously tied off each little short end with forceps. When he had finished he was slightly pop-eyed.

'Right, turn off the ether, Tristan,' he said as he pulled off half an inch of wool and primly wiped the wound down.

He turned to me and smiled gently. With dismay I saw that his patient look was spreading over his face. 'James, please don't misunderstand me. You've made a grand job of this dog but you've got to keep one eye on the economic side of things. I know it doesn't matter a hoot to you just now but some day, no doubt, you'll have your own practice and then you'll realise some of the worries I have on my shoulders.' He patted my arm and I steeled myself as he put his head on one side and a hint of roguishness crept into his smile.

'After all, James, you'll agree it is desirable to make some sort of profit in the end.'

It was a week later and I was kneeling on the neck of a sleeping colt in the middle of a field, the sun was hot on the back of my neck as I looked down at the peacefully closed eyes, the narrow face disappearing into the canvas chloroform muzzle. I tipped a few more drops of the anaesthetic on to the sponge and screwed the cap on to the bottle. He had had about enough now.

I couldn't count the number of times Siegfried and I have enacted this scene; the horse on his grassy bed, my employer cutting away at one end while I watched the head. Siegfried was a unique combination of born horseman and dexterous surgeon with which I couldn't compete, so I had inevitably developed into an anaesthetist. We liked to do the operations in the open; it was cleaner and if the horse was wild he stood less chance of injuring himself. We just hoped for a fine morning and today we were lucky. In the early haze I looked over the countless buttercups; the field was filled with them and it was like sitting in a shimmering yellow ocean. Their pollen had powdered my shoes and the neck of the horse beneath me.

Everything had gone off more or less as it

usually did. I had gone into the box with the colt, buckled on the muzzle underneath his head collar then walked him quietly out to a soft, level spot in the field. I left a man at the head holding a long shank on the head collar and poured the first half ounce of chloroform on to the sponge, watching the colt snuffling and shaking his head at the strange scent. As the man walked him slowly round I kept adding a little more chloroform till the colt began to stagger and sway; this stage always took a few minutes and I waited confidently for Siegfried's little speech which always came about now. I was not disappointed.

'He isn't going to go down, you know, James. Don't you think we should tie a foreleg up?'

I adopted my usual policy of feigning deafness and a few seconds later the colt gave a final lurch and collapsed on his side. Siegfried, released from his enforced inactivity, sprang into action. 'Sit on his head!' he yelled. 'Get a rope on that upper hind leg and pull it forward! Bring me that bucket of water over here! Come on — move!'

It was a violent transition. Just moments ago, peace and silence and now men scurrying in all directions, bumping into each other, urged on by Siegfried's cries.

Thirty years later I am still dropping horses for Siegfried and he is still saying 'He isn't going to go down, James'.

These days I mostly use an intravenous injection of Thiopentone and it puts a horse out in about ten seconds. It doesn't give Siegfried much time to say his piece but he usually gets it in somewhere between the seventh and tenth seconds.

This morning's case was an injury. But it was a pretty dramatic one, justifying general anaesthetic to repair it. The colt, bred from a fine hunter mare, had been galloping round his paddock and had felt the urge to visit the outside world. He had chosen the only sharp fence post to try to jump over and had been impaled between the forelegs; in his efforts to escape he had caused so much damage in the breast region that it looked like something from a butcher's shop with the skin extensively lacerated and the big sternal muscles hanging out, chopped through as though by a cleaver.

'Roll him on his back,' said Siegfried. 'That's better.' He took a probe from the tray which lay on the grass near by and carefully explored the wound. 'No damage to the bone,' he grunted, still peering into the depths. Then he took a pair of forceps and fished out all the loose debris he could find before turning to me.

'It's just a big stitching job. You can carry on if you like.'

As we changed places it occurred to me that he was disappointed it was not something more interesting. I couldn't see him asking me to take over in a rig operation or something like that. Then, as I picked up the needle, my mind clicked back to that gastrotomy on the dog. Maybe I was on trial for my wasteful ways. This time I would be on my guard.

I threaded the needle with a minute length of gut, took a bite at the severed muscle and, with an effort, stitched it back into place. But it was a laborious business tying the little short ends — it was taking me at least three times as long as it should. However, I stuck to it doggedly. I had been warned and I didn't want another lecture.

I had put in half a dozen sutures in this way when I began to feel the waves. My employer was kneeling close to me on the horse's neck and the foaming breakers of disapproval were crashing into me from close range. I held out for another two sutures then Siegfried exploded in a fierce whisper.

'What the hell are you playing at, James?'

'Well, just stitching. What do you mean?'

'But why are you buggering about with those little bits of gut? We'll be here all bloody day!'

I fumbled another knot into the muscle. 'For reasons of economy.' I whispered back virtuously.

Siegfried leaped from the neck as though the horse had bitten him. 'I can't stand any more of this! Here, let me have a go.'

He strode over to the tray, selected a needle and caught hold of the free end of the catgut protruding from the jar. With a scything sweep of his arm he pulled forth an enormous coil of gut, setting the bobbin inside the jar whirring wildly like a salmon reel with a big fish on the line. He returned to the horse, stumbling slightly as the gut caught round his ankles and began to stitch. It wasn't easy because even at the full stretch of his arm he was unable to pull the suture tight and had to keep getting up and down; by the time he had tacked the muscles back into their original positions he was puffing and I could see a faint dew of perspiration on his fore-head.

'Drop of blood seeping from somewhere down there,' he muttered and visited the tray again where he tore savagely at a huge roll of cotton wool. Trailing untidy white streamers over the buttercups he returned and swabbed out the wound with one corner of the mass.

Back to the tray again. 'Just a touch of powder before I stitch the skin,' he said lightly and seized a two pound carton. He poised for a moment over the wound then began to dispense the powder with extravagant jerks of the wrist. A considerable amount did go into the wound but much more floated over other parts of the horse, over me, over the but-tercups, and a particularly wayward flick obscured the sweating face of the man on the foot rope. When he had finished coughing he looked very like Coco the clown.

Siegfried completed the closure of the skin, using several yards of silk, and when he stood back and surveyed the tidy result I could see he was in excellent humour.

'Well now, that's fine. A young horse like that will heal in no time. Shouldn't be surprised if it doesn't even leave a mark.'

He came over and addressed me as I washed the instruments in the bucket. 'Sorry I pushed you out like that, James, but honestly I couldn't think what had come over you — you were like an old hen. You know it looks bad trying to work with piddling little amounts of materials. One has to operate with a certain . . . well . . . panache, if I can put it that way, and you just can't do that if you stint yourself.'

I finished washing the instruments, dried them off and laid them on the enamel tray. Then I lifted the tray and set off for the gate at the end of the field. Siegfried, walking alongside me, laid his hand on my shoulder. 'Mind you, don't think I'm blaming you, James. It's probably your Scottish upbringing. And don't misunderstand me, this same upbringing has inculcated in you so many of the qualities I admire — integrity, industry, loyalty. But I'm sure you will be the first to admit,' and here he stopped and wagged a finger at me 'that you Scots sometimes overdo the thrift.' He gave a light laugh. 'So remember, James, don't be too — er — canny when you are operating.'

I measured him up. If I dropped the tray quickly I felt sure I could fell him with a right hook.

Siegfried went on. 'But I know I don't have to ramble on at you, James. You always pay attention to what I say, don't you?'

I tucked the tray under my arm and set off again. 'Yes,' I replied. 'I do. Every single time.'

CHAPTER 38

'I can see you like pigs,' said Mr Worley as I edged my way into the pen.

'You can?'

'Oh yes, I can always tell. As soon as you went in there nice and quiet and scratched Queenie's back and spoke to her I said "There's a young man as likes pigs".'

'Oh good. Well, as a matter of fact you're absolutely right. I do like pigs.' I had, in truth, been creeping very cautiously past Queenie, wondering just how she was going to react. She was a huge animal and sows with litters can be very hostile to strangers. When I had come into the building she had got up from where she was suckling her piglets and eyed me with a non-committal grunt, reminding me of the number of times I had left a pig pen a lot quicker than I had gone in. A big, barking, gaping-mouthed sow has always been able to make me move very smartly.

Now that I was right inside the narrow pen, Queenie seemed to have accepted me. She grunted again, but peaceably, then carefully collapsed on the straw and exposed her udder to the eager little mouths. When she was in this position I was able to examine her foot.

'Aye, that's the one,' Mr Worley said anxiously. 'She could hardly hobble when she got up this morning.'

There didn't seem to be much wrong. A flap of the horn of one claw was a bit overgrown and was rubbing on the sensitive sole, but we didn't usually get called out for little things like that. I cut away the overgrown part and dressed the sore place with our multipurpose ointment, ung pini sedativum, while all the time Mr Worley knelt by Queenie's head and patted her and sort of crooned into her ear. I couldn't make out the words he used — maybe it was pig language because the sow really seemed to be answering him with little soft grunts. Anyway, it worked better than an anaesthetic and everybody was happy including the long row of piglets working busily at the double line of teats.

'Right, Mr Worley.' I straightened up and handed him the jar of ung pini. 'Keep rubbing in a little of that twice a day and I think she'll be sound in no time.'

'Thank ye, thank ye, I'm very grateful.' He shook my hand vigorously as though I had saved the animal's life. 'I'm very glad to meet you for the first time, Mr Herriot. I've known Mr Farnon for a year or two, of course, and I think a bit about him. Loves pigs does that man, loves them. And his young brother's been here once or twice — I reckon he's fond of pigs, too.'

'Devoted to them, Mr Worley.'

'Ah yes, I thought so. I can always tell.' He regarded me for a while with a moist eye, then smiled, well satisfied.

We went out into what was really the back yard of an inn. Because Mr Worley wasn't a regular farmer, he was the landlord of the Langthorpe Falls Hotel and his precious livestock were crammed into what had once been the stables and coach houses of the inn. They were all Tamworths and whichever door you opened you found yourself staring into the eyes of ginger-haired pigs; there were a few porkers and the odd one being fattened for bacon but Mr Worley's pride was his sows. He had six of them — Queenie, Princess, Ruby, Marigold, Delilah and Primrose.

For years expert farmers had been assuring Mr Worley that he'd never do any good with his sows. If you were going in for breeding, they said, you had to have proper premises; it wasn't a bit of use shoving sows into converted buildings like his. And for years Mr Worley's sows had responded by producing litters of unprecedented size and raising them with tender care. They were all good mothers and didn't savage their families or crush them clumsily under their bodies so it turned out with uncanny regularity that at the end of eight weeks Mr Worley had around twelve chunky weaners to take to market.

It must have spoiled the farmers' beer — none of them could equal that, and the pill was all the more bitter because the landlord had come from the industrial West Riding — Halifax, I think it was — a frail, short-sighted little retired newsagent with no agricultural background. By all the laws he just didn't have a chance.

Leaving the yard we came on to the quiet loop of road where my car was parked. Just beyond, the road dipped steeply into a tree-lined ravine where the Darrow hurled itself over a great broken shelf of rock in its passage to the lower Dale. I couldn't see down there from where I was standing, but I could hear the faint roar of the water and could picture the black cliff lifting sheer from the boiling river and on the other bank the gentle slope of turf where people from the towns came to sit and look in wonder.

Some of them were here now. A big, shiny car had drawn up and its occupants were disembarking. The driver, sleek, fat and impressive, strolled towards us and called out: 'We would like some tea.'

Mr Worley swung round on him. 'And you can 'ave some, maister, but when I'm ready. I have some very important business with this gentleman.' He turned his back on the man and began to ask me for final instructions about Queenie's foot.

The man was obviously taken aback and I couldn't blame him. It seemed to me that Mr Worley might have shown a little more tact — after all serving food and drink was his living — but as I came to know him better I realised that his pigs came first and everything else was an irritating intrusion.

Knowing Mr Worley better had its rewards. The time when I feel most like a glass of beer is not in the evening when the pubs are open but at around four-thirty on a hot afternoon after wrestling with young cattle in some stifling cowshed. It was delightful to retire, sweating and weary, to the shaded sanctuary of Mr Worley's back kitchen and sip at the bitter ale, cool, frothing, straight from the cellar below.

The smooth working of the system was facilitated by the attitude of the local constable, P.C. Dalloway, a man whose benign disposition and elastic interpretation of the licensing laws had made him deeply respected in the district. Occasionally he joined us, took off his uniform jacket and, in shirt and braces, consumed a pint with a massive dignity which was peculiar to him.

But mostly Mr Worley and I were on our own and when he had brought the tall jug up from the cellar he would sit down and say 'Well now, let's have a piggy talk!' His use of this particular phrase made me wonder if perhaps he had some humorous insight into his obsessive preoccupation with the porcine species. Maybe he had but for all that our conversations seemed to give him the deepest pleasure.

We talked about erysipelas and swine fever, brine poisoning and paratyphoid, the relative merits of dry and wet mash, while pictures of his peerless sows with their show rosettes looked down at us from the walls.

On one occasion, in the middle of a particularly profound discussion on the ventilation of farrowing houses Mr Worley stopped suddenly and, blinking rapidly behind his thick spectacles, burst out:

'You know, Mr Herriot, sitting here talking like this with you, I'm 'appy as king of England!'

His devotion resulted in my being called out frequently for very trivial things and I swore freely under my breath when I heard his voice on the other end of the line at one o'clock one morning.

'Marigold pigged this afternoon, Mr Herriot, and I don't think she's got much milk. Little pigs look very hungry to me. Will you come?'

I groaned my way out of bed and downstairs and through the long garden to the yard. By the time I had got the car out into the lane I had begun to wake up and when I rolled up to the inn was able to greet Mr Worley fairly cheerfully.

But the poor man did not respond. In the light from the oil lamp his face was haggard with worry.

'I hope you can do something quick. I'm real upset about her — she's just laid there doing nothin' and it's such a lovely litter. Fourteen she's had.'

I could understand his concern as I looked into the pen.

Marigold was stretched motionless on her side while the tiny piglets swarmed around her udder; they were rushing from teat to teat, squealing and falling over each other in their desperate quest for nourishment. And the little bodies had the narrow, empty look which meant they had nothing in their stomachs. I hated to see a litter die off from sheer starvation but it could happen so easily. There came a time when they stopped trying to suck and began to lie about the pen. After that it was hopeless.

Crouching behind the sow with my thermometer in her rectum I looked along the swelling flank, the hair a rich copper red in the light from the lamp. 'Did she eat anything tonight?'

'Aye, cleaned up just as usual.'

The thermometer reading was normal. I began to run my hands along the udder, pulling in turn at the teats. The ravenous piglets caught at my fingers with their sharp teeth as I pushed them to one side but my efforts failed to produce a drop of milk. The udder seemed full, even engorged, but I was unable to get even a bead down to the end of the teat.

'There's nowt there, is there?' Mr Worley whispered anxiously.

I straightened up and turned to him 'This is simply agalactia. There's no mastitis and Marigold isn't really ill, but there's something interfering with the let-down mechanism of the milk. She's got plenty of milk and there's an injection which ought to bring it down.'

I tried to keep the triumphant look off my face as I spoke, because this was one of my favourite party tricks. There is a flavour of magic in the injection of pituitrin in these cases; it works within a minute and though no skill is required the effect is spectacular.

Marigold didn't complain as I plunged in the needle and administered 3 c.c. deep into the muscle of her thigh. She was too busy conversing with her owner — they were almost nose to nose, exchanging soft pig noises.

After I had put away my syringe and listened for a few moments to the cooing sounds from the front end I thought it might be time. Mr Worley looked up in surprise as I reached down again to the udder.

'What are you doing now?'

'Having a feel to see if the milk's come down yet.'

'Why damn, it can't be! You've only just given t'stuff and she's bone dry!'

Oh, this was going to be good. A roll of drums would be appropriate at this moment. With finger and thumb I took hold of one of the teats at the turgid back end of the udder. I suppose it is a streak of exhibitionism in me which always makes me send the jet of milk spraying against the opposite wall in these circumstances; this time I thought it would be more impressive if I directed my shot past the innkeeper's left ear, but I got my trajectory wrong and sprinkled his spectacles instead.

He took them off and wiped them slowly as if he couldn't believe what he had seen. Then he bent over and tried for himself.

'It's a miracle!' he cried as the milk spouted eagerly over his hand. 'I've never seen owt like it!'

It didn't take the little pigs long to catch on. Within a few seconds they had stopped their fighting and squealing and settled down in a long, silent row. Their utterly rapt expressions all told the same story — they were going to make up for lost time.

I went into the kitchen to wash my hands and was using the towel hanging behind the door when I noticed something odd; there was a subdued hum of conversation, the low rumble of many voices. It seemed unusual in a pub at 2 a.m. and I looked through the partly open door into the bar. The place was crowded. In the light of a single weak electric bulb I could see a row of men drinking at the counter while others sat behind foaming pint pots on the wooden settles against the walls.

Mr Worley grinned as I turned to him in surprise.

'Didn't expect to see this lot, did you? Well, I'll tell you, the real drinkers don't come in till after closing time. Aye, it's a rum 'un — every night I lock front door and these lads come in the back.'

I pushed my head round the door for another look. It was a kind of rogue's gallery of Darrowby. All the dubious characters in the town seemed to be gathered in that room; the names which regularly enlivened the columns of the weekly newspaper with their activities. Drunk and disorderly, non-payment of rates, wife-beating, assault and battery — I could almost see the headings as I went from face to face.

I had been spotted. Beery cries of welcome rang out and I was suddenly conscious that all eyes were fixed on me in the smoky atmosphere. Above the rest a voice said 'Are you going to have a drink?' What I wanted most was to get back to my bed, but it wouldn't look so good just to close the door and go. I went inside and over to the bar. I seemed to have plenty of friends there and within seconds was in the centre of a merry group with a pint glass in my hand.

My nearest neighbour was a well-known Darrowby worthy called Gobber Newhouse, an enormously fat man who had always seemed able to get through life without working at all. He occupied his time with drinking, brawling and gambling. At the moment he was in a mellow mood and his huge, sweating face, pushed close to mine, was twisted into a comradely leer.

'Nah then, Herriot, ow's dog trade?' he enquired courteously.

I had never heard my profession described in this way and was wondering how to answer when I noticed that the company were looking at me expectantly. Mr Worley's niece who served behind the bar was looking at me expectantly too.

'Six pints of best bitter — six shillings please,' she said, clarifying the situation.

I fumbled the money from my pocket. Obviously my first impression that somebody had invited me to have a drink with them had been mistaken. Looking round the faces, there was no way of telling who had called out, and as the beer disappeared, the group round the bar thinned out like magic; the members just drifted away as though by accident till I found myself alone. I was no longer an object of interest and nobody paid any attention as I drained my glass and left.

The glow from the pig pen showed through the darkness of the yard and as I crossed over, the soft rumble of pig and human voices told me that Mr Worley was still talking things over with his sow. He looked up as I came in and his face in the dim light was ecstatic.

'Mr Herriot,' he whispered. 'Isn't that a beautiful sight?'

He pointed to the little pigs who were lying motionless in a layered heap, sprawled over each other without plan or pattern, eyes tightly closed, stomachs bloated with Marigold's bountiful fluid.

'It is indeed,' I said, prodding the sleeping mass with my finger but getting no response beyond the lazy opening of an eye. 'You'd have to go a long way to beat it.'

And I did share his pleasure; it was one of the satisfying little jobs. Climbing into the car I felt that the nocturnal visit had been worth while even though I had been effortlessly duped into buying a round with no hope of reciprocation. Not that I wanted to drink any more — my stomach wasn't used to receiving pints of ale at 2 a.m. and a few whimpers of surprise and indignation were already coming up — but I was just a bit ruffled by the offhand, professional way those gentlemen in the tap room had handled me.

But, winding my way home through the empty, moonlit roads, I was unaware that the hand of retribution was hovering over that happy band. This was, in fact, a fateful night, because ten minutes after I had left, Mr Worley's pub was raided. Perhaps that is a rather dramatic word, but it happened that it was the constable's annual holiday and the relief man, a young policeman who did not share Mr Dalloway's liberal views, had come up on his bicycle and pinched everybody in the place.

The account of the court proceedings in the *Darrowby and Houlton Times* made good reading. Gobber Newhouse and company were all fined £2 each and warned as to their future conduct. The magistrates, obviously a heartless lot, had remained unmoved by Gobber's passionate protestations that the beer in the glasses had all been purchased before closing time and that he and his friends had been lingering over it in light conversation for the subsequent four hours.

Mr Worley was fined £15 but I don't think he really minded; Marigold and her litter were doing well.

CHAPTER 39

This was the last gate. I got out to open it since Tristan was driving, and looked back at the farm, a long way below us now, and at the marks our tyres had made on the steep, grassy slopes. Strange places, some of these Dales farms; this one had no road to it — not even a track. From down there you just drove across the fields from gate to gate till you got to the main road above the valley. And this was the last one; ten minutes' driving and we'd be home.

Tristan was acting as my chauffeur, as my left hand had been infected after a bad calving and I had my arm in a sling. He didn't drive up through the gate but got out of the car, leaned his back against the gate post and lit a Woodbine.

Obviously he wasn't in any rush to leave. And with the sun warm on the back of his neck and the two bottles of Whitbread's nestling comfortably in his stomach I could divine that he felt pretty good. Come to think of it, it had been all right back there. He had taken some warts off a heifer's teats and the farmer had said he shaped well for a young 'un, ("Aye, you really framed at t'job, lad") and asked us in for a bottle of beer since it was so hot. Impressed by the ecstatic speed with which Tristan had consumed his, he had given him another.

Yes, it had been all right, and I could see Tristan thought so too. With a smile of utter content he took a long, deep gulp of moorland air and Woodbine smoke and closed his eyes.

He opened them quickly as a grinding noise came from the car. 'Christ! She's off, Jim!' he shouted.

The little Austin was moving gently backwards down the slope — it must have slipped out of gear and it had no brakes to speak of. We both leaped after it. Tristan was nearest and he just managed to touch the bonnet with one finger; the speed was too much for him. We gave it up and watched.

The hillside was steep and the little car rapidly gathered momentum, bouncing crazily over the uneven ground. I glanced at Tristan; his mind invariably worked quickly and clearly in a crisis and I had a good idea what he was thinking. It was only a fortnight since he had turned the Hillman over, taking a girl home from a dance. It had been a complete write-off and the insurance people had been rather nasty about it; and of course Siegfried had gone nearly berserk and had finished by sacking him finally, once and for all — never wanted to see his face in the place again.

But he had been sacked so often; he knew he had only to keep out of his way for a bit and his brother would forget. And he had been lucky this time because Siegfried had talked his bank manager into letting him buy a beautiful new Rover and this had blotted everything else from his mind.

It was distinctly unfortunate that this should happen when he, as driver, was technically in charge of the Austin. The car appeared now to be doing about 70 m.p.h. hurtling terrifyingly down the long, green hill. One by one the doors burst open till all four flapped wildly and the car swooped downwards looking like a huge, ungainly bird.

From the open doors, bottles, instruments, bandages, cotton wool cascaded out onto the turf, leaving a long, broken trail. Now and again a packet of nux vomica and bicarb stomach powder would fly out and burst like a bomb, splashing vivid white against the green.

Tristan threw up his arms. 'Look! The bloody thing's going straight for that hut.' He drew harder on his Woodbine.

There was indeed only one obstruction on the bare hillside — a small building near the foot where the land levelled out and the Austin, as if drawn by a magnet, was thundering straight towards it.

I couldn't bear to watch. Just before the impact I turned away and focused my attention on the end of Tristan's cigarette which was glowing bright red when the crash came. When I looked back down the hill the building was no longer there. It had been completely flattened and everything I had ever heard about houses of cards surged into my mind. On top of the shattered timbers the little car lay peacefully on its side, its wheels still turning lazily.

As we galloped down the hill it was easy to guess Tristan's thoughts. He wouldn't be looking forward to telling Siegfried he had wrecked the Austin; in fact it was something the mind almost refused to contemplate. But as we neared the scene of devastation, passing on our way syringes, scalpels, bottles of vaccine, it was difficult to see any other outcome.

Arriving at the car, we made an anxious inspection. The body had been so bashed and dented before that it wasn't easy to identify any new marks. Certainly the rear end was pretty well caved in but it didn't show up very much. The only obvious damage was a smashed rear light. Our hopes rising, we set off for the farm for help.

The farmer greeted us amiably. 'Now then,

you lads, hasta come back for more beer?'

'It wouldn't come amiss,' Tristan replied. 'We've had a bit of an accident.'

We went into the house and the hospitable man opened some more bottles. He didn't seem disturbed when he heard of the demolition of the hut. 'Nay, that's not mine. Belongs to t'golf club — it's t'club house.'

Tristan's eyebrows shot up. 'Oh no! Don't say we've flattened the headquarters of the Darrowby Golf Club!'

'Aye, lad, you must have. It's t'only wooden building in them fields. I rent that part of my land to the club and they've made a little nine hole course. Don't worry, hardly anybody plays on it — mainly t'bank manager and ah don't like that feller.'

Mr Prescott got a horse out of the stable and we went back to the car and pulled it upright again. Trembling a little, Tristan climbed in and pressed the starter. The sturdy little engine burst into a confident roar immediately and he drove carefully over the prostrate wooden walls on to the grass.

'Well thanks a lot, Mr Prescott,' he shouted. 'We seem to have got away with it.'

'Champion, lad, champion. You're as good as new.' Then the farmer winked and held up a finger. 'Now you say nowt about this job and I'll say nowt. Right?'

'Right! Come on, Jim, get in.' Tristan put his foot down and we chugged thankfully up the hill once more.

He seemed thoughtful on the way and didn't speak till we got on to the road. Then he turned to me.

'You know, Jim, it's all very well, but I've still got to confess to Siegfried about that rear light. And of course I'll get the lash again. Don't you think it's just a bit hard the way I get blamed for everything that happens to his cars? You've seen it over and over again — he gives me a lot of bloody old wrecks to drive and when they start to fall to bits it's always my fault. The bloody tyres are all down to the canvas but if I get a puncture there's hell to pay. It isn't fair.'

'Well Siegfried isn't the man to suffer in silence, you know,' I said. 'He's got to lash out and you're nearest.'

Tristan was silent for a moment then he took a deeper drag at his Woodbine, blew out his cheeks and assumed a judicial expression. 'Mind you, I'm not saying I was entirely blameless with regard to the Hillman — I was taking that sharp turn in Dringley at sixty with my arm round a little nurse — but all in all I've just had sheer bad luck. In fact, Jim, I'm a helpless victim of prejudice.'

Siegfried was out of sorts when we met in the surgery. He was starting a summer cold and was sniffly and listless, but he still managed to raise a burst of energy at the news.

'You bloody young maniac! It's the rear

400

light now, is it? God help me, I think all I work for is to pay for the repair bills you run up. You'll ruin me before you're finished. Go on, get to hell out of it. I'm finished with you.'

Tristan retired with dignity and followed his usual policy of lying low. He didn't see his brother until the following morning. Siegfried's condition had deteriorated; the cold had settled in his throat, always his weak spot, and he was down with laryngitis. His neck was swathed in vinegar-soaked Thermogene and when Tristan and I came into the bedroom he was feebly turning over the pages of the *Darrowby and Houlton Times.*

He spoke in a tortured whisper. 'Have you seen this? It says here that the golf clubhouse was knocked down yesterday and there's no clue as to how it happened. Damn funny thing. On Prescott's land, isn't it?' His head jerked suddenly from the pillow and he glared at his brother. 'You were there yesterday!' he croaked, then he fell back, muttering. 'Oh no, no, I'm sorry, it's too ridiculous — and it's wrong of me to blame you for everything.'

Tristan stared. He had never heard this kind of talk from Siegfried before. I too felt a pang of anxiety; could my boss be delirious?

Siegfried swallowed painfully. 'I've just had an urgent call from Armitage of Sorton. He's got a cow down with milk fever and I want you to drive James out there straight away. Go on, now — get moving.'

'Afraid I can't,' Tristan shrugged. 'Jim's car is in Hammond's garage. They're fixing that light — it'll take them about an hour.'

'Oh God, yes, and they said they couldn't let us have a spare. Well, Armitage is in a bit of a panic — that cow could be dead in an hour. What the hell can we do?'

'There's the Rover,' Tristan said quietly.

Siegfried's form stiffened suddenly under the blankets and wild terror flickered in his eyes. For a few moments his head rolled about on the pillow and his long, bony fingers picked nervously at the quilt, then with an effort he heaved himself on to his side and stared into his brother's eyes. He spoke slowly and the agonised hissing of his voice lent menace to his words.

'Right, so you'll have to take the Rover. I never thought I'd see the day when I'd let a wrecker like you drive it, but just let me tell you this. If you put a scratch on that car I'll kill you. I'll kill you with my own two hands.'

The old pattern was asserting itself. Siegfried's eyes had begun to bulge, a dark flush was creeping over his cheeks while Tristan's face had lost all expression.

Using the last remnants of his strength, Siegfried hoisted himself even higher. 'Now do you really think you are capable of driving that car five miles to Sorton and back without smashing it up? All right then, get on with it and just remember what I've said.'

Tristan withdrew in offended silence and as I followed him I took a last look at the figure in the bed. Siegfried had fallen back and was staring at the ceiling with feverish eyes. His lips moved feebly as though he were praying.

Outside the room, Tristan rubbed his hands delightedly. 'What a break, Jim! A chance in a lifetime! You know I never thought I'd get behind the wheel of that Rover in a hundred years.' He dropped his voice to a whisper. 'Just shows you — everything happens for the best.'

Five minutes later he was backing carefully out of the yard and into the lane and once on the Sorton road I saw he was beginning to enjoy himself. For two miles the way ahead stretched straight and clear except for a milk lorry approaching in the far distance; a perfect place to see what the Rover could do. He nestled down in the rich leather upholstery and pressed his foot hard on the accelerator.

We were doing an effortless eighty when I saw a car beginning to overtake the milk lorry; it was an ancient, square-topped, high-built vehicle like a biscuit tin on wheels and it had no business trying to overtake anything. I waited for it to pull back but it still came on. And the lorry, perhaps with a sporting driver, seemed to be spurting to make a race of it.

With increasing alarm I saw the two vehicles

abreast and bearing down on us only a few hundred yards away and not a foot of space on either side of them. Of course the old car would pull in behind the lorry — it had to, there was no other way — but it was taking a long time about it. Tristan jammed on his brakes. If the lorry did the same, the other car would just be able to dodge between. But within seconds I realised nothing like that was going to happen and as they thundered towards us I resigned myself with dumb horror to a head-on collision.

Just before I closed my eyes I had a fleeting glimpse of a large, alarmed face behind the wheel of the old car, then something hit the left side of the Rover with a rending crash.

When I opened my eyes we were stationary. There was just Tristan and myself staring straight ahead at the road, empty and quiet, curving ahead of us into the peaceful green of the hills.

I sat motionless, listening to my thumping heart then I looked over my shoulder and saw the lorry disappearing at high speed round a distant bend; in passing I studied Tristan's face with interest — I had never seen a completely green face before.

After quite a long time, feeling a draught from the left, I looked carefully round in that direction. There were no doors on that side — one was lying by the roadside a few yards back and the other hung from a single broken hinge; as I watched, this one too, clattered on to the tarmac with a note of flat finality. Slowly, as in a dream, I got out and surveyed the damage; the left side of the Rover was a desert of twisted metal where the old car, diving for the verge at the last split second, had ploughed its way.

Tristan had flopped down on the grass, his face blank. A nasty scratch on the paintwork might have sent him into a panic but this wholesale destruction seemed to have numbed his senses. But this state didn't last long; he began to blink, then his eyes narrowed and he felt for his Woodbines. His agile mind was back at work and it wasn't difficult to read his thoughts. What was he going to do now?

It seemed to me after a short appraisal of the situation that he had three possible courses of action. First, and most attractive, he could get out of Darrowby permanently — emigrate if necessary. Second, he could go straight to the railway station and board a train for Brawton where he could live quietly with his mother till this had blown over. Third, and it didn't bear thinking about, he could go back to Skeldale House and tell Siegfried he had smashed up his new Rover.

As I weighed up the possibilities I spotted the old car which had hit us; it was lying upside down in a ditch about fifty yards down the road. Hurrying towards it, I could hear a

405

loud cackling coming from the interior and I remembered it was market day and many of the farmers would be bringing in crates of hens and maybe twenty or thirty dozen eggs to sell. We peered in through a window and Tristan gasped. A fat man, obviously unhurt, was lying in a great pool of smashed eggs. His face wore a wide, reassuring smile — in fact, his whole expression was ingratiating as far as it could be seen through the mask of egg which covered his features. The rest of the interior was filled with frantic hens which had escaped from their crates in the crash and were hunting for a way out.

The fat man, smiling up happily from his bed of eggs, was shouting something, but it was difficult to hear him above the wild cackling. I managed to pick up odd phrases: 'Very sorry indeed — entirely my fault — I'll make good the damage.' The words floated up cheerfully while the hens scampered across the man's beaming face and yolks coursed sluggishly down his clothes.

With an effort, Tristan managed to wrench open a door and was driven back immediately by a rush of hens. Some of them galloped off in various directions till they were lost to sight, while their less adventurous companions began to peck about philosophically by the roadside.

'Are you all right?' Tristan shouted.

'Yes, yes, young man. I'm not hurt. Please

don't worry about me.' The fat man struggled vainly to rise from the squelching mass. 'Ee, I am sorry about this, but I'll see you right, you can be sure.'

He held up a dripping hand and we helped him out on to the road. Despite his saturated clothes and the pieces of shell sticking to his hair and moustache he hadn't lost his poise. In fact he radiated confidence, the same confidence, I thought, which made him think his old car could overtake that speeding lorry.

He laid a hand on Tristan's shoulder. 'There's a simple explanation, you know. The sun got in my eyes.'

It was twelve noon and the fat man had been driving due north, but there didn't seem much point in arguing.

We lifted the shattered doors from the road, put them inside the Rover, drove to Sorton, treated the milk fever cow and returned to Darrowby. Tristan gave me a single despairing look then squared his shoulders and marched straight to his brother's room. I followed close on his heels.

Siegfried was worse. His face was red with fever and his eyes burned deeply in their sockets. He didn't move when Tristan walked over to the foot of the bed.

'Well, how did you get on?' The whisper was barely audible.

'Oh fine, the cow was on her feet when we left. But there's just one thing — I had a bit of a bump with the car.'

Siegfried had been wheezing stertorously and staring at the ceiling but the breathing stopped as if it had been switched off. There was an eerie silence then from the completely motionless figure two strangled words escaped. 'What happened?'

'Wasn't my fault. Chap tried to overtake a lorry and didn't make it. Caught one side of the Rover.'

Again the silence and again the whisper.

'Much damage?'

'Front and rear wings pretty well mangled, I'm afraid — and both doors torn off the left side.'

As if operated by a powerful spring, Siegfried came bolt upright in the bed. It was startingly like a corpse coming to life and the effect was heightened by the coils of Thermogene which had burst loose and trailed in shroud-like garlands from the haggard head. The mouth opened wide in a completely soundless scream.

'You bloody fool! You're sacked!'

He crashed back on to the pillow as though the mechanism had gone into reverse and lay very still. We watched him for a few moments in some anxiety, but when we heard the breathing restart we tiptoed from the room.

On the landing Tristan blew out his cheeks and drew a Woodbine from its packet. 'A tricky little situation, Jim, but you know what

I always say.' He struck a match and pulled the smoke down blissfully. 'Things usually turn out better than you expect.'

CHAPTER 40

A lot of the Dales farms were anonymous and it was a help to find this one so plainly identified. 'Heston Grange' it said on the gate in bold black capitals.

I got out of the car and undid the latch. It was a good gate, too, and swung easily on its hinges instead of having to be dragged round with a shoulder under the top spar. The farmhouse lay below me, massive, grey-stoned, with a pair of bow windows which some prosperous Victorian had added to the original structure.

It stood on a flat, green neck of land in a loop of the river and the lushness of the grass and the quiet fertility of the surrounding fields contrasted sharply with the stark hills behind. Towering oaks and beeches sheltered the house and a thick pine wood covered the lower slopes of the fell.

I walked round the buildings shouting as I always did, because some people considered it a subtle insult to go to the house and ask if the farmer was in. Good farmers are indoors only at meal times. But my shouts drew no reply, so I went over and knocked at the door set deep among the weathered stones.

A voice answered 'Come in,' and I opened the door into a huge, stone-flagged kitchen with hams and sides of bacon hanging from hooks in the ceiling. A dark girl in a check blouse and green linen slacks was kneading dough in a bowl. She looked up and smiled.

'Sorry I couldn't let you in. I've got my hands full.' She held up her arms, floury-white to the elbow.

'That's all right. My name is Herriot. I've come to see a calf. It's lame, I understand.'

'Yes, we think he's broken his leg. Probably got his foot in a hole when he was running about. If you don't mind waiting a minute, I'll come with you. My father and the men are in the fields. I'm Helen Alderson, by the way.'

She washed and dried her arms and pulled on a pair of short Wellingtons. 'Take over this bread will you, Meg,' she said to an old woman who came through from an inner room. 'I have to show Mr Herriot the calf.'

Outside, she turned to me and laughed. 'We've got a bit of a walk, I'm afraid. He's in one of the top buildings. Look, you can just see it up there.' She pointed to a squat, stone barn, high on the fell-side. I knew all about these top buildings; they were scattered all over the high country and I got a lot of healthy exercise going round them. They were used for storing hay and other things and as shelters for the animals on the hill pastures.

I looked at the girl for a few seconds. 'Oh, that's all right, I don't mind. I don't mind in the least.'

We went over the field to a narrow bridge spanning the river, and, following her across, I was struck by a thought; this new fashion of women wearing slacks might be a bit revolutionary but there was a lot to be said for it. The path led upward through the pine wood and here the sunshine was broken up into islands of brightness among the dark trunks, the sound of the river grew faint and we walked softly on a thick carpet of pine needles. It was cool in the wood and silent except when a bird call echoed through the trees.

Ten minutes of hard walking brought us out again into the hot sun on the open moor and the path curved steeper still round a series of rocky outcrops. I was beginning to puff, but the girl kept up a brisk pace, swinging along with easy strides. I was glad when we reached the level ground on the top and the barn came in sight again.

When I opened the half door I could hardly see my patient in the dark interior which was heavy with the fragrance of hay piled nearly to the roof. He looked very small and sorry for himself with his dangling foreleg which trailed uselessly along the strawed floor as he tried to walk.

'Will you hold his head while I examine him, please?' I said.

The girl caught the calf expertly, one hand under its chin, the other holding an ear. As I felt my way over the leg the little creature stood trembling, his face a picture of woe.

'Well, your diagnosis was correct. Clean fracture of the radius and ulna, but there's very little displacement so it should do well with a plaster on it.' I opened my bag, took out some plaster bandages then filled a bucket with water from a near-by spring. I soaked one of the bandages and applied it to the leg, following it with a second and a third till the limb was encased in a rapidly hardening white sheath from elbow to foot.

'We'll just wait a couple of minutes till it hardens, then we can let him go.' I kept tapping the plaster till I was satisfied it was set like stone. 'All right,' I said finally. 'He can go now.'

The girl released the head and the little animal trotted away. 'Look,' she cried. 'He's putting his weight on it already! And doesn't he look a lot happier!' I smiled. I felt I had really done something. The calf felt no pain now that the broken ends of the bone were immobilised; and the fear which always demoralises a hurt animal had magically vanished.

'Yes,' I said. 'He certainly has perked up quickly.' My words were almost drowned by a tremendous bellow and the patch of blue above the half door was suddenly obscured by a large shaggy head. Two great liquid eyes stared down anxiously at the little calf and it answered with a high-pitched bawl. Soon a deafening duet was in progress.

'That's his mother,' the girl shouted above the din. 'Poor old thing, she's been hanging about here all morning wondering what we've done with her calf. She hates being separated from him.'

I straightened up and drew the bolt on the door. 'Well she can come in now.'

The big cow almost knocked me down as she rushed past me. Then she started a careful, sniffing inspection of her calf, pushing him around with her muzzle and making muffled lowing noises deep in her throat.

The little creature submitted happily to all the fuss and when it was over and his mother was finally satisfied, he limped round to her udder and began to suck heartily.

'Soon got his appetite back,' I said and we both laughed.

I threw the empty tins into my bag and closed it. 'He'll have to keep the plaster on for a month, so if you'll give me a ring then I'll come back and take it off. Just keep an eye on him and make sure his leg doesn't get sore round the top of the bandage.'

As we left the barn the sunshine and the sweet warm air met us like a high wave. I turned and looked across the valley to the soaring green heights, smooth, enormous, hazy in the noon heat. Beneath my feet the grassy slopes fell away steeply to where the river glimmered among the trees.

'It's wonderful up here,' I said. 'Just look at that gorge over there. And that great hill — I suppose you could call it a mountain.' I pointed at a giant which heaved its heather-mottled shoulders high above the others.

'That's Heskit Fell — nearly two and a half thousand feet. And that's Eddleton just beyond, and Wedder Fell on the other side and Colver and Sennor.' The names with their wild, Nordic ring fell easily from her tongue; she spoke of them like old friends and I could sense the affection in her voice.

We sat down on the warm grass of the hillside, a soft breeze pulled at the heads of the moorland flowers, somewhere a curlew cried. Darrowby and Skeldale House and veterinary practice seemed a thousand miles away.

'You're lucky to live here,' I said. 'But I don't think you need me to tell you that.'

'No, I love this country. There's nowhere else quite like it.' She paused and looked slowly around her. 'I'm glad it appeals to you too — a lot of people find it too bare and wild. It almost seems to frighten them.'

I laughed. 'Yes, I know, but as far as I'm concerned I can't help feeling sorry for all the thousands of vets who don't work in the Yorkshire Dales.'

I began to talk about my work, then almost without knowing, I was going back over my student days, telling her of the good times, the friends I had made and our hopes and aspirations.

I surprised myself with my flow of talk — I wasn't much of a chatterbox usually — and I felt I must be boring my companion. But she sat quietly looking over the valley, her arms around her green-clad legs, nodding at times as though she understood. And she laughed in all the right places.

I wondered too, at the silly feeling that I would like to forget all about the rest of the day's duty and stay up here on this sunny hillside. It came to me that it had been a long time since I had sat down and talked to a girl of my own age. I had almost forgotten what it was like.

I didn't hurry back down the path and through the scented pine wood but it seemed no time at all before we were walking across the wooden bridge and over the field to the farm.

I turned with my hand on the car door. 'Well, I'll see you in a month.' It sounded like an awful long time.

The girl smiled. 'Thank you for what you've done.' As I started the engine she waved and went into the house.

'Helen Alderson?' Siegfried said later over lunch. 'Of course I know her. Lovely girl.'

Tristan, across the table, made no comment, but he laid down his knife and fork, raised his eyes reverently to the ceiling and gave a long, low whistle. Then he started to eat again.

Siegfried went on. 'Oh yes, I know her very well. And I admire her. Her mother died a few years ago and she runs the whole place. Cooks and looks after her father and a younger brother and sister.' He spooned some mashed potatoes on to his plate. 'Any men friends? Oh, half the young bloods in the district are chasing her but she doesn't seem to be going steady with any of them. Choosy sort, I think.'

CHAPTER 41

It was when I was plodding up Mr Kay's field for the ninth time that it began to occur to me that this wasn't going to be my day. For some time now I had been an L.V.I., the important owner of a little certificate informing whosoever it may concern that James Herriot M.R.C.V.S. was a Local Veterinary Inspector of the Ministry of Agriculture and Fisheries. It meant that I was involved in a lot of routine work like clinical examinations and tuberculin testing. It also highlighted something which I had been suspecting for some time — the Dales farmers' attitude to time was different from my own.

It had been all right when I was calling on them to see a sick animal; they were usually around waiting for me and the beast would be confined in some building when I arrived. It was very different, however, when I sent them a card saying I was coming to inspect their dairy cows or test their herd. It stated quite clearly on the card that the animals must be assembled indoors and that I would be there at a certain time and I planned my day accordingly; fifteen minutes or so for a clinical and anything up to several hours for a test depending on the size of the herd. If I was kept waiting for ten minutes at every clinical while they got the cows in from the field it meant simply that after six visits I was running an hour late.

So when I drove up to Mr Kay's farm for a tuberculin test and found his cows tied up in their stalls I breathed a sigh of relief. We were through them in no time at all and I thought I was having a wonderful start to the day when the farmer said he had only half a dozen young heifers to do to complete the job. It was when I left the buildings and saw the group of shaggy roans and reds grazing contentedly at the far end of a large field that I felt the old foreboding.

'I thought you'd have them inside, Mr Kay,' I said apprehensively.

Mr Kay tapped out his pipe on to his palm, mixed the sodden dottle with a few strands of villainous looking twist and crammed it back into the bowl. 'Nay, nay,' he said, puffing appreciatively, 'Ah didn't like to put them in on a grand 'ot day like this. We'll drive them up to that little house.' He pointed to a tumbledown grey-stone barn at the summit of the long, steeply sloping pasture and blew out a cloud of choking smoke. 'Won't take many minutes.'

At his last sentence a cold hand clutched at me. I'd heard these dreadful words so many times before. But maybe it would be all right this time. We made our way to the bottom of the field and got behind the heifers.

'Cush, cush!' cried Mr Kay.

'Cush, cush!' I added encouragingly, slapping my hands against my thighs.

The heifers stopped pulling the grass and regarded us with mild interest, their jaws moving lazily, then in response to further cries they began to meander casually up the hill. We managed to coax them up to the door of the barn but there they stopped. The leader put her head inside for a moment then turned suddenly and made a dash down the hill. The others followed suit immediately and though we danced about and waved our arms they ran past us as if we weren't there. I looked thoughtfully at the young beasts thundering down the slope, their tails high, kicking up their heels like mustangs; they were enjoying this new game.

Down the hill once more and again the slow wheedling up to the door and again the sudden breakaway. This time one of them tried it on her own and as I galloped vainly to and fro trying to turn her the others charged with glee through the gap and down the slope again.

It was a long, steep hill and as I trudged up

for the third time with the sun blazing on my back I began to regret being so conscientious about my clothes; in the instructions to the new L.V.I.'s the Ministry had been explicit that they expected us to be properly attired to carry out our duties. I had taken it to heart and rigged myself out in the required uniform but I realised now that a long oilskin coat and Wellingtons was not an ideal outfit for the job in hand. The sweat was trickling into my eyes and my shirt was beginning to cling to me.

When, for the third time, I saw the retreating backs careering joyously down the hill, I thought it was time to do something about it.

'Just a minute,' I called to the farmer, 'I'm getting a bit warm.'

I took off the coat, rolled it up and placed it on the grass well away from the barn. And as I made a neat pile of my syringe, the box of tuberculin, my calipers, scissors, notebook and pencil, the thought kept intruding that I was being cheated in some way. After all, Ministry work was easy — any practitioner would tell you that. You didn't have to get up in the middle of the night, you had nice set hours and you never really had to exert yourself. In fact it was money for old rope — a pleasant relaxation from the real thing. I wiped my streaming brow and stood for a few seconds panting gently — this just wasn't fair.

We started again and at the fourth visit to the barn I thought we had won because all but one of the heifers strolled casually inside. But that last one just wouldn't have it. We cushed imploringly, waved and even got near enough to poke at its rump but it stood in the entrance regarding the interior with deep suspicion. Then the heads of its mates began to reappear in the doorway and I knew we had lost again; despite my frantic dancing and shouting they wandered out one by one before joining again in their happy downhill dash. This time I found myself galloping down after them in an agony of frustration.

We had another few tries during which the heifers introduced touches of variation by sometimes breaking away half way up the hill or occasionally trotting round the back of the barn and peeping at us coyly from behind the old stones before frisking to the bottom again.

After the eighth descent I looked appealingly at Mr Kay who was relighting his pipe calmly and didn't appear to be troubled in any way. My time schedule was in tatters but I don't think he had noticed that we had been going on like this for about forty minutes.

'Look, we're getting nowhere,' I said. 'I've got a lot of other work waiting for me. Isn't there anything more we can do?'

The farmer stamped down the twist with his thumb, drew deeply and pleasurably a few times then looked at me with mild surprise. 'Well, let's see. We could bring dog out but I don't know as he'll be much good. He's nobbut a young 'un.'

He sauntered back to the farmhouse and opened a door. A shaggy cur catapulted out, barking in delight, and Mr Kay brought him over to the field. 'Get away by!' he cried gesturing towards the cattle who had resumed their grazing and the dog streaked behind them. I really began to hope as we went up the hill with the hairy little figure darting in, nipping at the heels, but at the barn the rot set in again. I could see the heifers beginning to sense the inexperience of the dog and one of them managed to kick him briskly under the chin as he came in. The little animal yelped and his tail went down. He stood uncertainly, looking at the beasts, advancing on him now, shaking their horns threateningly, then he seemed to come to a decision and slunk away. The young cattle went after him at increasing speed and in a moment I was looking at the extraordinary spectacle of the dog going flat out down the hill with the heifers drumming close behind him. At the foot he disappeared under a gate and we saw him no more.

Something seemed to give way in my head. 'Oh God,' I yelled, 'we're never going to get these damn things tested! I'll just have to leave them. I don't know what the Ministry is going to say, but I've had enough!'

The farmer looked at me ruminatively. He seemed to recognise that I was at breaking point. 'Aye, it's no good,' he said, tapping his pipe out on his heel. 'We'll have to get Sam.'

'Sam?'

'Aye, Sam Broadbent. Works for me neighbour. He'll get 'em in all right.'

'How's he going to do that?'

'Oh, he can imitate a fly.'

For a moment my mind reeled. 'Did you say imitate a fly?'

'That's right. A warble fly, tha knows. He's a bit slow is t'lad but by gaw he can imitate a fly. I'll go and get him — he's only two fields down the road.'

I watched the farmer's retreating back in disbelief then threw myself down on the ground. At any other time I would have enjoyed lying there on the slope with the sun on my face and the grass cool against my sweating back; the air was still and heavy with the fragrance of clover and when I opened my eyes the gentle curve of the valley floor was a vision of peace. But my mind was a turmoil. I had a full day's Ministry work waiting for me and I was an hour behind time already. I could picture the long succession of farmers waiting for me and cursing me heartily. The tension built in me till I could stand it no longer; I jumped to my feet and ran down to the gate at the foot. I could see along the road from there and was relieved to find that Mr Kay was on his way back.

Just behind him a large, fat man was riding slowly on a very small bicycle, his heels on the pedals, his feet and knees sticking out at right angles. Tufts of greasy black hair stuck out at random from under a kind of skull cap which looked like an old bowler without the brim.

'Sam's come to give us a hand,' said Mr Kay with an air of quiet triumph.

'Good morning,' I said and the big man turned slowly and nodded. The eyes in the round, unshaven race were vacant and incurious and I decided that Sam did indeed look a bit slow. I found it difficult to imagine how he could possibly be of any help.

The heifers, standing near by, watched with languid interest as we came through the gate. They had obviously enjoyed every minute of the morning's entertainment and it seemed they were game for a little more fun if we so desired; but it was up to us, of course — they weren't worried either way.

Sam propped his bicycle against the wall and paced solemnly forward. He made a circle of his thumb and forefinger and placed it to his lips. His cheeks worked as though he was getting everything into place then he took a deep breath. And, from nowhere it seemed came a sudden swelling of angry sound, a vicious humming and buzzing which made me

425

look round in alarm for the enraged insect zooming in for the kill.

The effect on the heifers was electric. Their superior air vanished and was replaced by rigid anxiety; then, as the noise increased in volume, they turned and charged up the hill. But it wasn't the carefree frolic of before — no tossing heads, waving tails and kicking heels; this time they kept shoulder to shoulder in a frightened block.

Mr Kay and I, trotting on either side, directed them yet again up to the building where they formed a group, looking nervously around them.

We had to wait for a short while for Sam to arrive. He was clearly a one-pace man and ascended the slope unhurriedly. At the top he paused to regain his breath, fixed the animals with a blank gaze and carefully adjusted his fingers against his mouth. A moment's tense silence then the humming broke out again, even more furious and insistent than before.

The heifers knew when they were beaten. With a chorus of startled bellows they turned and rushed into the building and I crashed the half door behind them; I stood leaning against it unable to believe my troubles were over. Sam joined me and looked into the dark interior. As if to finally establish his mastery he gave a sudden sharp blast, this time without his fingers, and his victims huddled still closer against the far wall.

A few minutes later, after Sam had left us, I was happily clipping and injecting the necks. I looked up at the farmer. 'You know, I can still hardly believe what I saw there. It was like magic. That chap has a wonderful gift.'

Mr Kay looked over the half door and I followed his gaze down the grassy slope to the road. Sam was riding away and the strange black headwear was just visible, bobbing along the top of the wall.

'Aye, he can imitate a fly all right. Poor awd lad, it's t'only thing he's good at.'

CHAPTER 42

Hurrying away from Mr Kay's to my second test I reflected that if I had to be more than an hour late for an appointment it was a lucky thing that my next call was at the Hugills. The four brothers and their families ran a herd which, with cows, followers and calves must have amounted to nearly two hundred and I had to test the lot of them; but I knew that my lateness wouldn't bring any querulous remarks on my head because the Hugills had developed the Dales tradition of courtesy to an extraordinary degree. The stranger within their gates was treated like royalty.

As I drove into the yard I could see everybody leaving their immediate tasks and advancing on me with beaming faces. The brothers were in the lead and they stopped opposite me as I got out of the car, and I thought as I always did that I had never seen such healthy-looking men. Their ages ranged from Walter, who was about sixty, down through Thomas and Fenwick to William, the youngest, who would be in his late forties, and I should say their average weight would be about fifteen stones. They weren't fat, either, just huge, solid men with bright red, shining faces and clear eyes.

William stepped forward from the group and I knew what was coming; this was always his job. He leaned forward, suddenly solemn, and looked into my face.

'How are you today, sorr?' he asked.

'Very well, thank you, Mr Hugill,' I replied.

'Good!' said William fervently, and the other brothers all repeated 'Good, good, good,' with deep satisfaction.

William took a deep breath. 'And how is Mr Farnon?'

'Oh, he's very fit, thanks.'

'Good!' Then the rapid fire of the responses from behind him: 'Good, good, good.'

William hadn't finished yet. He cleared his throat. 'And how is young Mr Farnon?'

'In really top form.'

'Good!' But this time William allowed himself a gentle smile and from behind him came a few dignified ho-ho's. Walter closed his eyes and his great shoulders shook silently. They all knew Tristan.

William stepped back into line, his appointed task done and we all went into the byre. I braced myself as I looked at the long row of backs, the tails swishing at the flies. There was some work ahead here.

'Sorry I'm so late,' I said, as I drew the tuberculin into the syringe. 'I was held up at the last place. It's difficult to forecast how long these tests will take.'

All four brothers replied eagerly. 'Aye, you're right, sorr. It's difficult. It IS difficult. You're right, you're right, it's difficult.' They went on till they had thrashed the last ounce out of the statement.

I finished filling the syringe, got out my scissors and began to push my way between the first two cows. It was a tight squeeze and I puffed slightly in the stifling atmosphere.

'It's a bit warm in here,' I said.

Again the volley of agreement. 'You're right, sorr. Aye, it's warm. It IS warm. You're right. It's warm. It's warm. Aye, you're right.' This was all delivered with immense conviction and vigorous nodding of heads as though I had made some incredible discovery; and as I looked at the grave, intent faces still pondering over my brilliant remark, I could feel my tensions beginning to dissolve. I was lucky to work here. Where else but in the high country of Yorkshire would I meet people like these?

I pushed along the cow and got hold of its ear, but Walter stopped me with a gentle cough.

'Nay, Mr Herriot, you won't have to look in the ears. I have all t'numbers wrote down.'

'Oh, that's fine. It'll save us a lot of time.' I had always found scratching the wax away to find ear tattoos an overrated pastime. And it was good to hear that the Hugills were attending to the clerical side; there was a section in the Ministry form which said: 'Are the herd records in good order?' I always wrote 'Yes,' keeping my fingers crossed as I thought of the scrawled figures on the backs of old bills, milk recording sheets, anything.

'Aye,' said Walter. 'I have 'em all set down proper in a book.'

'Great! Can you go and get it, then?'

'No need, sorr, I have it 'ere.' Walter was the boss, there was no doubt about it. They all seemed to live in perfect harmony but when the chips were down Walter took over automatically. He was the organiser, the acknowledged brains of the outfit. The battered trilby which he always wore in contrast with the others' caps gave him an extra air of authority.

Everybody watched respectfully as he slowly and deliberately extracted a spectacle case from an inside pocket. He opened it and took out an old pair of steel-rimmed spectacles, blowing away fragments of the hay and corn chaff with which the interior of the case was thickly powdered. There was a quiet dignity and importance in the way he unhurriedly threaded the side pieces over his ears and stood grimacing slightly to work everything into place. Then he put his hand into his waistcoat pocket.

When he took it out he was holding some object but it was difficult to identify, being almost obscured by his enormous thumb. Then I saw that it was a tiny, black-covered miniature diary about two inches square — the sort of novelty people give each other at Christmas.

'Is that the herd record?' I asked.

'Yes, this is it. It's all set down in here.' Walter daintily flicked over the pages with a horny forefinger and squinted through his spectacles. 'Now that fust cow — she's number eighty-fower.'

'Splendid!' I said. 'I'll just check this one and then we can go by the book.' I peered into the ear. 'That's funny, I make it twenty-six.'

The brothers had a look. 'You're right, sorr, you're right. It IS twenty-six.'

Walter pursed his lips. 'Why, that's Blue-bell's calf isn't it?'

'Nay,' said Fenwick, 'she's out of awd Buttercup.'

'Can't be,' mumbled Thomas. 'Awd But-tercup was sold to Tim Jefferson afore this 'un was born. This is Brenda's calf.'

William shook his head. 'Ah'm sure we got her as a heifer at Bob Ashby's sale.'

'All right,' I said, holding up a hand. 'We'll put in twenty-six.' I had to cut in. It was in no way an argument, just a leisurely discus-sion but it looked as if it could go on for some time. I wrote the number in my notebook and injected the cow. 'Now how about this next one?'

'Well ah DO know that 'un,' said Walter confidently, stabbing at an entry in the diary. 'Can't make no mistake, she's number five.'

I looked in the ear. 'Says a hundred and thirty seven here.'

It started again. 'She was bought in, wasn't she?' 'Nay, nay, she's out of awd Dribbler.' 'Don't think so — Dribbler had nowt but bulls . . .'

I raised my hand again. 'You know, I really think it might be quicker to look in all the ears. Time's getting on.'

'Aye, you're right, sorr, it IS getting on.' Walter returned the herd record to his waist-coat pocket philosophically and we started the laborious business of clipping, measuring and injecting every animal, plus rubbing the inside of the ears with a cloth soaked in spirit to identify the numbers which had often faded to a few unrelated dots. Occasionally Walter referred to his tiny book. 'Ah, that's right, ninety-two. I thowt so. It's all set down here.'

Fighting with the loose animals in the boxes round the fold yard was like having a dirty Turkish bath while wearing oilskins. The brothers caught the big beasts effortlessly and even the strongest bullock grew quickly discouraged when it tried to struggle against those mighty arms. But I noticed one strange phenomenon: the men's fingers were so thick and huge that they often slipped out of the animals' noses through sheer immobility.

It took an awful long time but we finally got through. The last little calf had a space clipped in his shaggy neck and bawled heartily as he felt the needle, then I was out in the sweet air throwing my coat in the car boot. I looked at my watch — three o'clock. I was nearly two hours behind my schedule now and already I was hot and weary, with skinned toes on my right foot where a cow had trodden and a bruised left instep caused by the sudden descent of Fenwick's size thirteen hobnails during a particularly violent mêlée. As I closed the boot and limped round to the car door I began to wonder a little about this easy Ministry work.

Walter loomed over me and inclined his head graciously. 'Come in and sit down and have a drink o' tea.'

'It's very kind of you and I wish I could, Mr Hugill. But I've got a long string of inspections waiting and I don't know when I'll get round them. I've fixed up far too many and I completely underestimated the time needed for your test. I really am an absolute fool.'

And the brothers intoned sincerely. 'Aye, you're right, sorr, you're right, you're right.'

■ ■ ■ ■

Well, there was no more testing today, but ten inspections still to do and I should have been at the first one two hours ago. I roared off, feeling that little ball tightening in my stomach as it always did when I was fighting the clock. Gripping the wheel with one hand and exploring my lunch packet with the other, I pulled out a piece of Mrs Hall's ham and egg pie and began to gnaw at it as I went along.

But I had gone only a short way when reason asserted itself. This was no good. It was an excellent pie and I might as well enjoy it. I pulled off the unfenced road on to the grass, switched off the engine and opened the windows wide. The farm back there was like an island of activity in the quiet landscape and now that I was away from the noise and the stuffiness of the buildings the silence and the emptiness enveloped me like a soothing blanket. I leaned my head against the back of the seat and looked out at the checkered greens of the little fields along the flanks of the hills; thrusting upwards between their walls till they gave way to the jutting rocks and the harsh brown of the heather which flooded the wild country above.

I felt better when I drove away and didn't particularly mind when the farmer at the first inspection greeted me with a scowl.

'This isn't one o'clock, Maister!' he snapped. 'My cows have been in all afternoon and look at the bloody mess they've made. Ah'll never get the place clean again!'

I had to agree with him when I saw the muck piled up behind the cows; it was one of the snags about housing animals in grass time. And the farmer's expression grew blacker as most of them cocked their tails as though in welcome and added further layers to the heaps.

'I won't keep you much longer,' I said briskly, and began to work my way down the row. Before the tuberculin testing scheme came into being, these clinical examinations were the only means of detecting tuberculous cows and I moved from animal to animal palpating the udders for any unusual induration. The routine examinations were known jocularly in the profession as 'bag-snatching' or 'cow-punching' and it was a job that soon got tedious.

I found the only way to stop myself going nearly mad with boredom was to keep reminding myself what I was there for. So when I came to a gaunt red cow with a pendulous udder I straightened up and turned to the farmer.

'I'm going to take a milk sample from this one. She's a bit hard in that left hind quarter.'

The farmer sniffed. 'Please yourself. There's

nowt wrong with her but I suppose it'll make a job for somebody.'

Squirting milk from the quarter into a two ounce bottle, I thought about Siegfried's veterinary friend who always took a pint sample from the healthiest udder he could find to go with his lunchtime sandwiches.

I labelled the bottle and put it into the car. We had a little electric centrifuge at Skeldale House and tonight I would spin this milk and examine the sediment on a slide after staining by Ziehl-Neelsen. Probably I would find nothing but at times there was the strange excitement of peering down the microscope at a clump of bright red, iridescent T.B. bacilli. When that happened the cow was immediately slaughtered and there was always the thought that I might have lifted the death sentence from some child — the meningitis, the spinal and lung infections which were so common in those days.

Returning to the byre I finished the inspection by examining the wall in front of each cow.

The farmer watched me dourly. 'What you on with now?'

'Well, if a cow has a cough you can often find some spit on the wall.' I had, in truth, found more tuberculous cows this way than any other — by scraping a little sputum on to a glass slide and then staining it as for the milk.

The modern young vet just about never sees a T.B. cow, thank heavens, but 'screws' were all too common thirty years ago. There were very few in the high Pennines but in the low country on the plain you found them; the cows that 'weren't doing right', the ones with the soft, careful cough and slightly accelerated breathing. Often they were good milkers and ate well, but they were killers and I was learning to spot them. And there were the others, the big, fat, sleek animals which could still be riddled with the disease. They were killers of a more insidious kind and nobody could pick them out. It took the tuberculin test to do that.

At the next four places I visited, the farmers had got tired of waiting for me and had turned their cows out. They had all to be brought in from the field and they came slowly and reluctantly; there was nothing like the rodeo I had had with Mr Kay's heifers but a lot more time was lost. The animals kept trying to turn back to the field while I sped around their flanks like a demented sheep dog; and as I panted to and fro each farmer told me the same thing — that cows only liked to come in at milking time.

Milking time did eventually come and I caught three of my herds while they were being milked, but it was after six when I came tired and hungry to my second last inspection. A hush hung over the place and after shouting my way round the buildings without finding anybody I walked over to the house.

'Is your husband in, Mrs Bell?' I asked.

'No, he's had to go into t'village to get the horse shod but he won't be long before he's back. He's left cows in for you,' the farmer's wife replied.

That was fine. I'd soon get through this lot. I almost ran into the byre and started the old routine, feeling sick to death of the sight and smell of cows and fed up with pawing at their udders. I was working along almost automatically when I came to a thin, rangy cow with a narrow red and white face; she could be a crossed shorthorn-Ayrshire. I had barely touched her udder when she lashed out with the speed of light and caught me just above the kneecap.

I hopped round the byre on one leg, groaning and swearing in my agony. It was some time before I was able to limp back to have another try and this time I scratched her back and cush-cushed her in a wheedling tone before sliding my hand gingerly between her legs. The same thing happened again only this time the sharp-edged cloven foot smacked slightly higher up my leg.

Crashing back against the wall, I huddled there, almost weeping with pain and rage. After a few minutes I reached a decision. To hell with her. If she didn't want to be examined she could take her luck. I had had enough for one day — I was in no mood for heroics.

Ignoring her, I proceeded down the byre till I had inspected the others. But I had to pass her on my way back and paused to have another look; and whether it was sheer stubbornness or whether I imagined she was laughing at me, I don't know, but I decided to have just one more go. Maybe she didn't like me coming from behind. Perhaps if I worked from the side she wouldn't mind so much.

Carefully I squeezed my way between her and her neighbour, gasping as the craggy pelvic bones dug into my ribs. Once in the space beyond, I thought, I would be free to to do my job; and that was my big mistake. Because as soon as I had got there the cow went to work on me in earnest. Switching her back end round quickly to cut off my way of escape, she began to kick me systematically from head to foot. She kicked forward, reaching at times high on my chest as I strained back against the wall.

Since then I have been kicked by an endless variety of cows in all sorts of situations but never by such an expert as this one. There must be very few really venomous bovines and when one of them uses her feet it is usually an instinctive reaction to being hurt or frightened; and they kick blindly. But this cow measured me up before each blow and

440

her judgement of distance was beautiful. And as she drove me further towards her head she was able to hook me in the back with her horns by way of variety. I am convinced she hated the human race.

My plight was desperate. I was completely trapped and it didn't help when the apparently docile cow next door began to get into the act by prodding me off with her horns as I pressed against her.

I don't know what made me look up, but there, in the thick wall of the byre was a hole about two feet square where some of the crumbling stone had fallen out. I pulled myself up with an agility that amazed me and as I crawled through head first a sweet fragrance came up to me. I was looking into a hay barn and, seeing a deep bed of finest clover just below I launched myself into space and did a very creditable roll in the air before landing safely on my back.

Lying there, bruised and breathless, with the front of my coat thickly patterned with claw marks I finally abandoned any lingering illusions I had had that Ministry work was a soft touch.

I was rising painfully to my feet when Mr Bell strolled in. 'Sorry ah had to go out,' he said, looking me over with interest, 'But I'd just about given you up. You're 'ellish late.'

I dusted myself down and picked a few strands of hay from my hair. 'Yes, sorry about that. But never mind, I managed to get the job done.'

'But . . . were you havin' a bit of a kip, then?'

'No, not exactly. I had some trouble with one of your cows.' There wasn't much point in standing on my dignity. I told him the story.

Even the friendliest farmer seems to derive pleasure from a vet's discomfiture and Mr Bell listened with an ever-widening grin of delight. By the time I had finished he was doubled up, beating his breeches knees with his hands.

'I can just imagine it. That Ayrshire cross! She's a right bitch. Picked her up cheap at market last spring and thought ah'd got a bargain, but ah soon found out. Took us a fortnight to get bugger tied up!'

'Well, I just wish I'd known,' I said, rather tight lipped.

The farmer looked up at the hole in the wall. 'And you crawled through . . .' he went into another convulsion which lasted some time, then he took off his cap and wiped his eyes with the lining.

'Oh dear, oh dear,' he murmured weakly. 'By gaw, I wish I'd been here.'

My last call was just outside Darrowby and I could hear the church clock striking a quarter past seven as I got stiffly out of the car. After my easy day in the service of the government I felt broken in mind and body; I had to suppress a scream when I saw yet another long line of cows' backsides awaiting me. The sun was low, and dark thunder clouds piling up in the west had thrown the countryside into an eerie darkness; and in the old-fashioned, slit-windowed byre the animals looked shapeless and ill-defined in the gloom.

Right, no messing about. I was going to make a quick job of this and get off home; home to some food and an armchair. I had no further ambitions. So left hand on the root of the tail, right hand between the hind legs, a quick feel around and on to the next one. Eyes half closed, my mind numb, I moved from cow to cow going through the motions like a robot with the far end of the byre seeming like the promised land.

And finally here it was, the very last one up against the wall. Left hand on tail, right hand between legs . . . At first my tired brain didn't take in the fact that there was something different here, but there was . . . something vastly different. A lot of space and instead of the udder a deeply cleft, pendulous something with no teats anywhere.

I came awake suddenly and looked along the animal's side. A huge woolly head was turned towards me and two wide-set eyes regarded me enquiringly. In the dull light I could just see the gleam of the copper ring in the nose.

The farmer who had watched me in silence, spoke up.

'You're wasting your time there, young man. There's nowt wrong wi' HIS bag.'

CHAPTER 43

The card dangled above the old lady's bed. It read 'God is Near' but it wasn't like the usual religious text. It didn't have a frame or ornate printing. It was just a strip of cardboard about eight inches long with plain lettering which might have said 'No smoking' or 'Exit' and it was looped carelessly over an old gas bracket so that Miss Stubbs from where she lay could look up at it and read 'God is Near' in square black capitals.

There wasn't much more Miss Stubbs could see; perhaps a few feet of privet hedge through the frayed curtains but mainly it was just the cluttered little room which had been her world for so many years.

The room was on the ground floor and in the front of the cottage, and as I came up through the wilderness which had once been a garden I could see the dogs watching me from where they had jumped on to the old lady's bed. And when I knocked on the door the place almost erupted with their barking.

It was always like this. I had been visiting regularly for over a year and the pattern never changed; the furious barking, then Mrs Broadwith who looked after Miss Stubbs would push all the animals but my patient into the back kitchen and open the door and I would go in and see Miss Stubbs in the corner in her bed with the card hanging over it.

She had been there for a long time and would never get up again. But she never mentioned her illness and pain to me; all her concern was for her three dogs and two cats.

Today it was old Prince and I was worried about him. It was his heart — just about the most spectacular valvular incompetence I had ever heard. He was waiting for me as I came in, pleased as ever to see me, his long, fringed tail waving gently.

The sight of that tail used to make me think there must be a lot of Irish Setter in Prince but I was inclined to change my mind as I worked my way forward over the bulging black and white body to the shaggy head and upstanding Alsatian ears. Miss Stubbs often used to call him 'Mr Heinz' and though he may not have had 57 varieties in him his hybrid vigour had stood him in good stead. With his heart he should have been dead long ago.

'I thought I'd best give you a ring, Mr Herriot,' Mrs Broadwith said. She was a comfortable, elderly widow with a square, ruddy face contrasting sharply with the pinched features on the pillow. 'He's been coughing right bad this week and this morning he was a bit staggery. Still eats well, though.'

'I bet he does.' I ran my hands over the rolls of fat on the ribs. 'It would take something really drastic to put old Prince off his grub.'

Miss Stubbs laughed from the bed and the old dog, his mouth wide, eyes dancing, seemed to be joining in the joke. I put my stethoscope over his heart and listened, knowing well what I was going to hear. They say the heart is supposed to go 'Lub-dup, lub-dup', but Prince's went 'swish-swoosh, swish-swoosh'. There seemed to be nearly as much blood leaking back as was being pumped into the circulatory system. And another thing, the 'swish-swoosh' was a good bit faster than last time; he was on oral digitalis but it wasn't quite doing its job.

Gloomily I moved the stethoscope over the rest of the chest. Like all old dogs with a chronic heart weakness he had an ever-present bronchitis and I listened without enthusiasm to the symphony of whistles, rales, squeaks and bubbles which signalled the workings of Prince's lungs. The old dog stood very erect and proud, his tail still waving slowly. He always took it as a tremendous compliment when I examined him and there was no doubt he was enjoying himself now. Fortunately his was not a very painful ailment.

Straightening up, I patted his head and he responded immediately by trying to put his paws on my chest. He didn't quite make it and even that slight exertion started his ribs heaving and his tongue lolling. I gave him an intramuscular injection of digitalin and another of morphine hydrochloride which he accepted with apparent pleasure as part of the game.

'I hope that will steady his heart and breathing, Miss Stubbs. You'll find he'll be a bit dopey for the rest of the day and that will help, too. Carry on with the tablets, and I'm going to leave you some more medicine for his bronchitis.' I handed over a bottle of my old standby mixture of ipecacuanha and ammonium acetate.

The next stage of the visit began now as Mrs Broadwith brought in a cup of tea and the rest of the animals were let out of the kitchen. There were Ben, a Sealyham, and Sally, a Cocker Spaniel, and they started a deafening barking contest with Prince. They were closely followed by the cats, Arthur and Susie, who stalked in gracefully and began to rub themselves against my trouser legs.

It was the usual scenario for the many cups of tea I had drunk with Miss Stubbs under the little card which dangled above her bed.

'How are you today?' I asked.

'Oh, much better,' she replied and immediately, as always, changed the subject.

Mostly she liked to talk about her pets and the ones she had known right back to her girlhood. She spoke a lot, too, about the days when her family were alive. She loved to describe the escapades of her three brothers and today she showed me a photograph which Mrs Broadwith had found at the bottom of a drawer.

I took it from her and three young men in the knee breeches and little round caps of the nineties smiled up at me from the yellowed old print; they all held long church warden pipes and the impish humour in their expressions came down undimmed over the years.

'My word, they look really bright lads, Miss Stubbs,' I said.

'Oh, they were young rips!' she exclaimed. She threw back her head and laughed and for a moment her face was radiant, transfigured by her memories.

The things I had heard in the village came back to me; about the prosperous father and his family who lived in the big house many years ago. Then the foreign investments which crashed and the sudden change in circumstances. 'When t'owd feller died he was about skint,' one old man had said. 'There's not much brass there now.'

Probably just enough brass to keep Miss Stubbs and her animals alive and to pay Mrs Broadwith. Not enough to keep the garden dug or the house painted or for any of the normal little luxuries.

And, sitting there, drinking my tea, with the dogs in a row by the bedside and the cats making themselves comfortable on the bed itself, I felt as I had often felt before — a bit afraid of the responsibility I had. The one thing which brought some light into the life of the brave old woman was the transparent devotion of this shaggy bunch whose eyes were never far from her face. And the snag was that they were all elderly.

There had, in fact, been four dogs originally, but one of them, a truly ancient golden Labrador, had died a few months previously. And now I had the rest of them to look after and none of them less than ten years old.

They were perky enough but all showing some of the signs of old age; Prince with his heart, Sally beginning to drink a lot of water which made me wonder if she was starting with a pyometra, Ben growing steadily thinner with his nephritis. I couldn't give him new kidneys and I hadn't much faith in the hexamine tablets I had prescribed. Another peculiar thing about Ben was that I was always having to clip his claws; they grew at an extraordinary rate.

The cats were better, though Susie was a

bit scraggy and I kept up a morbid kneading of her furry abdomen for signs of lymphosarcoma. Arthur was the best of the bunch; he never seemed to ail anything beyond a tendency for his teeth to tartar up.

This must have been in Miss Stubbs' mind because, when I had finished my tea, she asked me to look at him. I hauled him across the bedspread and opened his mouth.

'Yes, there's a bit of the old trouble there. Might as well fix it while I'm here.'

Arthur was a huge, grey, neutered Tom, a living denial of all those theories that cats are cold-natured, selfish and the rest. His fine eyes, framed in the widest cat face I have ever seen, looked out on the world with an all-embracing benevolence and tolerance. His every movement was marked by immense dignity.

As I started to scrape his teeth his chest echoed with a booming purr like a distant outboard motor. There was no need for anybody to hold him; he sat there placidly and moved only once — when I was using forceps to crack off a tough piece of tartar from a back tooth and accidentally nicked his gum. He casually raised a massive paw as if to say 'Have a care, chum', but his claws were sheathed.

My next visit was less than a month later and was in response to an urgent summons from Mrs Broadwith at six o'clock in the evening. Ben had collapsed. I jumped straight into my car and in less than ten minutes was threading my way through the overgrown grass in the front garden with the animals watching from their window. The barking broke out as I knocked, but Ben's was absent. As I went into the little room I saw the old dog lying on his side, very still, by the bed.

D.O.A. is what we write in the day book. Dead on arrival. Just three words but they covered all kinds of situations — the end of milk fever cows, bloated bullocks, calves in fits. And tonight they meant that I wouldn't be clipping old Ben's claws any more.

It wasn't often these nephritis cases went off so suddenly but his urine albumen had been building up dangerously lately.

'Well, it was quick, Miss Stubbs. I'm sure the old chap didn't suffer at all.' My words sounded lame and ineffectual.

The old lady was in full command of herself. No tears, only a fixity of expression as she looked down from the bed at her companion for so many years. My idea was to get him out of the place as quickly as possible and I pulled a blanket under him and lifted him up. As I was moving away, Miss Stubbs said, 'Wait a moment.' With an effort she turned on to her side and gazed at Ben. Still without changing expression, she reached out and touched his head lightly. Then she lay back calmly as I hurried from the room.

In the back kitchen I had a whispered conference with Mrs Broadwith. 'I'll run down t'village and get Fred Manners to come and bury him,' she said. 'And if you've got time could you stay with the old lady while I'm gone. Talk to her, like, it'll do her good.'

I went back and sat down by the bed. Miss Stubbs looked out of the window for a few moments then turned to me. 'You know, Mr Herriot,' she said casually. 'It will be my turn next.'

'What do you mean?'

'Well, tonight Ben has gone and I'm going to be the next one. I just know it.'

'Oh, nonsense! You're feeling a bit low, that's all. We all do when something like this happens.' But I was disturbed. I had never heard her even hint at such a thing before.

'I'm not afraid,' she said. 'I know there's something better waiting for me. I've never had any doubts.' There was silence between us as she lay calmly looking up at the card on the gas bracket.

Then the head on the pillow turned to me again. 'I have only one fear.' Her expression changed with startling suddenness as if a mask had dropped. The brave face was almost unrecognisable. A kind of terror flickered in her eyes and she quickly grasped my hand.

'It's my dogs and cats, Mr Herriot. I'm afraid I might never see them when I'm gone

453

and it worries me so. You see, I know I'll be reunited with my parents and my brothers but . . . but . . .'

'Well, why not with your animals?'

'That's just it.' She rocked her head on the pillow and for the first time I saw tears on her cheeks. 'They say animals have no souls.'

'Who says?'

'Oh, I've read it and I know a lot of religious people believe it.'

'Well I don't believe it.' I patted the hand which still grasped mine. 'If having a soul means being able to feel love and loyalty and gratitude, then animals are better off than a lot of humans. You've nothing to worry about there.'

'Oh, I hope you're right. Sometimes I lie at night thinking about it.'

'I know I'm right, Miss Stubbs, and don't you argue with me. They teach us vets all about animals' souls.'

The tension left her face and she laughed with a return of her old spirit. 'I'm sorry to bore you with this and I'm not going to talk about it again. But before you go, I want you to be absolutely honest with me. I don't want reassurance from you — just the truth. I know you are very young but please tell me — what are your beliefs? Will my animals go with me?'

She stared intently into my eyes. I shifted in my chair and swallowed once or twice.

'Miss Stubbs, I'm afraid I'm a bit foggy about all this,' I said. 'But I'm absolutely certain of one thing. Wherever you are going, they are going too.'

She still stared at me but her face was calm again. 'Thank you, Mr Herriot, I know you are being honest with me. That is what you really believe, isn't it?'

'I do believe it,' I said. 'With all my heart I believe it.'

It must have been about a month later and it was entirely by accident that I learned I had seen Miss Stubbs for the last time. When a lonely, penniless old woman dies people don't rush up to you in the street to tell you. I was on my rounds and a farmer happened to mention that the cottage in Corby village was up for sale.

'But what about Miss Stubbs?' I asked.

'Oh, went off sudden about three weeks ago. House is in a bad state, they say — nowt been done at it for years.'

'Mrs Broadwith isn't staying on, then?'

'Nay, I hear she's staying at t'other end of village.'

'Do you know what's happened to the dogs and cats?'

'What dogs and cats?'

I cut my visit short. And I didn't go straight home though it was nearly lunch time. Instead I urged my complaining little car at top speed to Corby and asked the first person I saw where Mrs Broadwith was living. It was a tiny house but attractive and Mrs Broadwith answered my knock herself.

'Oh, come in, Mr Herriot. It's right good of you to call.' I went inside and we sat facing each other across a scrubbed table top.

'Well, it was sad about the old lady,' she said.

'Yes, I've only just heard.'

'Any road, she had a peaceful end. Just slept away at finish.'

'I'm glad to hear that.'

Mrs Broadwith looked round the room. 'I was real lucky to get this place — it's just what I've always wanted.'

I could contain myself no longer. 'What's happened to the animals?' I blurted out.

'Oh, they're in t'garden,' she said calmly. 'I've got a grand big stretch at back.' She got up and opened the door and with a surge of relief I watched my old friends pour in.

Arthur was on my knee in a flash, arching himself ecstatically against my arm while his outboard motor roared softly above the barking of the dogs. Prince, wheezy as ever, tail fanning the air, laughed up at me delightedly between barks.

'They look great, Mrs Broadwith. How long are they going to be here?'

'They're here for good. I think just as much about them as t'old lady ever did and I couldn't be parted from them. They'll have a good home with me as long as they live.'

I looked at the typical Yorkshire country face, at the heavy cheeks with their grim lines belied by the kindly eyes. 'This is wonderful,' I said. 'But won't you find it just a bit . . . er . . . expensive to feed them?'

'Nay, you don't have to worry about that. I 'ave a bit put away.'

'Well fine, fine, and I'll be looking in now and then to see how they are. I'm through the village every few days.' I got up and started for the door.

Mrs Broadwith held up her hand. 'There's just one thing I'd like you to do before they start selling off the things at the cottage. Would you please pop in and collect what's left of your medicines. They're in t'front room.'

I took the key and drove along to the other end of the village. As I pushed open the rickety gate and began to walk through the tangled grass the front of the cottage looked strangely lifeless without the faces of the dogs at the window; and when the door creaked open and I went inside the silence was like a heavy pall.

Nothing had been moved. The bed with its rumpled blankets was still in the corner. I moved around, picking up half empty bottles, a jar of ointment, the cardboard box with old

Ben's tablets — a lot of good they had done him.

When I had got everything I looked slowly round the little room. I wouldn't be coming here any more and at the door I paused and read for the last time the card which hung over the empty bed.

CHAPTER 44

I was spending Tuesday evening as I spent all the Tuesday evenings — staring at the back of Helen Alderson's head at the Darrowby Music Society. It was a slow way of getting to know her better but I had been unable to think of a better idea.

Since the morning on the high moor when I had set the calf's leg, I had scanned the day book regularly in the hope of getting another visit to the farm. But the Aldersons seemed to have lamentably healthy stock. I had to be content with the thought that there was the visit at the month end to take off the plaster. The really crushing blow came when Helen's father rang up to say that, since the calf was going sound he had removed the plaster himself. He was pleased to say that the fracture had knitted perfectly and there was no sign of lameness.

I had come to admire the self-reliance and initiative of the Dalesmen but I cursed it now at great length; and I joined the Music

459

Society. I had seen Helen going into the schoolroom where the meetings were held and, with the courage of desperation, had followed her inside.

That was weeks ago and, I reflected miserably, I had made no progress at all. I couldn't remember how many tenors, sopranos and male voice choirs had come and gone and on one occasion the local brass band had packed themselves into the little room and almost burst my ear drums; but I was no further forward.

Tonight a string quartet was scraping away industriously, but I hardly heard them. My eyes, as usual, were focused on Helen, several rows in front of me, sitting between the two old ladies she always seemed to bring with her. That was part of the trouble; those two old girls were always there, cutting out any chance of private conversation, even at the half-time break for tea. And there was the general atmosphere of the place; the members were nearly all elderly, and over everything hung the powerful schoolroom scent of ink and exercise books and chalk and lead pencils. It was the sort of place where you just couldn't say without warning 'Are you doing anything on Saturday night?'

The scraping stopped and everybody clapped. The vicar got up from the front row and beamed on the company. 'And now, ladies and gentlemen, I think we might stop for fifteen minutes as I see our willing helpers have prepared tea. The price, as usual is threepence.' There was laughter and a general pushing back of chairs.

I went to the back of the hall with the others, put my threepence on the plate and collected a cup of tea and a biscuit. This was when I tried to get near Helen in the blind hope that something might happen. It wasn't always easy, because I was often buttonholed by the school headmaster and others who regarded a vet who liked music as an interesting curiosity, but tonight I managed to edge myself as if by accident into her group.

She looked at me over the top of her cup. 'Good evening, Mr Herriot, are you enjoying it?' Oh God, she always said that. And Mr Herriot! But what could I do? 'Call me Jim', would sound great. I replied, as always, 'Good evening, Miss Alderson. Yes, it's very nice, isn't it.' Things were going with a bang again.

I munched my biscuit while the old ladies talked about Mozart. It was going to be the same as all the other Tuesdays. It was about time I gave up the whole thing. I felt beaten.

The vicar approached our group, still beaming. 'I'm afraid I have to call on somebody for the washing-up rota. Perhaps our two young friends would take it on tonight.' His friendly gaze twinkled from Helen to me and back again.

The idea of washing up teacups had never held much attraction for me but suddenly it was like sighting the promised land. 'Yes, certainly, delighted — that is if it's all right with Miss Alderson.'

Helen smiled. 'Of course it's all right. We all have to take a turn, don't we?'

I wheeled the trolley of cups and saucers into the scullery. It was a cramped, narrow place with a sink and a few shelves and there was just about room for the two of us to get inside.

'Would you like to wash or dry?' Helen asked.

'I'll wash,' I replied and began to run the hot water into the sink. It shouldn't be too difficult now, I thought, to work the conversation round to where I wanted it. I'd never have a better chance than now, jammed into this little room with Helen.

But it was surprising how the time went by. Five whole minutes and we hadn't talked about anything but music. With mounting frustration I saw that we had nearly got through the pile of crockery and I had achieved nothing. The feeling changed to near panic when I lifted the last cup from the soapy water.

It had to be now. I held out the cup to Helen and she tried to take it from me; but I kept a grip on the handle while I waited for inspiration. She pulled gently but I clung to it tenaciously. It was developing into a tug of war. Then I heard a hoarse croak which I only just recognised as my own voice. 'Can I see you some time?'

For a moment she didn't answer and I tried to read her face. Was she surprised, annoyed, even shocked? She flushed and replied, 'If you like.' I heard the croak again. 'Saturday evening?' She nodded, dried the cup and was gone.

I went back to my seat with my heart thudding. The strains of mangled Haydn from the quartet went unheeded. I had done it at last. But did she really want to come out? Had she been hustled into it against her will? My toes curled with embarrassment at the thought, but I consoled myself with the knowledge that for better or for worse it was a step forward. Yes, I had done it at last.

CHAPTER 45

At I sat at breakfast I looked out at the autumn mist dissolving in the early sunshine. It was going to be another fine day but there was a chill in the old house this morning, a shiveriness as though a cold hand had reached out to remind us that summer had gone and the hard months lay just ahead.

'It says here,' Siegfried said, adjusting his copy of the *Darrowby and Houlton Times* with care against the coffee-pot, 'that farmers have no feeling for their animals.'

I buttered a piece of toast and looked across at him.

'Cruel, you mean?'

'Well, not exactly, but this chap maintains that to a farmer, livestock are purely commercial — there's no sentiment in his attitude towards them, no affection.'

'Well, it wouldn't do if they were all like poor Kit Bilton, would it? They'd all go mad.'

Kit was a lorry driver who, like so many of the working men of Darrowby, kept a pig at the bottom of his garden for family consumption. The snag was that when killing time came, Kit wept for three days. I happened to go into his house on one of these occasions and found his wife and daughter hard at it cutting up the meat for pies and brawn while Kit huddled miserably by the kitchen fire, his eyes swimming with tears. He was a huge man who could throw a twelve stone sack of meal on to his wagon with a jerk of his arms, but he seized my hand in his and sobbed at me 'I can't bear it, Mr Herriot. He was like a Christian was that pig, just like a Christian.'

'No, I agree,' Siegfried leaned over and sawed off a slice of Mrs Hall's home-baked bread. 'But Kit isn't a real farmer. This article is about people who own large numbers of animals. The question is, is it possible for such men to become emotionally involved? Can the dairy farmer milking maybe fifty cows become really fond of any of them or are they just milk producing units?'

'It's an interesting point,' I said, 'And I think you've put your finger on it with the numbers. You know there are a lot of our farmers up in the high country who have only a few stock. They always have names for their cows — Daisy, Mabel, I even came across one called Kipperlugs the other day. I do think these small farmers have an affection for their animals but I don't see how the big men can possibly have.'

Siegfried rose from the table and stretched luxuriously. 'You're probably right. Anyway, I'm sending you to see a really big man this morning. John Skipton of Dennaby Close — he's got some tooth rasping to do. Couple of old horses losing condition. You'd better take all the instruments, it might be anything.'

I went through to the little room down the passage and surveyed the tooth instruments. I always felt at my most mediaeval when I was caught up in large animal dentistry and in the days of the draught horse it was a regular task. One of the commonest jobs was knocking the wolf teeth out of young horses. I have no idea how it got its name but you found the little wolf tooth just in front of the molars and if a young horse was doing badly it always got the blame.

It was no good the vets protesting that such a minute, vestigial object couldn't possibly have any effect on the horse's health and that the trouble was probably due to worms. The farmers were adamant; the tooth had to be removed.

We did this by having the horse backed into a corner, placing the forked end of a metal rod against the tooth and giving a sharp tap with an absurdly large wooden mallet. Since the tooth had no proper root the operation was not particularly painful, but the horse still didn't like it. We usually had a couple of fore-feet waving around our ears at each tap.

And the annoying part was that after we had done the job and pointed out to the farmer that we had only performed this bit of black magic to humour him, the horse would take an immediate turn for the better and thrive consistently from then on. Farmers are normally reticent about our successful efforts for fear we might put a bit more on the bill but in these cases they cast aside all caution. They would shout at us across the market place: 'Hey, remember that 'oss you knocked wolf teeth out of? Well he never looked back. It capped him.'

I looked again with distaste at the tooth instruments; the vicious forceps with two-feet-long arms, sharp-jawed shears, mouth gags, hammers and chisels, files and rasps; it was rather like a quiet corner in the Spanish Inquisition. We kept a long wooden box with a handle for carrying the things and I staggered out to the car with a fair selection.

Dennaby Close was not just a substantial farm, it was a monument to a man's endurance and skill. The fine old house, the extensive buildings, the great sweep of lush grass land along the lower slopes of the fell were all proof that old John Skipton had achieved the impossible; he had started as an uneducated farm labourer and he was now a wealthy landowner.

The miracle hadn't happened easily; old John had a lifetime of grinding toil behind him that would have killed most men, a lifetime with no room for a wife or family or creature comforts, but there was more to it than that; there was a brilliant acumen in agricultural matters that had made the old man a legend in the district. 'When all t'world goes one road, I go t'other' was one of his quoted sayings and it is true that the Skipton farms had made money in the hard times when others were going bankrupt. Dennaby was only one of John's farms; he had two large arable places of about four hundred acres each lower down the Dale.

He had conquered, but to some people it seemed that he had himself been conquered in the process. He had battled against the odds for so many years and driven himself so fiercely that he couldn't stop. He could be enjoying all kinds of luxuries now but he just hadn't the time; they said that the poorest of his workers lived in better style than he did.

I paused as I got out of the car and stood gazing at the house as though I had never seen it before; and I marvelled again at the elegance which had withstood over three hundred years of the harsh climate. People came a long way to see Dennaby Close and take photographs of the graceful manor with its tall, leaded windows, the massive chimneys towering over the old moss-grown tiles; or to wander through the neglected garden and climb up the sweep of steps to the entrance with its wide stone arch over the great studded door.

There should have been a beautiful woman in one of those pointed hats peeping out from that mullioned casement or a cavalier in ruffles and hose pacing beneath the high wall with its pointed copings. But there was just old John stumping impatiently towards me, his tattered, buttonless coat secured only by a length of binder twine round his middle.

'Come in a minute, young man,' he cried. 'I've got a little bill to pay you.' He led the way round to the back of the house and I followed, pondering on the odd fact that it was always a 'little bill' in Yorkshire. We went in through a flagged kitchen to a room which was graceful and spacious but furnished only with a table, a few wooden chairs and a collapsed sofa.

The old man bustled over to the mantelpiece and fished out a bundle of papers from behind the clock. He leafed through them, threw an envelope on to the table then produced a cheque book and slapped it down in front of me. I did the usual — took out the bill, made out the amount on the cheque and pushed it over for him to sign. He wrote with a careful concentration, the small-featured, weathered face bent low, the peak of the old cloth cap almost touching the pen. His trousers had ridden up his legs as he sat down showing the skinny calves and bare ankles. There were no socks underneath the heavy boots.

When I had pocketed the cheque, John jumped to his feet. 'We'll have to walk down to t'river; 'osses are down there.' He left the house almost at a trot.

I eased my box of instruments from the car boot. It was a funny thing but whenever I had heavy equipment to lug about, my patients were always a long way away. This box seemed to be filled with lead and it wasn't going to get any lighter on the journey down through the walled pastures.

The old man seized a pitch fork, stabbed it into a bale of hay and hoisted it effortlessly over his shoulder. He set off again at the same brisk pace. We made our way down from one gateway to another, often walking diagonally across the fields. John didn't reduce speed and I stumbled after him, puffing a little and trying to put away the thought that he was at least fifty years older than me.

About half way down we came across a group of men at the age-old task of 'walling' — repairing a gap in one of the dry stone walls which trace their patterns everywhere on the green slopes of the Dales. One of the men looked up. 'Nice mornin', Mr Skipton,' he sang out cheerfully.

'Bugger t'mornin'. Get on wi' some work,' grunted old John in reply and the man smiled contentedly as though he had received a compliment.

I was glad when we reached the flat land at the bottom. My arms seemed to have been stretched by several inches and I could feel a trickle of sweat on my brow. Old John appeared unaffected; he flicked the fork from his shoulder and the bale thudded on to the grass.

The two horses turned towards us at the sound. They were standing fetlock deep in the pebbly shallows just beyond a little beach which merged into the green carpet of turf; nose to tail, they had been rubbing their chins gently along each other's backs, unconscious of our approach. A high cliff overhanging the far bank made a perfect wind break while on either side of us clumps of oak and beech blazed in the autumn sunshine.

'They're in a nice spot, Mr Skipton,' I said.

'Aye, they can keep cool in the hot weather and they've got the barn when winter comes.' John pointed to a low, thick-walled building with a single door. 'They can come and go as they please.'

The sound of his voice brought the horses out of the river at a stiff trot and as they came near you could see they really were old. The mare was a chestnut and the gelding was a light bay but their coats were so flecked with grey that they almost looked like roans. This was most pronounced on their faces where the sprinkling of white hairs, the sunken eyes and the deep cavity above the eyes gave them a truly venerable appearance.

For all that, they capered around John with a fair attempt at skittishness, stamping their feet, throwing their heads about, pushing his cap over his eyes with their muzzles.

'Get by, leave off!' he shouted. 'Daft awd beggars.' But he tugged absently at the mare's forelock and ran his hand briefly along the neck of the gelding.

'When did they last do any work?' I asked.

'Oh, about twelve years ago, I reckon.'

I stared at John. 'Twelve years! And have they been down here all that time?'

'Aye, just lakin' about down here, retired like. They've earned it an' all.' For a few moments he stood silent, shoulders hunched, hands deep in the pockets of his coat, then he spoke quietly as if to himself. 'They were two slaves when I was a slave.' He turned and looked at me and for a revealing moment I read in the pale blue eyes something of the agony and struggle he had shared with the animals.

'But twelve years! How old are they, anyway?'

John's mouth twisted up at one corner. 'Well you're t'vet. You tell me.'

I stepped forward confidently, my mind buzzing with Galvayne's groove, shape of marks, degree of slope and the rest; I grasped the unprotesting upper lip of the mare and looked at her teeth.

'Good God!' I gasped, 'I've never seen anything like this.' The incisors were immensely long and projecting forward till they met at an angle of about forty-five degrees. There were no marks at all — they had long since gone.

I laughed and turned back to the old man. 'It's no good, I'd only be guessing. You'll have to tell me.'

'Well she's about thirty and gelding's a year or two younger. She's had fifteen grand foals and never ailed owt except a bit of teeth trouble. We've had them rasped a time or two and it's time they were done again, I reckon. They're both losing ground and dropping bits of half chewed hay from their mouths. Gelding's the worst — has a right job champin' his grub.'

I put my hand into the mare's mouth, grasped her tongue and pulled it out to one side. A quick exploration of the molars with my other hand revealed what I suspected; the outside edges of the upper teeth were overgrown and jagged and were irritating the cheeks while the inside edges of the lower molars were in a similar state and were slightly excoriating the tongue.

'I'll soon make her more comfortable, Mr Skipton. With those sharp edges rubbed off she'll be as good as new.' I got the rasp out of my vast box, held the tongue in one hand

473

and worked the rough surface along the teeth, checking occasionally with my fingers till the points had been sufficiently reduced.

'That's about right,' I said after a few minutes. 'I don't want to make them too smooth or she won't be able to grind her food.'

John grunted. 'Good enough. Now have a look at t'other. There's summat far wrong with him.'

I had a feel at the gelding's teeth. 'Just the same as the mare. Soon put him right, too.'

But pushing at the rasp, I had an uncomfortable feeling that something was not quite right. The thing wouldn't go fully to the back of the mouth; something was stopping it. I stopped rasping and explored again, reaching with my fingers as far as I could. And I came upon something very strange, something which shouldn't have been there at all. It was like a great chunk of bone projecting down from the roof of the mouth.

It was time I had a proper look. I got out my pocket torch and shone it over the back of the tongue. It was easy to see the trouble now; the last upper molar was overlapping the lower one resulting in a gross overgrowth of the posterior border. The result was a sabre-like barb about three inches long stabbing down into the tender tissue of the gum.

That would have to come off — right now. My jauntiness vanished and I suppressed a shudder; it meant using the horrible shears — those great long-handled things with the screw operated by a cross bar. They gave me the willies because I am one of those people who can't bear to watch anybody blowing up a balloon and this was the same sort of thing only worse. You fastened the sharp blades of the shears on to the tooth and began to turn the bar slowly, slowly. Soon the tooth began to groan and creak under the tremendous leverage and you knew that any second it would break off and when it did it was like somebody letting off a rifle in your ear. That was when all hell usually broke loose but mercifully this was a quiet old horse and I wouldn't expect him to start dancing around on his hind legs. There was no pain for the horse because the overgrown part had no nerve supply — it was the noise that caused the trouble.

Returning to my crate I produced the dreadful instrument and with it a Haussman's gag which I inserted on the incisors and opened on its ratchet till the mouth gaped wide. Everything was easy to see then and, of course, there it was — a great prong at the other side of the mouth exactly like the first. Great, great, now I had two to chop off.

The old horse stood patiently, eyes almost closed, as though he had seen it all and nothing in the world was going to bother him. I went through the motions with my toes curling and when the sharp crack came, the white-bordered eyes opened wide, but only in mild surprise. He never even moved. When I did the other side he paid no attention at all; in fact, with the gag prising his jaws apart he looked exactly as though he was yawning with boredom.

As I bundled the tools away, John picked up the bony spicules from the grass and studied them with interest. 'Well, poor awd beggar. Good job I got you along, young man. Reckon he'll feel a lot better now.'

On the way back, old John, relieved of his bale, was able to go twice as fast and he stumped his way up the hill at a furious pace, using the fork as a staff. I panted along in the rear, changing the box from hand to hand every few minutes.

About half way up, the thing slipped out of my grasp and it gave me a chance to stop for a breather. As the old man muttered impatiently I looked back and could just see the two horses; they had returned to the shallows and were playing together, chasing each other jerkily, their feet splashing in the water. The cliff made a dark backcloth to the picture — the shining river, the trees glowing bronze and gold and the sweet green of the grass.

Back in the farm yard, John paused awkwardly. He nodded once or twice, said 'Thank ye, young man,' then turned abruptly and walked away.

I was dumping the box thankfully into the boot when I saw the man who had spoken to us on the way down. He was sitting, cheerful as ever, in a sunny corner, back against a pile of sacks, pulling his dinner packet from an old army satchel.

'You've been down to see t'pensioners, then? By gaw, awd John should know the way.'

'Regular visitor, is he?'

'Regular? Every day God sends you'll see t'awd feller ploddin' down there. Rain, snow or blow, never misses. And allus has summat with him — bag o' corn, straw for their bedding.'

'And he's done that for twelve years?'

The man unscrewed his thermos flask and poured himself a cup of black tea. 'Aye, them 'osses haven't done a stroke o' work all that time and he could've got good money for them from the horse flesh merchants. Rum 'un, isn't it?'

'You're right,' I said, 'it is a rum 'un.'

Just how rum it was occupied my thoughts on the way back to the surgery. I went back to my conversation with Siegfried that morning; we had just about decided that the man with a lot of animals couldn't be expected to feel affection for individuals among them. But those buildings back there were full of John Skipton's animals — he must have hundreds.

Yet what made him trail down that hillside

every day in all weathers? Why had he filled the last years of those two old horses with peace and beauty? Why had he given them a final ease and comfort which he had withheld from himself?

It could only be love.

CHAPTER 46

The longer I worked in Darrowby the more
the charms of the Dales beguiled me. And
there was one solid advantage of which I
became more aware every day — the Dales
farmers were all stocksmen. They really knew
how to handle animals, and to a vet whose
patients are constantly trying to thwart him
or injure him it was a particular blessing.

So this morning I looked with satisfaction
at the two men holding the cow. It wasn't a
difficult job — just an intravenous injection
of magnesium lactate — but still it was reassuring to have two such sturdy fellows to
help me. Maurice Bennison, medium sized
but as tough as one of his own hill beasts,
had a horn in his right hand while the fingers
of his left gripped the nose; I had the comfortable impression that the cow wouldn't jump
very far when I pushed the needle in. His
brother George whose job it was to raise the
vein, held the choke rope limply in enormous
hands like bunches of carrots. He grinned

down at me amiably from his six feet four inches.

'Right, George,' I said. 'Tighten up that rope and lean against the cow to stop her coming round on me.' I pushed my way between the cow and her neighbour, past George's unyielding bulk and bent over the jugular vein. It was standing out very nicely. I poised the needle, feeling the big man's elbow on me as he peered over my shoulder, and thrust quickly into the vein.

'Lovely!' I cried as the dark blood fountained out and spattered thickly on the straw bedding beneath. 'Slacken your rope, George.' I fumbled in my pocket for the flutter valve. 'And for God's sake, get your weight off me!'

Because George had apparently decided to rest his full fourteen stones on me instead of the cow, and as I tried desperately to connect the tube to the needle I felt my knees giving way. I shouted again, despairingly, but he was inert, his chin resting on my shoulder, his breathing stertorous in my ear.

There could only be one end to it. I fell flat on my face and lay there writhing under the motionless body. My cries went unheeded; George was unconscious.

Mr Bennison, attracted by the commotion, came in to the byre just in time to see me crawling out from beneath his eldest son. 'Get him out, quick!' I gasped, 'before the cows trample on him.' Wordlessly, Maurice and his father took an ankle apiece and hauled away in unison. George shot out from under the cows, his head beating a brisk tattoo on the cobbles, traversed the dung channel, then resumed his sleep on the byre floor.

Mr Bennison moved back to the cow and waited for me to continue with my injection but I found the presence of the sprawled body distracting. 'Look, couldn't we sit him up against the wall and put his head between his legs?' I suggested apologetically. The others glanced at each other then, as though deciding to humour me, grabbed George's shoulders and trundled him over the floor with the expertise of men used to throwing around bags of fertiliser and potatoes. But even propped against the rough stones, his head slumped forward and his great long arms hanging loosely, the poor fellow still didn't look so good.

I couldn't help feeling a bit responsible. 'Don't you think we might give him a drink?'

But Mr Bennison had had enough. 'Nay, nay, he'll be right,' he muttered testily. 'Let's get on with t'job.' Evidently he felt he had pampered George too much already.

The incident started me thinking about this question of people's reactions to the sight of blood and other disturbing realities. Even though it was only my second year of practice I had already formulated certain rules about this and one was that it was always the biggest men who went down. (I had, by this time, worked out a few other, perhaps unscientific theories, e.g. big dogs were kept by people who lived in little houses and vice versa. Clients who said 'spare no expense' never paid their bills, ever. When I asked my way in the Dales and was told 'you can't miss it', I knew I'd soon be hopelessly lost.)

I had begun to wonder if perhaps country folk, despite their closer contact with fundamental things, were perhaps more susceptible than city people. Ever since Sid Blenkhorn had staggered into Skeldale House one evening. His face was ghastly white and he had obviously passed through a shattering experience. 'Have you got a drop o' whisky handy, Jim?' he quavered, and when I had guided him to a chair and Siegfried had put a glass in his hand he told us he had been at a first aid lecture given by Dr Allinson, a few doors down the street. 'He was talking about veins and arteries and things,' groaned Sid, passing a hand across his forehead. 'God, it was awful!' Apparently Fred Ellison the fishmonger had been carried out unconscious after only ten minutes and Sid himself had only just made it to the door. It had been a shambles.

I was interested because this sort of thing, I had found, was always just round the corner. I suppose we must have more trouble in this way than the doctors because in most cases when our medical colleagues have any cutting or carving to do they send their patients to hospital while the vets just have to get their jackets off and operate on the spot. It means that the owners and attendants of the animals are pulled in as helpers and are subjected to some unusual sights.

So, even in my short experience, I had become a fair authority on the various manifestations of 'coming over queer'. I suppose it was a bit early to start compiling statistics but I had never seen a woman or a little man pass out even though they might exhibit various shadings of the squeamish spectrum. The big chap was the best bet every time, especially the boisterous, super-confident type.

I have a vivid recollection of a summer evening when I had to carry out a rumenotomy on a cow. As a rule I was inclined to play for time when I suspected a foreign body — there were so many other conditions with similar symptoms that I was never in a hurry to make a hole in the animal's side. But this time diagnosis was easy; the sudden fall in milk yield, loss of cudding; grunting, and the rigid, sunken-eyed appearance of the cow. And to clinch it the farmer told me he had been repairing a hen house in the cow pasture — nailing up loose boards. I knew where one of the nails had gone.

The farm, right on the main street of the

village, was a favourite meeting place for the local lads. As I laid out my instruments on a clean towel draped over a straw bale a row of grinning faces watched from above the half door of the box; not only watched but encouraged me with ribald shouts. When I was about ready to start it occurred to me that an extra pair of hands would be helpful and I turned to the door. 'How would one of you lads like to be my assistant?' There was even more shouting for a minute or two, then the door was opened and a huge young man with a shock of red hair ambled into the box; he was a magnificent sight with his vast shoulders and the column of sunburned neck rising from the open shirt. It needed only the bright blue eyes and the ruddy, high-cheekboned face to remind me that the Norsemen had been around the Dales a thousand years ago. This was a Viking.

I had him roll up his sleeves and scrub his hands in a bucket of warm water and antiseptic while I infiltrated the cow's flank with local anaesthetic. When I gave him artery forceps and scissors to hold he pranced around, making stabbing motions at the cow and roaring with laughter.

'Maybe you'd like to do the job yourself?' I asked. The Viking squared his great shoulders. 'Aye, I'll 'ave a go,' and the heads above the door cheered lustily.

As I finally poised my Bard Parker scalpel

with its new razor-sharp blade over the cow, the air was thick with earthy witticisms. I had decided that this time I really would make the bold incision recommended in the surgery books; it was about time I advanced beyond the stage of pecking nervously at the skin. 'A veritable blow,' was how one learned author had described it. Well, that was how it was going to be.

I touched the blade down on the clipped area of the flank and with a quick motion of the wrist laid open a ten-inch wound. I stood back for a few seconds admiring the clean-cut edges of the skin with only a few capillaries spurting on to the glistening, twitching abdominal muscles. At the same time I noticed that the laughter and shouting from the heads had been switched off and was replaced by an eerie silence broken only by a heavy, thudding sound from behind me.

'Forceps please,' I said, extending my hand back. But nothing happened. I looked round; the top of the half door was bare — not a head in sight. There was only the Viking spreadeagled in the middle of the floor, arms and legs flung wide, chin pointing to the roof. The attitude was so theatrical that I thought he was still acting the fool, but a closer examination erased all doubts: the Viking was out cold. He must have gone straight over backwards like a stricken oak.

The farmer, a bent little man who couldn't

have scaled much more than eight stones, had been steadying the cow's head. He looked at me with the faintest flicker of amusement in his eyes. 'Looks like you and me for it, then, guvnor.' He tied the halter to a ring on the wall, washed his hands methodically and took up his place at my side. Throughout the operation, he passed me my instruments, swabbed away the seeping blood and clipped the sutures, whistling tunelessly through his teeth in a bored manner; the only time he showed any real emotion was when I produced the offending nail from the depths of the reticulum. He raised his eyebrows slightly, said ' 'ello, 'ello,' then started whistling again.

We were too busy to do anything for the Viking. Halfway through, he sat up, shook himself a few times then got to his feet and strolled with elaborate nonchalance out of the box. The poor fellow seemed to be hoping that perhaps we had noticed nothing unusual.

I don't suppose we could have done much to bring him round anyway. There was only one time I discovered a means of immediate resuscitation and that was by accident.

It was when Henry Dickson asked me to show him how to castrate a ruptured pig without leaving a swelling. Henry was going in for pigs in a big way and had a burning ambition to equip himself with veterinary skills.

When he showed me the young pig with the gross scrotal swelling I demurred. 'I really think this is a vet's job, Henry. Castrate your normal pigs by all means but I don't think you could make a proper job of this sort of thing.'

'How's that, then?'

'Well, there's the local anaesthetic, danger of infection — and you really need a knowledge of anatomy to know what you're doing.'

All the frustrated surgeon in Henry showed in his eyes. 'Gaw, I'd like to know how to do it.'

'I'll tell you what,' I said. 'How about if I do this one as a demonstration and you can make up your own mind. I'll give him a general anaesthetic so you don't have to hold him.'

'Right, that's a good idea.' Henry thought for a moment. 'What'll you charge me to do 'im?'

'Seven and six.'

'Well I suppose you have to have your pound of flesh. Get on.'

I injected a few cc's of Nembutal into the little pig's peritoneum and after some staggering he rolled over in the straw and lay still. Henry had rigged up a table in the yard and we laid the sleeping animal on it. I was preparing to start when Henry pulled out a ten-shilling note.

'Better pay you now before I forget.'

'All right, but my hands are clean now — push it into my pocket and I'll give you the change when we finish.'

I rather fancy myself as a teacher and soon warmed to my task. I carefully incised the skin over the inguinal canal and pulled out the testicle, intact in its tunics. 'See there, Henry, the bowels have come down the canal and are lying in with the testicle.' I pointed to the loops of intestine, pale pink through the translucent membranes. 'Now if I do this, I can push them right back into the abdomen, and if I press here, out they pop again. You see how it works? There, they've gone; now they're out again. Once more I make them disappear and whoops, there they are back with us! Now in order to retain them permanently in the abdomen I take the spermatic cord and wind it in its coverings tightly down to the . . .'

But my audience was no longer with me. Henry had sunk down on an upturned oil drum and lay slumped across the table, his head cradled on his arms. My disappointment was acute, and finishing off the job and inserting the sutures was a sad anticlimax with my student slumbering at the end of the table.

I put the pig back in his pen and gathered up my gear: then I remembered I hadn't given Henry his change. I don't know why I did it but instead of half-a-crown, I slapped down a shilling and sixpence on the wood a few inches from his face. The noise made him open his eyes and he gazed dully at the coins for a few seconds, then with almost frightening suddenness he snapped upright, ashen-faced but alert and glaring.

'Hey!' he shouted. 'I want another shillin'!'

CHAPTER 47

Vets are useless creatures, parasites on the agricultural community, expensive layabouts who really know nothing about animals or their diseases. You might as well get Jeff Mallock the knacker man as send for a vet.

At least that was the opinion, frequently expressed, of the Sidlow family. In fact, when you came right down to it, just about the only person for miles around who knew how to treat sick beasts was Mr Sidlow himself. If any of their cows or horses fell ill it was Mr Sidlow who stepped forward with his armoury of sovereign remedies. He enjoyed a God-like prestige with his wife and large family and it was an article of their faith that father was infallible in these matters; the only other being who had ever approached his skill was long-dead Grandpa Sidlow from whom father had learned so many of his cures.

Mind you, Mr Sidlow was a just and humane man. After maybe five or six days of dedicated nursing during which he would perhaps push half-a-pound of lard and raisins down the cow's throat three times a day, rub its udder vigorously with turpentine or maybe cut a bit off the end of the tail to let the bad out, he always in the end called the vet. Not that it would do any good, but he liked to give the animal every chance. When the vet arrived he invariably found a sunken-eyed, dying creature and the despairing treatment he gave was like a figurative administration of the last rites. The animal always died so the Sidlows were repeatedly confirmed in their opinion — vets were useless.

The farm was situated outside the normal area of the practice and we were the third firm Mr Sidlow had dealt with. He had been a client of Grier of Brawton but had found him wanting and moved to Wallace away over in Mansley. Wallace had disappointed him grievously so he had decided to try Darrowby. He had been with us for over a year but it was an uncomfortable relationship because Siegfried had offended him deeply on his very first visit. It was to a moribund horse, and Mr Sidlow, describing the treatment to date, announced that he had been pushing raw onions up the horse's rectum; he couldn't understand why it was so uneasy on its legs. Siegfried had pointed out that if he were to insert a raw onion in Mr Sidlow's rectum, he, Mr Sidlow, would undoubtedly be uneasy on his legs.

It was a bad start but there were really no other available vets left. He was stuck with us.

I had been uncannily lucky in that I had been at Darrowby for more than a year and had never had to visit this farm. Mr Sidlow rarely called us up during normal working hours as, after wrestling with his conscience for a few days, he always seemed to lose the battle around eleven o'clock at night (he made exceptions in the case of the occasional Sunday afternoon) and it had always landed on Siegfried's duty nights. It was Siegfried who had trailed out, swearing quietly, and returned, slightly pop-eyed in the small hours.

So when it did finally come round to my turn I didn't rush out with any great enthusiasm, even though the case was just a choking bullock and should present no difficulties. (This was when a beast got a piece of turnip or a potato stuck in its gullet, preventing regurgitation of gases and causing bloating which can be fatal. We usually either relieved the bloat by puncturing the stomach or we carefully pushed the obstruction down into the stomach by means of a long flexible leather instrument called a probang.) Anyway, they had realised they couldn't wait for days this time and by way of a change it was only four o'clock in the afternoon.

The farm was nearer Brawton than Darrowby and lay in the low country down on the Plain of York. I didn't like the look of the place; there was something depressing about the dilapidated brick buildings in the dreary setting of ploughing land with only the occasional mound of a potato clamp to relieve the flatness.

My first sight of Mr Sidlow reminded me that he and his family were members of a fanatically narrow religious sect. I had seen that gaunt, blue-jowled face with the tortured eyes staring at me from the pages of history books long ago. I had the feeling that Mr Sidlow would have burnt me at the stake without a qualm.

The bullock was in a gloomy box off the fold yard. Several of the family had filed in with us; two young men in their twenties and three teenage girls, all good-looking in a dark gipsy way, but all with the same taut, unsmiling look as their father. As I moved around, examining the animal, I noticed another peculiarity — they all looked at me, the bullock, each other, with quick sideways glances without any head movement. Nobody said anything.

I would have liked to break the silence but couldn't think of anything cheerful to say. This beast didn't have the look of an ordinary choke. I could feel the potato quite distinctly from the outside, half-way down the oesophagus but all around was an oedematous mass extending up and down the left side of the neck. Not only that, but there was a bloody foam dripping from the mouth. There was something funny here.

A thought struck me. 'Have you been trying to push the potato down with something?'

I could almost feel the battery of flitting glances, and the muscles of Mr Sidlow's clenched jaw stood out in a twitching ridge. He swallowed carefully. 'Aye, we've tried a bit.'

'What did you use?'

Again the rippling jaw muscles under the dark skin. 'Broom handle and a bit of hose pipe. Same as usual.'

That was enough; a sense of doom enveloped me. It would have been nice to be the first vet to make a good impression here but it wasn't to be. I turned to the farmer. 'I'm afraid you've ruptured the gullet. It's a very delicate tube, you know, and you only have to push a bit too hard and you're through. You can see the fluid collection round the rupture.'

A quivering silence answered me. I ploughed on. 'I've seen this happen before. It's a pretty black outlook.'

'All right,' Mr Sidlow ground out. 'What are you going to do about it?'

Well, we were at it now. What was I going to do about it? Maybe now, thirty years later, I might have tried to repair the gullet, packed the wound with antibiotic powder and given a course of penicillin injections. But there, in that cheerless place, looking at the patient animal gulping painfully, coughing up the gouts of blood, I knew I was whacked. A ruptured oesophagus was as near hopeless as anything could be. I searched my mind for a suitable speech.

'I'm sorry, Mr Sidlow, but I can't do anything about it.' The glances crackled around me and the farmer breathed in sharply through his nose. I didn't need to be told what they were all thinking — another no-good, useless vet. I took a deep breath and continued. 'Even if I shifted the potato the wound would get contaminated when the beast tried to eat. He'd have gangrene in no time and that means a painful death. He's in pretty good condition — if I were you I'd have him slaughtered immediately.'

The only reply was a virtuoso display from the jaw muscles. I tried another tack. 'I'll give you a certificate. I'm sure the meat will pass for the butcher.'

No cries of joy greeted this remark. If anything, Mr Sidlow's expression became still more bleak.

'That beast isn't ready for killin' yet,' he whispered.

'No, but you'd be sending him in before long — another month, maybe. I'm sure you won't lose much. I tell you what,' with a ghastly attempt at heartiness, 'if I can come into the house I'll write you this chit now and we'll get the job over. There's really nothing else for it.'

I turned and headed across the fold yard for the farm kitchen. Mr Sidlow followed wordlessly with the family. I wrote the certificate quickly, waves of disapproval washing around me in the silent room. As I folded the paper I had the sudden conviction that Mr Sidlow wasn't going to pay the slightest attention to my advice. He was going to wait a day or two to see how things turned out. The picture of the big, uncomprehending animal trying vainly to swallow as his hunger and thirst increased was too strong for me. I walked over to the phone on the window sill.

'I'll just give Harry Norman a ring at the abattoir. I know he'll come straight up if I ask him.' I made the arrangements, hung up the receiver and started for the door, addressing Mr Sidlow's profile as I left. 'It's fixed. Harry will be along within half-an-hour. Much better to get it done immediately.'

Going across the yard, I had to fight the impulse to break into a gallop. As I got into the car I recalled Siegfried's advice: 'In sticky situations always get your car backed round before you examine the animal. Leave the engine running if necessary. The quick getaway is essential.' He was right, it took a long time reversing and manoeuvring under the battery of unseen eyes. I don't blush easily but my face was burning as I finally left the farm.

That was my first visit to the Sidlows and I prayed that it might be my last. But my luck had run out. From then on, every time they sent for us it just happened to be me on duty. I would rather not say anything about the cases I treated there except to record that something went wrong every time. The very name Sidlow became like a jinx. Try as I might I couldn't do a thing right on that farm so that within a short time I was firmly established with the family as the greatest menace to the animal population they had ever encountered. They didn't think much of vets as a whole and they'd met some real beauties in their time, but I was by far the worst. My position as the biggest nincompoop of them all was unassailable.

It got so bad that if I saw any Sidlows in the town I would dive down an alley to avoid them and one day in the market place I had the unnerving experience of seeing the entire family, somehow jammed into a large old car, passing within a few feet of me. Every face looked rigidly to the front but every eye, I knew, was trained balefully on me. Fortunately I was just outside the Drovers' Arms, so I was able to reel inside and steady myself with a half-pint of Younger's Special Heavy.

However, the Sidlows were far from my mind on the Saturday morning when Siegfried asked me if I would go through and officiate at Brawton races.

'They've asked me to do it as Grier is on holiday,' he said. 'But I'd already promised to go through to Casborough to help Dick Henley with a rig operation. I can't let him down. There's nothing much to the race job: the regular course vet will be there and he'll keep you right.'

He hadn't been gone more than a few minutes when there was a call from the racecourse. One of the horses had fallen while being unloaded from its box and had injured its knee. Would I come right away.

Even now I am no expert on racehorses; they form a little branch of practice all by itself, with its own stresses, its own mystique. In my short spell in Darrowby I had had very little to do with them as Siegfried was fascinated by anything equine and usually gobbled up anything in that line which came along. So my practical experience was negligible.

I wasn't at all reassured when I saw my patient. The knee was a terrible mess. He had tripped at the bottom of the ramp and come down with his full weight on the stony ground. The lacerated skin hung down in bloody ribbons exposing the joint capsule over an area of about six inches and the extensor tendons gleamed through a tattered layer of fascia. The beautiful three-year-old held the limb up, trembling, with the toe just touching the ground; the ravaged knee made a violent contrast with the sleek, carefully groomed coat.

Examining the wound, gently feeling round the joint, I was immediately thankful for one thing — it was a quiet animal. Some light horses are so highly strung that the slightest touch sends them up in the air, but this one hardly moved as I tried to piece together the jigsaw of skin pieces Another lucky break — there was nothing missing.

I turned to the stable head lad, small, square, hands deep in his coat pockets who was standing watching. 'I'll clean up the wound and stitch it but he'll need some expert care when you get him home. Can you tell me who will be treating him?'

'Yes sir, Mr Brayley-Reynolds. He'll have charge of 'im.'

I came bolt upright from my crouching position. The name was like a trumpet call echoing down from my student days. When you talked about horses you usually talked about Brayley-Reynolds sooner or later. I could imagine the great man inspecting my handiwork. 'And who did you say treated this? Herriot . . . ? Herriot . . . ?'

I got down to the job again with my heart beating faster. Mercifully the joint capsule and tendon sheaths were undamaged — no escape of synovia. Using a solution of Chinosol, I swabbed out every last cranny of the wound till the ground around me was white with cotton wool pledgets, then I puffed in some iodoform powder and tacked down the loose shreds of fascia. Now the thing was to make a really good job of the skin to avoid disfigurement if possible. I chose some fine silk and a very small suture needle and squatted down again.

I must have stayed there for nearly an hour, pulling the flaps of skin carefully into position and fastening them down with innumerable tiny sutures. There is a fascination in repairing a ragged wound and I always took pains over it even without an imaginary Brayley-Reynolds peering over my shoulder. When I finally straightened up I did so slowly, like an old man, easing the kinks from neck and back. With shaking knees I looked down at the head lad almost without recognition. He was smiling.

'You've made a proper job of that,' he said. 'It looks nearly as good as new. I want to thank you, sir — he's one of my favourites, not just because he's a good 'orse, but he's kind.' He patted the three-year-old's flank.

'Well, I hope he does all right.' I got out a packet of gauze and a bandage. 'I'm just going to cover up the knee with this and then you can put on a stable bandage. I'll give him a shot against tetanus and that's it.'

I was packing my gear away in the car when the head lad hovered again at my side. 'Do you back 'orses?'

I laughed. 'No, hardly ever. Don't know much about it.'

'Well never mind.' The little man looked around him and lowered his voice. 'But I'll tell you something to back this afternoon. Kemal in the first race. He's one of ours and he's going to win. You'll get a nice price about him.'

'Well, thanks, it'll give me something to do. I'll have half-a-crown on him.'

The tough little face screwed up in disgust. 'No, no, put a fiver on him. This is the goods, I mean it. Keep it to yourself but get a fiver on him.' He walked rapidly away.

I don't know what madness took hold of me, but by the time I had got back to Darrowby I had decided to take his advice. There had been something compelling about that last hoarse whisper and the utter confidence in the black pebble eyes. The little chap was trying to do me a good turn. I had noticed him glancing at my old jacket and rumpled flannels, so different from the natty outfit of the typical horse vet; maybe he thought I needed the money.

I dropped in at the Midland Bank and drew out five pounds which at the time represented approximately half my available capital. I hurried round the remaining visits, had a quick lunch and got into my best suit. There was plenty of time to get to the course, meet the officials and get my fiver on Kemal before the first race at 2.30.

The phone rang just as I was about to leave the house. It was Mr Sidlow. He had a scouring cow which needed attention immediately. It was fitting, I thought dully, that in my moment of eager anticipation it should be my old jinx who should stretch out his cold hand and grasp me. And it was Saturday afternoon; that was fitting too. But I shook myself — the farm was near Brawton and it shouldn't take long to deal with a scouring cow; I could still make it.

When I arrived, my immaculate appearance set up an immediate flurry of oblique glances among the assembled family while Mr Sidlow's rigid lips and squared shoulders bore witness that he was prepared to endure another visit from me with courage.

A numbness filled me as we went into the byre. It continued as Mr Sidlow described how he had battled against this cow's recurring bouts of diarrhoea for several months; how he had started quietly with ground eggshells in gruel and worked up to his most powerful remedy, blue vitriol and dandelion tea, but all to no avail. I hardly heard him because it was fairly obvious at a glance that the cow had Jöhne's disease.

Nobody could be quite sure, of course, but the animal's advanced emaciation, especially in the hind end, and the stream of bubbly, foetid scour which she had ejected as I walked in were almost diagnostic. Instinctively I grasped her tail and thrust my thermometer into the rectum: I wasn't much interested in her temperature but it gave me a couple of minutes to think.

However, in this instance I got only about five seconds because, without warning, the thermometer disappeared from my fingers. Some sudden suction had drawn it inside the cow. I ran my fingers round just inside the rectum — nothing; I pushed my hand inside without success; with a feeling of rising panic I rolled up my sleeve and groped about in vain.

There was nothing else for it — I had to ask for a bucket of hot water, soap and a towel and strip off as though preparing for some large undertaking. Over my thirty-odd years in practice I can recall many occasions when I looked a complete fool, but there is a peculiarly piercing quality about the memory of myself, bare to the waist, the centre of a ring of hostile stares, guddling frantically inside that cow. At the time, all I could think of was that this was the Sidlow place; anything could happen here. In my mental turmoil I had discarded all my knowledge of pathology and anatomy and could visualise the little glass tube working its way rapidly along the intestinal tract until it finally pierced some vital organ. There was another hideous image of myself carrying out a major operation, a full-scale laparotomy on the cow to recover my thermometer.

It is difficult to describe the glorious relief which flooded through me when at last I felt the thing between my fingers; I pulled it out, filthy and dripping and stared down stupidly at the graduations on the tube.

Mr Sidlow cleared his throat. 'Well, wot does it say? Has she got a temperature?'

I whipped round and gave him a piercing look. Was it possible that this man could be making a joke? But the dark, tight-shut face was expressionless.

'No,' I mumbled in reply. 'No temperature.'

The rest of that visit has always been mercifully blurred in my mind. I know I got myself cleaned up and dressed and told Mr Sidlow that I thought his cow had Jöhne's disease which was incurable but I would take away a faeces sample to try to make sure. The details are cloudy but I do know that at no point was there the slightest gleam of light or hope.

I left the farm, bowed down by an ever greater sense of disgrace than usual and drove with my foot on the boards all the way to Brawton. I roared into the special car park at the racecourse, galloped through the owners' and trainers' entrance and seized the arm of the gatekeeper.

'Has the first race been run?' I gasped.

'Aye, just finished,' he replied cheerfully.

'Kemal won it — ten to one.'

I turned and walked slowly towards the paddock. Fifty pounds! A fortune snatched from my grasp by cruel fate. And hanging over the whole tragedy was the grim spectre of Mr Sidlow. I could forgive Mr Sidlow, I thought, for dragging me out at all sorts of ungodly hours; I could forgive him for presenting me with a long succession of hopeless cases which had lowered my self-esteem to rock bottom; I could forgive him for thinking I was the biggest idiot in Yorkshire and for proclaiming his opinion far and wide. But I'd never forgive him for losing me that fifty pounds.

CHAPTER 48

'The Reniston, eh?' I fidgeted uneasily. 'Bit grand, isn't it?'

Tristan lay rather than sat in his favourite chair and peered up through a cloud of cigarette smoke. 'Of course it's grand. It's the most luxurious hotel in the country outside of London, but for your purpose it's the only possible place. Look, tonight is your big chance isn't it? You want to impress this girl, don't you? Well, ring her up and tell her you're taking her to the Reniston. The food is wonderful and there's a dinner dance every Saturday night. And today is Saturday.' He sat up suddenly and his eyes widened. 'Can't you see it, Jim? The music oozing out of Benny Thornton's trombone and you, full of lobster thermidor, floating round the floor with Helen snuggling up to you. The only snag is that it will cost you a packet, but if you are prepared to spend about a fortnight's wages you can have a really good night.'

I hardly heard the last part, I was concentrating on the blinding vision of Helen snuggling up to me. It was an image which blotted out things like money and I stood with my mouth half open listening to the trombone. I could hear it quite clearly.

Tristan broke in. 'There's one thing — have you got a dinner jacket? You'll need one.'

'Well, I'm not very well off for evening-dress. In fact, when I went to Mrs Pumphrey's party I hired a suit from Brawton, but I wouldn't have time for that now.' I paused and thought for a moment. 'I do have my first and only dinner-suit but I got it when I was about seventeen and I don't know whether I'd be able to get into it.'

Tristan waved this aside. He dragged the Woodbine smoke into the far depths of his lungs and released it reluctantly in little wisps and trickles as he spoke. 'Doesn't matter in the least, Jim. As long as you're wearing the proper gear they'll let you in, and with a big, good-looking chap like you the fit of the suit is unimportant.'

We went upstairs and extracted the garment from the bottom of my trunk. I had cut quite a dash in this suit at the college dances and though it had got very tight towards the end of the course it had still been a genuine evening-dress outfit and as such had commanded a certain amount of respect.

But now it had a pathetic, lost look. The

fashion had changed and the trend was towards comfortable jackets and soft, un-starched shirts. This one was rigidly of the old school and included an absurd little waistcoat with lapels and a stiff, shiny-fronted shirt with a tall, winged collar.

My problems really started when I got the suit on. Hard work, Pennine air and Mrs Hall's good food had filled me out and the jacket failed to meet across my stomach by six inches. I seemed to have got taller, too, because there was a generous space between the bottom of the waistcoat and the top of the trousers. The trousers themselves were skin tight over the buttocks, yet seemed fool-ishly baggy lower down.

Tristan's confidence evaporated as I pa-raded before him and he decided to call on Mrs Hall for advice. She was an unemotional woman and endured the irregular life at Skel-dale House without noticeable reaction, but when she came into the bedroom and looked at me her facial muscles went into a long, twitching spasm. She finally overcame the weakness, however, and became very busi-nesslike.

'A little gusset at the back of your trousers will work wonders, Mr Herriot, and I think if I put a bit of silk cord across the front of your jacket it'll hold it nicely. Mind you, there'll be a bit of a space, like, but I shouldn't think that'll worry you. And I'll give the whole suit a good press — makes all the difference in the world.'

I had never gone in much for intensive grooming, but that night I really went to work on myself, scrubbing and anointing and trying a whole series of different partings in my hair before I was satisfied. Tristan seemed to have appointed himself master of the wardrobe and carried the suit tenderly upstairs, still warm from Mrs Hall's ironing board. Then, like a professional valet, he assisted in every step of the robing. The high collar gave most trouble and he drew strangled oaths from me as he trapped the flesh of my neck under the stud.

When I was finally arrayed he walked around me several times, pulling and patting the material and making delicate adjustments here and there.

Eventually he stopped his circling and surveyed me from the front. I had never seen him look so serious. 'Fine, Jim, fine — you look great. Distinguished, you know. It's not everybody who can wear a dinner jacket — so many people look like conjurers, but not you. Hang on a minute and I'll get your overcoat.'

I had arranged to pick up Helen at seven o'clock and as I climbed from the car in the darkness outside her house a strange unease crept over me. This was different. When I had come here before it had been as a veterinary surgeon — the man who knew, who was wanted, who came to render assistance in time of need. It had never occurred to me how much this affected my outlook every time I walked on to a farm. This wasn't the same thing at all. I had come to take this man's daughter out. He might not like it, might positively resent it.

Standing outside the farmhouse door I took a deep breath. The night was very dark and still. No sound came from the great trees near by and only the distant roar of the Darrow disturbed the silence. The recent heavy rains had transformed the leisurely, wandering river into a rushing torrent which in places overflowed its banks and flooded the surrounding pastures.

I was shown into the large kitchen by Helen's young brother. The boy had a hand over his mouth in an attempt to hide a wide grin. He seemed to find the situation funny. His little sister sitting at a table doing her homework was pretending to concentrate on her writing but she, too, wore a fixed smirk as she looked down at her book.

Mr Alderson was reading the *Farmer and Stockbreeder,* his breeches unlaced, his stockinged feet stretched out towards a blazing pile of logs. He looked up over his spectacles.

'Come in, young man, and sit by the fire,' he said absently. I had the uncomfortable impression that it was a frequent and boring experience for him to have young men calling for his eldest daughter.

I sat down at the other side of the fire and Mr Alderson resumed his study of the *Farmer and Stockbreeder.* The ponderous tick-tock of a large wall clock boomed out into the silence. I stared into the red depths of the fire till my eyes began to ache, then I looked up at a big oil painting in a gilt frame hanging above the mantelpiece. It depicted shaggy cattle standing knee-deep in a lake of an extraordinary bright blue; behind them loomed a backcloth of fearsome, improbable mountains, their jagged summits wreathed in a sulphurous mist.

Averting my eyes from this, I examined, one by one, the sides of bacon and the hams hanging from the rows of hooks in the ceiling. Mr Alderson turned over a page. The clock ticked on. Over by the table, spluttering noises came from the children.

After about a year I heard footsteps on the stairs, then Helen came into the room. She was wearing a blue dress — the kind, without shoulder straps, that seems to stay up by magic. Her dark hair shone under the single pressure lamp which lit the kitchen, shadowing the soft curves of her neck and shoulders. Over one white arm she held a camel-hair coat.

I felt stunned. She was like a rare jewel in

the rough setting of stone flags and white-washed walls. She gave me her quiet, friendly smile and walked towards me. 'Hello, I hope I haven't kept you waiting too long.'

I muttered something in reply and helped her on with her coat. She went over and kissed her father who didn't look up but waved his hand vaguely. There was another outburst of giggling from the table. We went out.

In the car I felt unusually tense and for the first mile or two had to depend on some inane remarks about the weather to keep a conversation going. I was beginning to relax when I drove over a little hump-backed bridge into a dip in the road. Then the car suddenly stopped. The engine coughed gently and then we were sitting silent and motion-less in the darkness. And there was something else; my feet and ankles were freezing cold.

'My God!' I shouted. 'We've run into a bit of flooded road. The water's right into the car.' I looked round at Helen. 'I'm terribly sorry about this — your feet must be soaked.'

But Helen was laughing. She had her feet tucked up on the seat, her knees under her chin. 'Yes, I am a bit wet, but it's no good sitting about like this. Hadn't we better start pushing?'

Wading out into the black icy waters was a nightmare but there was no escape. Merci-fully it was a little car and between us we managed to push it beyond the flooded patch. Then by torchlight I dried the plugs and got the engine going again.

Helen shivered as we squelched back into the car. 'I'm afraid I'll have to go back and change my shoes and stockings. And so will you. There's another road back through Fensley. You take the first turn on the left.'

Back at the farm, Mr Alderson was still reading the *Farmer and Stockbreeder* and kept his finger on the list of pig prices while he gave me a baleful glance over his spectacles. When he learned that I had come to borrow a pair of his shoes and socks he threw the paper down in exasperation and rose, groaning, from his chair. He shuffled out of the room and I could hear him muttering to himself as he mounted the stairs.

Helen followed him and I was left alone with the two young children. They studied my sodden trousers with undisguised delight. I had wrung most of the surplus water out of them but the final result was remarkable. Mrs Hall's knife-edge crease reached to just below the knee, but then there was chaos. The trousers flared out at that point in a crumpled, shapeless mass and as I stood by the fire to dry them a gentle steam rose about me. The children stared at me, wide-eyed and happy. This was a big night for them.

Mr Alderson reappeared at length and dropped some shoes and rough socks at my feet. I pulled on the socks quickly but shrank back when I saw the shoes. They were a pair of dancing slippers from the early days of the century and their cracked patent leather was topped by wide, black silk bows.

I opened my mouth to protest but Mr Alderson had dug himself deep into his chair and had found his place again among the pig prices. I had the feeling that if I asked for another pair of shoes Mr Alderson would attack me with the poker. I put the slippers on.

We had to take a roundabout road to avoid the floods but I kept my foot down and within half-an-hour we had left the steep sides of the Dale behind us and were heading out on to the rolling plain. I began to feel better. We were making good time and the little car, shuddering and creaking, was going well. I was just thinking that we wouldn't be all that late when the steering-wheel began to drag to one side.

I had a puncture most days and recognised the symptoms immediately. I had become an expert at changing wheels and with a word of apology to Helen was out of the car like a flash. With my rapid manipulation of the rusty jack and brace the wheel was off within three minutes. The surface of the crumpled tyre was quite smooth except for the lighter, frayed parts where the canvas showed through. Working like a demon, I screwed on the spare, cringing inwardly as I saw that this tyre was in exactly the same condition as the other. I steadfastly refused to think of what I would do if its frail fibres should give up the struggle.

By day, the Reniston dominated Brawton like a vast mediaeval fortress, bright flags fluttering arrogantly from its four turrets, but tonight it was like a dark cliff with a glowing cavern at street level where the Bentleys discharged their expensive cargoes. I didn't take my vehicle to the front entrance but tucked it away quietly at the back of the car park. A magnificent commissionaire opened the door for us and we trod noiselessly over the rich carpeting of the entrance hall.

We parted there to get rid of our coats, and in the men's cloakroom I scrubbed frantically at my oily hands. It didn't do much good; changing that wheel had given my finger nails a border of deep black which defied ordinary soap and water. And Helen was waiting for me.

I looked up in the mirror at the white-jacketed attendant hovering behind me with a towel. The man, clearly fascinated by my ensemble, was staring down at the wide-bowed pierrot shoes and the rumpled trouser bottoms. As he handed over the towel he smiled broadly as if in gratitude for this little bit of extra colour in his life.

I met Helen in the reception hall and we went over to the desk. 'What time does the dinner dance start?' I asked.

The girl at the desk looked surprised. 'I'm sorry, sir, there's no dance tonight. We only have them once a fortnight.'

I turned to Helen in dismay but she smiled encouragingly. 'It doesn't matter,' she said. 'I don't really care what we do.'

'We can have dinner, anyway,' I said. I tried to speak cheerfully but a little black cloud seemed to be forming just above my head. Was anything going to go right tonight? I could feel my morale slumping as I padded over the lush carpet and my first sight of the dining-room didn't help.

It looked as big as a football field with great marble pillars supporting a carved, painted ceiling. The Reniston had been built in the late Victorian period and all the opulence and ornate splendour of those days had been retained in this tremendous room. Most of the tables were occupied by the usual clientele, a mixture of the county aristocracy and industrialists from the West Riding. I had never seen so many beautiful women and masterful-looking men under one roof and I noticed with a twinge of alarm that, though the men were wearing everything from dark lounge suits to hairy tweeds, there wasn't another dinner jacket in sight.

A majestic figure in white tie and tails bore down on us. With his mane of white hair falling back from the lofty brow, the bulging waistline, the hooked nose and imperious expression he looked exactly like a Roman emperor. His eyes flickered expertly over me and he spoke tonelessly.

'You want a table, sir?'

'Yes please,' I mumbled, only just stopping myself saying 'sir' to the man in return. 'A table for two.'

'Are you staying, sir?'

This question baffled me. How could I possibly have dinner here if I wasn't staying.

'Yes, I am staying.'

The emperor made a note on a pad. 'This way, sir.'

He began to make his way with great dignity among the tables while I followed abjectly in his wake with Helen. It was a long way to the table and I tried to ignore the heads which turned to have a second look at me as I passed. It was Mrs Hall's gusset that worried me most and I imagined it standing out like a beacon below the short jacket. It was literally burning my buttocks by the time we arrived.

The table was nicely situated and a swarm of waiters descended on us, pulling out our chairs and settling us into them, shaking out our napkins and spreading them on our laps. When they had dispersed the emperor took charge again. He poised a pencil over his pad.

'May I have your room number, sir?'

I swallowed hard and stared up at him over

my dangerously billowing shirt front. 'Room number? Oh, I'm not living in the hotel.'

'Ah, NOT staying.' He fixed me for a moment with an icy look before crossing out something on the pad with unnecessary violence. He muttered something to one of the waiters and strode away.

It was about then that the feeling of doom entered into me. The black cloud over my head spread and descended, enveloping me in a dense cloud of misery. The whole evening had been a disaster and would probably get worse. I must have been mad to come to this sumptuous place dressed up like a knock-about comedian. I was as hot as hell inside this ghastly suit and the stud was biting viciously into my neck.

I took a menu card from a waiter and tried to hold it with my fingers curled inwards to hide my dirty nails. Everything was in French and in my numbed state the words were largely meaningless, but somehow I ordered the meal and, as we ate, I tried desperately to keep a conversation going. But long deserts of silence began to stretch between us; it seemed that only Helen and I were quiet among all the surrounding laughter and chatter.

Worst of all was the little voice which kept telling me that Helen had never really wanted to come out with me anyway. She had done it out of politeness and was getting through a boring evening as best she could.

The journey home was a fitting climax. We stared straight ahead as the headlights picked out the winding road back into the Dales. We made stumbling remarks then the strained silence took over again. By the time we drew up outside the farm my head had begun to ache.

We shook hands and Helen thanked me for a lovely evening. There was a tremor in her voice and in the moonlight her face was anxious and withdrawn. I said goodnight, got into the car and drove away.

CHAPTER 49

If only my car had had any brakes I would
certainly have enjoyed looking down on Worton village from the high moor. The old stone
houses straggling unevenly along the near
bank of the river made a pleasant splash of
grey on the green floor of the valley and the
little gardens with their clipped lawns gave a
touch of softness to the bare, rising sweep of
the fellside on the other side of the Dale.

But the whole scene was clouded by the
thought that I had to get down that road with
its 1 in 4 gradient and those two villainous S
bends. It was like a malevolent snake coiling
almost headlong from where I sat. And, as I
said, I had no brakes.

Of course the vehicle had originally been
fitted with the means of bringing it to a halt,
and during most of the year I had ridden in
it a violent pressure on the pedal would have
the desired effect even though it caused a
certain amount of veering about on the road.
But lately the response had been growing

weaker and now it was nil.

During the gradual deterioration I had brought the matter up with Siegfried now and then and he had expressed sympathy and concern.

'That won't do at all, James. I'll have a word with Hammond about it. Leave it with me.'

And then a few days later when I made a further appeal.

'Oh Lord, yes. I've been meaning to fix it up with Hammond. Don't worry, James, I'll see to it.'

Finally I had to tell him that when I put my foot on the pedal there was nothing at all and the only way I had of stopping the car was to crash it into bottom gear.

'Oh bad luck, James. Must be a nuisance for you. But never mind, I'll arrange everything.'

Some time later I asked Mr Hammond down at the garage if he had heard anything from Siegfried, but he hadn't. The motor man did, however, hop into the car and drive it slowly down the street. He came to a jerking, shuddering halt about fifty yards away and then got out. He made no attempt to back up but walked thoughtfully towards me. Normally an imperturbable man, he had gone rather pale and he looked at me wonderingly.

'And you mean to tell me, lad, that you do all your rounds in that car?'

'Well, yes, I do.'

'You ought to have a medal, then. I dursn't drive across market place in that bloody thing.'

There wasn't much I could do. The car was Siegfried's property and I'd have to await his pleasure. Of course I had had experience of this sort of thing before in the shape of the movable passenger seat he had in his own vehicle when I first came to Darrowby. He never seemed to notice when I went over backwards every time I sat in it and I don't suppose he would ever have done anything about it but for an incident one market day when he noticed an old lady with a large basket of vegetables walking into Darrowby and courteously offered her a lift.

'Poor old girl's feet went straight up in the air and she just disappeared into the back. Had a hell of a job getting her out — thought we'd have to get a block and tackle. Cabbages and cauliflowers rolling all over the place.'

I looked again down the steep track. The sensible thing, of course, would be to go back into Darrowby and take the low road into Worton. No danger that way. But it meant a round trip of nearly ten miles and I could actually see the smallholding I wanted to visit just a thousand feet below. The calf with joint ill was in that shed with the green door — in fact there was old Mr Robinson coming out of the house now and pottering across the yard with a bucket. I could almost reach out and touch him.

I thought, not for the first time, that if you had to drive a car with no brakes one of the last places in England you'd want to be was the Yorkshire Dales. Even on the flat it was bad enough but I got used to it after a week or two and often forgot all about it. As when one day I was busy with a cow and the farmer jumped into my car to move it so that one of his men could get past with a tractor. I never said a word as the unsuspecting man backed round quickly and confidently and hit the wall of the barn with a sickening crash. With typical Yorkshire understatement, all he said was; 'Your brakes aren't ower savage, mister.'

Anyway, I had to make up my mind. Was it to be back to Darrowby or straight over the top? It had become a common situation and every day I had the experience of sitting wrestling with myself on the edge of a hill with my heart thumping as it was now. There must have been scores of these unwitnessed dramas played out in the green silence of the fells. At last, I started the engine and did what I always did — took the quick way down.

But this hill really was a beauty, a notorious road even in this country, and as I nosed gingerly on to it, the whole world seemed to drop away from me. With the gear lever in bottom and my hand jammed against it I headed, dry-mouthed, down the strip of tarmac which now looked to be almost vertical.

It is surprising what speed you can attain in bottom gear if you have nothing else to hold you back and as the first bend rushed up at me the little engine started a rising scream of protest. When I hit the curve, I hauled the wheel round desperately to the right, the tyres spun for a second in the stones and loose soil of the verge, then we were off again.

This was a longer stretch and even steeper and it was like being on the big dipper with the same feeling of lack of control over one's fate. Hurtling into the bend, the idea of turning at this speed was preposterous but it was that or straight over the edge. Terror-stricken, I closed my eyes and dragged the wheel to the left. This time, one side of the car lifted and I was sure we were over, then it rocked back on to the other side and for a horrible second or two kept this up till it finally decided to stay upright and I was once more on my way.

Again a yawning gradient. But as the car sped downwards, engine howling, I was aware of a curious numbness. I seemed to have reached the ultimate limits of fear and hardly noticed as we shot round the third bend. One more to go and at last the road was levelling out; my speed dropped rapidly and at the last bend I couldn't have been doing more than twenty. I had made it.

It wasn't till I was right on to the final straight that I saw the sheep. Hundreds of them, filling the road. A river of woolly backs lapping from wall to wall. They were only yards from me and I was still going downhill. Without hesitation I turned and drove straight into the wall.

There didn't seem to be much damage. A few stones slithered down as the engine stalled and fell silent.

Slowly I sank back in my seat, relaxing my clenched jaws, releasing, finger by finger, the fierce grip on the wheel. The sheep continued to flow past and I took a sideways glance at the man who was shepherding them. He was a stranger to me and I prayed he didn't recognise me either because at that moment the role of unknown madman seemed to be the ideal one. Best not to say anything; appearing round a corner and driving deliberately into a wall is no basis for a rewarding conversation.

The sheep were still passing by and I could hear the man calling to his dogs. 'Get by, Jess. Come by, Nell.' But I kept up a steady stare at the layered stones in front of me, even though he passed within a few feet.

I suppose some people would have asked me what the hell I was playing at, but not a Dales shepherd. He went quietly by without invading my privacy, but when I looked in the mirror after a few moments I could see him in the middle of the road staring back at me, his sheep temporarily forgotten.

My brakeless period has always been easy to recall. There is a piercing clarity about the memory which has kept it fresh over the years. I suppose it lasted only a few weeks but it could have gone on indefinitely if Siegfried himself hadn't become involved.

It was when we were going to a case together. For some reason he decided to take my car and settled in the driver's seat. I huddled apprehensively next to him as he set off at his usual brisk pace.

Hinchcliffe's farm lies about a mile on the main road outside Darrowby. It is a massive place with a wide straight drive leading down to the house. We weren't going there, but as Siegfried spurted to full speed I could see Mr Hinchcliffe in his big Buick ahead of us proceeding in a leisurely way along the middle of the road. As Siegfried pulled out to overtake, the farmer suddenly stuck out his hand and began to turn right towards his farm — directly across our path. Siegfried's foot went hard down on the brake pedal and his eyebrows shot right up as nothing happened. We were going straight for the side of the Buick and there was no room to go round on the left.

Siegfried didn't panic. At the last moment he turned right with the Buick and the two cars roared side by side down the drive, Mr Hinchcliffe staring at me with bulging eyes from close range. The farmer stopped in the yard, but we continued round the back of the house because we had to.

Fortunately, it was one of those places where you could drive right round and we rattled through the stackyard and back to the front of the house behind Mr Hinchcliffe who had got out and was looking round the corner to see where we had gone. The farmer whipped round in astonishment and, open-mouthed watched us as we passed, but Siegfried, retaining his aplomb to the end, inclined his head and gave a little wave before we shot back up the drive.

Before we returned to the main road I had a look back at Mr Hinchcliffe. He was still watching us and there was a certain rigidity in his pose which reminded me of the shepherd.

Once on the road, Siegfried steered carefully into a layby and stopped. For a few moments he stared straight ahead without speaking and I realised he was having a little difficulty in getting his patient look properly adjusted; but when he finally turned to me his face was transfigured, almost saintly.

I dug my nails into my palms as he smiled at me with kindly eyes.

'Really, James,' he said, 'I can't understand why you keep things to yourself. Heaven knows how long your car has been in this condition, yet never a word from you.' He raised a forefinger and his patient look was replaced by one of sorrowing gravity. 'Don't you realise we might have been killed back there? You really ought to have told me.'

CHAPTER 50

There didn't seem much point in a millionaire filling up football pools coupons but it was one of the motive forces in old Harold Denham's life. It made a tremendous bond between us because, despite his devotion to the pools, Harold knew nothing about football, had never seen a match and was unable to name a single player in league football; and when he found that I could discourse knowledgeably not only about Everton and Preston North End but even about Arbroath and Cowdenbeath the respect with which he had always treated me deepened into a wide-eyed deference.

Of course we had first met over his animals. He had an assortment of dogs, cats, rabbits, budgies and goldfish which made me a frequent visitor to the dusty mansion whose Victorian turrets peeping above their sheltering woods could be seen for miles around Darrowby. When I first knew him, the circumstances of my visits were entirely normal —

his fox terrier had cut its pad or the old grey tabby was having trouble with its sinusitis, but later on I began to wonder. He called me out so often on a Wednesday and the excuse was at times so trivial that I began seriously to suspect that there was nothing wrong with the animal but that Harold was in difficulties with his Nine Results or the Easy Six.

I could never be quite sure, but it was funny how he always received me with the same words. 'Ah, Mr Herriot, how are your pools?' He used to say the word in a long-drawn, loving way — poools. This enquiry had been unvarying ever since I had won sixteen shillings one week on the Three Draws. I can never forget the awe with which he fingered the little slip from Littlewoods, looking unbelievingly from it to the postal order. That was the only time I was a winner but it made no difference — I was still the oracle, unchallenged, supreme. Harold never won anything, ever.

The Denhams were a family of note in North Yorkshire. The immensely wealthy industrialists of the last century had become leaders in the world of agriculture. They were 'gentlemen farmers' who used their money to build up pedigree herds of dairy cows or pigs; they ploughed out the high, stony moorland and fertilised it and made it grow crops, they drained sour bogs and made them yield potatoes and turnips; they were the chairmen of committees, masters of fox hounds, leaders of the county society.

But Harold had opted out of all that at an early age. He had refuted the age old dictum that you can't be happy doing absolutely nothing; all day and every day he pottered around his house and his few untidy acres, uninterested in the world outside, not entirely aware of what was going on in his immediate vicinity, but utterly content. I don't think he ever gave a thought to other people's opinions which was just as well because they were often unkind; his brother, the eminent Basil Denham, referred to him invariably as 'that bloody fool' and with the country people it was often 'nobbut ninepence in t'shillin'.'

Personally I always found something appealing in him. He was kind, friendly, with a sense of fun and I enjoyed going to his house. He and his wife ate all their meals in the kitchen and in fact seemed to spend most of their time there, so I usually went round the back of the house.

On this particular day it was to see his Great Dane bitch which had just had pups and seemed unwell; since it wasn't Wednesday I felt that there really might be something amiss with her and hurried round. Harold gave me his usual greeting; he had the most attractive voice — round, fruity, mellow, like a bishop's, and for the hundredth time I thought how odd it was to hear those organ-

531

like vocal cords intoning such incongruities as Mansfield Town or Bradford City.

'I wonder if you could advise me, Mr Herriot,' he said as we left the kitchen and entered a long, ill-lit passage. 'I'm searching for an away winner and I wondered about Sunderland at Aston Villa?'

I stopped and fell into an attitude of deep thought while Harold regarded me anxiously. 'Well, I'm not sure, Mr Denham,' I replied. 'Sunderland are a good side but I happen to know that Raich Carter's auntie isn't too well at present and it could easily affect his game this Saturday.'

Harold looked crestfallen and he nodded his head gravely a few times; then he looked closely at me for a few seconds and broke into a shout of laughter. 'Ah, Mr Herriot, you're pulling my leg again.' He seized my arm, gave it a squeeze and shuffled off along the passage, chuckling deeply.

We traversed a labyrinth of gloomy, cob-webbed passages before he led the way into a little gun room. My patient was lying on a raised wooden dog bed and I recognised her as the enormous Dane I had seen leaping around at previous visits. I had never treated her, but my first sight of her had dealt a blow at one of my new-found theories — that you didn't find big dogs in big houses. Times without number I had critically observed Bull Mastiffs, Alsatians and Old English Sheep

Dogs catapulting out of the tiny, back street dwellings of Darrowby, pulling their helpless owners on the end of a lead, while in the spacious rooms and wide acres of the stately homes I saw nothing but Border Terriers and Jack Russells. But Harold would have to be different.

He patted the bitch's head. 'She had the puppies yesterday and she's got a nasty dark discharge. She's eating well, but I'd like you to look her over.'

Great Danes, like most of the big breeds, are usually placid animals and the bitch didn't move as I took her temperature. She lay on her side, listening contentedly to the squeals of her family as the little blind creatures climbed over each other to get at the engorged teats.

'Yes, she's got a slight fever and you're right about the discharge.' I gently palpated the long hollow of the flank. 'I don't think there's another pup there but I'd better have a feel inside her to make sure. Could you bring me some warm water, soap and towel please?'

As the door closed behind Harold I looked idly around the gun room. It wasn't much bigger than a cupboard and, since another of Harold's idiosyncrasies was that he never killed anything, was devoid of guns. The glass cases contained only musty bound volumes of *Blackwood's Magazine* and *Country Life*. I stood there for maybe ten minutes, wondering why the old chap was taking so long, then I turned to look at an old print on the wall; it was the usual hunting scene and I was peering through the grimy glass and wondering why they always drew those horses flying over the stream with such impossible long legs when I heard a sound behind me.

It was a faint growl, a deep rumble, soft but menacing. I turned and saw the bitch rising very slowly from her bed. She wasn't getting to her feet in the normal way of dogs, it was as though she were being lifted up by strings somewhere in the ceiling, the legs straightening almost imperceptibly, the body rigid, every hair bristling. All the time she glared at me unblinkingly and for the first time in my life I realised the meaning of blazing eyes. I had only once seen anything like this before and it was on the cover of an old copy of *The Hound of the Baskervilles.* At the time I had thought the artist ridiculously fanciful but here were two eyes filled with the same yellow fire and fixed unwaveringly on mine.

She thought I was after her pups, of course. After all, her master had gone and there was only this stranger standing motionless and silent in the corner of the room, obviously up to no good. One thing was sure — she was going to come at me any second, and I blessed the luck that had made me stand right by the door. Carefully I inched my left hand towards the handle as the bitch still rose with terrifying slowness, still rumbling deep in her chest. I had almost reached the handle when I made the mistake of making a quick grab for it. Just as I touched the metal the bitch came out of the bed like a rocket and sank her teeth into my wrist.

I thumped her over the head with my right fist and she let go and seized me high up on the inside of the left thigh. This really made me yell out and I don't know just what my immediate future would have been if I hadn't bumped up against the only chair in the room; it was old and flimsy but it saved me. As the bitch, apparently tiring of gnawing my leg, made a sudden leap at my face I snatched the chair up and fended her off.

The rest of my spell in the gun room was a sort of parody of a lion-taming act and would have been richly funny to an impartial observer. In fact, in later years I have often wished I could have a cine film of the episode; but at the time, with that great animal stalking me round those few cramped yards of space, the blood trickling down my leg and only a rickety chair to protect me I didn't feel a bit like laughing. There was a dreadful dedication in the way she followed me and those maddened eyes never left my face for an instant.

The pups, furious at the unceremonious removal of their delightful source of warmth and nourishment, were crawling blindly across the bed and bawling, all nine of them, at the top of their voices. The din acted as a spur to the bitch and the louder it became the more she pressed home her attack. Every few seconds she would launch herself at me and I would prance about, stabbing at her with my chair in best circus fashion. Once she bore me back against the wall, chair and all; on her hind legs she was about as tall as me and I had a disturbing close-up of the snarling gaping jaws.

My biggest worry was that my chair was beginning to show signs of wear; the bitch had already crunched two of the spars effortlessly away and I tried not to think of what would happen if the whole thing finally disintegrated. But I was working my way back to the door and when I felt the handle at my back I knew I had to do something about it. I gave a final, intimidating shout, threw the remains of the chair at the bitch and dived out into the corridor. As I slammed the door behind me and leaned against it I could feel the panels quivering as the big animal threw herself against the wood.

I was sitting on the floor with my back against the passage wall, pants round my ankles, examining my wounds when I saw Harold pass across the far end, pottering vaguely along with a basin of steaming water held in front of him and a towel over his shoulder. I could understand now why he had been so long — he had been wandering around like that all the time; being Harold it was just possible he had been lost in his own house. Or maybe he was just worrying about his Four Aways.

Back at Skeldale House I had to endure some unkind remarks about my straddling gait, but later, in my bedroom, the smile left Siegfried's face as he examined my leg.

'Right up there, by God.' He gave a low, awed whistle. 'You know, James, we've often made jokes about what a savage dog might do to us one day. Well, I tell you boy, it damn nearly happened to you.'

CHAPTER 51

This was my second winter in Darrowby so I didn't feel the same sense of shock when it started to be really rough in November. When they were getting a drizzle of rain down there on the plain the high country was covered in a few hours by a white blanket which filled in the roads, smoothed out familiar landmarks, transformed our world into something strange and new. This was what they meant on the radio when they talked about 'snow on high ground'.

When the snow started in earnest it had a strangling effect on the whole district. Traffic crawled laboriously between the mounds thrown up by the snow ploughs. Herne Fell hung over Darrowby like a great gleaming whale and in the town the people dug deep paths to their garden gates and cleared the drifts from their front doors. They did it without fuss, with the calm of long use and in the knowledge that they would probably have to do it again tomorrow.

Every new fall struck a fresh blow at the vets. We managed to get to most of our cases but we lost a lot of sweat in the process. Sometimes we were lucky and were able to bump along in the wake of a council plough but more often we drove as far as we could and walked the rest of the way.

On the morning when Mr Clayton of Pike House rang up we had had a night of continuous snow.

'Young beast with a touch o' cold,' he said. 'Will you come?'

To get to his place you had to cross over Pike Edge and then drop down into a little valley. It was a lovely drive in the summer, but I wondered.

'What's the road like?' I asked.

'Road? road?' Mr Clayton's reaction was typically airy. Farmers in the less accessible places always brushed aside such queries. 'Road's right enough. Just tek a bit o' care and you'll get here without any trouble.'

Siegfried wasn't so sure. 'You'll certainly have to walk over the top and it's doubtful whether the ploughs will have cleared the lower road. It's up to you.'

'Oh, I'll have a go. There's not much doing this morning and I feel like a bit of exercise.'

In the yard I found that old Boardman had done a tremendous job in his quiet way; he had dug open the big double doors and cleared a way for the cars to get out. I put what I thought I would need into a small rucksack — some expectorant mixture, a tub of electuary, a syringe and a few ampoules of pneumonia serum. Then I threw the most important item of my winter equipment, a broad-bladed shovel, into the back and left.

The bigger roads had already been cleared by the council ploughs which had been clanking past Skeldale House since before dawn, but the surface was rough and I had a slow, bumpy ride. It was more than ten miles to the Clayton farm and it was one of those iron days when the frost piled thickly on the windscreen blotting out everything within minutes. But this morning I was triumphant. I had just bought a wonderful new invention — a couple of strands of wire mounted on a strip of bakelite and fastened to the windscreen with rubber suckers. It worked from the car batteries and cleared a small space of vision.

No more did I have to climb out wearily and scrub and scratch at the frozen glass every half mile or so. I sat peering delightedly through a flawlessly clear semicircle about eight inches wide at the countryside unwinding before me like a film show; the grey stone villages, silent and withdrawn under their smothering white cloak; the low, burdened branches of the roadside trees.

I was enjoying it so much that I hardly noticed the ache in my toes. Freezing feet were the rule in those days before car heaters, especially when you could see the road flashing past through the holes in the floor boards. On long journeys I really began to suffer towards the end. It was like that today when I got out of the car at the foot of the Pike Edge road; my fingers too, throbbed painfully as I stamped around and swung my arms.

The ploughs hadn't even attempted to clear the little side road which wound its way upwards and into the valley beyond. Its solid, creamy, wall-to-wall filling said 'No, you can't come up here', with that detached finality I had come to know so well. But as always, even in my disappointment, I looked with wonder at the shapes the wind had sculpted in the night; flowing folds of the most perfect smoothness tapering to the finest of points, deep hollows with knife-edge rims, soaring cliffs with overhanging margins almost transparent in their delicacy.

Hitching the rucksack on my shoulder I felt a kind of subdued elation. With a leather golf jacket buttoned up to my neck and an extra pair of thick socks under my Wellingtons I felt ready for anything. No doubt I considered there was something just a bit dashing and gallant in the picture of the dedicated young vet with his magic potions on his back battling against the odds to succour a helpless animal.

I stood for a moment gazing at the fell,

curving clean and cold into the sullen sky. An expectant hush lay on the fields, the frozen river and the still trees as I started off.

I kept up a good pace. First over a bridge with the river white and silent beneath then up and up, picking my way over the drifts till the road twisted, almost invisible, under some low cliffs. Despite the cold, the sweat was beginning to prick on my back when I got to the top.

I looked around me. I had been up here several times in June and July and I could remember the sunshine, the smell of the warm grass, and the scent of flowers and pines that came up the hill from the valley below. But it was hard to relate the smiling landscape of last summer with this desolation.

The flat moorland on the fell top was a white immensity rolling away to the horizon with the sky pressing down like a dark blanket. I could see the farm down there in its hollow and it, too, looked different; small, remote, like a charcoal drawing against the hills bulking smooth and white beyond. A pine wood made a dark smudge on the slopes but the scene had been wiped clean of most of its familiar features.

I could see the road only in places — the walls were covered over most of their length, but the farm was visible all the way. I had gone about half a mile towards it when a sudden gust of wind blew up the surface snow into a cloud of fine particles. Just for a few seconds I found myself completely alone. The farm, the surrounding moor, everything disappeared and I had an eerie sense of isolation till the veil cleared.

It was hard going in the deep snow and in the drifts I sank over the tops of my Wellingtons. I kept at it, head down, to within a few hundred yards of the stone buildings. I was just thinking that it had all been pretty easy, really, when I looked up and saw a waving curtain of a million black dots bearing down on me. I quickened my steps and just before the blizzard hit me I marked the position of the farm. But after ten minutes' stumbling and slithering I realised I had missed the place. I was heading for a shape that didn't exist; it was etched only in my mind.

I stood for a few moments feeling again the chilling sense of isolation. I was convinced I had gone too far to the left and after a few gasping breaths, struck off to the right. It wasn't long before I knew I had gone in the wrong direction again. I began to fall into deep holes, up to the arm-pits in the snow reminding me that the ground was not really flat on these high moors but pitted by countless peat haggs.

As I struggled on I told myself that the whole thing was ridiculous. I couldn't be far from the warm fireside at Pike House — this wasn't the North Pole. But my mind went back to the great empty stretch of moor beyond the farm and I had to stifle a feeling of panic.

The numbing cold seemed to erase all sense of time. Soon I had no idea of how long I had been falling into the holes and crawling out. I did know that each time it was getting harder work dragging myself out. And it was becoming more and more tempting to sit down and rest, even sleep; there was something hypnotic in the way the big, soft flakes brushed noiselessly across my skin and mounted thickly on my closed eyes.

I was trying to shut out the conviction that if I fell down many more times I wouldn't get up when a dark shape hovered suddenly ahead. Then my outflung arms touched something hard and rough. Unbelievingly I felt my way over the square stone blocks till I came to a corner. Beyond that was a square of light — it was the kitchen window of the farm.

Thumping on the door, I leaned against the smooth timbers, mouth gaping, chest heaving agonisingly. My immense relief must have bordered on hysteria because it seemed to me that when the door was opened the right thing would be to fall headlong into the room. My mind played with the picture of the family crowding round the prostrate figure, plying him with brandy.

When the door did open, however, something kept me on my feet. Mr Clayton stood there for a few seconds, apparently unmoved by the sight of the distraught snowman in front of him.

'Oh, it's you, Mr Herriot. You couldn't have come better — I've just finished me dinner. Hang on a minute till I get me 'at. Beast's just across yard.'

He reached behind the door, stuck a battered trilby on his head, put his hands in his pockets and sauntered over the cobbles, whistling. He knocked up the latch of the calf house and with a profound sense of release I stepped inside; away from the relentless cold, the sucking swirling snow into an animal warmth and the scent of hay.

As I rid myself of my rucksack, four long-haired little bullocks regarded me calmly from over a hurdle, their jaws moving rhythmically. They appeared as unconcerned at my appearance as their owner. They showed a mild interest, nothing more. Behind the shaggy heads I could see a fifth small beast with a sack tied round it and a purulent discharge coming from its nose.

It reminded me of the reason for my visit. As my numb fingers fumbled in a pocket for my thermometer a great gust of wind buffeted the door, setting the latch clicking softly and sending a faint powdering of snow into the dark interior.

Mr Clayton turned and rubbed the pane of the single small window with his sleeve. Picking his teeth with his thumb-nail he peered out at the howling blizzard.

'Aye,' he said, and belched pleasurably. 'It's a plain sort o' day.'

CHAPTER 52

As I waited for Siegfried to give me my morning list I pulled my scarf higher till it almost covered my ears, turned up the collar of my overcoat and buttoned it tightly under my chin. Then I drew on a pair of holed woollen gloves.

A biting north wind was driving the snow savagely past the window almost parallel with the ground, obliterating the street and everything else with big, swirling flakes.

Siegfried bent over the day book. 'Now let's see what we've got. Barnett, Gill, Sunter, Dent, Cartwright . . .' He began to scribble on a pad. 'Oh, and I'd better see Scruton's calf — you've been attending it, I know, but I'm going right past the door. Can you tell me about it?'

'Yes, it's been breathing a bit fast and running a temperature around 103 — I don't think there's any pneumonia there. In fact I rather suspect it may be developing diphtheria — it has a bit of a swelling on the jaw and the throat glands are up.'

All the time I was speaking, Siegfried continued to write on the pad and only stopped once to whisper to Miss Harbottle. Then he looked up brightly. 'Pneumonia, eh? How have you been treating it?'

'No, I said I didn't think it was pneumonia. I've been injecting Prontosil and I left some liniment to rub into the throat region.'

But Siegfried was writing hard again. He said nothing till he had made out two lists. He tore one from the pad and gave it to me. 'Right, you've been applying liniment to the chest. Suppose it might do a bit of good. Which liniment exactly?'

'Lin. methyl. sal., but they're rubbing it on the calf's throat, not the chest.' But Siegfried had turned away to tell Miss Harbottle the order of his visits and I found myself talking to the back of his head.

Finally he straightened up and came away from the desk. 'Well, that's fine. You have your list — let's get on.' But half way across the floor he hesitated in his stride and turned back. 'Why the devil are you rubbing that liniment on the calf's throat?'

'Well, I thought it might relieve the inflammation a bit.'

'But James, why should there be any inflammation there? Don't you think the liniment would do more good on the chest wall?' Siegfried was wearing his patient look again.

'No, I don't. Not in a case of calf diphtheria.'

Siegfried put his head on one side and a smile of saintly sweetness crept over his face. He laid his hand on my shoulder. 'My dear old James, perhaps it would be a good idea if you started right at the beginning. Take all the time you want — there's no hurry. Speak slowly and calmly and then you won't become confused. You told me you were treating a calf with pneumonia — now take it from there.'

I thrust my hands deep into my coat pockets and began to churn among the thermometers and scissors and little bottles which always dwelt there. 'Look, I told you right at the start that I didn't think there was any pneumonia but that I suspected early diphtheria. There was also a bit of fever — 103.'

Siegfried was looking past me at the window. 'God, just look at that snow. We're going to have some fun getting round today.' He dragged his eyes back to my face. 'Don't you think that with a temperature of 103 you should be injecting some Prontosil?' He raised his arms sideways and let them fall. 'Just a suggestion, James — I wouldn't interfere for the world but I honestly think that the situation calls for a little Prontosil.'

'But hell, I am using it!' I shouted. 'I told you that way back but you weren't listening. I've been doing my damnedest to get this across to you but what chance have I got . . .'

'Come come, dear boy, come come. No need to upset yourself.' Siegfried's face was transfigured by an internal radiance. Sweetness and charity, forgiveness, tolerance and affection flowed from him in an enveloping wave. I battled with an impulse to kick him swiftly on the shin.

'James, James.' The voice was caressing. 'I've not the slightest doubt you tried in your own way to tell me about this case, but we haven't all got the gift of communication. You're the most excellent fellow but must apply yourself to this. It is simply a matter of marshalling your facts and presenting them in an orderly manner. Then you wouldn't get confused and mixed up as you've done this morning; it's only a question of practice, I'm sure.' He gave an encouraging wave of the hand and was gone.

I strode quickly through to the stock room and, seeing a big, empty cardboard box on the floor, dealt it a vicious kick. I put so much venom into it that my foot went clear through the cardboard and I was trying to free myself when Tristan came in. He had been stoking the fire and had witnessed the conversation.

He watched silently as I plunged about the room swearing and trying to shake the box loose. 'What's up, Jim? Has my big brother been getting under your skin?'

I got rid of the box at last and sank down

on one of the lower shelves. 'I don't know. Why should he be getting under my skin now? I've known him quite a long time and he's always been the same. He's never been any different but it hasn't bothered me before — not like this, anyway. Any other time I'd laugh that sort of thing off. What the hell's wrong with me?'

Tristan put down his coal bucket and looked at me thoughtfully. 'There's nothing much wrong with you, Jim, but I can tell you one thing — you've been just a bit edgy since you went out with the Alderson woman.'

'Oh God,' I groaned and closed my eyes. 'Don't remind me. Anyway, I've not seen her or heard from her since, so that's the end of that and I can't blame her.'

Tristan pulled out his Woodbines and squatted down by the coal bucket. 'Yes, that's all very well, but look at you. You're suffering and there's no need for it. All right, you had a disastrous night and she's given you the old heave ho. Well, so what? Do you know how many times I've been spurned?'

'Spurned? I never even got started.'

'Very well then, but you're still going around like a bullock with bellyache. Forget it, lad, and get out into the big world. The rich tapestry of life is waiting for you out there. I've been watching you — working all hours and when you're not working you're reading up your cases in the text books —

and I tell you this dedicated vet thing is all right up to a point. But you've got to live a little. Think of all the lovely little lasses in Darrowby — you can hardly move for them. And every one just waiting for a big handsome chap like you to gallop up on his white horse. Don't disappoint them.' He leaned over and slapped my knee. 'Tell you what. Why don't you let me fix something up? A nice little foursome — just what you need.'

'Ach I don't know. I'm not keen, really.'

'Nonsense!' Tristan said. 'I don't know why I haven't thought of it before. This monkish existence is bad for you. Leave all the details to me.'

I decided to have an early night and was awakened around eleven o'clock by a heavy weight crashing down on the bed. The room was dark but I seemed to be enveloped in beer-scented smoke. I coughed and sat up. 'Is that you, Triss?'

'It is indeed,' said the shadowy figure on the end of the bed. 'And I bring you glad tidings. You remember Brenda?'

'That little nurse I've seen you around with?'

'The very same. Well, she's got a pal, Connie, who's even more beautiful. The four of us are going dancing at the Poulton Institute on Tuesday night.' The voice was thick with beery triumph.

'You mean me, too?'

'By God I do, and you're going to have the best time you've ever had. I'll see to that.' He blew a last choking blast of smoke into my face and left, chuckling.

CHAPTER 53

'We're having a 'ot dinner and entertainers.'

My reaction to the words surprised me. They stirred up a mixture of emotions, all of them pleasant; fulfilment, happy acceptance, almost triumph.

I know by now that there is not the slightest chance of anybody asking me to be President of the Royal College of Veterinary Surgeons, but if they had, I wonder if I'd have been more pleased than when I heard about the 'ot dinner.

The reason, I suppose, was that the words reflected the attitude of a typical Dales farmer towards myself. And this was important because, though after just over a year I was becoming accepted as a vet, I was always conscious of the gulf which was bound to exist between these hill folk and a city product like me. Much as I admired them I was aware always that we were different; it was inevitable, I knew, but it still rankled so that a sincere expression of friendship from one of them struck a deep answering chord in me.

Especially when it came from somebody like Dick Rudd. I had first met Dick last winter on the doorstep of Skeldale House at six o'clock on the kind of black morning when country vets wonder about their choice of profession. Shivering as the ever-present passage draught struck at my pyjamaed legs, I switched on the light and opened the door. I saw a small figure muffled in an old army greatcoat and balaclava leaning on a bicycle. Beyond him the light spilled onto a few feet of streaming pavement where the rain beat down in savage swathes.

'Sorry to ring your bell at this hour, guvnor,' he said. 'My name's Rudd, Birch Tree Farm, Coulston. I've got a heifer calvin' and she's not getting on with t'job. Will you come?'

I looked closer at the thin face, at the water trickling down the cheeks and dripping from the end of the nose. 'Right, I'll get dressed and come straight along. But why don't you leave your bike here and come with me in the car? Coulston's about four miles isn't it and you must be soaked through.'

'Nay, nay, it'll be right.' The face broke into the most cheerful of grins and under the sopping balaclava a pair of lively blue eyes glinted at me. 'I'd only have to come back and get it another time. I'll get off now and you won't be there long afore me.'

He mounted his bike quickly and pedalled

away. People who think farming is a pleasant, easy life should have been there to see the hunched figure disappear into the blackness and the driving rain. No car, no telephone, a night up with the heifer, eight miles biking in the rain and a back-breaking day ahead of him. Whenever I thought of the existence of the small farmer it made my own occasional bursts of activity seem small stuff indeed.

I produced a nice live heifer calf for Dick that first morning and later, gratefully drinking a cup of hot tea in the farmhouse kitchen, I was surprised at the throng of young Rudds milling around me; there were seven of them and they were unexpectedly grown up. Their ages ranged from twenty odd down to about ten and I hadn't thought of Dick as middle-aged; in the dim light of the doorway at Skeldale House and later in the byre lit only by a smoke-blackened oil lamp his lively movements and perky manner had seemed those of a man in his thirties. But as I looked at him now I could see that the short, wiry hair was streaked with grey and a maze of fine wrinkles spread from around his eyes onto his cheeks.

In their early married life the Rudds, anxious like all farmers for male children, had observed with increasing chagrin the arrival of five successive daughters. 'We nearly packed up then,' Dick confided to me once; but they didn't and their perseverance was rewarded at last by the appearance of two fine boys. A farmer farms for his sons and Dick had something to work for now.

As I came to know them better I used to observe the family with wonder. The five girls were all tall, big-limbed, handsome, and already the two chunky young boys gave promise of massive growth. I kept looking from them to their frail little parents — 'not a pickin' on either of us', as Mrs Rudd used to say — and wonder how the miracle had happened.

It puzzled me, too, how Mrs Rudd, armed only with the milk cheque from Dick's few shaggy cows, had managed to feed them all, never mind bring them to this state of physical perfection. I gained my first clue one day when I had been seeing some calves and I was asked to have a 'bit o' dinner' with them. Butcher's meat was a scarce commodity on the hill farms and I was familiar with the usual expedients for filling up the eager stomachs before the main course — the doughy slab of Yorkshire pudding or the heap of suet dumplings. But Mrs Rudd had her own method — a big bowl of rice pudding with lots of milk was her *hors d'oeuvres*. It was a new one on me and I could see the family slowing down as they ploughed their way through. I was ravenous when I sat down but after the rice I viewed the rest of the meal with total detachment.

Dick believed in veterinary advice for everything so I was a frequent visitor at Birch Tree Farm. After every visit there was an unvarying ritual; I was asked into the house for a cup of tea and the whole family downed tools and sat down to watch me drink it. On weekdays the eldest girl was out at work and the boys were at school but on Sundays the ceremony reached its full splendour with myself sipping the tea and all nine Rudds sitting around in what I can only call an admiring circle. My every remark was greeted with nods and smiles all round. There is no doubt it was good for my ego to have an entire family literally hanging on my words, but at the same time it made me feel curiously humble.

I suppose it was because of Dick's character. Not that he was unique in any way — there were thousands of small farmers just like him — but he seemed to embody the best qualities of the Dalesman; the indestructibility, the tough philosophy, the unthinking generosity and hospitality. And there were the things that were Dick's own; the integrity which could be read always in his steady eyes and the humour which was never very far away. Dick was no wit but he was always trying to say ordinary things in a funny way. If I asked him to get hold of a cow's nose for me he would say solemnly 'Ah'll endeavour to do so', or I remember when I was trying to lift a square of plywood which was penning a calf in a corner he said 'Just a minute till ah raise portcullis'. When he broke into a smile a kind of radiance flooded his pinched features.

When I held my audiences in the kitchen with all the family reflecting Dick's outlook in their eager laughter I marvelled at their utter contentment with their lot. None of them had known ease or softness but it didn't matter; and they looked on me as a friend and I was proud.

Whenever I left the farm I found something on the seat of my car — a couple of home-made scones, three eggs. I don't know how Mrs Rudd spared them but she never failed.

Dick had a burning ambition — to upgrade his stock until he had a dairy herd which would live up to his ideals. Without money behind him he knew it would be a painfully slow business but he was determined. It probably wouldn't be in his own lifetime but some time, perhaps when his sons were grown up, people would come and look with admiration at the cows of Birch Tree.

I was there to see the very beginning of it. When Dick stopped me on the road one morning and asked me to come up to his place with him I knew by his air of suppressed excitement that something big had happened. He led me into the byre and stood silent. He didn't need to say anything because I was staring unbelievingly at a bovine aristocrat.

Dick's cows had been scratched together over the years and they were a motley lot. Many of them were old animals discarded by more prosperous farmers because of their pendulous udders or because they were 'three titted 'uns'. Others had been reared by Dick from calves and tended to be rough-haired and scruffy. But half way down the byre, contrasting almost violently with her neighbours was what seemed to me a perfect Dairy shorthorn cow.

In these days when the Friesian has surged over England in a black and white flood and inundated even the Dales which were the very home of the shorthorn, such cows as I looked at that day at Dick Rudd's are no longer to be seen, but she represented all the glory and pride of her breed. The wide pelvis tapering to fine shoulders and a delicate head, the level udder thrusting back between the hind legs, and the glorious colour — dark roan. That was what they used to call a 'good colour' and whenever I delivered a dark roan calf the farmer would say 'It's a good-coloured 'un', and it would be more valuable accordingly. The geneticists are perfectly right, of course: the dark roaned cows gave no more milk than the reds or the whites, but we loved them and they were beautiful.

'Where did she come from, Dick?' I said, still staring.

Dick's voice was elaborately casual. 'Oh, ah

went over to Weldon's of Cranby and picked her out. D'you like her?'

'She's a picture — a show cow. I've never seen one better.' Weldons were the biggest pedigree breeders in the northern Dales and I didn't ask whether Dick had cajoled his bank manager or had been saving up for years just for this.

'Aye, she's a seven galloner when she gets goin' and top butter fat, too. Reckon she'll be as good as two of my other cows and a calf out of her'll be worth a bit.' He stepped forward and ran his hand along the perfectly level, smoothly-fleshed back. 'She's got a great fancy pedigree name but missus 'as called her Strawberry.'

I knew as I stood there in the primitive, cobbled byre with its wooden partitions and rough stone walls that I was looking not just at a cow but at the foundation of the new herd, at Dick Rudd's hopes for the future.

It was about a month later that he phoned me. 'I want you to come and look at Strawberry for me,' he said. 'She's been doing grand, tipplin' the milk out, but there's summat amiss with her this morning.'

The cow didn't really look ill and, in fact, she was eating when I examined her, but I noticed that she gulped slightly when she swallowed. Her temperature was normal and her lungs clear but when I stood up by her head I could just hear a faint snoring sound.

'It's her throat, Dick,' I said. 'It may be just a bit of inflammation but there's a chance that she's starting a little abscess in there.' I spoke lightly but I wasn't happy. Post-pharyngeal abscesses were, in my limited experience, nasty things. They were situated in an inaccessible place, right away behind the back of the throat and if they got very large could interfere seriously with the breathing. I had been lucky with the few I had seen; they had either been small and regressed or had ruptured spontaneously.

I gave an injection of Prontosil and turned to Dick. 'I want you to foment this area behind the angle of the jaw with hot water and rub this salve well in afterwards. You may manage to burst it that way. Do this at least three times a day.'

I kept looking in at her over the next ten days and the picture was one of steady development of the abscess. The cow was still not acutely ill but she was eating a lot less, she was thinner and was going off her milk. Most of the time I felt rather helpless as I knew that only the rupture of the abscess would bring relief and the various injections I was giving her were largely irrelevant. But the infernal thing was taking a long time to burst.

It happened that just then Siegfried went off to an equine conference which was to last a week; for a few days I was at full stretch and hardly had time to think about Dick's cow until he biked in to see me one morning. He was cheerful as usual but he had a strained look.

'Will you come and see Strawberry? She's gone right down t'nick over the last three days. I don't like look of her.'

I dashed straight out and was in the byre at Birch Tree before Dick was half way home. The sight of Strawberry stopped me in mid-stride and I stared, dry-mouthed at what had once been a show cow. The flesh had melted from her incredibly and she was little more than a hide-covered skeleton. Her rasping breathing could be heard all over the byre and she exhaled with a curious out-puffing of the cheeks which I had never seen before. Her terrified eyes were fixed rigidly on the wall in front of her. Occasionally she gave a painful little cough which brought saliva drooling from her mouth.

I must have stood there a long time because I became aware of Dick at my shoulder.

'She's the worst screw in the place now,' he said grimly.

I winced inwardly. 'Hell, Dick, I'm sorry. I'd no idea she'd got to this state. I can't believe it.'

'Aye well it all happened sudden like. I've never seen a cow alter so fast.'

'The abscess must be right at its peak,' I said. 'She hasn't much space to breathe through now.' As I spoke the cow's limbs began to tremble and for a moment I thought she would fall. I ran out to the car and got a tin of Kaolin poultice. 'Come on, let's get this on to her throat. It just might do the trick.'

When we had finished I looked at Dick. 'I think tonight will do it. It's just got to burst.'

'And if it doesn't she'll snuff it tomorrow,' he grunted. I must have looked very woebegone because suddenly his undefeated grin flashed out. 'Never mind, lad, you've done everything anybody could do.'

But as I walked away I wasn't so sure. Mrs Rudd met me at the car. It was her baking day and she pushed a little loaf into my hand. It made me feel worse.

CHAPTER 54

That night I sat alone in the big room at Skeldale House and brooded. Siegfried was still away, I had nobody to turn to and I wished to God I knew what I was going to do with that cow of Dick's in the morning. By the time I went up to bed I had decided that if nothing further had happened I would have to go in behind the angle of the jaw with a knife.

I knew just where the abscess was but it was a long way in and en route there were such horrific things as the carotid artery and the jugular vein. I tried hard to keep them out of my mind but they haunted my dreams; huge, throbbing, pulsating things with their precious contents threatening to burst at any moment through their fragile walls. I was awake by six o'clock and after an hour of staring miserably at the ceiling I could stand it no longer. I got up and, without washing or shaving, drove out to the farm.

As I crept fearfully into the byre I saw with

a sick dismay that Strawberry's stall was empty. So that was that. She was dead. After all, she had looked like it yesterday. I was turning away when Dick called to me from the doorway.

'I've got her in a box on t'other side of the yard. Thought she'd be a bit more comfortable in there.'

I almost ran across the cobbles and as we approached the door the sound of the dreadful breathing came out to us. Strawberry was off her legs now — it had cost her the last of her strength to walk to the box and she lay on her chest, her head extended straight in front of her, nostrils dilated, eyes staring, cheeks puffing in her desperate fight for breath.

But she was alive and the surge of relief I felt seemed to prick me into action, blow away my hesitations.

'Dick,' I said, 'I've just got to operate on your cow. This thing is never going to burst in time, so it's now or never. But there's one thing I want you to know — the only way I can think of doing it is to go in from behind the jaw. I've never done this before, I've never seen it before and I've never heard of anybody doing it. If I nick any of those big blood vessels in there it'll kill her within a minute.'

'She can't last much longer like this,' Dick grunted. 'There's nowt to lose — get on with it.'

In most operations in large bovines we have to pull the animal down with ropes and then use general anaesthesia, but there was no need for this with Strawberry. She was too far gone. I just pushed gently at her shoulder and she rolled on to her side and lay still.

I quickly infiltrated the area from beneath the ear to the angle of the jaw with local anaesthetic then laid out my instruments.

'Stretch her head straight out and slightly back, Dick,' I said. Kneeling in the straw I incised the skin, cut carefully through the long thin layer of the brachiocephalic muscle and held the fibres apart with retractors. Somewhere down there was my objective and I tried to picture the anatomy of the region clearly in my mind. Just there the maxillary veins ran together to form the great jugular and, deeper and more dangerous, was the branching, ramifying carotid. If I pushed my knife straight in there, behind the mandibular salivary gland, I'd just about hit the spot. But as I held the razor-sharp blade over the small space I had cleared, my hand began to tremble. I tried to steady it but I was like a man with malaria. The fact had to be faced that I was too scared to cut any further. I put the scalpel down, lifted a pair of long artery forceps and pushed them steadily down through the hole in the muscle. It seemed that I had gone an incredibly long way when, almost unbelievingly, I saw a thin trickle of pus along the gleaming metal. I was into the abscess.

Gingerly, I opened the forceps as wide as possible to enlarge the drainage hole and as I did the trickle became a creamy torrent which gushed over my hand, down the cow's neck and onto the straw. I stayed quite still till it had stopped, then withdrew the forceps.

Dick looked at me from the other side of the head. 'Now what, boss?' he said softly.

'Well, I've emptied the thing, Dick,' I said, 'and by all the laws she should soon be a lot better. Come on, let's roll her on to her chest again.'

When we had got the cow settled comfortably with a bale of straw supporting her shoulder, I looked almost entreatingly at her. Surely she would show some sign of improvement. She must feel some relief from that massive evacuation. But Strawberry looked just the same. The breathing, if anything, was worse.

I dropped the soiled instruments into a bucket of hot water and antiseptic and began to wash them. 'I know what it is. The walls of the abscess have become indurated — thickened and hardened, you know — because it's been there a long time. We'll have to wait for them to collapse.'

Next day as I hurried across the yard I felt buoyantly confident. Dick was just coming out of the loose box and I shouted across to him, 'Well, how is she this morning?'

He hesitated and my spirits plummeted to zero. I knew what this meant; he was trying to find something good to say.

'Well, I reckon she's about t'same.'

'But dammit,' I shouted, 'she should be much better! Let's have a look at her.'

The cow wasn't just the same, she was worse. And on top of all the other symptoms she had a horribly sunken eye — the sign, usually, of approaching death in the bovine.

We both stood looking at the grim wreck of the once beautiful cow, then Dick broke the silence, speaking gently. 'Well, what do you think? Is it Mallock for her?'

The sound of the knacker man's name added the final note of despair. And indeed, Strawberry looked just like any of the other broken down animals that man came to collect.

I shuffled my feet miserably. 'I don't know what to say, Dick. There's nothing more I can do.' I took another look at the gasping staring head, the mass of bubbling foam around the lips and nostrils. 'You don't want her to suffer any more and neither do I. But don't get Mallock yet — she's distressed but not actually in pain, and I want to give her another day. If she's just the same tomorrow, send her in.' The very words sounded futile — every instinct told me the thing was hopeless. I turned to go, bowed down by a sense of failure heavier than I had ever known. As I went out into the yard, Dick called after me.

'Don't worry, lad, these things happen. Thank ye for all you've done.'

The words were like a whip across my back. If he had cursed me thoroughly I'd have felt a lot better. What had he to thank me for with his cow dying back there, the only good cow he'd ever owned? This disaster would just about floor Dick Rudd and he was telling me not to worry.

When I opened the car door I saw a cabbage on the seat. Mrs Rudd, too, was still at it. I leaned my elbow on the roof of the car and the words flowed from me. It was as if the sight of the cabbage had tapped the deep well of my frustration and I directed a soliloquy at the unheeding vegetable in which I ranged far over my many inadequacies. I pointed out the injustice of a situation where kindly people like the Rudds, in dire need of skilled veterinary assistance, had called on Mr Herriot who had responded by falling flat on his face. I drew attention to the fact that the Rudds, instead of hounding me off the place as I deserved, had thanked me sincerely and started to give me cabbages.

I went on for quite a long time and when I had finally finished I felt a little better. But not much, because, as I drove home I could not detect a glimmer of hope. If the walls of that abscess had been going to collapse they would have done so by now. I should have sent her in — she would be dead in the morning anyway.

I was so convinced of this that I didn't hurry to Birch Tree next day. I took it in with the round and it was almost midday when I drove through the gates. I knew what I would find — the usual grim signs of a vet's failure; the box door open and the drag marks where Mallock had winched the carcass across the yard on to his lorry. But everything was as usual and as I walked over to the silent box I steeled myself. The knacker man hadn't arrived yet but there was nothing surer than that my patient was lying dead in there. She couldn't possibly have hung on till now. My fingers fumbled at the catch as though something in me didn't want to look inside, but with a final wrench I threw the door wide.

Strawberry was standing there, eating hay from the rack; and not just eating it but jerking it through the bars almost playfully as cows do when they are really enjoying their food. It looked as though she couldn't get it down fast enough, pulling down great fragrant tufts and dragging them into her mouth with her rasp-like tongue. As I stared at her an organ began to play somewhere in the back of my mind; not just a little organ but a mighty instrument with gleaming pipes climbing high into the shadows of the cathedral roof. I went into the box, closed the door behind me and sat down in the straw in a corner. I had waited a long time for this. I was going to enjoy it.

The cow was almost a walking skeleton with her beautiful dark roan skin stretched tightly over the jutting bones. The once proud udder was a shrivelled purse dangling uselessly above her hocks. As she stood, she trembled from sheer weakness, but there was a light in her eye, a calm intensity in the way she ate which made me certain she would soon fight her way back to her old glory.

There was just the two of us in the box and occasionally Strawberry would turn her head towards me and regard me steadily, her jaws moving rhythmically. It seemed like a friendly look to me — in fact I wouldn't have been surprised if she had winked at me.

I don't know just how long I sat in there but I savoured every minute. It took some time for it to sink in that what I was watching was really happening; the swallowing was effortless, there was no salivation, no noise from her breathing. When I finally went out and closed the door behind me the cathedral organ was really blasting with all stops out, the exultant peals echoing back from the vaulted roof.

The cow made an amazing recovery. I saw her three weeks later and her bones were magically clothed with flesh, her skin shone and, most important, the magnificent udder bulged turgid beneath her, a neat little teat proudly erect at each corner.

I was pretty pleased with myself but of course a cold assessment of the case would show only one thing — that I had done hardly anything right from start to finish. At the very beginning I should have been down that cow's throat with a knife, but at that time I just didn't know how. In later years I have opened many a score of these abscesses by going in through a mouth gag with a scalpel tied to my fingers. It was a fairly heroic undertaking as the cow or bullock didn't enjoy it and was inclined to throw itself down with me inside it almost to the shoulder. It was simply asking for a broken arm.

When I talk about this to the present-day young vets they are inclined to look at me blankly because most of these abscesses undoubtedly had a tuberculous origin and since attestation they are rarely seen. But I can imagine it might bring a wry smile to the faces of my contemporaries as their memories are stirred.

The post-pharyngeal operation had the attraction that recovery was spectacular and rapid and I have had my own share of these little triumphs. But none of them gave me as much satisfaction as the one I did the wrong way.

It was a few weeks after the Strawberry

episode and I was back in my old position in the Rudds' kitchen with the family around me. This time I was in no position to drop my usual pearls of wisdom because I was trying to cope with a piece of Mrs Rudd's apple tart. Mrs Rudd, I knew, could make delicious apple tarts but this was a special kind she produced for ' 'lowance' time — for taking out to Dick and the family when they were working in the fields. I had chewed at the two-inch pastry till my mouth had dried out. Somewhere inside there was no doubt a sliver of apple but as yet I had been unable to find it. I didn't dare try to speak in case I blew out a shower of crumbs and in the silence which followed I wondered if anybody would help me out. It was Mrs Rudd who spoke up.

'Mr Herriot,' she said in her quiet matter-of-fact way, 'Dick has something to say to you.'

Dick cleared his throat and sat up straighter in his chair. I turned towards him expectantly, my cheeks still distended by the obdurate mass. He looked unusually serious and I felt a twinge of apprehension.

'What I want to say is this,' he said. 'It'll soon be our silver wedding anniversary and we're going to 'ave a bit of a do. We want you to be our guest.'

I almost choked. 'Dick, Mrs Rudd, that's very kind of you. I'd love that — I'd be honoured to come.'

Dick inclined his head gravely. He still looked portentous as though there was something big to follow. 'Good, I think you'll enjoy it, because it's goin' to be a right do. We've got a room booked at t'King's Head at Carsley.'

'Gosh, sounds great!'

'Aye, t'missus and me have worked it all out.' He squared his thin shoulders and lifted his chin proudly.

'We're having a 'ot dinner and entertainers.'

CHAPTER 55

As time passed and I painfully clothed the bare bones of my theoretical knowledge with practical experience I began to realise there was another side to veterinary practice they didn't mention in the books. It had to do with money. Money has always formed a barrier between the farmer and the vet. I think this is because there is a deeply embedded, maybe subconscious conviction in many farmers' minds that they know more about their stock than any outsider and it is an admission of defeat to pay somebody else to doctor them.

The wall was bad enough in those early days when they had to pay the medical practitioners for treating their own ailments and when there was no free agricultural advisory service. But it is worse now when there is the Health Service and N.A.A.S. and the veterinary surgeon stands pitilessly exposed as the only man who has to be paid.

Most farmers, of course, swallow the pill and get out their cheque books, but there is a proportion — maybe about ten per cent — who do their best to opt out of the whole business.

We had our own ten per cent in Darrowby and it was a small but constant irritation. As an assistant I was not financially involved and it didn't seem to bother Siegfried unduly except when the quarterly bills were sent out. Then it really got through to him.

Miss Harbottle used to type out the accounts and present them to him in a neat pile and that was when it started. He would go through them one by one and it was a harrowing experience to watch his blood pressure gradually rising.

I found him crouched over his desk one night. It was about eleven o'clock and he had had a hard day. His resistance was right down. He was scrutinising each bill before placing it face down on a pile to his left. On his right there was a smaller pile and whenever he placed one there it was to the accompaniment of a peevish muttering or occasionally a violent outburst.

'Would you believe it?' he grunted as I came in. 'Henry Bransom — more than two years since we saw a penny of his money, yet he lives like a sultan. Never misses a market for miles around, gets as tight as an owl several nights a week and I saw him putting ten pounds on a horse at the races last month.'

He banged the piece of paper down and

went on with his job, breathing deeply. Then he froze over another account. 'And look at this one! Old Summers of Low Ness. I bet he's got thousands of pounds hidden under his bed but by God he won't part with any of it to me.'

He was silent for a few moments as he transferred several sheets to the main pile then he swung round on me with a loud cry, waving a paper in my face.

'Oh no! Oh Christ, James, this is too much! Bert Mason here owes me twenty-seven and sixpence. I must have spent more than that sending him bills year in year out and do you know I saw him driving past the surgery yesterday in a brand new car. The bloody scoundrel!'

He hurled the bill down and started his scrutiny again. I noticed he was using only one hand while the other churned among his hair. I hoped fervently that he might hit upon a seam of good payers because I didn't think his nervous system could take much more. And it seemed that my hopes were answered because several minutes went by with only the quiet lifting and laying of the paper sheets. Then Siegfried stiffened suddenly in his chair and sat quite motionless as he stared down at his desk. He lifted an account and held it for several seconds at eye level. I steeled myself. This must be a beauty.

But to my surprise Siegfried began to giggle

softly then he threw back his head and gave a great bellow of laughter. He laughed until he seemed to have no strength to laugh any more, then he turned to me.

'It's the Major, James,' he said weakly. 'The dear old gallant Major. You know, you can't help admiring the man. He owed my predecessor a fair bit when I bought the practice and he still owes it. And I've never had a sou for all the work I've done for him. The thing is he's the same with everybody and yet he gets away with it. He's a genuine artist — these other fellows are just fumbling amateurs by comparison.'

He got up, reached up into the glass-fronted cupboard above the mantelpiece and pulled out the whisky bottle and two glasses. He carelessly tipped a prodigal measure into each glass and handed one to me, then he sank back into his chair, still grinning. The Major had magically restored his good humour.

Sipping my drink, I reflected that there was no doubt Major Bullivant's character had a rich, compelling quality. He presented an elegant, patrician front to the world; beautiful Shakespearean actor voice, impeccable manners and an abundance of sheer presence. Whenever he unbent sufficiently to throw me a friendly word I felt honoured even though I knew I was doing his work for nothing.

He had a small, cosy farm, a tweed-clad wife and several daughters who had ponies and were active helpers for the local hunt. Everything in his entire ménage was right and fitting. But he never paid anybody.

He had been in the district about three years and on his arrival the local tradesmen, dazzled by his façade, had fallen over each other to win his custom. After all, he appeared to be just their type because they preferred inherited wealth in Darrowby. In contrast to what I had always found in Scotland, the self-made man was regarded with deep suspicion and there was nothing so damning among the townsfolk as the darkly muttered comment: 'He had nowt when he first came 'ere.'

Of course, when the scales had fallen from their eyes they fought back, but ineffectually. The local garage impounded the Major's ancient Rolls Royce and hung on to it fiercely for a while but he managed to charm it back. His one failure was that his telephone was always being cut off; it seemed that the Postmaster General was one of the few who were immune to his blandishments.

But time runs out for even the most dedicated expert. I was driving one day through Hollerton, a neighbouring market town about ten miles away, and I noticed the Bullivant girls moving purposefully among the shops armed with large baskets. The Major, it seemed, was having to cast his net a little wider and I wondered at the time if perhaps he was ready to move on. He did, in fact, disappear from the district a few weeks later leaving a lot of people licking their wounds. I don't know if he ever paid anybody before he left but Siegfried didn't get anything.

Even after his departure Siegfried wasn't at all bitter, preferring to regard the Major as a unique phenomenon, a master of his chosen craft. 'After all, James,' he said to me once, 'putting ethical considerations to one side, you must admit that anybody who can run up a bill of fifty pounds for shaves and haircuts at the Darrowby barber's shop must command a certain amount of respect.'

Siegfried's attitude to his debtors was remarkably ambivalent. At times he would fly into a fury at the mention of their names, at others he would regard them with a kind of wry benevolence. He often said that if ever he threw a cocktail party for the clients he'd have to invite the non-payers first because they were all such charming fellows.

Nevertheless he waged an inexorable war against them by means of a series of letters graduated according to severity which he called his P.N.S. system (Polite, Nasty, Solicitor's) and in which he had great faith. It was a sad fact, however, that the system seldom worked with the real hard cases who were accustomed to receiving threatening letters with their morning mail. These people yawned over the polite and nasty ones and were unimpressed by the solicitor's because they knew from experience that Siegfried always shrank from following through to the limit of the law.

When the P.N.S. system failed Siegfried was inclined to come up with some unorthodox ideas to collect his hard-earned fees. Like the scheme he devised for Dennis Pratt. Dennis was a tubby, bouncy little man and his high opinion of himself showed in the way he always carried his entire five feet three inches proudly erect. He always seemed to be straining upwards, his chest thrust forward, his fat little bottom stuck out behind him at an extraordinary angle.

Dennis owed the practice a substantial amount and about eighteen months ago had been subjected to the full rigour of the P.N.S. system. This had induced him to part with five pounds 'on account' but since then nothing more had been forthcoming. Siegfried was in a quandary because he didn't like getting tough with such a cheerful, hospitable man.

Dennis was always either laughing or about to laugh. I remember when we had to anaesthetise a cow on his farm to remove a growth from between its cleats. Siegfried and I went to the case together and on the way we were talking about something which had amused us. As we got out of the car we were both laughing helplessly and just then the farmhouse door opened and Dennis emerged.

We were at the far end of the yard and we must have been all of thirty yards away. He couldn't possibly have heard anything of our conversation but when he saw us laughing he threw back his head immediately and joined in at the top of his voice. He shook so much on his way across the yard that I thought he would fall over. When he arrived he was wiping the tears from his eyes.

After a job he always asked us in to sample Mrs Pratt's baking. In fact on cold days he used to keep a thermos of hot coffee ready for our arrival and he had an endearing habit of sloshing rum freely into each cup before pouring in the coffee.

'You can't put a man like that in court,' Siegfried said. 'But we've got to find some way of parting him from his brass.' He looked ruminatively at the ceiling for a few moments then thumped a fist into his palm.

'I think I've got it, James! You know it's quite possible it just never occurs to Dennis to pay a bill. So I'm going to pitch him into an environment where it will really be brought home to him. The accounts have just gone out and I'll arrange to meet him in here at two o'clock next market day. I'll say I want to discuss his mastitis problem. He'll be right in the middle of all the other farmers paying their bills and I'll deliberately leave him with them for half an hour or so. I'm sure it will give him the notion.'

I couldn't help feeling dubious. I had known Siegfried long enough to realise that some of his ideas were brilliant and others barmy; and he had so many ideas and they came in such a constant torrent that I often had difficulty in deciding which was which. Clearly in this case he was working on the same lines as a doctor who turns on a water tap full force to induce a pent up patient to urinate into a bottle.

The scheme may have merit — it was possible that the flutter of cheque books, the chink of coins, the rustle of notes might tap the long-buried well of debt in Dennis and bring it gushing from him in a mighty flood; but I doubted it.

My doubts must have shown on my face because Siegfried laughed and thumped me on the shoulder. 'Don't look so worried — we can only try. And it'll work. Just you wait.'

After lunch on market day I was looking out of the window when I saw Dennis heading our way. The street was busy with the market bustle but he was easy to pick out. Chin in air, beaming around him happily, every springing step taking him high on tiptoe he was a distinctive figure. I let him in at the front door and he strutted past me along the passage, the back of his natty sports jacket ly-

ing in a neat fold over his protruding buttocks.

Siegfried seated him strategically by Miss
Harbottle's elbow, giving him an unimpeded
view of the desk. Then he excused himself,
saying he had a dog to attend to in the
operating room. I stayed behind to answer
the clients' queries and to watch develop-
ments. I hadn't long to wait; the farmers
began to come in, a steady stream of them,
clutching their cheque books. Some of them
stood patiently by the desk, others sat in the
chairs along the walls waiting their turn.

It was a typical bill-paying day with the
usual quota of moans. The most common
expression was that Mr Farnon had been
'ower heavy wi' t'pen' and many of them
wanted a 'bit knockin' off'. Miss Harbottle
used her discretion in these matters and if
the animal had died or the bill did seem
unduly large she would make some reduction.

There was one man who didn't get away
with it. He had truculently demanded a 'bit
of luck' on an account and Miss Harbottle
fixed him with a cold eye.

'Mr Brewiss,' she said. 'This account has
been owing for over a year. You should really
be paying us interest. I can only allow dis-
count when a bill is paid promptly. It's too
bad of you to let it run on for this length of
time.'

Dennis, sitting bolt upright, his hands resting on his knees, obviously agreed with every word. He pursed his lips in disapproval as he looked at the farmer and turned towards me with a positively scandalised expression.

Among the complaints was an occasional bouquet. A stooping old man who had received one of the polite letters was full of apologies. 'I'm sorry I've missed paying for a few months. The vets allus come out straight away when I send for them so I reckon it's not fair for me to keep them waiting for their money.'

I could see that Dennis concurred entirely with this sentiment. He nodded vigorously and smiled benevolently at the old man.

Another farmer, a hard-looking character, was walking out without his receipt when Miss Harbottle called him back. 'You'd better take this with you or we might ask you to pay again,' she said with a heavy attempt at roguishness.

The man paused with his hand on the door knob. 'I'll tell you summat, missis, you're bloody lucky to get it once — you'd never get it twice.'

Dennis was right in the thick of it all. Watching closely as the farmers slapped their cheque books on the desk for Miss Harbottle to write (they never wrote their own cheques) then signed them slowly and painstakingly. He looked with open fascination at the neat bundles of notes being tucked away in the desk drawer and I kept making little provocative remarks like 'It's nice to see the money coming in. We can't carry on without that, can we?'

The queue began to thin out and sometimes we were left alone in the room. On these occasions we conversed about many things — the weather, Dennis's stock, the political situation. Finally, Siegfried came in and I left to do a round.

When I got back, Siegfried was at his evening meal. I was eager to hear how his scheme had worked out but he was strangely reticent. At length I could wait no longer.

'Well, how did it go?' I asked.

Siegfried speared a piece of steak with his fork and applied some mustard. 'How did what go?'

'Well — Dennis. How did you make out with him?'

'Oh, fine. We went into his mastitis problem very thoroughly. I'm going out there on Tuesday morning to infuse every infected quarter in the herd with acriflavine solution. It's a new treatment — they say it's very good.'

'But you know what I mean. Did he show any sign of paying his bill?'

Siegfried chewed impassively for a few moments and swallowed. 'No, never a sign.' He put down his knife and fork and a haggard look spread over his face. 'It didn't work, did it?'

'Oh well, never mind. As you said, we could only try.' I hesitated. 'There's something else, Siegfried. I'm afraid you're going to be annoyed with me. I know you've told me never to dish out stuff to people who don't pay, but he talked me into letting him have a couple of bottles of fever drink. I don't know what came over me.'

'He did, did he?' Siegfried stared into space for a second then gave a wintry smile. 'Well, you can forget about that. He got six tins of stomach powder out of me.'

CHAPTER 56

There was one client who would not have been invited to the debtors' cocktail party. He was Mr Horace Dumbleby, the butcher of Aldgrove. As an inveterate non-payer he fulfilled the main qualification for the function but he was singularly lacking in charm.

His butcher shop in the main street of picturesque Aldgrove village was busy and prosperous but most of his trade was done in the neighbouring smaller villages and among the scattered farmhouses of the district. Usually the butcher's wife and married daughter looked after the shop while Mr Dumbleby himself did the rounds. I often saw his blue van standing with the back doors open and a farmer's wife waiting while he cut the meat, his big, shapeless body hunched over the slab. Sometimes he would look up and I would catch a momentary glimpse of a huge, bloodhound face and melancholy eyes.

Mr Dumbleby was a farmer himself in a small way. He sold milk from six cows which he kept in a tidy little byre behind his shop and he fattened a few bullocks and pork pigs which later appeared as sausages, pies, roasting cuts and chops in his front window. In fact Mr Dumbleby seemed to be very nicely fixed and it was said he owned property all over the place. But Siegfried had only infrequent glimpses of his money.

All the slow payers had one thing in common — they would not tolerate slowness from the vets. When they were in trouble they demanded immediate action. 'Will you come at once?', 'How long will you be?', 'You won't keep me waiting, will you?', 'I want you to come out here straight away'. It used to alarm me to see the veins swelling on Siegfried's forehead, the knuckles whitening as he gripped the phone.

After one such session with Mr Dumbleby at ten o'clock on a Sunday night he had flown into a rage and unleashed the full fury of the P.N.S. system on him. It had no loosening effect on the butcher's purse strings but it did wound his feelings deeply. He obviously considered himself a wronged man. From that time on, whenever I saw him with his van out in the country he would turn slowly and direct a blank stare at me till I was out of sight. And strangely, I seemed to see him more and more often — the thing became unnerving.

And there was something worse. Tristan

and I used to frequent the little Aldgrove pub where the bar was cosy and the beer measured up to Tristan's stringent standards. I had never taken much notice of Mr Dumbleby before although he always occupied the same corner, but now, every time I looked up, the great sad eyes were trained on me in disapproval. I tried to forget about him and listen to Tristan relating his stories from the backs of envelopes but all the time I could feel that gaze upon me. My laughter would trail away and I would have to look round. Then the excellent bitter would be as vinegar in my mouth.

In an attempt to escape, I took to visiting the snug instead of the bar and Tristan, showing true nobility of soul, came with me into an environment which was alien to him; where there was a carpet on the floor, people sitting around at little shiny tables drinking gin and hardly a pint in sight. But even this sacrifice was in vain because Mr Dumbleby changed his position in the bar so that he could look into the snug through the communicating hatch. The odd hours I was able to spend there took on a macabre quality. I was like a man trying desperately to forget. But quaff the beer as I might, laugh, talk, even sing, half of me was waiting in a state of acute apprehension for the moment when I knew I would have to look round. And when I did, the great sombre face looked even more forbidding framed by the wooden surround of the hatch. The hanging jowls, the terraced chins, the huge, brooding eyes — all were dreadfully magnified by their isolation in that little hole in the wall.

It was no good, I had to stop going to the place. This was very sad because Tristan used to wax lyrical about a certain unique, delicate nuttiness which he could discern in the draught bitter. But it had lost its joy for me; I just couldn't take any more of Mr Dumbleby.

In fact I did my best to forget all about the gentleman, but he was brought back forcibly into my mind when I heard his voice on the phone at 3 a.m. one morning. It was nearly always the same thing when the bedside phone exploded in your ear in the small hours — a calving.

Mr Dumbleby's call was no exception but he was more peremptory than might have been expected. There was no question about apologising about ringing at such an hour as most farmers would do. I said I would come immediately but that wasn't good enough — he wanted to know exactly in minutes how long I would be. In a sleepy attempt at sarcasm I started to recite a programme of so many minutes to get up and dressed, so many to go downstairs and get the car out etc. but I fear it was lost on him.

When I drove into the sleeping village a

light was showing in the window of the butcher's shop. Mr Dumbleby almost trotted out into the street and paced up and down, muttering, as I fished out my ropes and instruments from the boot. Very impatient, I thought, for a man who hadn't paid his vet bill for over a year.

We had to go through the shop to get to the byre in the rear. My patient was a big, fat white cow which didn't seem particularly perturbed by her situation. Now and then she strained, pushing a pair of feet a few inches from her vulva. I took a keen look at those feet — it is the vet's first indication of how tough the job is going to be. Two huge hooves sticking out of a tiny heifer have always been able to wipe the smile off my face. These feet were big enough but not out of the way, and in truth the mother looked sufficiently roomy. I wondered what was stopping the natural sequence.

'I've had me hand in,' said Mr Dumbleby. 'There's a head there but I can't shift owt. I've been pulling them legs for half an hour.'

As I stripped to the waist (it was still considered vaguely cissy to wear a calving overall) I reflected that things could be a lot worse. So many of the buildings where I had to take my shirt off were primitive and draughty but this was a modern cow house and the six cows provided a very adequate central heating. And there was electricity in place of the usual smoke-blackened oil lamp.

When I had soaped and disinfected my arms I made my first exploration and it wasn't difficult to find the cause of the trouble.

There was a head and two legs all right, but they belonged to different calves.

'We've got twins here,' I said. 'These are hind legs you've been pulling — a posterior presentation.'

'Arse fust, you mean?'

'If you like. And the calf that's coming the right way has both his legs back along his sides. I'll have to push him back out of the way and get the other one first.'

This was going to be a pretty tight squeeze. Normally I like a twin calving because the calves are usually so small, but these seemed to be quite big. I put my hand against the little muzzle in the passage, poked a finger into the mouth and was rewarded by a jerk and flip of the tongue; he was alive, anyway.

I began to push him steadily back into the uterus, wondering at the same time what the little creature was making of it all. He had almost entered the world — his nostrils had been a couple of inches from the outside air — and now he was being returned to the starting post.

The cow didn't think much of the idea either because she started a series of straining heaves with the object of frustrating me.

594

She did a pretty fair job, too, since a cow is a lot stronger than a man, but I kept my arm rigid against the calf and though each heave forced me back I maintained a steady pressure till I had pushed him to the brim of the pelvis.

I turned to Mr Dumbleby and gasped: 'I've got this head out of the way. Get hold of those feet and pull the other calf out.'

The butcher stepped forward ponderously and each of his big, meaty hands engulfed a foot. Then he closed his eyes and with many facial contortions and noises of painful effort he began to go through the motions of tugging. The calf didn't move an inch and my spirits drooped. Mr Dumbleby was a grunter. (This expression had its origin in an occasion when Siegfried and a farmer had a foot apiece at a calving and the farmer was making pitiful sounds without exerting himself in the slightest. Siegfried had turned to him and said: 'Look, let's come to an arrangement — you do the pulling and I'll do the grunting.')

It was clear I was going to get no help from the big butcher and decided to have one go by myself. I might be lucky. I let go the muzzle and made a quick grab for those hind feet, but the cow was too quick for me. I had just got a slippery grasp when she made a single expulsive effort and pushed calf number two into the passage again. I was back where I started.

Once more I put my hand against the wet little muzzle and began the painful process of repulsion. And as I fought against the big cow's straining I was reminded that it was 4 a.m. when none of us feels very strong. By the time I had worked the head back to the pelvic inlet I was feeling the beginning of that deadly creeping weakness and it seemed as though somebody had removed most of the bones from my arm.

This time I took a few seconds to get my breath back before I made my dive for the feet, but it was no good. The cow beat me easily with a beautifully timed contraction. Again that intruding head was jammed tight in the passage.

I had had enough. And it occurred to me that the little creature inside must also be getting a little tired of this back and forth business. I shivered my way through the cold, empty shop out into the silent street and collected the local anaesthetic from the car. Eight cc's into the epidural space and the cow, its uterus completely numbed, lost all interest in the proceedings. In fact she pulled a little hay from her rack and began to chew absently.

From then on it was like working inside a mail bag; whatever I pushed stayed put instead of surging back at me. The only snag was that once I had got everything straight there were no uterine contractions to help

596

me. It was a case of pulling. Leaning back on a hind leg and with Mr Dumbleby panting in agony on the other, the posterior presentation was soon delivered. He had inhaled a fair amount of placental fluid but I held him upside down till he had coughed it up. When I laid him on the byre floor he shook his head vigorously and tried to sit up.

Then I had to go in after my old friend the second calf. He was lying well inside now, apparently sulking. When I finally brought him snuffling and kicking into the light I couldn't have blamed him if he had said 'Make up your mind, will you!'

Towelling my chest I looked with the sharp stab of pleasure I always felt at the two wet little animals wriggling on the floor as Mr Dumbleby rubbed them down with a handful of straw.

'Big 'uns for twins,' the butcher muttered.

Even this modest expression of approval surprised me and it seemed I might as well push things along a bit.

'Yes, they're two grand calves. Twins are often dead when they're mixed up like that — good job we got them out alive.' I paused a moment. 'You know, those two must be worth a fair bit.'

Mr Dumbleby didn't answer and I couldn't tell whether the shaft had gone home.

I got dressed, gathered up my gear and followed him out of the byre and into the silent shop past the rows of beef cuts hanging from hooks, the trays of offal, the mounds of freshly-made sausages. Near the outside door the butcher halted and stood, irresolute, for a moment. He seemed to be thinking hard. Then he turned to me.

'Would you like a few sausages?'

I almost reeled in my astonishment. 'Yes, thank you very much, I would.' It was scarcely credible but I must have touched the man's heart.

He went over, cut about a pound of links, wrapped them quickly in grease-proof paper and handed the parcel to me.

I looked down at the sausages, feeling the cold weight on my hand. I still couldn't believe it. Then an unworthy thought welled in my mind. It wasn't fair, I know — the poor fellow couldn't have known the luxury of many generous impulses — but some inner demon drove me to put him to the test. I put a hand in my trouser pocket, jingled my loose change and looked him in the eye.

'Well, how much will that be?' I asked.

Mr Dumbleby's big frame froze suddenly into immobility and he stood for a few seconds perfectly motionless. His face, as he stared at me, was almost without expression, but a single twitch of the cheek and a slowly rising anguish in the eyes betrayed the internal battle which was raging. When he did speak it was in a husky whisper as though the words had been forced from him by a power beyond his control.

'That' he said, 'will be two and sixpence.'

CHAPTER 57

It was a new experience for me to be standing outside the hospital waiting for the nurses to come off duty, but it was old stuff to Tristan who was to be found there several nights a week. His experience showed in various ways, but mainly in the shrewd position he took up in a dark corner of the doorway of the gas company office just beyond the splash of light thrown by the street lamp. From there he could look straight across the road into the square entrance of the hospital and the long white corridor leading to the nurses' quarters. And there was the other advantage that if Siegfried should happen to pass that way, Tristan would be invisible and safe.

At half past seven he nudged me. Two girls had come out of the hospital and down the steps and were standing expectantly in the street. Tristan looked warily in both directions before taking my arm. 'Come on, Jim, here they are. That's Connie on the left —

the coppery blonde — lovely little thing.'

We went over and Tristan introduced me with characteristic charm. I had to admit that if the evening had indeed been arranged for therapeutic purposes I was beginning to feel better already. There was something healing in the way the two pretty girls looked up at me with parted lips and shining eyes as though I was the answer to every prayer they had ever offered.

They were remarkably alike except for the hair. Brenda was very dark but Connie was fair with a deep, fiery glow where the light from the doorway touched her head. Both of them projected a powerful image of bursting health — fresh cheeks, white teeth, lively eyes and something else which I found particularly easy to take; a simple desire to please.

Tristan opened the back door of the car with a flourish. 'Be careful with him in there Connie, he looks quiet but he's a devil with women. Known far and wide as a great lover.'

The girls giggled and studied me with even greater interest. Tristan leaped into the driver's seat and we set off at breakneck speed.

As the dark countryside hastened past the windows I leaned back in the corner and listened to Tristan who was in full cry; maybe in a kindly attempt to cheer me or maybe because he just felt that way, but his flow of chatter was unceasing. The girls made an ideal audience because they laughed in delight at everything he said. I could feel Connie shaking against me. She was sitting very close with a long stretch of empty seat on the other side of her. The little car swayed round a sharp corner and threw her against me and she stayed there quite naturally with her head on my shoulder. I felt her hair against my cheek. She didn't use much perfume but smelt cleanly of soap and antiseptic. My mind went back to Helen — I didn't think much about her these days. It was just a question of practice; to scotch every thought of her as soon as it came up. I was getting pretty good at it now. Anyway, it was over — all over before it had begun.

I put my arm round Connie and she lifted her face to me. Ah well, I thought as I kissed her. Tristan's voice rose in song from the front seat, Brenda giggled, the old car sped over the rough road with a thousand rattles.

We came at last to Poulton, a village on the road to nowhere. Its single street straggled untidily up the hillside to a dead end where there was a circular green with an ancient stone cross and a steep mound on which was perched the institute hall.

This was where the dance was to be held, but Tristan had other plans first. 'There's a lovely little pub here. We'll just have a toothful to get us in the mood.' We got out of the car and Tristan ushered us into a low stone building.

There was nothing of the olde worlde about the place; just a large, square, whitewashed room with a black cooking range enclosing a bright fire and a long high-backed wooden settle facing it. Over the fireplace stretched a single immense beam, gnarled and pitted with the years and blackened with smoke.

We hurried over to the settle, feeling the comfort of it as a screen against the cold outside. We had the place to ourselves.

The landlord came in. He was dressed informally — no jacket, striped, collarless shirt, trousers and braces which were re-inforced by a broad, leather belt around his middle. His cheerful round face lit up at the sight of Tristan. 'Now then, Mr Farnon, are you very well?'

'Never better, Mr Peacock, and how are you?'

'Nicely, sir, very nicely. Can't complain. And I recognise the other gentleman. Been in my place before, haven't you?'

I remembered then. A day's testing in the Poulton district and I had come in here for a meal, freezing and half starved after hours of wrestling with young beasts on the high moor. The landlord had received me unemotionally and had set to immediately with his frying-pan on the old black range while I sat looking at his shirt back and the braces and the shining leather belt. The meal had taken up the whole of the round oak table by the fire — a thick steak of home cured ham overlapping the plate with two fresh eggs nestling on its bosom, a newly baked loaf with the knife sticking in it, a dish of farm butter, some jam, a vast pot of tea and a whole Wensleydale cheese, circular, snow white, about eighteen inches high.

I could remember eating unbelievingly for a long time and finishing with slice after slice of the moist, delicately flavoured cheese. The entire meal had cost me half a crown.

'Yes, Mr Peacock, I have been here before and if I'm ever starving on a desert island I'll think of that wonderful meal you gave me.'

The landlord shrugged. 'Well it was nowt much, sir. Just t'usual stuff.' But he looked pleased.

'That's fine, then,' Tristan said impatiently. 'But we haven't come to eat, we've come for a drink and Mr Peacock keeps some of the finest draught Magnet in Yorkshire. I'd welcome your opinion on it, Jim. Perhaps you would be kind enough to bring us up two pints and two halves, Mr Peacock.'

I noticed there was no question of asking the girls what they would like to have, but they seemed quite happy with the arrangement. The landlord reappeared from the cellar, puffing slightly. He was carrying a tall, white enamelled jug from which he poured a thin brown stream, varying the height expertly till he had produced a white, frothy head on each glass.

Tristan raised his pint and looked at it with quiet reverence. He sniffed it carefully and then took a sip which he retained in his mouth for a few seconds while his jaw moved rapidly up and down. After swallowing he smacked his lips a few times with the utmost solemnity then closed his eyes and took a deep gulp. He kept his eyes closed for a long time and when he opened them they were rapturous, as though he had seen a beautiful vision.

'It's an experience coming here,' he whispered. 'Keeping beer in the wood is a skilful business, but you, Mr Peacock, are an artist.'

The landlord inclined his head modestly and Tristan, raising his glass in salute, drained it with an easy upward motion of the elbow.

Little oohs of admiration came from the girls but I saw that they, in their turn, had little difficulty in emptying their glasses. With an effort I got my own pint down and the enamel jug was immediately in action again.

I was always at a disadvantage in the company of a virtuoso like Tristan, but as the time passed and the landlord kept revisiting the cellar with his jug it seemed to become easier. In fact, a long time later, as I drew confidently on my eighth pint, I wondered why I had ever had difficulty with large amounts of fluid. It was easy and it soothed and comforted.

Tristan was right — I had been needing this.

It puzzled me that I hadn't realised until now that Connie was one of the most beautiful creatures I had ever seen. Back there in the street outside the hospital she had seemed attractive, but obviously the light had been bad and I had failed to notice the perfection of her skin, the mysterious greenish depths of her eyes and the wonderful hair catching lights of gold and deep red-bronze from the flickering fire. And the laughing mouth, shining, even teeth and little pink tongue — she hardly ever stopped laughing except to drink her beer. Everything I said was witty, brilliantly funny in fact, and she looked at me all the time, peeping over the top of her glass in open admiration. It was profoundly reassuring.

As the beer flowed, time slowed down and finally lurched to a halt and there was neither past nor future, only Connie's face and the warm, untroubled present.

I was surprised when Tristan pulled at my arm, I had forgotten he was there and when I focused on him it was the same as with Connie — there was just the face swimming disembodied in an empty room. Only this face was very red and puffy and glassy-eyed.

'Would you care for the mad conductor?' the face said.

I was deeply touched. Here was another sign of my friend's concern for me. Of all

Tristan's repertoire his imitation of a mad conductor was the most exacting. It involved tremendous expenditure of energy and since Tristan was unused to any form of physical activity, it really took it out of him. Yet here he was, ready and willing to sacrifice himself. A wave of treacly sentiment flooded through me and I wondered for a second if it might not be the proper thing to burst into tears; but instead I contented myself with wringing Tristan's hand.

'There's nothing I would like more, my dear old chap,' I said thickly. 'I greatly appreciate the kind thought. And may I take this opportunity of telling you that I consider that in all Yorkshire there is no finer gentleman breathing than T. Farnon.'

The big red face grew very solemn. 'You honour me with those words, old friend.'

'Not a bit of it,' I slurred. 'My stumbling sentences cannot hope to express my extremely high opinion of you.'

'You are too kind,' hiccuped Tristan.

'Nothing of the sort. It's a privlish, a rare privlish to know you.'

'Thank you, thank you,' Tristan nodded gravely at me from a distance of about six inches. We were staring into each other's eyes with intense absorption and the conversation might have gone on for a long time if Brenda hadn't broken in.

'Hey, when you two have finished rubbing

noses I'd rather like another drink.'

Tristan gave her a cold look. 'You'll have to wait just a few minutes. There's something I have to do.' He rose, shook himself and walked with dignity to the centre of the floor. When he turned to face his audience he looked exalted. I felt that this would be an outstanding performance.

Tristan raised his arms and gazed imperiously over his imaginary orchestra, taking in the packed rows of strings, the woodwind, brass and tympani in one sweeping glance. Then with a violent downswing he led them into the overture. Rossini, this time, I thought or maybe Wagner as I watched him throwing his head about, bringing in the violins with a waving clenched fist or exhorting the trumpets with a glare and a trembling, outstretched hand.

It was somewhere near the middle of the piece that the rot always set in and I watched enthralled as the face began to twitch and the lips to snarl. The arm waving became more and more convulsive then the whole body jerked with uncontrollable spasms. It was clear that the end was near — Tristan's eyes were rolling, his hair hung over his face and he had lost control of the music which crashed and billowed about him. Suddenly he grew rigid, his arms fell to his sides and he crashed to the floor.

I was joining in the applause and laughter

when I noticed that Tristan was very still. I bent over him and found that he had struck his head against the heavy oak leg of the settle and was almost unconscious. The nurses were quickly into action. Brenda expertly propped up his head while Connie ran for a basin of hot water and a cloth. When he opened his eyes they were bathing a tender lump above his ear. Mr Peacock hovered anxiously in the background. 'Ista all right? Can ah do anything?'

Tristan sat up and sipped weakly at his beer. He was very pale. 'I'll be all right in a minute and there is something you can do. You can bring us one for the road and then we must be getting on to this dance.'

The landlord hurried away and returned with the enamel jug brimming. The final pint revived Tristan miraculously and he was soon on his feet. Then we shook hands affectionately with Mr Peacock and took our leave. After the brightness of the inn the darkness pressed on us like a blanket and we groped our way up the steep street till we could see the institute standing on its grassy mound. Faint rays of light, escaped through the chinks in the curtained windows and we could hear music and a rhythmic thudding.

A cheerful young farmer took our money at the door and when we went into the hall we were swallowed up in a tight mass of dancers. The place was packed solidly with young men in stiff-looking dark suits and girls in bright dresses all sweating happily as they swayed and wheeled to the music.

On the low platform at one end, four musicians were playing their hearts out — piano, accordion, violin and drums. At the other end, several comfortable, middle-aged women stood behind a long table on trestles, presiding over the thick sandwiches of ham and brawn, home made pies, jugs of milk and trifles generously laid with cream.

All round the walls more lads were standing, eyeing the unattached girls. I recognised a young client. 'What do you call this dance?' I yelled above the din.

'The Eva Three Step,' came back the reply.

This was new to me but I launched out confidently with Connie. There was a lot of twirling and stamping and when the men brought their heavy boots down on the boards the hall shook and the noise was deafening. I loved it — I was right on the peak and I whirled Connie effortlessly among the throng. I was dimly aware of bumping people with my shoulders but, try as I might, I couldn't feel my feet touching the floor. The floating sensation was delicious. I decided that I had never been so happy in my life.

After half a dozen dances I felt ravenous and floated with Connie towards the food table. We each ate an enormous wedge of ham and egg pie which was so exquisite that we had the same again. Then we had some trifle and plunged again into the crush. It was about half way through a St. Bernard's Waltz that I began to feel my feet on the boards again — quite heavy and dragging somewhat. Connie felt heavy too. She seemed to be slumped in my arms.

She looked up. Her face was very white. 'Jus' feeling a bit queer — 'scuse me.' She broke away and began to tack erratically towards the ladies' room. A few minutes later she came out and her face was no longer white. It was green. She staggered over to me. 'Could do with some fresh air. Take me outside.'

I took her out into the darkness and it was as if I had stepped aboard a ship; the ground pitched and heaved under my feet and I had to straddle my legs to stay upright. Holding Connie's arm, I retreated hastily to the wall of the institute and leaned my back against it. This didn't help a great deal because the wall, too, was heaving about. Waves of nausea swept over me. I thought of the ham and egg pie and groaned loudly.

Open mouthed, gulping in the sharp air, I looked up at the clean, austere sweep of the night sky and at the ragged clouds driving across the cold face of the moon. 'Oh God,' I moaned at the unheeding stars, 'Why did I drink all that bloody beer?'

But I had to look after Connie. I put my

611

arm round her. 'Come on, we'd better start walking.' We began to reel blindly round the building, pausing after every two or three circuits while I got my breath back and shook my head violently to try to clear my brain.

But our course was erratic and I forgot that the institute was perched on a little steep-sided hill. There was an instant when we were treading on nothing, then we were sprawling down a muddy bank. We finished in a tangled heap on the hard road at the bottom.

I lay there peacefully till I heard a pitiful whimpering near by. Connie! Probably a compound fracture at least; but when I helped her up I found she was unhurt and so, surprisingly, was I. After our large intake of alcohol we must have been as relaxed as rag dolls when we fell.

We went back into the institute and stood just inside the door. Connie was unrecognisable; her beautiful hair hung across her face in straggling wisps, her eyes were vacant and tears coursed slowly through the muddy smears on her cheeks. My suit was plastered with clay and I could feel more of it drying on one side of my face. We stood close, leaning miserably on each other in the doorway. The dancers were a shapeless blur. My stomach heaved and tossed.

Then I heard somebody say 'Good evening'. It was a woman's voice and very close. There were two figures looking at us with interest.

612

They seemed to have just come through the door.

I concentrated fiercely on them and they swam into focus for a few seconds. It was Helen and a man. His pink, scrubbed-looking face, the shining fair hair plastered sideways across the top of his head was in keeping with the spotless British warm overcoat. He was staring at me distastefully. They went out of focus again and there was only Helen's voice. 'We thought we would just look in for a few moments to see how the dance was going. Are you enjoying it?'

Then, unexpectedly, I could see her clearly. She was smiling her kind smile but her eyes were strained as she looked from me to Connie and back again. I couldn't speak but stood gazing at her dully, seeing only her calm beauty in the crush and noise. It seemed, for a moment, that it would be the most natural thing in the world to throw my arms around her but I discarded the idea and, instead, just nodded stupidly.

'Well then, we must be off,' she said and smiled again. 'Good night.'

The fair haired man gave me a cold nod and they went out.

CHAPTER 58

It looked as though I was going to make it back to the road all right. And I was thankful for it because seven o'clock in the morning with the wintry dawn only just beginning to lighten the eastern rim of the moor was no time to be digging my car out of the snow.

This narrow, unfenced road skirted a high tableland and gave on to a few lonely farms at the end of even narrower tracks. It hadn't actually been snowing on my way out to this early call — a uterine haemorrhage in a cow — but the wind had been rising steadily and whipping the top surface from the white blanket which had covered the fell-tops for weeks. My headlights had picked out the creeping drifts; pretty, pointed fingers feeling their way inch by inch across the strip of tarmac.

This was how all blocked roads began, and at the farm as I injected pituitrin and packed the bleeding cervix with a clean sheet I could hear the wind buffeting the byre door and wondered if I would win the race home.

On the way back the drifts had stopped being pretty and lay across the road like white bolsters; but my little car had managed to cleave through them, veering crazily at times, wheels spinning, and now I could see the main road a few hundred yards ahead, reassuringly black in the pale light

But just over there on the left, a field away, was Cote House. I was treating a bullock there — he had eaten some frozen turnips — and a visit was fixed for today. I didn't fancy trailing back up here if I could avoid it and there was a light in the kitchen window. The family were up, anyway. I turned and drove down into the yard.

The farmhouse door lay within a small porch and the wind had driven the snow inside forming a smooth, two-foot heap against the timbers. As I leaned across to knock, the surface of the heap trembled a little, then began to heave. There was something in there, something quite big. It was eerie standing in the half light watching the snow parting to reveal a furry body. Some creature of the wild must have strayed in, searching for warmth — but it was bigger than a fox or anything else I could think of.

Just then the door opened and the light from the kitchen streamed out. Peter Trenholm beckoned me inside and his wife smiled at me from the bright interior. They were a cheerful young couple.

'What's that?' I gasped, pointing at the animal which was shaking the snow vigorously from its coat.

'That?' Peter grinned, 'That's awd Tip.'

'Tip? Your dog? But what's he doing under a pile of snow?'

'Just blew in on him, I reckon. That's where he sleeps, you know, just outside back door.'

I stared at the farmer. 'You mean he sleeps there, out in the open, every night?'

'Aye, allus. Summer and winter. But don't look at me like that Mr Herriot — it's his own choice. The other dogs have a warm bed in the cow house but Tip won't entertain it. He's fifteen now and he's been sleeping out there since he were a pup. I remember when me father was alive he tried all ways to get t'awd feller to sleep inside but it was no good.'

I looked at the old dog in amazement. I could see him more clearly now; he wasn't the typical sheep dog type, he was bigger boned, longer in the hair, and he projected a bursting vitality that didn't go with his fifteen years. It was difficult to believe that any animal living in these bleak uplands should choose to sleep outside — and thrive on it. I had to look closely to see any sign of his great age. There was the slightest stiffness in his gait as he moved around, perhaps a fleshless look about his head and face and of course the tell-tale lens opacity in the depths of his eyes. But the general impression was of an unquenchable jauntiness.

He shook the last of the snow from his coat, pranced jerkily up to the farmer and gave a couple of reedy barks. Peter Trenholm laughed. 'You see he's ready to be off — he's a beggar for work is Tip.' He led the way towards the buildings and I followed, stumbling over the frozen ruts, like iron under the snow, and bending my head against the knife-like wind. It was a relief to open the byre door and escape into the sweet bovine warmth.

There was a fair mixture of animals in the long building. The dairy cows took up most of the length, then there were a few young heifers, some bullocks and finally, in an empty stall deeply bedded with straw, the other farm dogs. The cats were there too, so it had to be warm. No animal is a better judge of comfort than a cat and they were just visible as furry balls in the straw. They had the best place, up against the wooden partition where the warmth came through from the big animals.

Tip strode confidently among his colleagues — a young dog and a bitch with three half-grown pups. You could see he was boss.

One of the bullocks was my patient and he was looking a bit better. When I had seen him yesterday his rumen (the big first stomach) had been completely static and atonic following an over eager consumption of frozen turnips. He had been slightly bloated and groaning with discomfort. But today as I leaned with my ear against his left side I could hear the beginnings of the surge and rumble of the normal rumen instead of the deathly silence of yesterday. My gastric lavage had undoubtedly tickled things up and I felt that another of the same would just about put him right. Almost lovingly I got together the ingredients of one of my favourite treatments, long since washed away in the flood of progress; the ounce of formalin, the half pound of common salt, the can of black treacle from the barrel which you used to find in most cow houses, all mixed up in a bucket with two gallons of hot water.

I jammed the wooden gag into the bullock's mouth and buckled it behind the horns, then as Peter held the handles I passed the stomach tube down into the rumen and pumped in the mixture. When I had finished the bullock opened his eyes wide in surprise and began to paddle his hind legs. Listening again at his side, I could hear the reassuring bubbling of the stomach contents. I smiled to myself in satisfaction. It worked it always worked.

Wiping down the tube I could hear the hiss-hiss as Peter's brother got on with the morning's milking, and as I prepared to leave he came down the byre with a full bucket on the way to the cooler. As he passed the dogs' stall he tipped a few pints of the warm milk into their dishes and Tip strolled forward casually for his breakfast. While he was drinking, the young dog tried to push his way in but a soundless snap from Tip's jaws missed his nose by a fraction and he retired to another dish. I noticed, however, that the old dog made no protest as the bitch and pups joined him. The cats, black and white, tortoise-shell, tabby grey, appeared, stretching, from the straw and advanced in a watchful ring. Their turn would come.

Mrs Trenholm called me in for a cup of tea and when I came out it was full daylight. But the sky was a burdened grey and the sparse trees near the house strained their bare branches against the wind which drove in long, icy gusts over the white empty miles of moor. It was what the Yorkshiremen called a 'thin wind' or sometimes a 'lazy wind' — the kind that couldn't be bothered to blow round you but went straight through instead. It made me feel that the best place on earth was by the side of that bright fire in the farmhouse kitchen.

Most people would have felt like that, but not old Tip. He was capering around as Peter loaded a flat cart with some hay bales for the young cattle in the outside barns; and as Peter shook the reins and the cob set off over the fields, he leapt on to the back of the cart.

As I threw my tackle into the boot I looked

back at the old dog, legs braced against the uneven motion, tail waving, barking defiance at the cold world. I carried away the memory of Tip who scorned the softer things and slept in what he considered the place of honour — at his master's door.

A little incident like this has always been able to brighten my day and fortunately I have the kind of job where things of this kind happened. And sometimes it isn't even a happening — just a single luminous phrase.

As when I was examining a cow one morning while its neighbour was being milked. The milker was an old man and he was having trouble. He was sitting well into the cow, his cloth-capped head buried in her flank, the bucket gripped tightly between his knees, but the stool kept rocking about as the cow fidgeted and weaved. Twice she kicked the bucket over and she had an additional little trick of anointing her tail with particularly liquid faeces then lashing the old man across the face with it.

Finally he could stand it no longer. Leaping to his feet he dealt a puny blow at the cow's craggy back and emitted an exasperated shout.

'Stand still, thou shittin' awd bovril!'

Or the day when I had to visit Luke Benson at his smallholding in Hillom village. Luke was a powerful man of about sixty and had the unusual characteristic of speaking always through his clenched teeth. He literally articulated every word by moving only his lips, showing the rows of square, horse-like incisors clamped tightly together. It leant a peculiar intensity to his simplest utterance; and as he spoke, his eyes glared.

Most of his conversation consisted of scathing remarks about the other inhabitants of Hillom. In fact he seemed to harbour a cordial dislike of the human race in general. Yet strangely enough I found him a very reasonable man to deal with; he accepted my diagnoses of his animals' ailments without question and appeared to be trying to be friendly by addressing me repeatedly as 'Jems', which was the nearest he could get to my name with his teeth together.

His fiercest hatred was reserved for his neighbour and fellow smallholder, a little lame man called Gill to whom Luke referred invariably and unkindly as 'Yon 'oppin youth'. A bitter feud had raged between them for many years and I had seen Luke smile on only two occasions — once when Mr Gill's sow lost its litter and again when he had a stack burnt down.

When Mr Gill's wife ran away with a man who came round the farms selling brushes it caused a sensation. Nothing like that had ever happened in Hillom before and a wave of delighted horror swept through the village. This, I thought, would be the high point of Luke Benson's life and when I had to visit a heifer of his I expected to find him jubilant. But Luke was gloomy.

As I examined and treated his animal he remained silent and it wasn't until I went into the kitchen to wash my hands that he spoke. He glanced round warily at his wife, a gaunt, grim-faced woman who was applying black-lead to the grate.

'You'll have heard about yon 'oppin youth's missus runnin' off?' he said.

'Yes,' I replied. 'I did hear about it.' I waited for Luke to gloat but he seemed strangely ill at ease. He fidgeted until I had finished drying my hands then he glared at me and bared his strong teeth.

'Ah'll tell you something, Jems,' he ground out. 'Ah wish somebody would tek MA bugger!'

And there was that letter from the Bramleys — that really made me feel good. You don't find people like the Bramleys now; radio, television and the motorcar have carried the outside world into the most isolated places so that the simple people you used to meet on the lonely farms are rapidly becoming like people anywhere else. There are still a few left, of course — old folk who cling to the ways of their fathers and when I come across any of them I like to make some excuse to sit down and talk with them and listen to the old Yorkshire words and expressions which have almost disappeared.

But even in the thirties when there were many places still untouched by the flood of progress the Bramleys were in some ways unique. There were four of them; three brothers, all middle-aged bachelors, and an older sister, also unmarried, and their farm lay in a wide, shallow depression in the hills. You could just see the ancient tiles of Scar House through the top branches of the sheltering trees if you stood outside the pub in Drewburn village and in the summer it was possible to drive down over the fields to the farm. I had done it a few times, the bottles in the boot jingling and crashing as the car bounced over the rig and furrow. The other approach to the place was right on the other side through Mr Broom's stackyard and then along a track with ruts so deep that only a tractor could negotiate it.

There was, in fact, no road to the farm, but that didn't bother the Bramleys because the outside world held no great attraction for them. Miss Bramley made occasional trips to Darrowby on market days for provisions and Herbert, the middle brother, had come into town in the spring of 1929 to have a tooth out, but apart from that they stayed contentedly at home.

A call to Scar House always came as rather a jolt because it meant that at least two hours had been removed from the working day. In all but the driest weather it was safer to leave the car at Mr Broom's and make the journey on foot. One February night at about eight o'clock I was splashing my way along the track, feeling the mud sucking at my Wellingtons; it was to see a horse with colic and my pockets were stuffed with the things I might need — arecoline, phials of morphia, a bottle of Paraphyroxia. My eyes were half closed against the steady drizzle but about half a mile ahead I could see the lights of the house winking among the trees.

After twenty minutes of slithering in and out of the unseen puddles and opening a series of broken, string-tied gates, I reached the farm yard and crossed over to the back door. I was about to knock when I stopped with my hand poised. I found I was looking through the kitchen window and in the interior, dimly lit by an oil lamp, the Bramleys were sitting in a row.

They weren't grouped round the fire but were jammed tightly on a long, high-backed wooden settle which stood against the far wall. The strange thing was the almost exact similarity of their attitudes; all four had their arms folded, chins resting on their chests, feet stretched out in front of them. The men had removed their heavy boots and were stocking-footed, but Miss Bramley wore an old pair of carpet slippers.

I stared, fascinated by the curious immobility of the group. They were not asleep, not talking or reading or listening to the radio — in fact they didn't have one — they were just sitting.

I had never seen people just sitting before and I stood there for some minutes to see if they would make a move or do anything at all, but nothing happened. It occurred to me that this was probably a typical evening; they worked hard all day, had their meal, then they just sat till bedtime.

A month or two later I discovered another unsuspected side of the Bramleys when they started having trouble with their cats. I knew they were fond of cats by the number and variety which swarmed over the place and perched confidently on my car bonnet on cold days with their unerring instinct for a warm place. But I was unprepared for the family's utter desolation when the cats started to die. Miss Bramley was on the doorstep at Skeldale House nearly every day carrying an egg basket with another pitiful patient — a cat or sometimes a few tiny kittens — huddling miserably inside.

Even today with the full range of modern antibiotics, the treatment of feline enteritis is unrewarding and I had little success with my salicylates and non-specific injections. I did my best. I even took some of the cats in and kept them at the surgery so that I could attend them several times a day, but the mortality rate was high.

The Bramleys were stricken as they saw their cats diminishing. I was surprised at their grief because most farmers look on cats as pest killers and nothing more. But when Miss Bramley came in one morning with a fresh consignment of invalids she was in a sorry state. She stared at me across the surgery table and her rough fingers clasped and unclasped on the handle of the egg basket.

'Is it going to go through 'em all?' she quavered.

'Well, if it's very infectious and it looks as though most of your young cats will get it anyway.'

For a moment Miss Bramley seemed to be struggling with herself, then her chin began to jerk and her whole face twitched uncontrollably. She didn't actually break down but her eyes brimmed and a couple of tears wandered among the network of wrinkles on her cheeks. I looked at her helplessly as she stood there, wisps of grey hair straggling untidily from under the incongruous black beret which she wore pulled tightly over her ears.

'It's Topsy's kittens I'm worried about,' she gasped out at length. 'There's five of 'em and they're the best we've got.'

I rubbed my chin. I had heard a lot about

Topsy, one of a strain of incomparable ratters and mousers. Her last family were only about ten weeks old and it would be a crushing blow to the Bramleys if anything happened to them. But what the devil could I do? There was, as yet, no protective vaccine against the disease — or wait a minute, was there? I remembered that I'd heard a rumour that Burroughs Wellcome were working on one.

I pulled out a chair. 'Just sit down a few minutes, Miss Bramley. I'm going to make a phone call.' I was soon through to the Wellcome Laboratory and half expected a sarcastic reply. But they were kind and co-operative. They had had encouraging results with the new vaccine and would be glad to let me have five doses if I would inform them of the result.

I hurried back to Miss Bramley. 'I've ordered something for your kittens. I can't guarantee anything but there's nothing else to do. Have them down here on Tuesday morning.'

The vaccine arrived promptly and as I injected the tiny creatures Miss Bramley extolled the virtues of the Topsy line. 'Look at the size of them ears! Did you ever see bigger 'uns on kittens?'

I had to admit that I hadn't. The ears were enormous, sail-like and they made the ravishingly pretty little faces look even smaller.

Miss Bramley nodded and smiled with

satisfaction. 'Aye, you can allus tell. It's the sure sign of a good mouser.'

The injection was repeated a week later. The kittens were still looking well.

'Well that's it,' I said. 'We'll just have to wait now. But remember I want to know the outcome of this, so please don't forget to let me know.'

I didn't hear from the Bramleys for several months and had almost forgotten about the little experiment when I came upon a grubby envelope which had apparently been pushed under the surgery door. It was the promised report and was, in its way, a model of conciseness. It communicated all the information I required without frills or verbiage.

It was in a careful, spidery scrawl and said simply: 'Dere Sir, Them kittens is now big cats. Yrs trly, R. Bramley.'

CHAPTER 59

As I stopped my car by the group of gipsies I felt I was looking at something which should have been captured by a camera. The grass verge was wide on this loop of the road and there were five of them squatting round the fire; it seemed like the mother and father and three little girls. They sat very still, regarding me blankly through the drifting smoke while a few big snowflakes floated across the scene and settled lazily on the tangled hair of the children. Some unreal quality in the wild tableau kept me motionless in my seat, staring through the glass, forgetful of the reason for my being here. Then I wound down the window and spoke to the man.

'Are you Mr Myatt? I believe you have a sick pony.' The man nodded. 'Aye, that's right. He's over here.' It was a strange accent with no trace of Yorkshire in it. He got up from the fire, a thin, dark-skinned unshaven little figure, and came over to the car holding out something in his hand. It was a ten shilling note and I recognised it as a gesture of good faith.

The gipsies who occasionally wandered into Darrowby were always regarded with a certain amount of suspicion. They came, unlike the Myatts, mainly in the summer to camp down by the river and sell their horses and we had been caught out once or twice before. A lot of them seemed to be called Smith and it wasn't uncommon to go back on the second day and find that patient and owner had gone. In fact Siegfried had shouted to me as I left the house this morning: 'Get the brass if you can.' But he needn't have worried — Mr Myatt was on the up and up.

I got out of the car and followed him over the grass, past the shabby, ornate caravan and the lurcher dog tied to the wheel to where a few horses and ponies were tethered. My patient was easy to find; a handsome piebald of about thirteen hands with good, clean legs and a look of class about him. But he was in a sorry state. While the other animals moved around on their tethers, watching us with interest, the piebald stood as though carved from stone.

Even from a distance I could tell what was wrong with him. Only acute laminitis could produce that crouching posture and as I moved nearer I could see that all four feet were probably affected because the pony had his hind feet right under his body in a desperate attempt to take his full weight on his heels.

I pushed my thermometer into the rectum. 'Has he been getting any extra food, Mr Myatt?'

'Aye, he getten into a bag of oats last night.' The little man showed me the big, half empty sack in the back of the caravan. It was difficult to understand him but he managed to convey that the pony had broken loose and gorged himself on the oats. And he had given him a dose of castor oil — he called it 'casta ile'.

The thermometer read 104 and the pulse was rapid and bounding. I passed my hand over the smooth, trembling hooves, feeling the abnormal heat, then I looked at the taut face, the dilated nostrils and terrified eyes. Anybody who has had an infection under a finger-nail can have an inkling of the agony a horse goes through when the sensitive laminae of the foot are inflamed and throbbing against the unyielding wall of the hoof.

'Can you get him to move?' I asked.

The man caught hold of the head collar and pulled, but the pony refused to budge.

I took the other side of the collar. 'Come on, it's always better if they can get moving.'

We pulled together and Mrs Myatt slapped the pony's rump. He took a couple of stumbling steps but it was as though the ground was red hot and he groaned as his feet came down. Within seconds he was crouching again with his weight on his heels.

'It seems he just won't have it.' I turned and went back to the car. I'd have to do what I could to give him relief and the first thing was to get rid of as much as possible of that bellyful of oats. I fished out the bottle of arecoline and gave an injection into the muscle of the neck, then I showed the little man how to tie cloths round the hooves so that he could keep soaking them with cold water.

Afterwards I stood back and looked again at the pony. He was salivating freely from the arecoline and he had cocked his tail and evacuated his bowel; but his pain was undiminished and it would stay like that until the tremendous inflammation subsided — if it ever did. I had seen cases like this where serum had started to ooze from the coronet; that usually meant shedding of the hooves — even death.

As I turned over the gloomy thoughts the three little girls went up to the pony. The biggest put her arms round his neck and laid her cheek against his shoulder while the others stroked the shivering flanks. There were no tears, no change in the blank expressions, but it was easy to see that that pony really meant something to them.

Before leaving I handed over a bottle of tincture of aconite mixture. 'Get a dose of this down him every four hours, Mr Myatt, and be sure to keep putting cold water on the feet. I'll come and see him in the morning.'

I closed the car door and looked through the window again at the slow-rising smoke, the drifting snowflakes and the three children with their ragged dresses and uncombed hair still stroking the pony.

'Well you got the brass, James,' Siegfried said at lunch, carelessly stuffing the ten shilling note into a bulging pocket. 'What was the trouble?'

'Worst case of laminitis I've ever seen. Couldn't move the pony at all and he's going through hell. I've done the usual things but I'm pretty sure they aren't going to be enough.'

'Not a very bright prognosis, then?'

'Really black. Even if he gets over the acute stage he'll have deformed feet, I'd like to bet. Grooved hooves, dropped soles, the lot. And he's a grand little animal, lovely piebald. I wish to God there was something else I could do.'

Siegfried sawed two thick slices off the cold mutton and dropped them on my plate. He looked thoughtfully at me for a moment. 'You've been a little distrait since you came back. These are rotten jobs, I know, but it's no good worrying.'

'Ach, I'm not worrying, exactly, but I can't get it off my mind. Maybe it's those people

— the Myatts. They were something new to me. Right out of the world. And three raggedy little girls absolutely crazy about that pony. They aren't going to like it at all.'

As Siegfried chewed his mutton I could see the old glint coming into his eyes; it showed when the talk had anything to do with horses. I knew he wouldn't push in but he was waiting for me to make the first move. I made it.

'I wish you'd come along and have a look with me. Maybe there's something you could suggest. Do you think there could be?'

Siegfried put down his knife and fork and stared in front of him for a few seconds, then he turned to me. 'You know, James, there just might be. Quite obviously this is a right pig of a case and the ordinary remedies aren't going to do any good. We have to pull something out of the bag and I've got an idea. There's just one thing.' He gave me a crooked smile. 'You may not like it.'

'Don't bother about me,' I said. 'You're the horseman. If you can help this pony I don't care what you do.'

'Right, eat up then and we'll go into action together.' We finished our meal and he led me through to the instrument room. I was surprised when he opened the cupboard where old Mr Grant's instruments were kept. It was a kind of museum.

When Siegfried had bought the practice from the old vet who had worked on into his eighties these instruments had come with it and they lay there in rows, unused but undisturbed. It would have been logical to throw them out, but maybe Siegfried felt the same way about them as I did. The polished wooden boxes of shining, odd-shaped scalpels, the enema pumps and douches with their perished rubber and brass fittings, the seaton needles, the ancient firing irons — they were a silent testament to sixty years of struggle. I often used to open that cupboard door and try to picture the old man wrestling with the same problems as I had, travelling the same narrow roads as I did. He had done it absolutely on his own and for sixty years. I was only starting but I knew a little about the triumphs and disasters, the wondering and worrying, the hopes and disappointments — and the hard labour. Anyway, Mr Grant was dead and gone, taking with him all the skills and knowledge I was doggedly trying to accumulate.

Siegfried reached to the back of the cupboard and pulled out a long flat box. He blew the dust from the leather covering and gingerly unfastened the clasp. Inside, a fleam, glittering on its bed of frayed velvet, lay by the side of a round, polished blood stick.

I looked at my employer in astonishment. 'You're going to bleed him, then?'

'Yes, my boy, I'm going to take you back to the Middle Ages.' He looked at my startled face and put a hand on my arm. 'But don't start beating me over the head with all the scientific arguments against blood-letting. I've no strong views either way.'

'But have you ever done it? I've never seen you use this outfit.'

'I've done it. And I've seen some funny things after it, too.' Siegfried turned away as if he wanted no more discussion. He cleaned the fleam thoroughly and dropped it into the steriliser. His face was expressionless as he stood listening to the hiss of the boiling water.

The gipsies were again hunched over the fire when we got there and Mr Myatt, sensing that reinforcements had arrived, scrambled to his feet and shuffled forward, holding out another ten shilling note.

Siegfried waved it away. 'Let's see how we get on, Mr Myatt,' he grunted. He strode across the grass to where the pony still trembled in his agonised crouch. There was no improvement; in fact the eyes stared more wildly and I could hear little groans as the piebald carefully eased himself from foot to foot.

Siegfried spoke softly without looking at me, 'Poor beggar. You weren't exaggerating, James. Bring that box from the car, will you?'

When I came back he was tying a choke rope round the base of the pony's neck. 'Pull it up tight,' he said. As the jugular rose up tense and turgid in its furrow he quickly clipped and disinfected a small area and inserted a plaque of local anaesthetic. Finally he opened the old leather-covered box and extracted the fleam, wrapped in sterile lint.

Everything seemed to start happening then. Siegfried placed the little blade of the fleam against the bulging vein and without hesitation gave it a confident smack with the stick. Immediately an alarming cascade of blood spouted from the hole and began to form a dark lake on the grass. Mr Myatt gasped and the little girls set up a sudden chatter. I could understand how they felt. In fact I was wondering how long the pony could stand this tremendous outflow without dropping down.

It didn't seem to be coming out fast enough for Siegfried, however, because he produced another stick from his pocket, thrust it into the pony's mouth and began to work the jaws. And as the animal champed, the blood gushed more fiercely.

When at least a gallon had come away Siegfried seemed satisfied. 'Slacken the rope, James,' he cried, then rapidly closed the wound on the neck with a pin suture. Next he trotted over the grass and looked over a gate in the roadside wall. 'Thought so,' he shouted. 'There's a little beck in that field. We've got to get him over to it. Come on, lend a hand everybody!'

He was clearly enjoying himself and his

presence was having its usual effect. The Myatts were spurred suddenly into action and began to run around aimlessly, bumping into each other. I was gripped by a sudden tension and preparedness and even the pony seemed to be taking an interest in his surroundings for the first time.

All five of the gipsies pulled at the halter, Siegfried and I looped our arms behind the pony's thighs, everybody gave encouraging shouts and at last he began to move forward. It was a painful process but he kept going — through the gate and across the field to where the shallow stream wandered among its rushes. There were no banks to speak of and it was easy to push him out into the middle. As he stood there with the icy water rippling round his inflamed hooves I fancied I could read in his eyes a faint dawning of an idea that things were looking up at last.

'Now he must stand in there for an hour,' Siegfried said. 'And then you'll have to make him walk round the field. Then another hour in the beck. As he gets better you can give him more and more exercise but he must come back to the beck. There's a lot of work for somebody here, so who's going to do it?'

The three little girls came shyly round him and looked up, wide-eyed, into his face. Siegfried laughed. 'You three want the job, do you? Right, I'll tell you just what to do.'

He pulled out the bag of peppermint drops

which was an ever-present among his widely-varied pocket luggage and I settled myself for a long wait. I had seen him in action with the children on the farms and when that bag of sweets came out, everything stopped. It was the one time Siegfried was never in a hurry.

The little girls each solemnly took a sweet, then Siegfried squatted on his heels and began to address them like a professor with his class. They soon began to thaw and put a word in for themselves. The smallest launched into a barely intelligible account of the remarkable things the pony had done when he was a foal and Siegfried listened intently, nodding his head gravely now and then. There was all the time in the world.

His words obviously went home because, over the next few days whenever I passed the gipsy camp I could see the three wild little figures either grouped around the pony in the beck or dragging him round the field on a long halter shank. I didn't need to butt in — I could see he was improving all the time.

It was about a week later that I saw the Myatts on their way out of Darrowby, the red caravan rocking across the market place with Mr Myatt up front wearing a black velvet cap, his wife by his side. Tethered to various parts of the caravan the family of horses clopped along and right at the rear was the piebald, a bit stiff perhaps, but going very well. He'd be all right.

The little girls were looking out of the back door and as they spotted me I waved. They looked back at me unsmilingly until they had almost turned the corner into Hallgate then one of them shyly lifted her hand. The others followed suit and my last sight was of them waving eagerly back.

I strolled into the Drovers and took a thoughtful half pint into a corner. Siegfried had done the trick there all right but I was wondering what to make of it because in veterinary practice it is difficult to draw definite conclusions even after spectacular results. Was it my imagination or did that pony seem to feel relief almost immediately after the blood-letting? Would we ever have got him moving without it? Was it really the right thing in these cases to bash a hole in the jugular and release about a bucketful of the precious fluid? I still don't have the answers because I never dared try it for myself.

CHAPTER 60

'Could Mr Herriot see my dog, please?'

Familiar enough words coming from the waiting-room but it was the voice that brought me to a slithering halt just beyond the door.

It couldn't be, no of course it couldn't, but it sounded just like Helen. I tiptoed back and applied my eye without hesitation to the crack in the door. Tristan was standing there looking down at somebody just beyond my range of vision. All I could see was a hand resting on the head of a patient sheep dog, the hem of a tweed skirt and two silk stockinged legs.

They were nice legs — not skinny — and could easily belong to a big girl like Helen. My cogitations were cut short as a head bent over to speak to the dog and I had a close up in profile of the small straight nose and the dark hair falling across the milky smoothness of the cheek.

I was still peering, bemused, when Tristan shot out of the room and collided with me.

Stifling an oath, he grabbed my arm and hauled me along the passage into the dispensary. He shut the door and spoke in a hoarse whisper.

'It's her! The Alderson woman! And she wants to see you! Not Siegfried, not me, but you, Mr Herriot himself!'

He looked at me wide-eyed for a few moments then, as I stood hesitating he opened the door and tried to propel me into the passage.

'What the hell are you waiting for?' he hissed.

'Well, it's a bit embarrassing, isn't it? After that dance, I mean. Last time she saw me I was a lovely sight — so pie-eyed I couldn't even speak.'

Tristan struck his forehead with his hand. 'God help us! You worry about details, don't you? She's asked to see you — what more do you want? Go on, get in there!'

I was shuffling off irresolutely when he raised a hand. 'Just a minute. Stay right there.' He trotted off and returned in a few seconds holding out a white lab coat.

'Just back from the laundry,' he said as he began to work my arms into the starched sleeves. 'You'll look marvellous in this, Jim — the immaculate young surgeon.'

I stood unresisting as he buttoned me into the garment but struck away his hand when he started to straighten my tie. As I left him he gave me a final encouraging wave before heading for the back stairs.

I didn't give myself any more time to think but marched straight into the waiting-room. Helen looked up and smiled. And it was just the same smile. Nothing behind it. Just the same friendly, steady-eyed smile as when I first met her.

We faced each other in silence for some moments then when I didn't say anything she looked down at the dog.

'It's Dan in trouble this time,' she said. 'He's our sheep dog but we're so fond of him that he's more like one of the family.'

The dog wagged his tail furiously at the sound of his name but yelped as he came towards me. I bent down and patted his head. 'I see he's holding up a hind leg.'

'Yes, he jumped over a wall this morning and he's been like that ever since. I think it's something quite bad — he can't put any weight on the leg.'

'Right bring him through to the other room and I'll have a look at him. But take him on in front of me, will you, and I'll be able to watch how he walks.'

I held the door open and she went through ahead of me with the dog.

Watching how Helen walked distracted me over the first few yards, but it was a long passage and by the time we had reached the second bend I had managed to drag my attention back to my patient.

And glory be, it was a dislocated hip. It had to be with that shortening of the limb and the way he carried it underneath his body with the paw just brushing the ground.

My feelings were mixed. This was a major injury but on the other hand the chances were I could put it right quickly and look good in the process. Because I had found, in my brief experience, that one of the most spectacular procedures in practice was the reduction of a dislocated hip. Maybe I had been lucky, but with the few I had seen I had been able to convert an alarmingly lame animal into a completely sound one as though by magic.

In the operating room I hoisted Dan on to the table. He stood without moving as I examined the hip. There was no doubt about it at all — the head of the femur was displaced upwards and backwards, plainly palpable under my thumb.

The dog looked round only once — when I made a gentle attempt to flex the limb — but turned away immediately and stared resolutely ahead. His mouth hung open a little as he panted nervously but like a lot of the placid animals which arrived on our surgery table he seemed to have resigned himself to his fate. I had the strong impression that I could have started to cut his head off and he wouldn't have made much fuss.

'Nice, good-natured dog,' I said. 'And a bonny one, too.'

Helen patted the handsome head with the broad blaze of white down the face; the tail waved slowly from side to side.

'Yes,' she said. 'He's just as much a family pet as a working dog. I do hope he hasn't hurt himself too badly.'

'Well, he has a dislocated hip. It's a nasty thing but with a bit of luck I ought to be able to put it back.'

'What happens if it won't go back?'

'He'd have to form a false joint up there. He'd be very lame for several weeks and probably always have a slightly short leg.'

'Oh dear, I wouldn't like that,' Helen said. 'Do you think he'll be all right?'

I looked at the docile animal still gazing steadfastly to his front. 'I think he's got a good chance, mainly because you haven't hung about for days before bringing him in. The sooner these things are tackled the better.'

'Oh good. When will you be able to start on him?'

'Right now.' I went over to the door. 'I'll just give Tristan a shout. This is a two man job.'

'Couldn't I help?' Helen said. 'I'd very much like to if you wouldn't mind.'

I looked at her doubtfully. 'Well I don't know. You mightn't like playing tug of war with Dan in the middle. He'll be anaesthetised of course but there's usually a lot of pulling.'

Helen laughed. 'Oh, I'm quite strong. And not a bit squeamish. I'm used to animals, you know, and I like working with them.'

'Right,' I said. 'Slip on this spare coat and we'll begin.'

The dog didn't flinch as I pushed the needle into his vein and as the Nembutal flowed in, his head began to slump against Helen's arm and his supporting paw to slide along the smooth top of the table. Soon he was stretched unconscious on his side.

I held the needle in the vein as I looked down at the sleeping animal. 'I might have to give him a bit more. They have to be pretty deep to overcome the muscular resistance.'

Another cc. and Dan was as limp as any rag doll. I took hold of the affected leg and spoke across the table. 'I want you to link your hands underneath his thigh and try to hold him there when I pull. O.K.? Here we go, then.'

It takes a surprising amount of force to pull the head of a displaced femur over the rim of the acetabulum. I kept up a steady traction with my right hand, pressing on the head of the femur at the same time with my left. Helen did her part efficiently, leaning back against the pull, her lips pushed forward in a little pout of concentration.

I suppose there must be a foolproof way of doing this job — a method which works the very first time — but I have never been able to find it. Success has always come to me only after a fairly long period of trial and error and it was the same today. I tried all sorts of angles, rotations and twists on the flaccid limb, trying not to think of how it would look if this just happened to be the one I couldn't put back. I was wondering what Helen, still hanging on determinedly to her end, must be thinking of this wrestling match when I heard the muffled click. It was a sweet and welcome sound.

I flexed the hip joint once or twice. No resistance at all now. The femoral head was once more riding smoothly in its socket.

'Well that's it,' I said. 'Hope it stays put — we'll have to keep our fingers crossed. The odd one does pop out again but I've got a feeling this is going to be all right.'

Helen ran her hand over the silky ears and neck of the sleeping dog. 'Poor old Dan. He wouldn't have jumped over that wall this morning if he'd known what was in store for him. How long will it be before he comes round?'

'Oh, he'll be out for the rest of the day. When he starts to wake up tonight I want you to be around to steady him in case he falls and puts the thing out again. Perhaps you'd give me a ring. I'd like to know how things are.'

I gathered Dan up in my arms and was carrying him along the passage, staggering under his weight, when I met Mrs Hall. She was carrying a tray with two cups.

'I was just having a drink of tea, Mr Herriot,' she said. 'I thought you and the young lady might fancy a cup.'

I looked at her narrowly. This was unusual. Was it possible she had joined Tristan in playing Cupid? But the broad, dark-skinned face was as unemotional as ever. It told me nothing.

'Well, thanks very much, Mrs Hall. I'll just put this dog outside first.' I went out and settled Dan on the back seat of Helen's car; with only his eyes and nose sticking out from under a blanket he looked at peace with the world.

Helen was already sitting with a cup in her lap and I thought of the other time I had drunk tea in this room with a girl. On the day I had arrived in Darrowby. She had been one of Siegfried's followers and surely the toughest of them all.

This was a lot different. During the struggle in the operating room I had been able to observe Helen at close range and I had discovered that her mouth turned up markedly at the comers as though she was just going to smile or had just been smiling; also that the deep warm blue of the eyes under the smoothly arching brows made a dizzying partnership with the rich black-brown of her hair.

And this time the conversation didn't lag. Maybe it was because I was on my own ground — perhaps I never felt fully at ease unless there was a sick animal involved somewhere, but at any rate I found myself prattling effortlessly just as I had done up on that hill when we had first met.

Mrs Hall's teapot was empty and the last of the biscuits gone before I finally saw Helen off and started on my round.

The same feeling of easy confidence was on me that night when I heard her voice on the phone.

'Dan is up and walking about,' she said. 'He's still a bit wobbly but he's perfectly sound on that leg.'

'Oh great, he's got the first stage over. I think everything's going to be fine.'

There was a pause at the other end of the line, then: 'Thank you so much for what you've done. We were terribly worried about him, especially my young brother and sister. We're very grateful.'

'Not at all, I'm delighted too. He's a grand dog.' I hesitated for a moment — it had to be now. 'Oh, you remember we were talking about Scotland today. Well, I was passing the Plaza this afternoon and I see they're showing a film about the Hebrides. I thought maybe . . . I wondered if perhaps, er . . . you might like to come and see it with me.'

Another pause and my heart did a quick thud-thud.

'All right.' Helen said. 'Yes, I'd like that. When? Friday night? Well, thank you — goodbye till then.'

I replaced the receiver with a trembling hand. Why did I make such heavy weather of these things? But it didn't matter — I was back in business.

CHAPTER 61

Rheumatism is a terrible thing in a dog. It is painful enough in humans but an acute attack can reduce an otherwise healthy dog to terrified, screaming immobility.

Very muscular animals suffered most and I went carefully as my fingers explored the bulging triceps and gluteals of the little Staffordshire bull terrier. Normally a tough little fellow, afraid of nothing, friendly, leaping high in an attempt to lick people's faces; but today, rigid, trembling, staring anxiously in front of him. Even to turn his head a little brought a shrill howl of agony.

Mercifully it was something you could put right and quickly too. I pulled the Novalgin into the syringe and injected it rapidly. The little dog, oblivious to everything but the knife-like stabbing of the rheumatism did not stir at the prick of the needle. I counted out some salicylate tablets into a box, wrote the directions on the lid and handed the box to the owner.

'Give him one of those as soon as the injection has eased him, Mr Tavener. Then repeat in about four hours. I'm pretty sure he'll be greatly improved by then.'

Mrs Tavener snatched the box away as her husband began to read the directions. 'Let me see it,' she snapped. 'No doubt I'll be the one who has the job to do.'

It had been like that all the time, ever since I had entered the beautiful house with the terraced gardens leading down to the river. She had been at him ceaselessly while he was holding the dog for me. When the animal had yelped she had cried: 'Really, Henry, don't grip the poor thing like that, you're hurting him!' She had kept him scuttling about for this and that and when he was out of the room she said: 'You know, this is all my husband's fault. He will let the dog swim in the river. I knew this would happen.'

Half-way through, daughter Julia had come in and it was clear from the start that she was firmly on Mama's side. She helped out with plenty of 'How could you, Daddy!' and 'For God's sake, Daddy!' and generally managed to fill in the gaps when her mother wasn't in full cry.

The Taveners were in their fifties. He was a big, floridly handsome man who had made millions in the Tyneside shipyards before pulling out of the smoke to this lovely place. I had taken an instant liking to him; I had expected a tough tycoon and had found a warm, friendly, curiously vulnerable man, obviously worried sick about his dog.

I had reservations about Mrs Tavener despite her still considerable beauty. Her smile had a switched-on quality and there was a little too much steel in the blue of her eyes. She had seemed less concerned about the dog than with the necessity of taking it out on her husband.

Julia, a scaled-down model of her mother, drifted about the room with the aimless, bored look of the spoiled child; glancing blankly at the dog or me, staring without interest through the window at the smooth lawns, the tennis court, the dark band of river under the trees.

I gave the terrier a final reassuring pat on the head and got up from my knees. As I put away the syringe, Tavener took my arm. 'Well, that's fine, Mr Herriot. We're very grateful to you for relieving our minds. I must say I thought the old boy's time had come when he started yelling. And now you'll have a drink before you go.'

The man's hand trembled on my arm as he spoke. It had been noticeable, too, when he had been holding the dog's head and I had wondered; maybe Parkinson's disease, or nerves, or just drink. Certainly he was pouring a generous measure of whisky into his glass, but as he tipped up the bottle his hand was seized by an even more violent tremor and he slopped the spirit on to the polished sideboard.

'Oh God! Oh God!' Mrs Tavener burst out. There was a bitter note of oh no, not again, in her cry and Julia struck her forehead with her hand and raised her eyes to heaven. Tavener shot a single hunted look at the women then grinned as he handed me my glass.

'Come and sit down, Mr Herriot,' he said. 'I'm sure you have time to relax for a few minutes.'

We moved over to the fireside and Tavener talked pleasantly about dogs and the countryside and the pictures which hung on the walls of the big room. Those pictures were noted in the district; many of them were originals by famous painters and they had become the main interest in Tavener's life. His other passion was clocks and as I looked round the room at the rare and beautiful timepieces standing among elegant period furniture it was easy to believe the rumours I had heard about the wealth within these walls.

The women did not drink with us; they had disappeared when the whisky was brought out, but as I drained my glass the door was pushed open and they stood there, looking remarkably alike in expensive tweed coats and fur-trimmed hats. Mrs Tavener pulling on a pair of motoring gloves, looked with distaste at her husband. 'We're going into Brawton,' she said. 'Don't know when we'll be back.'

Behind her, Julia stared coldly at her father; her lip curled slightly.

Tavener did not reply. He sat motionless as I listened to the roar of the car engine and the spatter of whipped-up gravel beyond the window; then he looked out, blank-faced, empty-eyed at the drifting cloud of exhaust smoke in the drive.

There was something in his expression which chilled me. I put down my glass and got to my feet. 'Afraid I must be moving on, Mr Tavener. Thanks for the drink.'

He seemed suddenly to be aware of my presence; the friendly smile returned. 'Not at all. Thank you for looking after the old boy. He seems better already.'

In the driving mirror, the figure at the top of the steps looked small and alone till the high shrubbery hid him from my view.

The next call was to a sick pig, high on Marstang Fell. The road took me at first along the fertile valley floor, winding under the riverside trees past substantial farmhouses and rich pastures; but as the car left the road and headed up a steep track the country began to change. The transition was almost violent as the trees and bushes thinned out and gave way to the bare, rocky hillside and the miles of limestone walls.

And though the valley had been rich with the fresh green of the new leaves, up here the buds were unopened and the naked branches stretched against the sky still had the look of winter.

Tim Alton's farm lay at the top of the track and as I pulled up at the gate I wondered as I always did how the man could scrape a living from those few harsh acres with the grass flattened and yellowed by the wind which always blew. At any rate, many generations had accomplished the miracle and had lived and struggled and died in that house with its outbuildings crouching in the lee of a group of stunted, wind-bent trees, its massive stones crumbling under three centuries of fierce weathering.

Why should anybody want to build a farm in such a place? I turned as I opened the gate and looked back at the track threading between the walls down and down to where the white stones of the river glittered in the spring sunshine. Maybe the builder had stood here and looked across the green vastness and breathed in the cold, sweet air and thought it was enough.

I saw Tim Alton coming across the yard. There had been no need to lay down concrete or cobbles here; they had just swept away the thin soil and there, between house and buildings was a sloping stretch of fissured rock. It was more than a durable surface — it was everlasting.

'It's your pig this time, then, Tim,' I said and the farmer nodded seriously.

'Aye, right as owt yesterday and laid flat like a dead 'un this morning. Never looked up when I filled his trough and by gaw when a pig won't tackle his grub there's summat far wrong.' Tim dug his hands inside the broad leather belt which encircled his over-sized trousers and which always seemed to be about to nip his narrow frame in two and led the way gloomily into the sty. Despite the bitter poverty of his existence he was a man who took misfortune cheerfully. I had never seen him look like this and I thought I knew the reason; there is something personal about the family pig.

Smallholders like Tim Alton made their meagre living from a few cows; they sold their milk to the big dairies or made butter. And they killed a pig or two each year and cured it themselves for home consumption. On the poorer places it seemed to me that they ate little else; whatever meal I happened to stumble in on, the cooking smell was always the same — roasting fat bacon.

It appeared to be a matter of pride to make the pig as fat as possible; in fact, on these little wind-blown farms where the people and the cows and the dogs were lean and spare, the pig was about the only fat thing to be seen.

I had seen the Alton pig before. I had been stitching a cow's torn teat about a fortnight ago and Tim had patted me on the shoulder and whispered: 'Now come along wi' me, Mr Herriot and I'll show tha summat.' We had looked into the sty at a twenty-five-stone monster effortlessly emptying a huge trough of wet meal. I could remember the pride in the farmer's eyes and the way he listened to the smacking and slobbering as if to great music.

It was different today. The pig looked, if possible, even more enormous as it lay on its side, eyes closed, filling the entire floor of the sty like a beached whale. Tim splashed a stick among the untouched meal in the trough and made encouraging noises but the animal never stirred. The farmer looked at me with haggard eyes.

'He's bad, Mr Herriot. It's serious whatever it is.'

I had been taking the temperature and when I read the thermometer I whistled. 'A hundred and seven. That's some fever.'

The colour drained from Tim's face. 'Oh 'ell! A hundred and seven! It's hopeless, then. It's ower with him.'

I had been feeling along the animal's side and I smiled reassuringly. 'No, don't worry, Tim. I think he's going to be all right. He's got erysipelas. Here, put your fingers along his back. You can feel a lot of flat swellings on his skin — those are the diamonds. He'll have a beautiful rash within a few hours but at the moment you can't see it, you can only feel it.'

'And you can make him better?'

'I'm nearly sure I can. I'll give him a whacking dose of serum and I'd like to bet you he'll have his nose in that trough in a couple of days. Most of them get over it all right.'

'Well that's a bit o' good news, any road,' said Tim, a smile flooding over his face. 'You had me worried there with your hundred and seven, dang you!'

I laughed. 'Sorry, Tim, didn't mean to frighten you. I'm often happier to see a high temperature than a low one. But it's a funny time for erysipelas. We usually see it in late summer.'

'All right, I'll let ye off this time. Come in and wash your hands.'

In the kitchen I ducked my head but couldn't avoid bumping the massive side of bacon hanging from the beamed ceiling. The heavy mass rocked gently on its hooks; it was about eight inches thick in parts — all pure white fat. Only by close inspection was it possible to discern a thin strip of lean meat.

Mrs Alton produced a cup of tea and as I sipped I looked across at Tim who had fallen back into a chair and lay with his hands hanging down; for a moment he closed his eyes and his face became a mask of weariness. I thought for the hundredth time about the endless labour which made up the lives of these little farmers. Alton was only forty but his body was already bent and ravaged by the constant demands he made on it; you could read his story in the corded forearm, the rough, work-swollen fingers. He told me once that the last time he missed a milking was twelve years ago and that was for his father's funeral.

I was taking my leave when I saw Jennie. She was the Altons' eldest child and was pumping vigorously at the tyre of her bicycle which was leaning against the wall just outside the kitchen door.

'Going somewhere?' I asked and the girl straightened up quickly, pushing back a few strands of dark hair from her forehead. She was about eighteen with delicate features and large, expressive eyes; in her wild, pinched prettiness there was something of the wheeling curlews, the wind and sun, the wide emptiness of the moors.

'I'm going down to t'village.' She stole a glance into the kitchen. 'I'm going to get a bottle of Guinness for dad.'

'The village! It's a long way to go for a bottle of Guinness. It must be two miles and then you've got to push back up this hill. Are you going all that way just for one bottle?'

'Ay, just one,' she whispered, counting out a sixpence and some coppers into her palm with calm absorption. 'Dad's been up all night waiting for a heifer to calve — he's tired out. I won't be long and he can have his Guinness with his dinner. That's what he likes.' She looked up at me conspiratorially. 'It'll be a surprise for him.'

As she spoke, her father, still sprawled in the chair, turned his head and looked at her; he smiled and for a moment I saw a serenity in the steady eyes, a nobility in the seamed face.

Jennie looked at him for a few seconds, a happy secret look from under her lowered brows; then she turned quickly, mounted her bicycle and began to pedal down the track at surprising speed.

I followed her more slowly, the car, in second gear, bumping and swaying over the stones. I stared straight ahead, lost in thought. I couldn't stop my mind roaming between the two houses I had visited; between the gracious mansion by the river and the crumbling farmhouse I had just left; from Henry Tavener with his beautiful clothes, his well-kept hands, his rows of books and pictures and clocks to Tim Alton with his worn, chest-high trousers nipped in by that great belt, his daily, monthly, yearly grind to stay alive on that unrelenting hilltop.

But I kept coming back to the daughters; to the contempt in Julia Tavener's eyes when she looked at her father and the shining tenderness in Jennie Alton's.

It wasn't so easy to work out as it seemed; in fact it became increasingly difficult to decide who was getting the most out of their different lives. But as I guided the car over the last few yards of the track and pulled on to the smooth tarmac of the road it came to me with unexpected clarity. Taking it all in all, if I had the choice to make, I'd settle for the Guinness.

CHAPTER 62

Tristan was unpacking the U.C.M.'s. These bottles contained a rich red fluid which constituted our last line of defence in the battle with animal disease. Its full name, Universal Cattle Medicine, was proclaimed on the label in big black type and underneath it pointed out that it was highly efficacious for coughs, chills, scours, garget, milk fever, pneumonia, felon and bloat. It finished off on a confident note with the assurance: 'Never Fails to Give Relief' and we had read the label so often that we half believed it.

It was a pity it didn't do any good because there was something compelling about its ruby depths when you held it up to the light and about the solid camphor-ammonia jolt when you sniffed at it and which made the farmers blink and shake their heads and say 'By gaw, that's powerful stuff,' with deep respect. But our specific remedies were so few and the possibilities of error so plentiful that it was comforting in cases of doubt to be able to hand over a bottle of the old standby. Whenever an entry of Siegfried's or mine appeared in the day book stating 'Visit attend cow, advice, 1 U.C.M.' it was a pretty fair bet we didn't know what was wrong with the animal.

The bottles were tall and shapely and they came in elegant white cartons, so much more impressive than the unobtrusive containers of the antibiotics and steroids which we use today. Tristan was lifting them out of the tea chest and stacking them on the shelves in deep rows. When he saw me he ceased his labours, sat on the chest and pulled out a packet of Woodbines. He lit one, pulled the smoke a long way down then fixed me with a non-committal stare.

'You're taking her to the pictures then?'

Feeling vaguely uneasy under his eye, I tipped a pocketful of assorted empties into the waste basket. 'Yes, that's right. In about an hour.'

'Mm.' He narrowed his eyes against the slowly escaping smoke. 'Mm, I see.'

'Well what are you looking like that for?' I said defensively. 'Anything wrong with going to the pictures?'

'No-no. No-no-no. Nothing at all, Jim. Nothing, nothing. A very wholesome pursuit.'

'But you don't think I should be taking Helen there.'

'I never said that. No, I'm sure you'll have

a nice time. It's just that . . .' He scratched his head. 'I thought you might have gone in for something a bit more . . . well . . . enterprising.'

I gave a bitter laugh. 'Look, I tried enterprise at the Reniston. Oh, I'm not blaming you, Triss, you meant well, but as you know it was a complete shambles. I just don't want anything to go wrong tonight. I'm playing safe.'

'Well, I won't argue with you there,' Tristan said. 'You couldn't get much safer than the Darrowby Plaza.'

And later, shivering in the tub in the vast, draughty bathroom, I couldn't keep out the thought that Tristan was right. Taking Helen to the local cinema was a form of cowardice, a shrinking away from reality into what I hoped would be a safe, dark intimacy. But as I towelled myself, hopping about to keep warm, and looked out through the fringe of wistaria at the darkening garden there was comfort in the thought that it was another beginning, even though a small one.

And as I closed the door of Skeldale House and looked along the street to where the first lights of the shops beckoned in the dusk I felt a lifting of the heart. It was as though a breath from the near-by hills had touched me. A fleeting fragrance which said winter had gone. It was still cold — it was always cold in Darrowby until well into May — but the promise was there, of sunshine and warm grass and softer days.

You had to look closely or you could easily miss the Plaza, tucked in as it was between Pickersgills the ironmongers and Howarths the chemists. There had never been much attempt at grandeur in its architecture and the entrance was hardly wider than the average shop front. But what puzzled me as I approached was that the place was in darkness. I was in good time but the show was due to start in ten minutes or so and there was no sign of life.

I hadn't dared tell Tristan that my precautions had extended as far as arranging to meet Helen here. With a car like mine there was always an element of doubt about arriving anywhere in time or indeed at all and I had thought it prudent to eliminate all transport hazards.

'Meet you outside the cinema.' My God, it wasn't very bright was it? It took me back to my childhood, to the very first time I had taken a girl out. I was just fourteen and on my way to meet her I tendered my only half-crown to a bloody-minded Glasgow tram conductor and asked for a penny fare. He vented his spleen on me by ransacking his bag and giving me my change entirely in half-pennies. So when the cinema queue reached the pay box I had to stand there with my little partner and everybody else watching while I paid for our shilling tickets with great hand-fuls of copper. The shame of it left a scar — it was another four years before I took out a girl again.

But the black thoughts were dispelled when I saw Helen picking her way across the market-place cobbles. She smiled and waved cheerfully as if being taken to the Darrowby Plaza was the biggest treat a girl could wish for, and when she came right up to me there was a soft flush on her cheeks and her eyes were bright.

Everything was suddenly absolutely right. I felt a surging conviction that this was going to be a good night — nothing was going to spoil it. After we had said hello she told me that Dan was running about like a puppy with no trace of a limp and the news was another wave on the high tide of my euphoria.

The only thing that troubled me was the blank, uninhabited appearance of the cinema entrance.

'Strange there's nobody here,' I said. 'It's nearly starting time. I suppose the place is open?'

'Must be,' Helen said. 'It's open every night but Sunday. Anyway, I'm sure these people are waiting too.'

I looked around. There was no queue as such but little groups were standing here and there; a few couples, mostly middle-aged, a bunch of small boys rolling and fighting on the pavement. Nobody seemed worried.

And indeed there was no cause. Exactly two minutes before the picture was due to start a figure in a mackintosh coat pedalled furiously round the corner of the street, head down, legs pistoning, the bicycle lying over at a perilous angle with the ground. He came to a screeching halt outside the entrance, inserted a key in the lock and threw wide the doors. Reaching inside, he flicked a switch and a single neon strip flickered fitfully above our heads and went out. It did this a few times and seemed bent on mischief till he stood on tiptoe and beat it into submission with a masterful blow of his fist. Then he whipped off the mackintosh revealing faultless evening-dress. The manager had arrived.

While this was going on a very fat lady appeared from nowhere and wedged herself into the pay box. The show was ready to roll.

We all began to shuffle inside. The little boys put down their ninepences and punched each other as they passed through a curtain into the stalls, while the rest of us proceeded decorously upstairs to the one-and-sixpenny seats in the balcony. The manager, his white shirt front and silk lapels gleaming, smiled and bowed with great courtesy as we passed.

We paused at a row of pegs at the top of the stairs while some people hung up their coats. I was surprised to see Maggie Robinson the blacksmith's daughter there, taking

668

the tickets, and she appeared to be intrigued by the sight of us. She simpered and giggled, darted glances at Helen and did everything but dig me in the ribs. Finally she parted the curtains and we went inside.

It struck me immediately that the management were determined that their patrons wouldn't feel cold because if it hadn't been for the all-pervading smell of old sofas we might have been plunging into a tropical jungle. Maggie steered us through the stifling heat to our places and as I sat down I noticed that there was no arm between the two seats.

'Them's the courting seats,' she blurted out and fled with her hand to her mouth.

The lights were still on and I looked round the tiny balcony. There were only about a dozen people dotted here and there sitting in patient silence under the plain distempered walls. By the side of the screen the hands of a clock stood resolutely at twenty-past four.

But it was all right sitting there with Helen. I felt fine except for a tendency to gasp like a goldfish in the airless atmosphere. I was settling down cosily when a little man seated in front of us with his wife turned slowly round. The mouth in the haggard face was pursed grimly and he fixed his eyes on mine in a long, challenging stare. We faced each other for several silent moments before he finally spoke.

'She's dead,' he said.

A thrill of horror shot through me. 'Dead?'

'Aye, she is. She's dead.' He dragged the word out slowly with a kind of mournful satisfaction while his eyes still stared into mine.

I swallowed a couple of times. 'Well, I'm sorry to hear that. Truly sorry.'

He nodded grimly and continued to regard me with a peculiar intensity as though he expected me to say more. Then with apparent reluctance he turned away and settled in his seat.

I looked helplessly at the rigid back, at the square, narrow shoulders muffled in a heavy overcoat. Who in God's name was this? And what was he talking about? I knew the face from somewhere — must be a client. And what was dead? Cow? Ewe? Sow? My mind began to race over the cases I had seen during the past week but that face didn't seem to fit in anywhere.

Helen was looking at me questioningly and I managed a wan smile. But the spell was shattered. I started to say something to her when the little man began to turn again with menacing deliberation.

He fixed me once more with a hostile glare. 'Ah don't think there was ever owt wrong with her stomach,' he declared.

'You don't, eh?'

'No, young man, ah don't.' He dragged his eyes unwillingly from my face and turned towards the screen again.

The effect of this second attack was heightened because the lights went off suddenly and an incredible explosion of noise blasted my ear drums. It was the Gaumont News. The sound machine, like the heating system, had apparently been designed for something like the Albert Hall and for a moment I cowered back under the assault. As a voice bellowed details of fortnight-old events I closed my eyes and tried again to place the man in front of me.

I often had trouble identifying people outside their usual environment and had once discussed the problem with Siegfried.

He had been airy. 'There's an easy way, James. Just ask them how they spell their names. You'll have no trouble at all.'

I had tried this on one occasion and the farmer had looked at me strangely, replied 'S-M-I-T-H' and hurried away. So there seemed nothing to do now but sit sweating with my eyes on the disapproving back and search through my memory. When the news finished with a raucous burst of music I had got back about three weeks without result.

There was a blessed respite of a few seconds before the uproar broke out again. This was the main feature — the film about Scotland was on later — and was described outside as a tender love story. I can't remember the title but there was a lot of embracing which would have been all right except that every kiss was accompanied by a chorus of long-drawn sucking noises from the little boys downstairs. The less romantic blew raspberries.

And all the time it got hotter. I opened my jacket wide and unbuttoned my shirt collar but I was beginning to feel decidedly light-headed. The little man in front, still huddled in his heavy coat, seemed unperturbed. Twice the projector broke down and we stared for several minutes at a blank screen while a storm of whistling and stamping came up from the stalls.

Maggie Robinson, standing in the dim light by the curtain, still appeared to be fascinated by the sight of Helen and me. Whenever I looked up I found her eyes fixed upon us with a knowing leer. About half-way through the film, however, her concentration was disturbed by a commotion on the other side of the curtain and she was suddenly brushed aside as a large form burst through.

With a feeling of disbelief I recognised Gobber Newhouse. I had had previous experience of his disregard of the licensing laws and it was clear he had been at it again. He spent most afternoons in the back rooms of the local pubs and here he was, come to relax after a rough session.

He reeled up the aisle, turned, to my dismay, into our row, rested briefly on Helen's lap, trod on my toe and finally spread his enormous carcass over the seat on my left. Fortunately it was another courting seat with no central arm to get in his way but for all that he had great difficulty in finding a comfortable position. He heaved and squirmed about and the wheezing and snuffling and grunting in the darkness might have come from a pen of bacon pigs. But at last he found a spot and with a final cavernous belch composed himself for slumber.

The tender love story never did have much of a chance but Gobber sounded its death knell. With his snores reverberating in my ear and a dense pall of stale beer drifting over me I was unable to appreciate any of the delicate nuances.

It was a relief when the last close-up came to an end and the lights went up. I was a bit worried about Helen. I had noticed as the evening wore on that her lips had a tendency to twitch occasionally and now and then she drew her brows down in a deep frown. I wondered if she was upset. But Maggie appeared providentially with a tray round her neck and stood over us, still leering while I purchased two chocolate ices.

I had taken only one bite when I noticed a stirring under the overcoat in front of me. The little man was returning to the attack. The eyes staring from the grim mask were as chilling as ever.

'Ah knew,' he said. 'Right from start, that

673

you were on the wrong track.'

'Is that so?'

'Aye, I've been among beasts for fifty years and they never go on like that when it's the stomach.'

'Don't they? You're probably right.'

The little man twisted higher in his seat and for a moment I thought he was going to climb over at me. He raised a forefinger. 'For one thing a beast wi' a bad stomach is allus hard in its muck.'

'I see.'

'And if you think back, this un's muck was soft, real soft.'

'Yes, yes, quite,' I said hastily, glancing across at Helen. This was great — just what I needed to complete the romantic atmosphere.

He sniffed and turned away and once again, as if the whole thing had been stage-managed, we were plunged into blackness and the noise blasted out again. I was lying back quivering when it came through to me that something was wrong. What was this strident Western music? Then the title flashed on the screen. Arizona Guns.

I turned to Helen in alarm. 'What's going on? This is supposed to be the Scottish film, isn't it? The one we came to see?'

'It's supposed to be.' Helen paused and looked at me with a half-smile. 'But I'm afraid it isn't going to be. The thing is they often change the supporting film without warning. Nobody seems to mind.'

I slumped wearily in my seat. Well I'd done it again. No dance at the Reniston, wrong picture tonight. I was a genius in my own way.

'I'm sorry,' I said. 'I hope you don't mind too much.'

She shook her head. 'Not a bit. Anyway, let's give this one a chance. It may be all right.'

But as the ancient horse opera crackled out its cliché-ridden message I gave up hope. This was going to be another of those evenings. I watched apathetically as the posse galloped for the fourth time past the same piece of rock and I was totally unprepared for the deafening fusillade of shots which rang out. It made me jump and it even roused Gobber from his sleep.

' 'Ellow! 'ellow! 'ellow!' he bawled jerking upright and thrashing around him with his arms. A backhander on the side of the head drove me violently against Helen's shoulder and I was beginning to apologise when I saw that her twitching and frowning had come on again. But this time it spread and her whole face seemed to break up. She began to laugh, silently and helplessly.

I had never seen a girl laugh like this. It was as though it was something she had wanted to do for a long time. She abandoned herself utterly to it, lying back with her head on the back of the seat, legs stretched out in front of her, arms dangling by her side. She took her time and waited until she had got it all out of her system before she turned to me.

She put her hand on my arm. 'Look,' she said faintly. 'Next time, why don't we just go for a walk?'

I settled down. Gobber was asleep again and his snores, louder than ever, competed with the bangs and howls from the screen. I still hadn't the slightest idea who that little man in front could be and I had the feeling he wasn't finished with me yet. The clock still stood at twenty-past four. Maggie was still staring at us and a steady trickle of sweat ran down my back.

The environment wasn't all I could have desired, but never mind. There was going to be a next time.

CHAPTER 63

Siegfried had a habit of pulling at the lobe of his ear and staring blankly ahead when preoccupied. He was doing it now, his other hand, outstretched, crumbling a crust of bread on his plate.

I didn't usually pry into my boss's meditations and anyway, I wanted to be off on the morning round, but there was something portentous in his face which made me speak.

'What's the matter? Something on your mind?'

Siegfried turned his head slowly and his eyes glared sightlessly for a few moments until recognition dawned. He stopped his lobe-pulling, got to his feet, walked over to the window and looked out at the empty street.

'There is, James, there is indeed. In fact, I was just about to ask your advice. It's about this letter I got this morning.' He ransacked his pockets impatiently, pulling out handkerchiefs, thermometers, crumpled bank-notes, lists of calls, till he found a long blue envelope. 'Here, read it.'

I opened the envelope and quickly scanned the single sheet. I looked up, puzzled. 'Sorry, I don't get it. All it says here is that H. W. St. J. Ransom, Maj. Gen., would like the pleasure of your company at Brawton races on Saturday. No problem there, is there? You like racing.'

'Ah, but it's not so simple as that,' Siegfried said, starting again on the lobe. 'This is in the nature of a trial. General Ransom is one of the big boys in the North West Racing Circuit and he's bringing one of his pals along on Saturday to vet me. They're going to examine me for soundness.'

I must have looked alarmed because he grinned. 'Look, I'd better start at the beginning. And I'll cut it short. The officials of the North West Circuit are looking for a veterinary surgeon to supervise all meetings. You know the local man attends if there's a racecourse in his town and he is on call in case of injury to the horses, but this would be different. This supervisory vet would deal with cases of suspected doping and the like — in fact he'd have to be a bit of a specialist. Well I've had a whisper that they think I might be the man for the job and that's what Saturday's about. I know old Ransom but I haven't met his colleague. The idea is to have a day at the races with me and size me up.'

'If you got the job would it mean giving up general practice?' I asked. And a chill wind seemed to creep around me at the idea.

'No, no, but it would mean spending something like three days a week on racecourses and I'm wondering if that wouldn't be just a bit much.'

'Well, I don't know,' I finished my coffee and pushed back my chair. 'I'm not really the one to advise you on this. I haven't had a lot of experience with racehorses and I'm not interested in racing. You'll have to make up your own mind. But you've often talked of specialising in horse work and you love the atmosphere of a racecourse.'

'You're right there, James, I do. And there's no doubt the extra money would come in very useful. It's what every practice needs — a contract of some sort, a regular income from somewhere to make you less dependent on the farmers paying their bills.' He turned away from the window. 'Anyway, I'll go to Brawton races with them on Saturday and we'll see how it turns out. And you must come too.'

'Me! Why?'

'Well it says in the letter "and partner".'

'That means some woman. They'll have their wives with them, no doubt.'

'Doesn't matter what it means, James, you're coming with me. A day out and a bit of free food and booze will do you good. Tristan can hold the fort for a few hours.'

It was nearly noon on Saturday when I answered the door bell. As I walked along the passage it was easy to identify the people beyond the glass door.

General Ransom was short and square with a moustache of surprising blackness thrusting aggressively from his upper lip. Colonel Tremayne was tall, hawk-nosed and stooping but he shared with his companion the almost tangible aura of authority which comes from a lifetime of command. Two tweedy women stood behind them on the lower step.

I opened the door, feeling my shoulders squaring and my heels coming together under the battery of fierce, unsmiling glares.

'Mr Farnon!' barked the general. 'Expectin' us, I think.'

I retreated a pace and opened the door. 'Oh yes, certainly, please come in.'

The two women swept in first, Mrs Ransom as squat and chunky and even tougher-looking than her husband, then Mrs Tremayne, much younger and attractive in a hard-boiled fashion. All of them completely ignored me except the colonel who brought up the rear and fixed me for a moment with a fishy eye.

I had been instructed to dispense sherry, and once inside the sitting-room I began to pour from a decanter. I was half-way up the second glass when Siegfried walked in. I spilt some of the sherry. My boss had really spruced up for the occasion. His lean frame was draped in cavalry twill of flawless cut; the long, strong-boned face was freshly shaven, the small sandy moustache neatly clipped. He swept off a brand-new bowler as he came in and I put down my decanter and gazed at him with proprietary pride. Maybe there had been a few dukes or the odd earl in Siegfried's family tree but be that as it may, the two army men seemed in an instant to have become low bred and a trifle scruffy.

There was something almost ingratiating in the way the general went up to Siegfried. 'Farnon, me dear feller, how are you? Good to see you again. Let me introduce you to me wife, Mrs Tremayne, Colonel Tremayne.'

The colonel astonishingly dug up a twisted smile, but my main interest was in the re-action of the ladies. Mrs Ransom, looking up at Siegfried as he bent over her, just went to pieces. It was unbelievable that this formi-dable fortress should crumble at the first shot, but there it was; the tough lines melted from her face and she was left with a big sloppy smile looking like anybody's dear old mum.

Mrs Tremayne's response was different but no less dramatic. As the steady grey eyes swept her she seemed to wither and it was as if a spasm of exquisite pain twisted her cheeks. She controlled herself with an effort but looked after Siegfried with wistful hunger as he turned back to the men.

I began to slosh the sherry violently into the glasses. Damn it, there it was again. The same old thing. And yet he didn't do anything. Just looked at them. Hell, it wasn't fair.

Sherry over, we moved outside and installed ourselves in Siegfried's Rover on which an immaculate coach-building job had been done since the disaster of last summer. It was an impressive turnout. The car, after a morning's forced labour by Tristan with hose and leather, shone like a mirror. Siegfried, in the driver's seat, extended an elegant arm to his brother as we drove away. I couldn't help feeling that the only superfluous object was myself, squatting uncomfortably on a little let-down seat, facing the two army men who sat to attention in the back seat, their bowlers pointing rigidly to the front. Between them Mrs Tremayne stared wonderingly at the back of Siegfried's head.

We lunched on the course, Siegfried comfortably at home with the smoked salmon, the cold chicken and the champagne. There was no doubt he had scored a tremendous success during the meal, discussing racing knowledgeably with the men and dispensing charm equally to their wives. The tough Mrs Ransom positively simpered as he marked her card for her. It was quite certain that if the new appointment hung upon his behaviour today, a vote at this time would have seen him home and dry.

After lunch we went down to the paddock and had a look at the horses parading for the first race. I could see Siegfried expanding as he took in the scene; the jostling crowds, the shouting bookies, the beautiful animals pacing round, the jockeys, tiny, colourful, durable, chatting to the trainers out in the middle. He had got through enough champagne at lunch to sharpen his appreciation and he was the very picture of a man who just knew he was going to have a successful day.

Merryweather, the course vet, joined us to watch the first race. Siegfried knew him slightly and they were chatting after the race when the 'vet wanted' sign went up. A man hurried up to Merryweather. 'That horse that slipped at the last bend is still down and doesn't look like getting up.'

The vet started for his car which was parked in readiness near the rails. He turned towards us 'You two want to come?' Siegfried looked enquiringly at his party and received gracious nods of assent. We hurried after our colleague.

Within seconds we were racing down the course towards the last bend. Merryweather, hanging on to the wheel as we sped over the grass, grunted half to himself: 'Hell, I hope this thing hasn't got a fracture — if there's one thing I mortally hate it's shooting horses.'

It didn't look good when we got to the spot. The sleek animal lay flat on its side showing no movement apart from the laboured rise and fall of its ribs. The jockey, blood streaming from a cut brow, knelt by its head. 'What do you think, sir? Has he broken a leg?'

'Let's have a look.' Merryweather began to palpate the extended limbs, running strong fingers over one bone then another, carefully flexing the joints of fetlock, knee, shoulder, hock. 'Nothing wrong there. Certainly no fracture.' Then he pointed suddenly at the head. 'Look at his eyes.'

We looked; they were glazed and there was a slight but unmistakable nystagmus.

'Concussion?' Siegfried said.

'That's it, he's just had a bang on the head.' Merryweather got off his knees, looking happier. 'Come on, we'll push him on to his chest. I think he ought to be able to get up with a bit of help.'

There were plenty of helpers from the crowd and the horse was rolled easily till he rested on his sternum, forelegs extended forward. After a couple of minutes in this position he struggled to his feet and stood swaying slightly. A stable lad walked him away.

Merryweather laughed. 'Well, that wasn't

so bad. Good horse that. I think he'll be all right after a rest.'

Siegfried had started to reply when we heard a 'Psst, psst!' from beyond the rails. We looked up and saw a stout, red-faced figure gesturing at us eagerly. 'Hey! Hey!' it was saying. 'Come over here a minute.'

We went over. There was something about the face which Siegfried seemed to find intriguing. He looked closer at the grinning, pudgy features, the locks of oily black hair falling over the brow and cried out in delight.

'God help us! Stewie Brannon! Here, James, come and meet another colleague — we came through college together.'

Siegfried had told me a lot about Stewie Brannon. So much, in fact, that I seemed to be shaking hands with an old, well-remembered friend. Sometimes, when the mood was on us, Siegfried and I would sit up nearly till dawn over a bottle in the big room at Skeldale House chewing over old times and recalling the colourful characters we had known. I remembered he had told me he had overtaken Stewie about half way through the course and had qualified while Stewie was still battling in his third year. Siegfried had described him as totally unambitious, averse to study, disinclined to wash or shave; in fact, his idea of the young man least likely to suc-ceed. But there had been something touching about him; the ingenuousness of a child, a

685

huge, all-embracing affection for his fellow humans, an impregnable cheerfulness.

Siegfried called over to Merryweather. 'Will you give my apologies to my friends when you go back? There's a chap here I have to see — I'll only be a few minutes.'

Merryweather waved, got into his car and drove back up the course as we ducked under the rails.

Siegfried seized the bulky figure by the arm. 'Come on, Stewie, where can we get a drink?'

CHAPTER 64

We went into a long, low bar under the stand and I experienced a slight shock of surprise. This was the four and sixpenny end and the amenities were rather different from the paddock. The eating and drinking was done mainly in the vertical position and the cuisine seemed to consist largely of pies and sausage rolls.

Siegfried fought his way to the bar and collected three whiskies. We sat down at one of the few available tables — an unstable, metal-topped structure. At the next table a sharp faced character studied the *Pink 'Un* while he took great swigs at a pint and tore savagely at a pork pie.

'Now, my lad,' Siegfried said. 'What have you been doing for the past six years?'

'Well, let's see,' said Stewie, absently downing his whisky at a gulp. 'I got into finals shortly after you left and I didn't do so bad at all, really. Pipped them both first go, then I had a bit of bother with surgery a couple of times, but I was launched on the unsuspecting animal population four years ago. I've been around quite a lot since then. North, South, even six months in Ireland. I've been trying to find a place with a living wage. This three or four quid a week lark isn't much cop when you have a family to keep.'

'Family? You're married then?'

'Not half. You remember little Meg Hamilton — I used to bring her to the college dances. We got married when I got into final year. We've got five kids now and another on the way.'

Siegfried choked on his whisky. 'Five kids! For God's sake, Stewie!'

'Ah, it's wonderful really, Siegfried. You probably wonder how we manage to exist. Well I couldn't tell you. I don't know myself. But we've kept one jump ahead of ruin and we've been happy, too. I think we're going to be O.K. now. I stuck up my plate in Hensfield a few months ago and I'm doing all right. Been able to clear the housekeeping and that's all that matters.'

'Hensfield, eh?' Siegfried said. I pictured the grim West Riding town. A wilderness of decaying brick bristling with factory chimneys. It was the other Yorkshire. 'Mainly small animal, I suppose?'

'Oh yes. I earn my daily bread almost entirely by separating the local torn cats from their knackers. Thanks to me, the feline females of Hensfield can walk the streets unmolested.'

Siegfried laughed and caught the only waitress in the place lightly by the arm as she hurried by. She whipped round with a frown and an angry word but took another look and smiled. 'Yes, sir?'

Siegfried looked into her face seriously for a few moments, still holding her arm. Then he spoke quietly. 'I wonder if you'd be kind enough to bring us three large whiskies and keep repeating the order whenever you see our glasses are empty. Would you be able to do that?'

'Certainly, sir, of course.' The waitress was over forty but she was blushing like a young girl.

Stewie's chins quivered with silent laugher. 'You old bugger, Farnon. It does me good to see you haven't changed.'

'Really? Well that's rather nice, isn't it?'

'And the funny thing is I don't think you really try.'

'Try? Try what?'

'Ah, nothing. Forget it — here's our whisky.'

As the drinks kept coming they talked and talked. I didn't butt in — I sat listening, wrapped in a pleasant euphoria and pushing every other glassful unobtrusively round to Stewie who put it out of sight with a careless jerk of the wrist.

As Siegfried sketched out his own progress,

I was struck by the big man's total absence of envy. He was delighted to hear about the rising practice, the pleasant house, the assistant. Siegfried had described him as plump in the old days but he was fat now, despite his hard times. And I had heard about that overcoat; it was the 'navy nap' which had been his only protection through the years at college. It couldn't have looked so good then, but it was a sad thing now, the seams strained to bursting by the bulging flesh.

'Look, Stewie.' Siegfried fumbled uncomfortably with his glass. 'I'm sure you're going to do well at Hensfield but if by some mischance things got a bit rough, I hope you wouldn't hesitate to turn to me. I'm not so far off in Darrowby, you know. In fact.' He paused and swallowed. 'Are you all right now? If a few quid would help, I've got 'em here.'

Stewie tossed back what must have been the tenth double whisky and gazed at his old friend with gentle benevolence. 'You're a kind old bugger, Siegfried, but no thanks. As I said we're clearing the housekeeping and we'll be O.K. But I appreciate it — you always were kind. A strange old bugger, but kind.'

'Strange?' Siegfried was interested.

'No, not strange. Wrong word. Different, That's it, you were as different as hell.'

'Different?' queried Siegfried, swallowing his whisky as if it had stopped tasting of

690

anything a long time ago. 'I'm sure you're wrong there, Stewie.'

'Don't worry your head about it,' Stewie said, and reached across the table to thump his friend on the shoulder. But his judgement was way out and instead he swept Siegfried's bowler from his head. It rolled to the feet of the man at the next table.

During the conversation I had been aware of this gentleman rushing out and trailing slowly back to resume his study of the *Pink 'Un* and renew his attack on the food and drink. The man looked down at the hat. His face was a picture of misery and frustration born of too much beer, semi-masticated pork pies and unwise investment. Convulsively he lashed out with a foot at the bowler and looked better immediately.

The hat, deeply dented, soared back to Siegfried who caught it and replaced it on his head with unruffled aplomb. He didn't seem in the least annoyed; apparently considered the man's reaction perfectly normal.

We all stood up and I was mildly surprised by a slight swaying and blurring of my surroundings. When things came to rest I had another surprise; the big bar was nearly empty. The beer machines were hidden by white cloths. The barmaids were collecting the empty glasses.

'Stewie,' Siegfried said. 'The meeting's over. Do you realise we've been nattering here for over two hours?'

'And very nice, too. Far better than giving the hard-earned coppers to the bookies.' As Stewie rose to his feet he clutched at the table and stood blinking for a few seconds.

'There's one thing, though,' Siegfried said. 'My friends. I came here with a party and they must be wondering where I've got to. Tell you what, come and meet them. They'll understand when they realise we haven't seen each other for years.'

We worked our way round to the paddock. No sign of the general and company. We finally found them in the car park grouped unsmilingly around the Rover. Most of the other cars had gone. Siegfried strode up confidently, his dented bowler cocked at a jaunty angle.

'I'm sorry to have left you but a rather wonderful thing happened back there. I would like to present Mr Stewart Brannon, a professional colleague and a very dear friend.'

Four blank stares turned on Stewie. His big, meaty face was redder than ever and he smiled sweetly through a faint dew of perspiration. I noticed that he had made a lopsided job of buttoning the navy nap overcoat; there was a spare button hole at the top and a lack of alignment at the bottom. It made the straining, tortured garment look even more grotesque.

The general nodded curtly, the colonel appeared to be grinding his teeth, the ladies froze visibly and looked away.

'Yes, yes, quite,' grunted the general. 'But we've been waitin' here some time and we want to be gettin' home.' He stuck out his jaw and his moustache bristled.

Siegfried waved a hand. 'Certainly, certainly, by all means. We'll leave right away.' He turned to Stewie. 'Well, goodbye for now, my lad. We'll get together again soon. I'll ring you.'

He began to feel through his pockets for his ignition key. He started quite slowly but gradually stepped up his pace. After he had explored the pockets about five times he stopped, closed his eyes and appeared to give himself over to intense thought. Then, as though he had decided to do the thing systematically, he commenced to lay out the contents of his pockets one by one, using the car bonnet as a table, and as the pile grew so did my conviction that doom was very near.

It wasn't just the key that worried me. Siegfried had consumed a lot more whisky than I had and with its usual delayed action it had begun to creep up on him. He was swaying slightly, his dented bowler had slid forward over one eyebrow and he kept dropping things as he pulled them from his pocket and examined them owlishly.

A man with a long brush and a handcart was walking slowly across the car park when

Siegfried grabbed his arm. 'Look, I want you to do something for me. Here's five bob.'

'Right, mister.' The man pocketed the money. 'What d'you want me to do?'

'Find my car key.'

The man began to peer round Siegfried's feet. 'I'll do me best. Dropped it round 'ere, did you?'

'No, no. I've no idea where I dropped it.' Siegfried waved vaguely. 'It's somewhere on the course.'

The man looked blank for a moment then he gazed out over the acres of littered ground, the carpet of discarded race cards, torn up tickets. He turned back to Siegfried and giggled suddenly then he walked away, still giggling.

I stole a glance at our companions. They had watched the search in stony silence and none of them seemed to be amused. The general was the first to explode.

'Great heavens, Farnon, have you got the blasted key or haven't you? If the damn thing's lost, then we'd better make other arrangements. Can't keep the ladies standing around here.'

A gentle cough sounded in the background. Stewie was still there. He shambled forward and whispered in his friend's ear and after a moment Siegfried wrung his hand fervently.

'By God, Stewie, that's kind of you! You've saved the situation.' He turned back to the party. 'There's nothing to worry about — Mr Brannon has kindly offered to provide us with transport. He's gone to get his car from the other park.' He pointed triumphantly at the shiny back of the bulging navy overcoat navigating unsteadily through the gate.

Siegfried did his best to keep a conversation going but it was hard slogging. Nobody replied to any of his light sallies and he stopped abruptly when he saw a look of rage and disbelief spread over the general's face. Stewie had come back.

The car was a tiny Austin Seven dwarfed even further by the massive form in the driver's seat. I judged from the rusted maroon paintwork and cracked windows that it must be one of the very earliest models, a 'tourer' whose hood had long since disintegrated and been replaced by a home-made canvas cover fastened to the twisted struts by innumerable loops of string.

Stewie struggled out, dragged open the passenger door and inclined his head with modest pride. He motioned towards a pile of sacks which lay on the bare boards where the passenger seat should have been; there were no seats in the back either, only a couple of rough wooden boxes bearing coloured labels with the legend 'Finest American Apples'. From the boxes peeped a jumble of medicine bottles, stethoscopes, powders, syringe cases.

'I thought,' said Stewie. 'If we put the sacks on top of the boxes . . .'

The general didn't let him finish. 'Dammit, is this supposed to be a joke?' His face was brick red and the veins on his neck were swelling dangerously. 'Are you tryin' to insult me friend and these ladies? You want horsewhippin' for this afternoon's work, Farnon. That's what you want — horsewhippin'!'

He was halted by a sudden roar from the Rover's engine. The colonel, a man of resource as befitted his rank, had shorted the ignition. Fortunately the doors were not locked.

The ladies took their places in the back with the colonel and I slunk miserably on to my little seat. The general had regained control of himself. 'Get in! I'll drive!' he barked at Siegfried as though addressing an erring lance corporal.

But Siegfried held up a restraining hand. 'Just one moment,' he slurred. 'The windscreen is very dirty. I'll give it a rub for you.'

The ladies watched him silently as he weaved round to the back of the car and began to rummage in the boot. The love light had died from their eyes. I don't know why he took the trouble; possibly it was because, through the whisky mists, he felt he must reestablish himself as a competent and helpful member of the party.

But the effort fell flat; the effect was entirely

spoiled He was polishing the glass with a dead hen.

It was a couple of weeks later, again at the breakfast table that Siegfried, reading the morning paper with his third cup of coffee, called out to me.

'Ah, I see Herbert Jarvis M.R.C.V.S., one time Captain R.A.V.C., has been appointed to the North West Circuit as supervisory veterinary surgeon. I know Jarvis. Nice chap. Just the man for the job.'

I looked across at my boss for some sign of disappointment or regret. I saw none.

Siegfried put down his cup, wiped his lips on his napkin and sighed contentedly. 'You know, James, everything happens for the best. Old Stewie was sent by providence or heaven or anything you like. I was never meant to get that job and I'd have been as miserable as hell if I had got it. Come on, lad, let's get off into those hills.'

CHAPTER 65

After my night at the cinema with Helen I just seemed to drift naturally into the habit of dropping in to see her on an occasional evening. And before I knew what was happening I had developed a pattern; around eight o'clock my feet began to make of their own accord for Heston Grange. Of course I fought the impulse — I didn't go every night; there was my work which often occupied me round the clock, there was a feeling of propriety, and there was Mr Alderson.

Helen's father was a vague little man who had withdrawn into himself to a great extent since his wife's death a few years ago. He was an expert stocksman and his farm could compare with the best, but a good part of his mind often seemed to be elsewhere. And he had acquired some little peculiarities; when things weren't going well he carried on long muttered conversations with himself, but when he was particularly pleased about something he was inclined to break into a loud, tuneless humming. It was a penetrating sound and on my professional visits I could often locate him by tracking down this characteristic droning among the farm buildings.

At first when I came to see Helen I'm sure he never even noticed me — I was just one of the crowd of young men who hung around his daughter; but as time went on and my visits became more frequent he suddenly seemed to become conscious of me, and began to regard me with an interest which deepened rapidly into alarm. I couldn't blame him, really. He was devoted to Helen and it was natural that he should desire a grand match for her. And there was at least one such in the offing — young Richard Edmundson, whose father was an old friend of the Aldersons and farmed nearly a thousand acres. They were rich, powerful people and Richard was very keen indeed. Compared with him, an unknown, impecunious young vet was a poor bargain.

When Mr Alderson was around, my visits were uncomfortable affairs. We always seemed to be looking at each other out of the corners of our eyes; whenever I glanced his way he was invariably in the act of averting his gaze, and I must admit that if he looked over at me suddenly I couldn't help switching my eyes away.

It was a pity because I instinctively liked

him. He had an amiable, completely inoffensive nature which was very appealing and under other conditions we would have got along very well. But there was no getting round the fact that he resented me. And it wasn't because he wanted to hang on to Helen — he was an unselfish man and anyway, he had an excellent housekeeper in his sister who had been recently widowed and had come to live with the Aldersons. Auntie Lucy was a redoubtable character and was perfectly capable of running the household and looking after the two younger children. It was just that he had got used to the comfortable assumption that one day his daughter would marry the son of his old friend and have a life of untroubled affluence; and he had a stubborn streak which rebelled fiercely against any prospect of change.

So it was always a relief when I got out of the house with Helen. Everything was right then; we went to the little dances in the village institutes, we walked for miles along the old grassy mine tracks among the hills, or sometimes she came on my evening calls with me. There wasn't anything spectacular to do in Darrowby but there was a complete lack of strain, a feeling of being self-sufficient in a warm existence of our own that made everything meaningful and worthwhile.

Things might have gone on like this indefinitely but for a conversation I had with

Siegfried. We were sitting in the big room at Skeldale House as we often did before bed-time, talking over the day's events, when he laughed and slapped his knee.

'I had old Harry Forster in tonight paying his bill. He was really funny — sat looking round the room and saying, "It's a nice little nest you have here, Mr Farnon, a nice little nest," and then, very sly, "It's time there was a bird in this nest, you know, there should be a little bird in here."'

I laughed too. 'Well, you should be used to it by now. You're the most eligible bachelor in Darrowby. People are always having a dig at you — they won't be happy till they've got you married off.'

'Wait a minute, not so fast.' Siegfried eyed me thoughtfully. 'I don't think for a moment that Harry was talking about me; it was you he had in mind.'

'What do you mean?'

'Well, just think. Didn't you say you had run into the old boy one night when you were walking over his land with Helen? He'd be on to a thing like that in a flash. He thinks it's time you were hitched up, that's all.'

I lay back in my chair and gave myself over to laughter. 'Me! Married! That'll be the day. Can you imagine it? Poor old Harry.'

Siegfried leaned forward. 'What are you laughing at, James? He's quite right — it's time you were married.'

'What's that?' I looked at him incredulously. 'What are you on about now?'

'It's quite simple,' he said. 'I'm saying you ought to get married, and soon.'

'Oh come on, Siegfried, you're joking!'

'Why should I be?'

'Well, damn it, I'm only starting my career, I've no money, no nothing. I've never even thought about it.'

'You've never even . . . well tell me this, are you courting Helen Alderson or aren't you?'

'Well I'm . . . I've been . . . oh I suppose you could call it that.'

Siegfried settled back comfortably on his chair, put his fingertips together and assumed a judicial expression. 'Good, good. You admit you're courting the girl. Now let us take it a step further. She is, from my own observation, extremely attractive — in fact she nearly causes a traffic pileup when she walks across the cobbles on market day. It's common knowledge that she is intelligent, equable and an excellent cook. Perhaps you would agree with this?'

'Of course I would,' I said, nettled at his superior air. 'But what's this all about? Why are you going on like a high court judge?'

'I'm only trying to establish my point, James, which is that you seem to have an ideal wife lined up and you are doing nothing about it. In fact, not to put too fine a point on it, I wish you'd stop playing around and let us see a little action.'

'But it's not as simple as that,' I said, my voice rising. 'I've told you already I'd have to be a lot better off, and anyway, give me a chance, I've only been going to the house for a few weeks — surely you don't start thinking of getting married as soon as that. And there's another thing — her old man doesn't like me.'

Siegfried put his head on one side and I gritted my teeth as a saintly expression began to settle on his face. 'Now old lad, don't get angry, but there's something I have to tell you for your own good. Caution is often a virtue, but in your case you carry it too far. It's a little flaw in your character and it shows in a multitude of ways. In your wary approach to problems in your work, for instance — you are always too apprehensive, proceeding fearfully step by step when you should be plunging boldly ahead. You keep seeing dangers when there aren't any — you've got to learn to take a chance, to lash out a bit. As it is, you are confined to a narrow range of activity by your own doubts.'

'The original stick-in-the-mud in fact, eh?'

'Oh come now, James, I didn't say that, but while we're talking, there's another small point I want to bring up. I know you won't mind my saying this. Until you get married I'm afraid I shall fail to get the full benefit of your assistance in the practice because frankly you are becoming increasingly besotted and bemused to the extent that I'm sure you don't know what you're doing half the time.'

'What the devil are you talking about? I've never heard such . . .'

'Kindly hear me out, James. What I'm saying is perfectly true — you're walking about like a man in a dream and you've developed a disturbing habit of staring into space when I'm talking to you. There's only one cure, my boy.'

'And it's a simple little cure, isn't it!' I shouted. 'No money, no home, but leap into matrimony with a happy cry. There's not a thing to worry about!'

'Ah-ah, you see, there you go again, looking for difficulties.' He gave a light laugh and gazed at me with pitying affection. 'No money, you say. Well one of these days you'll be a partner here. Your plate will be out on those railings in front of the house, so you'll never be short of your daily bread. And as regards a home — look at all the empty rooms in this house. You could set up a private suite upstairs without any trouble. So that's just a piffling little detail.'

I ran my hand distractedly through my hair. My head was beginning to swim. 'You make it all sound so easy.'

'But it IS easy!' Siegfried shot upright in his chair. 'Go out and ask that girl without further delay and get her into church before the month is out!' He wagged a finger at me. 'Learn to grasp the nettle of life, James. Throw off your hesitant ways and remember' — he clenched his fist and struck an attitude — 'there is a tide in the affairs of men which, taken at the flood . . .'

'O.K., O.K.,' I said, rising wearily from my chair, 'that's enough, I get the message. I'm going to bed now.'

I don't suppose I am the first person to have had his life fundamentally influenced by one of Siegfried's chance outbursts. I thought his opinions ridiculous at the time but he planted a seed which germinated and flowered almost overnight. There is no doubt he is responsible for the fact that I was the father of a grown-up family while I was still a young man, because when I brought the subject up with Helen she said yes, she'd like to marry me and we set our eyes on an early date. She seemed surprised at first — maybe she had the same opinion of me as Siegfried and expected it would take me a few years to get off the ground.

Anyway, before I had time to think much more about it everything was neatly settled and I found I had made a magical transition from jeering at the whole idea to making plans for furnishing our prospective bedsitter at Skeldale House.

It was a blissful time with only one cloud

on the horizon; but that cloud bulked large and forbidding. As I walked hand in hand with Helen, my thoughts in the air, she kept bringing me back to earth with an appealing look.

'You know, Jim, you'll really have to speak to Dad. It's time he knew.'

CHAPTER 66

I had been warned long before I qualified that country practice was a dirty, stinking job. I had accepted the fact and adjusted myself to it but there were times when this side of my life obtruded itself and became almost insupportable. Like now, when even after a long hot bath I still smelt.

As I hoisted myself from the steaming water I sniffed at my arm and there it was; the malodorous memory of that horrible cleansing at Tommy Dearlove's striking triumphantly through all the soap and antiseptic, almost as fresh and pungent as it had been at four o'clock this afternoon. Nothing but time would remove it.

But something in me rebelled at the idea of crawling into bed in this state and I looked with something like desperation along the row of bottles on the bathroom shelf. I stopped at Mrs Hall's bath salts, shining violent pink in their big glass jar. This was something I'd never tried before and I tipped a small handful into the water round my feet. For a moment my head swam as the rising steam was suddenly charged with an aggressive sweetness then on an impulse I shook most of the jar's contents into the bath and lowered myself once more under the surface.

For a long time I lay there smiling to myself in triumph as the oily liquid lapped around me. Not even Tommy Dearlove's cleansing could survive this treatment.

The whole process had a stupefying effect on me and I was half asleep even as I sank back on the pillow. There followed a few moments of blissful floating before a delicious slumber claimed me. And when the bedside phone boomed in my ear the sense of injustice and personal affront was even stronger than usual. Blinking sleepily at the clock which said 1.15 a.m. I lifted the receiver and mumbled into it, but I was jerked suddenly wide awake when I recognised Mr Alderson's voice. Candy was calving and something was wrong. Would I come right away?

There has always been a 'this is where I came in' feeling about a night call. And as my lights swept the cobbles of the deserted market place it was there again, a sense of returning to fundamentals, of really being me. The silent houses, the tight-drawn curtains, the long, empty street giving way to the stone walls of the country road flipping endlessly past on either side. At these times I was usually in a state of suspended animation, just sufficiently awake to steer the car in the right direction, but tonight I was fully alert, my mind ticking over anxiously.

Because Candy was something special. She was the house cow, a pretty little Jersey and Mr Alderson's particular pet. She was the sole member of her breed in the herd but whereas the milk from the shorthorns went into the churns to be collected by the big dairy, Candy's rich yellow offering found its way on to the family porridge every morning or appeared heaped up on trifles and fruit pies or was made into butter, a golden creamy butter to make you dream.

But apart from all that, Mr Alderson just liked the animal. He usually stopped opposite her on his way down the byre and began to hum to himself and gave her tall head a brief scratch as he passed. And I couldn't blame him because I sometimes wish all cows were Jerseys: small, gentle, doe-eyed creatures you could push around without any trouble; with padded corners and fragile limbs. Even if they kicked you it was like a love tap compared with the clump from a craggy Friesian.

I just hoped it would be something simple with Candy, because my stock wasn't high with Mr Alderson and I had a nervous conviction that he wouldn't react favourably if I started to make a ham-fisted job of calving his little favourite. I shrugged away my fears; obstetrics in the Jersey was usually easy.

Helen's father was an efficient farmer. As I pulled up in the yard I could see into the lighted loose box where two buckets of water were steaming in readiness for me. A towel was draped over the half door and Stan and Bert, the two long-serving cowmen, were standing alongside their boss. Candy was lying comfortably in deep straw. She wasn't straining and there was nothing visible at the vulva but the cow had a preoccupied, inward look as though all was not well with her.

I closed the door behind me. 'Have you had a feel inside her, Mr Alderson?'

'Aye, I've had me hand in and there's nowt there.'

'Nothing at all?'

'Not a thing. She'd been on for a few hours and not showing so I popped me hand in and there's no head, no legs, nowt. And not much room, either. That's when I rang you.'

This sounded very strange. I hung my jacket on a nail and began thoughtfully to unbutton my shirt. It was when I was pulling it over my head that I noticed Mr Alderson's nose wrinkling. The farm men, too, began to sniff and look at each other wonderingly. Mrs Hall's bath salts, imprisoned under my clothing, had burst from their bondage in a sickly wave, filling the enclosed space with their strident message. Hurriedly I began to wash my arms in the hope that the alien odour might pass away but it seemed to get worse, welling from my warm skin, competing incongruously with the honest smells of cow, hay and straw. Nobody said anything. These men weren't the type to make the ribald remark which would have enabled me to laugh the thing off. There was no ambiguity about this scent; it was voluptuously feminine and Bert and Stan stared at me open-mouthed. Mr Alderson, his mouth turned down at the corners, his nostrils still twitching, kept his eyes fixed on the far wall.

Cringing inwardly I knelt behind the cow and in a moment my embarrassment was forgotten. The vagina was empty; a smooth passage narrowing rapidly to a small, ridged opening just wide enough to admit my hand. Beyond I could feel the feet and head of a calf. My spirits plummeted. Torsion of the uterus. There was going to be no easy victory for me here.

I sat back on my heels and turned to the farmer. 'She's got a twisted calf bed. There's a live calf in there all right but there's no way out for it — I can barely get my hand through.'

'Aye, I thought it was something peculiar.' Mr Alderson rubbed his chin and looked at me doubtfully. 'What can we do about it, then?'

'We'll have to try to correct the twist by rolling the cow over while I keep hold of the calf. It's a good job there's plenty of us here.'

'And that'll put everything right, will it?'

I swallowed. I didn't like these jobs. Sometimes rolling worked and sometimes it didn't and in those days we hadn't quite got round to performing caesareans on cows. If I was unsuccessful I had the prospect of telling Mr Alderson to send Candy to the butcher. I banished the thought quickly.

'It'll put everything right,' I said. It had to. I stationed Bert at the front legs, Stan at the hind and had the farmer holding the cow's head on the floor. Then I stretched myself on the hard concrete, pushed in a hand and grasped the calf's foot.

'Now roll her,' I gasped, and the men pulled the legs round in a clockwise direction. I held fiercely to the little foot as the cow flopped on to her other side. Nothing seemed to be happening inside.

'Push her on to her chest,' I panted.

Stan and Bert expertly tucked the legs under the cow and rolled her on to her brisket and as she settled there I gave a yell of pain.

'Get her back, quick! We're going the wrong way!' The smooth band of tissue had tightened on my wrist in a numbing grip of frightening power. For a moment I had the panicky impression that I'd never get out of there again.

But the men worked like lightning. Within

seconds Candy was stretched out on her original side, the pressure was off my arm and we were back where we started.

I gritted my teeth and took a fresh grip on the calf's foot. 'O.K., try her the other way.'

This time the roll was anti-clockwise and we went through 180 degrees without anything happening. I only just kept my grasp on the foot — the resistance this time was tremendous. Taking a breather for a few seconds I lay face down while the sweat sprang out on my back, sending out fresh exotic vapours from the bath salts.

'Right. One more go!' I cried and the men hauled the cow further over.

And oh it was beautiful to feel everything magically unravelling and my arm lying free in a wide uterus with all the room in the world and the calf already beginning to slide towards me.

Candy summed up the situation immediately and for the first time gave a determined heaving strain. Sensing victory just round the corner she followed up with another prolonged effort which popped the calf wet and wriggling into my arms.

'By gum, it was quick at t'finish,' Mr Alderson murmured wonderingly. He seized a wisp of hay and began to dry off the little creature.

Thankfully I soaped my arms in one of the buckets. After every delivery there is a feeling of relief but in this case it was overwhelming.

It no longer mattered that the loose box smelt like a ladies' hairdressing salon, I just felt good. I said good night to Bert and Stan as they returned to their beds, giving a final incredulous sniff as they passed me. Mr Alderson was pottering about, having a word with Candy, then starting again on the calf which he had already rubbed down several times. He seemed fascinated by it. And I couldn't blame him because it was like something out of Disney; a pale gold fawn, unbelievably tiny with large dark limpid eyes and an expression of trusting innocence. It was a heifer, too.

The farmer lifted it as if it were a whippet dog and laid it by its mother's head. Candy nosed the little animal over, rumbling happily in her throat, then she began to lick it. I watched Mr Alderson. He was standing, hands clasped behind him, rocking backwards and forwards on his heels, obviously enchanted by the scene. Any time now, I thought. And I was right; the tuneless humming broke out, even louder than usual, like a joyful paean.

I stiffened in my Wellingtons. There would never be a better time. After a nervous cough I spoke up firmly.

'Mr Alderson,' I said and he half turned his head. 'I would like to marry your daughter.'

The humming was switched off abruptly and he turned slowly till he was facing me.

He didn't speak but his eyes searched my face unhappily. Then he bent stiffly, picked up the buckets one by one, tipped out the water and made for the door.

'You'd better come in the house,' he said.

The farmhouse kitchen looked lost and forsaken with the family abed. I sat in a high-backed wooden chair by the side of the empty hearth while Mr Alderson put away his buckets, hung up the towel and washed his hands methodically at the sink, then he pottered through to the parlour and I heard him bumping and clinking about in the sideboard. When he reappeared he bore a tray in front of him on which a bottle of whisky and two glasses rattled gently. The tray lent the simple procedure an air of formality which was accentuated by the heavy cut crystal of the glasses and the virgin, unopened state of the bottle.

Mr Alderson set the tray down on the kitchen table which he dragged nearer to us before settling in the chair at the other side of the fireplace. Nobody said anything. I waited in the lengthening silence while he peered at the cap of the bottle like a man who had never seen one before then unscrewed it with slow apprehension as though he feared it might blow up in his face.

Finally he poured out two measures with the utmost gravity and precision, ducking his head frequently to compare the levels in the two glasses, and with a last touch of ceremony proffered the laden tray.

I took my drink and waited expectantly.

Mr Alderson looked into the lifeless fireplace for a minute or two then he directed his gaze upwards at the oil painting of the paddling cows which hung above the mantelpiece. He pursed his lips as though about to whistle but appeared to change his mind and without salutation took a gulp of his whisky which sent him into a paroxysm of coughing from which it took him some time to recover. When his breathing had returned to normal he sat up straight and fixed me with two streaming eyes. He cleared his throat and I felt a certain tension.

'Aye well,' he said, 'it's grand hay weather.'

I agreed with him and he looked round the kitchen with the interested stare of a total stranger. Having completed his inspection he took another copious swallow from his glass, grimaced, closed his eyes, shook his head violently a few times, then leaned forward.

'Mind you,' he said, 'a night's rain would do a lot o' good.'

I gave my opinion that it undoubtedly would and the silence fell again. It lasted even longer this time and my host kept drinking his whisky as though he was getting used to it. And I could see that it was having a relaxing effect; the strained lines on his face were beginning to smooth out and his eyes were losing their hunted look.

Nothing more was said until he had replenished our glasses, balancing the amounts meticulously again. He took a sip at his second measure then he looked down at the rug and spoke in a small voice.

'James,' he said, 'I had a wife in a thousand.'

I was so surprised I hardly knew what to say. 'Yes, I know,' I murmured. 'I've heard a lot about her.'

Mr Alderson went on, still looking down, his voice full of gentle yearning.

'Aye, she was the grandest lass for miles around and the bonniest.' He looked up at me suddenly with the ghost of a smile. 'Nobody thought she'd ever have a feller like me, you know. But she did.' He paused and looked away. 'Aye, she did.'

He began to tell me about his dead wife. He told me calmly, without self-pity, but with a wistful gratitude for the happiness he had known. And I discovered that Mr Alderson was different from a lot of the farmers of his generation because he said nothing about her being a 'good worker'. So many of the women of those times seemed to be judged mainly on their working ability and when I had first come to Darrowby I had been shocked when I commiserated with a newly-widowed old man. He had brushed a tear from his eye and said 'Aye, she was a grand worker.'

But Mr Alderson said only that his wife had

been beautiful, that she had been kind, and that he had loved her very much. He talked about Helen, too, about the things she had said and done when she was a little girl, about how very like her mother she was in every way. He never said anything about me but I had the feeling all the time that he meant it to concern me; and the very fact that he was talking so freely seemed a sign that the barriers were coming down.

Actually he was talking a little too freely. He was half way down his third huge whisky and in my experience Yorkshiremen just couldn't take the stuff. I had seen burly ten-pint men from the local pubs keel over after a mere sniff at the amber fluid and little Mr Alderson hardly drank at all. I was getting worried.

But there was nothing I could do, so I let him ramble on happily. He was lying right back in his chair now, completely at ease, his eyes, alight with his memories, gazing somewhere above my head. In fact I am convinced he had forgotten I was there because after one long passage he dropped his eyes, caught sight of me and stared for a moment without recognition. When he did manage to place me it seemed to remind him of his duties as a host. But as he reached again for the bottle he caught sight of the clock on the wall.

'Well dang it, it's four o'clock. We've been here long enough. It's hardly worth goin' to bed, but I suppose we'd better have an hour or two's sleep.' He tipped the last of the whisky down his throat, jumped briskly to his feet, looked around him for a few moments in a business-like sort of way then pitched head first with a sickening clatter among the fire irons.

Frozen with horror, I started forward to help the small figure scrabbling on the hearth but I needn't have worried because he bounced back to his feet in a second or two and looked me in the eye as if nothing had happened.

'Well, I'd better be off,' I said. 'Thanks for the drink.' There was no point in staying longer as I realised that the chances of Mr Alderson saying 'Bless you, my son,' or anything like that were remote. But I had a comforting impression that all was going to be well.

As I made my way to the door the farmer made a creditable attempt to usher me out but his direction was faulty and he tacked helplessly away from me across the kitchen floor before collapsing against a tall dresser. From under a row of willow pattern dinner plates his face looked at me with simple bewilderment.

I hesitated then turned back. 'I'll just walk up the stairs with you, Mr Alderson,' I said in a matter-of-fact voice and the little man made no resistance as I took his arm and guided him towards the door in the far corner.

As we creaked our way upstairs he stumbled and would have gone down again had I not grabbed him round the waist. As I caught him he looked up at me and grunted 'Thanks, lad,' and we grinned at each other for a moment before restarting the climb.

I supported him across the landing to his bedroom door and he stood hesitating as though about to say something. But finally he just nodded to me a couple of times before ducking inside.

I waited outside the door, listening in some anxiety to the bumps and thumps from within; but I relaxed as a loud, tuneless humming came through the panels. Everything most certainly was going to be all right.

CHAPTER 67

Considering we spent our honeymoon tuberculin testing it was a big success. It compared favourably, at any rate, with the experiences of a lot of people I know who celebrated this milestone in their lives by cruising for a month on sunny seas and still wrote it off as a dead loss. For Helen and me it had all the ingredients; laughter, fulfilment and camaraderie, and yet it only lasted a week. And, as I say, we spent it tuberculin testing.

The situation had its origins one morning at the breakfast table when Siegfried, red-eyed after a bad night with a colicky mare, was opening the morning mail. He drew his breath in sharply as a thick roll of forms fell from an official envelope.

'God almighty! Look at all that testing!' He smoothed out the forms on the tablecloth and read feverishly down the long list of farm premises. 'And they want us to start this lot around Ellerthorpe next week without fail — it's very urgent.' He glared at me for a moment. 'That's when you're getting married, isn't it?'

I shifted uncomfortably in my chair. 'Yes, I'm afraid it is.'

Siegfried snatched a piece of toast from the rack and began to slap butter on it like an exasperated bricklayer. 'Well this is just great, isn't it? The practice going mad, a week's testing right at the top of the Dale, away in the back of beyond, and your bloody wedding smack in the middle of it. You'll be drifting gaily off on your honeymoon without a care in the world while I'm rushing around here nearly disappearing up my own backside!' He bit a piece from the toast and began to crunch it savagely.

'I'm sorry, Siegfried,' I said. 'I didn't mean to land you in the cart like this. I couldn't know the practice was going to get so busy right now and I never expected them to throw all this testing at us.'

Siegfried paused in his chewing and pointed a finger at me. 'That's just it, James, that's your trouble — you don't look ahead. You just go belting straight on without a thought. Even when it comes to a bloody wedding you're not worried — oh no, let's get on with it, to hell with the consequences.' He paused to cough up a few crumbs which he had inhaled in his agitation. 'In fact I can't see what all the hurry is — you've got all the time in the world to get married, you're just a boy.

And another thing — you hardly know this girl, you've only been seeing her regularly for a few weeks.'

'But wait a minute, you said . . .'

'No, let me finish, James. Marriage is a very serious step, not to be embarked upon without long and serious thought. Why in God's name does it have to be next week? Next year would have been soon enough and you could have enjoyed a nice long engagement. But no, you've got to rush in and tie the knot and it isn't so easily untied you know.'

'Oh hell, Siegfried, this is too bad! You know perfectly well it was you who . . .'

'One moment more. Your precipitate marital arrangements are going to cause me a considerable headache but believe me I wish you well. I hope all turns out for the best despite your complete lack of foresight, but at the same time I must remind you of the old saying: "Marry in haste, repent at leisure".'

I could stand no more. I leaped to my feet, thumped a fist on the table and yelled at him.

'But damn it, it was your idea! I was all for leaving it for a bit but you . . .'

Siegfried wasn't listening. He had been cooling off all the time and now his face broke into a seraphic smile. 'Now, now, now, James, you're getting excited again. Sit down and calm yourself. You mustn't mind my speaking to you like this — you are very young and it's my duty. You haven't done anything wrong at all; I suppose it's the most natural thing in the world for people of your age to act without thinking ahead, to jump into things with never a thought of the morrow. It's just the improvidence of youth.' Siegfried was about six years older than I but he had donned the mantle of the omniscient greybeard without effort.

I dug my fingers into my knees and decided not to pursue the matter. I had no chance anyway, and besides, I was beginning to feel a bit worried about clearing off and leaving him snowed under with work. I got up and walked to the window where I watched old Will Varley pushing a bicycle up the street with a sack of potatoes balanced on the handlebars as I had watched him a hundred times before. Then I turned back to my employer. I had had one of my infrequent ideas.

'Look, Siegfried, I wouldn't mind spending my honeymoon round Ellerthorpe. It's wonderful up there at this time of the year and we could stay at the Wheat Sheaf. I could do the testing from there.'

He looked at me in astonishment. 'Spend it at Ellerthorpe? And testing? It's impossible — what would Helen say?'

'She wouldn't mind. In fact she could do the writing for me. We were only going off touring in the car so we haven't made any plans, and anyway it's funny, but Helen and I have often said we'd like to stay at the Wheat Sheaf some time — there's something about that little pub.'

Siegfried shook his head decisively. 'No, James, I won't hear of it. In fact you're beginning to make me feel guilty. I'll get through the work all right so forget about it and go away and have a good time.'

'No, I've made up my mind. I'm really beginning to like the idea.' I scanned the list quickly. 'I can start testing at Allen's and do all those smaller ones around there on Tuesday, get married on Wednesday and go back for the second injection and readings on Thursday and Friday. I can knock hell out of that list by the end of the week.'

Siegfried looked at me as though he was seeing me for the first time. He argued and protested but for once I got my way. I fished the Ministry notification cards from the desk drawer and began to make the arrangements for my honeymoon.

On Tuesday at 12 noon I had finished testing Allen's huge herd scattered for miles over the stark fells at the top of the Dale and was settling down with the hospitable folk for the inevitable 'bit o' dinner'. Mr Allen was at the head of the scrubbed table and facing me were his two sons, Jack, aged about twenty, and Robbie, about seventeen. The young men were superbly fit and tough and I had been watching all morning in something like awe as they manhandled the wild, scattered beasts, chasing and catching tirelessly hour after hour. I had stared incredulously as Jack had run down a galloping heifer on the open moor, seized its horns and borne it slowly to the ground for me to inject; it struck me more than once that it was a pity that an Olympic Selector was unlikely to stray into this remote corner of high Yorkshire — he would have seen material to beat the world.

I always had to stand a bit of leg-pulling from Mrs Allen, a jolly talkative woman; on previous visits she had ribbed me mercilessly about being a slowcoach with the girls, the disgrace of having nothing better than a housekeeper to look after me. I knew she would start on me again today but I bided my time; I had a devastating riposte up my sleeve. She had just opened the oven door, filling the room with a delectable fragrance, and as she dumped a huge slab of roast ham on the table she looked down at me with a smile.

'Now then, Mr Herriot, when are we going to get you married off? It's time you found a nice girl, you know I'm always at you but you take not a bit o' notice.' She giggled as she bustled back to the cooking range for a bowl of mashed potatoes.

I waited until she had returned before I

dropped my bombshell. 'Well, as a matter of fact, Mrs Allen,' I said airily, 'I've decided to accept your advice. I'm getting married tomorrow.'

The good woman, mounding mashed potatoes on to my plate, stopped with her spoon in mid air. 'Married tomorrow?' Her face was a study in blank astonishment.

'That's right. I thought you'd be pleased.'

'But . . . but . . . you're coming back here on Thursday and Friday.'

'Well of course. I have to finish the test, haven't I? I'll be bringing my wife with me — I'm looking forward to introducing her to you.'

There was a silence. The young men stared at me, Mr Allen stopped sawing at the ham and regarded me stolidly, then his wife gave an uncertain laugh.

'Oh come on, I don't believe it. You're kidding us. You'd be off on your honeymoon if you were getting married tomorrow.'

'Mrs Allen,' I said with dignity, 'I wouldn't joke about a serious matter like that. Let me repeat — tomorrow is my wedding day and I'll be bringing my wife along on Thursday to see you.'

Completely deflated, she heaped our plates and we all fell to in silence. But I knew she was in agony; she kept darting little glances at me and it was obvious she was dying to ask me more. The boys, too, seemed intrigued; only Mr Allen, a tall, quiet man who, I'm sure, wouldn't have cared if I'd been going to rob a bank tomorrow, ploughed calmly through his food.

Nothing more was said until I was about to leave, then Mrs Allen put a hand on my arm.

'You really don't mean it, do you?' Her face was haggard with strain.

I got into the car and called out through the window. 'Goodbye and thank you. Mrs Herriot and I will be along first thing on Thursday.'

I can't remember much about the wedding. It was a 'quiet do' and my main recollection is of desiring to get it all over with as soon as possible. I have only one vivid memory; of Siegfried, just behind me in the church booming 'Amen' at regular intervals throughout the ceremony — the only time I have ever heard a best man do this.

It was an incredible relief when Helen and I were ready to drive away and when we were passing Skeldale House Helen grasped my hand.

'Look!' she cried excitedly. 'Look over there!'

Underneath Siegfried's brass plate which always hung slightly askew on the iron railings was a brand new one. It was of the modern bakelite type with a black background and bold white letters which read 'J.

Herriot M.R.C.V.S. Veterinary Surgeon', and it was screwed very straight and level on the metal.

I looked back down the street to try to see Siegfried but we had said our goodbyes and I would have to thank him later. So I drove out of Darrowby with a feeling of swelling pride because I knew what the plate meant — I was a partner, a man with a real place in the world. The thought made me slightly breathless. In fact we were both a little dizzy and we cruised for hours around the countryside, getting out when we felt like it, walking among the hills, taking no account of time. It must have been nine o'clock in the evening and darkness coming in fast when we realised we had gone far out of our way.

We had to drive ten miles over a desolate moor on the fell top and it was very dark when we rattled down the steep, narrow road into Ellerthorpe. The Wheat Sheaf was an unostentatious part of the single long village street, a low grey stone building with no light over the door, and as we went into the slightly musty-smelling hallway the gentle clink of glasses came from the public bar on our left. Mrs Burn, the elderly widow who owned the place, appeared from a back room and scrutinised us unemotionally.

'We've met before, Mrs Burn,' I said and she nodded. I apologised for our lateness and was wondering whether I dare ask for a few sandwiches at this time of night when the old lady spoke up, quite unperturbed.

'Nay,' she said, 'it's all right. We've been expecting you and your supper's waiting.' She led us to the dining-room where her niece, Beryl, served a hot meal in no time. Thick lentil soup, followed by what would probably be called a goulash these days but which was in fact simply a delicious stew with mushrooms and vegetables obviously concocted by a culinary genius. We had to say no to the gooseberry pie and cream.

It was like that all the time at the Wheat Sheaf. The whole place was aggressively unfashionable; needing a lick of paint, crammed with hideous Victorian furniture, but it was easy to see how it had won its reputation. It didn't have stylish guests, but fat, comfortable men from the industrial West Riding brought their wives at the weekends and did a bit of fishing or just took in the incomparable air between the meal times, which were the big moments of the day. There was only one guest while we were there and he was a permanent one — a retired draper from Darlington who was always at the table in good time, a huge white napkin tucked under his chin, his eyes gleaming as he watched Beryl bring in the food.

But it wasn't just the home-fed ham, the Wensleydale cheese, the succulent steak and kidney pies, the bilberry tarts and mountainous Yorkshire puddings which captivated Helen and me. There was a peace, a sleepy insinuating charm about the old pub which we always recall with happiness. I still often pass the Wheat Sheaf, and as I look at its ancient stone frontage, quite unaltered by the passage of a mere thirty years, the memories are still fresh and warm; our footsteps echoing in the empty street when we took our last walk at night, the old brass bedstead almost filling the little room, the dark rim of the fells bulking against the night sky beyond our window, faint bursts of laughter from the farmers in the bar downstairs.

I particularly enjoyed, too, our very first morning when I took Helen to do the test at Allen's. As I got out of the car I could see Mrs Allen peeping round the curtains in the kitchen window. She was soon out in the yard and her eyes popped when I brought my bride over to her. Helen was one of the pioneers of slacks in the Dales and she was wearing a bright purple pair this morning which would in modern parlance knock your eye out. The farmer's wife was partly shocked, partly fascinated but she soon found that Helen was of the same stock as herself and within seconds the two women were chattering busily. I judged from Mrs Allen's vigorous head-nodding and her ever widening smile that Helen was putting her out of her pain by explaining all the circumstances. It took a long time and finally Mr Allen had to break into the conversation.

'If we're goin' we'll have to go,' he said gruffly and we set off to start the second day of the test.

We began on a sunny hillside where a group of young animals had been penned. Jack and Robbie plunged in among the beasts while Mr Allen took off his cap and courteously dusted the top of the wall.

'Your missus can sit 'ere,' he said.

I paused as I was about to start measuring. My missus! It was the first time anybody had said that to me. I looked over at Helen as she sat cross-legged on the rough stones, her notebook on her knee, pencil at the ready, and as she pushed back the shining dark hair from her forehead she caught my eye and smiled; and as I smiled back at her I became aware suddenly of the vast, swelling glory of the Dales around us, and of the Dales scent of clover and warm grass, more intoxicating than any wine. And it seemed that my first two years at Darrowby had been leading up to this moment; that the first big step of my life was being completed right here with Helen smiling at me and the memory, fresh in my mind, of my new plate hanging in front of Skeldale House.

I might have stood there indefinitely, in a sort of trance, but Mr Allen cleared his throat in a marked manner and I turned back to the job in hand.

'Right,' I said, placing my callipers against the beast's neck. 'Number thirty-eight, seven millimetres and circumscribed,' I called out to Helen. 'Number thirty-eight, seven, C.'

'Thirty-eight, seven, C,' my wife repeated as she bent over her book and started to write.

The employees of Thorndike Press hope you have enjoyed this Large Print book. All our Thorndike, Wheeler, and Kennebec Large Print titles are designed for easy reading, and all our books are made to last. Other Thorndike Press Large Print books are available at your library, through selected bookstores, or directly from us.

For information about titles, please call:

(800) 223-1244

or visit our Web site at:

http://gale.cengage.com/thorndike

To share your comments, please write:

Publisher
Thorndike Press
10 Water St., Suite 310
Waterville, ME 04901